ent
.... in
Alberta

Government and Politics in Alberta

Edited by
Allan Tupper and
Roger Gibbins

The University of Alberta Press

First published by
The University of Alberta Press
Athabasca Hall
Edmonton, Alberta
Canada T6G 2E8

Copyright © The University of Alberta Press 1992

ISBN 0-88864-243-1

Canadian Cataloguing in Publication Data

Main entry under title:

Government and Politics in Alberta

Includes bibliographical references and index.
ISBN 0-88864-243-1

1. Alberta—Politics and government—1971–
I. Tupper, Allan, 1950–   II. Gibbins, Roger, 1947–
JL336.G69 1992   320.97123'09'045   C92-091396-2

Printed on acid-free paper.

Typesetting by Pièce de Résistance Ltée., Edmonton, Alberta, Canada
Printed by Quality Color Ltd., Edmonton, Alberta, Canada

Contents

Preface

The origins of this volume lie in a telephone conversation between the editors in the fall of 1989. At that time we lamented the absence of a readily available, relatively comprehensive and easily accessible volume on modern Alberta politics. Several themes were implicit in the wide-ranging discussion that followed—these themes remained central to our subsequent deliberations and thus exerted a marked influence on the shape of the book at hand. The first important notion was that Alberta's politics were changing dramatically as the 1980s were ending. And while we had many ideas about the source and possible consequences of these changes, we had seldom committed our thoughts to prose. Perhaps, we agreed, we should do something about it! At the same time, we also concluded that neither of us was prepared to undertake the large task of preparing a co-authored volume. A perhaps better approach was to bring together the specialized talents of our colleagues and to prepare a collection of essays on a range of important topics. Such an approach had several merits. First, it allowed us to bring to bear the views, talents and skills of a diverse group of Alberta's scholars. To a degree, therefore, we sought to encourage an interchange among each other. Second, the project brought together scholars from the province's two largest universities in an undertaking that led each of us to think deeply about at least one important aspect of Alberta's changing political landscape. Without any false modesty, several contributors, when first approached, remarked that they did not see themselves as Alberta politics "specialists" and hence were reluctant to contribute. Our standard response to this concern was twofold—none of us is really an Alberta "specialist" and that we wanted papers that, if possible, placed Alberta in a broader context of political, social and economic change. In other words, we asked contributors to ponder modern Alberta, not necessarily as a "special case," but in the light of their ongoing research and teaching interests. Our initially reluctant contributors rose to the occasion in every instance and enthusiastically pursued their mandate. Our final concern was that we prepare a volume that would be accessible to diverse readers including university audiences especially at the senior undergraduate level, informed general readers and students of provincial and national politics. At the same time, we urged contributors to employ the accepted tools of our discipline as they saw fit and to avoid oversimplification even in the face of a broad and diverse audience. In this vein, we walked a familiar tightrope for social scientists as we struggled to communicate clearly sometimes complex ideas. We hope we have succeeded but we leave judgement on this question to our readers.

Canadian political science has never accorded the study of provincial politics a status comparable to that conferred on the study of national events, although this state of affairs may finally be changing. Various factors account for this disciplinary bias but the neglect of provincial affairs is paradoxical given Canadian political science's incessant assertions about the political, social and economic significance of contemporary provincial governments. Our book is not designed to enjoin the sometimes arcane debate about the relative political significance of federal and provincial governments. But we hope that it will inspire further research into the complex politics of Alberta and the other provinces. A clearer understanding of the dynamics of provincial politics is valuable in its own right. It may also provide important insights into the behaviour of provincial governments on the national stage and hence partially illuminate the vexing problems of national unity that beset us as we write in 1992.

Acknowledgements

Many debts are accumulated in the preparation of a volume such as this one. The few words that follow are a decidedly modest tribute to the many contributors to the final result. First, our contributors deserve high praise for their commitment, their enthusiasm and their professionalism. They diligently and good naturedly endured the demands of their several editors. Many of them put aside other pressing research projects to join with us in an important collective effort. The contribution of two, anonymous referees also merits high praise. Their reviews of the manuscript were thorough, fair and extraordinarily helpful. Their contributions added much to the ultimate quality of our volume and gave real meaning and substance to the badly overused phrase "constructive criticism."

Many others contributed to the volume although their contributions are less obvious and less visible than those already cited. First, many Albertans assisted in the project by submitting to interviews with the individual authors. We extend a collective thank you to those who gave of their time, their expertise and their views in this way. And of course, our colleagues contributed to our deliberations, often unknowingly, during the incessant conversations and informal debates that characterize life in a university. As we all know, such contributions are very important yet hard to pinpoint and acknowledge formally. Our students are also important, yet seldom recognized, contributors to our intellectual undertakings. Our teaching and our research interact in complex ways. For example, important points are clarified, new research topics emerge and old ideas are routinely challenged in classroom discussions. Our many students are thus ongoing participants in our work even though they themselves might not realize their important contributions. We thank them for their thoughts, for their enthusiasm and for their commitment to scholarship.

We formally acknowledge the financial contribution of the Alberta government through its program of grants, especially the Alberta Foundation for the Arts that provided funds towards this publication, the Canada Council for its general support of University presses and the University of Alberta for its continuing commitment to its Press and hence to scholarly publishing in this country.

Norma Gutteridge, Director of the University of Alberta Press, supported the project from its conception. Her commitment moved the project through to completion. Mary Mahoney-Robson, Editor of the University of Alberta Press, skillfully and energetically guided the volume through the editorial and production stages. Her good judgement, her helpful counsel, her tact and her knowledge were invaluable. She grasped our intellectual goals and made sure that technical considerations were always subordinate to, or meshed with, the broader purposes being pursued.

We must thank our colleagues in support positions at the University of Alberta and the University of Calgary who played a key role in the production of this book. In particular, the support staff in the Department of Political Science at the University of Alberta—especially Pam Ouimet, Bonnie Muirhead and Terry Brown "word processed" the entire document through to its final form. Their expertise, their commitment and their good humour in the performance of their role merits formal recognition. Perhaps more often than ever the editors, they wondered whether "it" would indeed ever be done!

Contributors

Keith Archer is Associate Professor of Political Science at the University of Calgary. He is the author of *Political Choices and Electoral Consequences* and articles on political parties and voting behaviour. His current research is on New Democratic Party conventions.

Edward Bell is an SSHRC Post-Doctoral Fellow in the Department of Sociology at the University of Calgary. His work has appeared in the *Canadian Journal of Sociology* and the *Canadian Journal of Political Science*. He is currently writing a book on the Social Credit movement in Alberta.

Frederick C. Engelmann is Professor Emeritus of Political Science, University of Alberta. He is the co-author of *Canadian Political Parties: Origin, Character, Impact* and of numerous chapters and articles. His current research focuses on Alberta, Canadian and Austrian politics.

Thomas Flanagan is Professor of Political Science at the University of Calgary. He is the author of numerous articles and books on native affairs, including *Riel and the Rebellion: 1885 Reconsidered* and *Metis Lands in Manitoba*. In 1991, he became Director of Policy, Strategy and Communications for the Reform Party of Canada.

Roger Gibbins is Professor and Head, Department of Political Science, University of Calgary. He has published extensively on such topics as political parties, western Canadian politics, regionalism in a comparative perspective and constitutional developments. He is the editor of the *Canadian Journal of Political Science*.

Jack Masson is Professor of Political Science at the University of Alberta. A specialist in local and urban government, he is currently working on *Alberta's Local Governments: Politics and Democracy*, an updated revision to his *Alberta's Local Governments and Their Politics*.

J. Peter Meekison is University Professor, Department of Political Science at the University of Alberta. A former deputy minister of the Alberta Department of Federal and Intergovernmental Affairs, he also holds the Belzberg Chair in Constitutional Studies in the University of Alberta's Faculty of Law. He has written on many aspects of Canadian federalism.

Leslie A. Pal is Professor, School of Public Administration, Carleton University. His publications include *State, Class and Bureaucracy, The Real Worlds of Canadian Politics*, 2nd ed. (with Robert M. Campbell) and *Public Policy Analysis*, 2nd ed.

Larry Pratt is Professor of Political Science at the University of Alberta. He has published extensively on Alberta politics, resource development and international relations. He is the co-author of *Prairie Capitalism: Power and Influence in the New West*.

Denise Savage-Hughes has an M.A. from the Graduate Program in Communication Studies at the University of Calgary and is currently special assistant to the Minister of State for grains and oilseeds and the Minister Responsible for Western Diversification.

David Taras is Director of the Canadian Studies Program at the University of Calgary. He is the author of *The Newsmakers: The Media's Influence on Canadian Politics* and the editor of *Seeing Ourselves: Media Power and Policy in Canada* (with Helen Holmes) and *Prime Ministers and Premiers* (with Leslie Pal).

Linda Trimble is Assistant Professor of Political Science at the University of Alberta. Her major research interest is women and Canadian Politics. She has published articles on several topics.

Allan Tupper is Professor and Chair, Department of Political Science, University of Alberta. He has published extensively in such areas as public administration, Alberta politics and Crown corporations. He is now working on a book on the ethical conduct of Canadian public officials.

Ian Urquhart is Assistant Professor of Political Science at the University of Alberta. His research and teaching interests include public policy, public administration and constitutional affairs.

Alberta Politics:
Change and Continuity

Alberta's rich and complex political life evokes conflicting images and emotions both within and without the province. Consider several common, yet confusing and perhaps contradictory, views. Alberta politics, with their tradition of overwhelming legislative support for a single party, are portrayed as staid, "businesslike" and uninspired by deeper debates about the nature of political life. And as immortalized by C.B. Macpherson's interpretation, Alberta is often seen as a politically and socially homogeneous province preoccupied with its dependent relationship with other parts of the country.[1] But the province has spawned iconoclastic political movements, like Social Credit and the Reform Party, which have rejected the political status quo and, in so doing, have exerted an influence far beyond the province's boundaries. Moreover, the province's political history, far from revealing a politically homogeneous populace, is marked by deep conflicts between ethnic groups, social classes and regions. In a related vein, perhaps the strongest stereotype of Alberta politics is the alleged political conservatism of its people and their governments' apparent preference for "right wing" policies. But Alberta's Progressive Conservative governments have been and remain interventionist, especially in their efforts to alter the province's economic structure; the interventionist state, in Alberta as elsewhere, has been a potent weapon in the hands of ambitious elites. Interestingly, public opinion data reveal that Albertans' attitudes about major policy issues differ little from those of other Canadians although Albertans perceive themselves as quite conservative.[2] An allegedly conservative electorate has returned the New

Democrats as the Official Opposition in the 1986 and 1989 provincial general elections.

In national affairs, Alberta is often simplistically portrayed as a bellicose defender of provincial autonomy and a decentralized federation. Yet this image is confounded by the continuing participation of Albertans in national political discourse and by a desire to have the province's voice strengthened in national institutions. Moreover, the province's anger and bitter opposition to federal energy policies in the 1970s and early 1980s has subsided and the extent of Albertans', if not their governments', discontent with federalism is debatable. Put differently, Albertans' frustrations with modern Canadian political structures and practices may not now differ much from those of other "English" Canadians.

Despite its lingering and romantic image as a rural and agrarian society, modern Alberta is a heavily urbanized province integrated into Canadian, continental and international commercial and political circles and deeply influenced by modern mass culture. In writing about the province in the 1970s, Tamara and Howard Palmer neatly capture the gap between Alberta's rural past and its modern urban reality.

> . . . the way of life of most Albertans differed only marginally from people living in other metropolitan centres across Canada. A growing number were considerably less familiar with the smell of the barnyard and the work of the cowboy and the farmer than they were with Toronto and New York stock markets, international travel, and gourmet cuisine.[3]

A final perennial tension in Alberta politics concerns, for lack of more precise terms, the provincial character and mood. Here we note stark contrasts over time in the thinking of citizens and their leaders about the province's potential. For example, Lewis G. Thomas described the province's mood in 1905 as "optimistic, self-confident, even euphoric."[4] Such self-confidence has been deeply shaken on several occasions in this century, notably during the Depression which took a cruel toll in the province and in the mid 1980s when the combined effects of the National Energy Program, a severe international recession and the collapse of prices for Alberta's resources shattered a provincial economy that had boomed in the 1970s. Alberta's politics are marked by powerful, contrasting and shifting emotions as its people and elites struggle to reconcile their optimism and ambitions with the harsh realities of an unpredictable political economy, a volatile national political scene and a rapidly changing world order.

It is against this complex backdrop of conflicting images that we probe our central concern—the interplay between change and continuity in modern Alberta politics. How have such powerful forces as continuing urbanization, changing immigration patterns and the seemingly unstoppable influences of technological change and economic "globalization" shaped Alberta politics? In the aftermath of Meech Lake and in the transformation of the national political landscape, where does the province fit into vital national debates about Canada's political future? Such questions highlight the impact of social, economic and political change on Alberta society. But major changes in the environment of provincial politics, to be understood, must be seen in context with forces of continuity. Modern Alberta faces an uncertain future, not with a clean slate, but rather with the trappings of traditional assumptions, institutions and political practices. An abiding concern with the power of central Canadian interests, an uneasiness about the domestic and international economy, and even in a technological age, a sense of physical and even psychological isolation from metropolitan centres will influence Alberta's response to the major issues of the 1990s and beyond. Policy-making and electoral practices will continue to be shaped by the province's political institutions and political culture as they have developed since 1905.

The theme of change and continuity is a large and potentially unwieldy one. Our approach, therefore, is to examine the main concern by probing particular institutions, political processes and issues. Like all serious students of Alberta politics, we realize the acute importance of the province's brief political history, but our focus is primarily on the last two decades. The electoral victory of the Progressive Conservatives under Peter Lougheed in 1971 is generally seen as a watershed in the province's political development and as the start of the "modern" phase in provincial politics. As such, it provides a natural point of departure for several of our authors.

We approach Alberta's political future armed with a knowledge of the past and some insights into present problems, but without crystal balls. Nonetheless, a related objective is to provide "informed speculation" about the future course of provincial affairs. Our intention and preference is to be provocative, controversial and future oriented.

In a compelling analysis of the literature on provincial politics in the Canadian Maritimes, R.A. Young convincingly argues that particular themes are given extraordinary attention while other important topics are ignored.[5] In the case of the Maritimes, perennial themes are the party system and political patronage, while almost no sustained attention is paid to political modernization or to the role and growth of governments and their attendant bureaucracies. In Alberta, similar tendencies are to be noted. "Alienation," "one-party dominance" and the emergence of "third parties" are often discussed, although much controversy remains. Our objective is to examine further the traditional debates about Alberta's party system and patterns of electoral competition. Keith Archer's chapter examines the modern party system and highlights considerable changes in the electorate, the party system and the individual parties. But we also stress several issues and themes that are seldom explicitly analyzed. Linda Trimble's chapter on gender politics examines an issue that has assumed much greater prominence in the 1980s and 1990s and promises to become even more important in Alberta's political discourse. The chapter by Denise Savage-Hughes and David Taras focuses on the political role of the Alberta mass media, a topic which is seldom examined rigorously despite its obvious importance in modern democratic politics and its particular significance in the political development of Alberta. They show how Peter Lougheed consciously employed television as a crucial medium in the construction of the modern Progressive Conservative Party. More generally, their analysis highlights the emergence of the modern media as a major political actor.

Tom Flanagan's thorough analysis of the Lubicon Lake dispute demonstrates the nuances of policy-making in this complex area. Jack Masson's assessment of provincial-municipal relations reveals the political problems and contradictions induced by the concentration of Alberta's population in Edmonton and Calgary, two large, almost equally populated, yet very different and competitive cities. Economic decline and the election in the 1980s of mayors in Edmonton closely identified with provincial opposition parties adds new complexity to the provincial-municipal nexus. Allan Tupper, Larry Pratt and Ian Urquhart examine the role of the provincial government in light of considerable economic, social and political change in the 1980s and early 1990s. Analysis of these and other issues adds breadth to our knowledge of Alberta politics and moves us away from a single-minded focus on the party system.

Our final objective is to stimulate further research on Alberta politics. In this context, an interesting point arises. The major literature on Alberta government, while quantitatively modest, is among the most influential in the Canadian social sciences. The province's politics have long attracted considerable scholarly interest. C.B. Macpherson's classic study, *Democracy in Alberta*, which is carefully critiqued in Edward Bell's chapter, remains a prism through which Alberta politics are routinely examined.[6] Perhaps more importantly, his work is seen as a compelling application of Marxist analysis to the development of a democratic political system. Other major studies on Social Credit, notably J.R. Mallory's *Social Credit and the Federal Power in Canada*, remain as core works in the literature on political parties, federalism and political economy.[7] More recently, John Richards and Larry Pratt's *Prairie Capitalism: Power and Influence in the New West*, which probes the development of resource policy in modern Alberta and Saskatchewan, provides a standard reference and a model for other students of Canadian provincial politics.[8] Particularly influential and controversial is their view that the rise of Peter Lougheed's Progressive Conservatives in the 1970s reflects the political advent of a "new middle class" committed to extracting maximum local benefit from the exploitation of Alberta's valuable natural resources. Another impressive recent contribution is *Alberta: A New History* by Howard and Tamara Palmer.[9] This ambitious volume emphasizes Alberta's social history as well as its complex political and economic development. Alvin Finkel and Edward Bell have made major contributions to our understanding of the Social Credit era.[10] Finkel provides important insights into Social Credit as a government as well as a social movement and a political party. The development and problems of the Alberta New Democrats are probed in Larry Pratt's edited volume, *Essays in Honour of Grant Notley: Socialism and Democracy in Alberta*.[11] Howard Leeson's biography of the New Democrats former leader Grant Notley, who died tragically in 1984, follows Notley's political career in the context of Alberta's social, economic and political change in the 1970s and early 1980s.[12] A group of prominent Alberta journalists and authors capture the province's changing political, social and economic climate in the late 1980s in their polemical volume, *Running on Empty: Alberta after the Boom*.[13] Alberta's volatile economy and the elusive quest for economic diversification and stability are the subjects of *Strength in Adversity: A Study of the Alberta Economy* by Michael Percy and Robert Mansell.[14] The province's complex, often difficult, relationship with the federal government and other parts of the country is captured in essays in *Canadian Political Life: An Alberta Perspective*, edited by Roger Gibbins, Keith Archer and Stan Drabek.[15]

These contributions, and hopefully this one, add new insights and interpretations. However, substantial gaps remain in our knowledge, and we hope to stimulate the abiding interest of researchers. For example, we lack a general study of the modern Alberta Progressive Conservative Party, despite that party's obvious importance to provincial and to a degree, national political life. The civil service, although the subject of incessant partisan controversy and public debate, remains a virtually untouched area for researchers. For example, how have two decades of uninterrupted Progressive Conservative government shaped the organization, staffing and political neutrality of the civil service? We lack comprehensive studies of policy development in such important areas as health care, education and the provincial welfare state. The history and changing roles of important government departments and agencies are seldom explored systematically. The list could be easily extended, and we could also enter the larger debate among specialists about how best to study Canadian provincial politics. But our modest objective at this point is to note several glaring gaps in our knowledge, to urge others to explore uncharted areas and to continue the debate about established interpretations.

Our format reflects a decision to concentrate the expertise and specialized knowledge of various authors on the core theme of change and continuity. Within the broad framework established by the interplay between change and continuity, our authors enjoyed considerable freedom to define their questions, to pursue their research and to generate original essays on aspects of provincial politics. The result is a volume that reflects the considerable methodological diversity of modern political science. For example, Tom Flanagan's use of rational choice analysis stands in contrast to the historical approach adopted by Leslie A. Pal in his heady interpretation of Alberta's political leadership. Keith Archer and Denise Savage-Hughes and David Taras employ the insights of modern political sociology and communications theories respectively to plumb their topics. The chapters thus reflect various approaches and, perhaps more importantly, considerable intellectual and political heterogeneity. No "party line" governed the selection of authors, their methodologies or their conclusions. The result is a volume that reflects a range of opinions. The volume's internal diversity is well reflected in J. Peter Meekison's and Roger Gibbins's chapters on Alberta's constitutional positions. They differ markedly in their interpretations of Alberta's influence on the national stage; Gibbins sees Alberta as an increasingly marginalized constitutional actor while Meekison sees the province as playing a major role in future constitutional developments. They also differ about the political implications of Alberta's alliance with successive Quebec governments in the 1970s and 1980s and the provincial government's ability to respond to such new constitutional actors as women's groups, aboriginal peoples and ethnic minorities.

In a related but different vein, all the authors are "Albertans," at least insofar as we all live and work in the province. In either mysterious, or perhaps to our readers, obvious ways, our examination of Alberta politics is probably shaped by this basic fact. Although no obvious biases or flaws occur to us, it is an interesting intellectual exercise to ponder how, for example, a group of informed Ontarians, Australians, Texans or Quebecois might analyze modern Alberta.

Studying Alberta Politics

A number of themes run through our chapters. The first, not surprisingly to even casual observers of Alberta politics, embraces the intertwined notions of alienation and economic dependence, instability and vulnerability. Indeed, virtually every contributor notes the political impact of Alberta's rapid descent from what Lewis G. Thomas called the province's "vulgarly rich" condition of the 1970s to its present economic condition in the early 1990s.[16] Among other things, "boom and bust" strengthened the political opposition and highlighted political cleavages within the province—between men and women, between aboriginals and others, between workers and employers—that were masked by the affluence of the 1970s. As Allan Tupper, Larry Pratt and Ian Urquhart argue in their chapter, the achievement of economic stability and economic diversification remain preoccupations of Alberta's elites who fear unpredictable and uncontrollable economic and political forces. Fiscal restraint has severely constrained government's room for manoeuvre. Jack Masson's chapter on provincial-municipal relations stresses the impact of provincial restraint as the province's cities recoil against what they perceive as an unjust transfer of provincial indebtedness onto their shoulders. Alberta's position in Canada has also changed with the return to economic normalcy. The imperative of defending provincial resources against "external" intrusions has lessened as international markets have changed, as new provincial issues have emerged and as Canadians ponder wrenching adjustments to their political order.

Efforts to assess the political impact of Alberta's chronic economic instability raise several basic questions. First, without embracing a crude economic determinism, do the province's economic structure and circumstances ultimately exert a profound impact on its politics and the policy options available to its governments? Without directly answering this question, several commentators speculate that a change of government in the next provincial election might not change Alberta politics profoundly. New political elites may find themselves severely constrained, despite their heady opposition rhetoric, by the province's fiscal problems and by its financial dependence on volatile and decreasing natural resource revenues. Second, are Alberta politics, under the pressure of changing economic circumstances, becoming more "normal" at least in comparison to other Canadian provinces? Is the province losing its status as English Canada's most politically distinctive province? Neither clear nor uniform answers emerge to these complex questions. Indeed, our contributors views on this question are partially shaped by their methodologies and their perspectives. For example, Keith Archer's application of several broad concepts from modern political sociology to Alberta's political behaviour makes the contemporary provincial scene appear much like that prevailing elsewhere in Canada and to a lesser degree, other parts of the modern democratic world. Leslie A. Pal's chapter on traditions of political leadership in the province evokes images of a distinct political culture, one underpinned by unique social and economic circumstances. This having been said, the "bust," by robbing the provincial government of enormous resource revenues, has raised questions about taxation and expenditure policy to new prominence in modern Alberta politics. Like their counterparts elsewhere in the democratic world, Alberta governments are now constrained by a static economy, by the economic imperatives of a changing world order and by the limits imposed by a relatively bare Treasury. Such circumstances have altered Alberta's politics and the province's relationships with other parts of the country.

The most revered theme in the discussion of Alberta politics is the province's tradition of long periods of "one-party dominance" of the legislature, if not the society. The question as to why this occurs continues to fascinate observers of provincial politics even in light of the changed electoral competition of the late 1980s and early 1990s. Inevitably, many of our contributors address the question of one-party dominance either directly or indirectly. Several note how overwhelming legislative majorities are noteworthy in other provinces and are not unique to Alberta as measured by either the magnitude of majorities or by the length of governments' tenure. But more importantly, Keith Archer, Edward Bell, and Leslie A. Pal all argue in their chapters that one-party dominance, far from reflecting a politically monolithic, united society, is shaped by the political system itself. Of particular importance is the "first past the post" electoral system which, in the face of a significant but divided opposition, often generates substantial *legislative* majorities. The partisan composition of the Legislative Assembly and hence of the government, as shaped by this institutional context, is certainly not a perfect reflector of the province's range of political preferences. Seen in this light, one can readily dismiss some of the journalistic interpretations of Albertans' lemming-like electoral behaviour.

A related, but ultimately different question, is the future of partisan competition in the province. Will the intense three-party competition seen in the 1986 and 1989 elections continue indefinitely in major urban centres or will one party gain the upper hand? Will Edmonton continue to support the New Democrats? Are the Conservatives becoming a rural rump sustained by the electoral system and by electoral boundaries that overrepresent rural voters? Might the Reform Party still enter provincial politics and if so, with what results? Is the Progressive Conservative Party becoming, despite its name, a provincial version of the federal Reform Party? Will the provincial Liberals replace the Conservatives as the province's dominant party by portraying themselves as an uptempo, more focussed version of the now aging Conservatives? No clear or easy answers emerge to these questions. Contributors' views are shaped by their assessment of the relative importance of leadership, the impact of economic change and diversification, the pattern of federal partisan competition and the emergence of new cleavages and issues.

A third concern is the consequences of long-term one-party dominance. How has long-term Conservative rule shaped Alberta politics and society? Despite its importance, this question has seldom been systematically addressed. Our contributors advance several answers. For example, Frederick C. Engelmann maintains that the Legislative Assembly bears the imprint of Conservative dominance throughout its operations. Moreover, Conservative control of the Assembly has been little disturbed by the recent advent of larger oppositions. The legislature is geared to the needs of a powerful cabinet, although legislative reform is emerging as an important issue in the early 1990s. Gender equality issues, Alberta's constitutional positions and economic diversification remain underpinned by several principles through two decades of Conservative rule. Alberta's modern public bureaucracy has been nurtured by successive Tory governments in distinctive ways. Ties have been forged with foreign governments and with provincial, national and international business elites. These and many other consequences suggest that, even if soon ended electorally, two decades of uninterrupted Conservative rule will exert long-term influences on Alberta's governance.

A third important theme concerns the "emergence" of a new provincial agenda of issues and interests. In modern Alberta politics, a significant environmental movement has emerged, gender issues are more important and aboriginal peoples are better organized, more politically skilled and more aggressive in demanding the resolution of their grievances. Tensions now abound in provincial politics about the role of government and the balance, for example, between support for the welfare state and spending on economic development. Senior citizens are more politically vocal and in the post Meech Lake era, Albertans, like other Canadians, are interested in basic questions about their democratic governance including representation, the ethics of our governors and the effectiveness of political institutions. In recognizing these significant developments, our contributors point to a range of possible explanations and implications. Several see the decline in federal-provincial tensions over resource policy as a development which lessens the seductiveness of calls for united provincial fronts against external threats and thereby makes easier the emergence of a different, more obviously provincial agenda. The Charter of Rights and Freedoms has also awakened the political interests of aboriginals, women and representatives of linguistic minorities and ethnic groups. Such heightened political involvement manifests itself in provincial as well as national politics and leads to calls for different policies and often, for greater public involvement in policy making and administration. The government's continuing commitment to expenditure restraint led many groups into the political arena to defend public programs that in the 1970s and early 1980s were justified by oil rich Conservative governments as something akin to an Albertan birthright. Politically active environmental and peace groups are provincial versions of international developments and movements. Their emergence reflects the impact of global developments on

Alberta's political life. The implications of such developments are not fully understood but, if nothing else, the new agenda belies Alberta's reputation as a politically staid province.

Finally, we are concerned with the Alberta government's economic and social roles. The province's reputation as an island paradise of free enterprise in a Canadian sea of interventionism reflects neither historical traditions nor contemporary realities. Successive Alberta governments have been deeply committed to the development of economic infrastructure, public education, provincial resources and a welfare state, subject in each case to the opportunities and constraints imposed by federalism. A particular skill of successful Alberta politicians is their capacity to wed the rhetoric of limited government with the practice of active government. As Tupper, Pratt and Urquhart argue, the government's rapid development of northern Alberta's forests raised complex questions about economic diversification and the overall costs and benefits especially in the face of cutbacks to important social services. But questions about economic development are only parts of a broader agenda. Alberta governments, like their counterparts elsewhere in Canada, are facing demands for intervention in support of employment equity, the protection of minority rights and the regulation and definition of such controversial issues as pornography and religious freedom. Canadians' burgeoning ''rights'' consciousness, combined with changing immigration patterns, will force this agenda on even the most reluctant governments. And as J. Peter Meekison's and Roger Gibbins's chapters argue, either a substantially revised federalism or more dramatically still, a Canada without Quebec, will force Albertans and their leaders to think hard, and hopefully creatively, about the sort of society they envision. A crucial element of this debate will be a discussion of the roles government should play and assuming some sort of federalism, which level(s) of government is best equipped to undertake different activities.

The Future of Alberta Politics

In a political world marked by sudden, dramatic and fundamental change, the future is even harder to predict than the present is to explain. Political scientists must cope with very cloudy crystal balls; our conceptual tools and historical analogies sometimes provide limited guidance in turbulent political environments. Will Canada survive? What patterns of political competition might emerge in Alberta? How will immigration shape future political events? Will political institutions adapt easily to new social, political and economic forces?

At the same time, however, the themes of continuity and change provide at least some parameters on the future direction of Alberta politics. We know that the province's course will be plotted by a number of constants: the Alberta economy will remain vulnerable to unstable resource markets, the provincial population will not overtake that of Ontario or Quebec, Alberta will not move from the geographic margins of the continental economy and the United States will continue to dominate continental policy-making. Yet we also know that these fixed points of reference, and others, still permit a good deal of latitude, a good deal of manoeuvrability, as Albertans move toward the twenty-first century. The continuities of the past constrain but do not fix the future. The dynamics of change are thus important to understand, and it is to those dynamics, charted against the continuities of the past, that we now turn.

NOTES

1. C.B. Macpherson, *Democracy in Alberta: Social Credit and the Party System* (Toronto: University of Toronto Press, 1953).

2. Roger Gibbins, Keith Archer and Stan Drabek, "Public Opinion and Policy Preferences in the Canadian Regions," in *Canadian Political Life: An Alberta Perspective*, Roger Gibbins, Keith Archer and Stan Drabek, eds. (Dubuque, Iowa: Kendall-Hunt, 1990), pp. 229-38.

3. Howard Palmer with Tamara Palmer, *Alberta: A New History* (Edmonton: Hurtig Publishers, 1990), p. 337.

4. Lewis G. Thomas, "Alberta 1905-1980: The Uneasy Society" in *Rancher's Legacy*, Patrick A. Dunae, ed. (Edmonton: The University of Alberta Press, 1986), p. 187.

5. R.A. Young, "Teaching and Research in Maritime Politics: Old Stereotypes and New Directions," *Journal of Canadian Studies* 21, no. 2 (Summer 1986): 133-55.

6. Macpherson, *Democracy in Alberta*.

7. J.R. Mallory, *Social Credit and the Federal Power in Canada* (Toronto: University of Toronto Press, 1954).

8. Larry Pratt and John Richards, *Prairie Capitalism: Power and Influence in the New West* (Toronto: McLelland and Stewart, 1979).

9. Palmer with Palmer, *Alberta: A New History.*

10. Alvin Finkel, *The Social Credit Phenomenon in Alberta* (Toronto: University of Toronto Press, 1988) and Edward Bell, "Class Voting in the First Alberta Social Credit Election," *Canadian Journal of Political Science* 23, no. 3 (September 1990): 519-30.

11. *Essays in Honour of Grant Notley: Socialism and Democracy in Alberta,* Larry Pratt, ed. (Edmonton: NeWest Press, 1986).

12. Howard Leeson, *Grant Notley: The Social Conscience of Alberta* (Edmonton: University of Alberta Press, 1992).

13. *Running on Empty: Alberta after the Boom,* Andrew Nikiforuk, Sheila Pratt and Don Wanagas, eds. (Edmonton: NeWest Press, 1987).

14. Robert L. Mansell and Michael B. Percy, *Strength in Adversity: A Study of the Alberta Economy* (Edmonton: The University of Alberta Press, 1990).

15. *Canadian Political Life: An Alberta Perspective,* Roger Gibbins, Keith Archer and Stan Drabek, eds. (Dubuque, Iowa: Kendall-Hunt, 1990).

16. Thomas, "Alberta 1905-1980: The Uneasy Society," p. 211.

1

The Political Executive and Political Leadership in Alberta

Leslie A. Pal

To outsiders, and even to many insiders, Alberta's political history seems exotic and bizarre. This is the province of "Bible Bill" Aberhart, of social credit funny money theory, populism, farmers' movements, wealth, envy and angst. For many eastern Canadians, Alberta is the nation's epicentre of red-necked conservatism, the most recent expression of which is the Reform party. Regional alienation in Nova Scotia or New Brunswick seems resigned and melancholy; Alberta's provincialism is aggressive. Alberta also has the dubious reputation of appearing uninterested in strong opposition parties and legislative democracy. Albertans seem to vote en masse for the dominant party, and like to keep it in power for decades on end. Provincial premiers, looked at from afar, resemble benign Latin American caudillos who are superficially populist but in fact rule their nations with iron will. When Albertans decide they want another party and leader in government, they vote as a bloc, make the change, and then settle down once again for a long stretch of single party dominance.

These images are myth, and we cannot understand the province's executive and political leadership unless they are dispelled. First, if Albertans like long periods of one-party rule, it is a taste they share with most other Canadian provinces. Think of the Co-operative Commonwealth Federation (CCF) in Saskatchewan (1944-1964; 1971-1982), the Conservatives in Ontario (1943-1985) and the Union Nationale in Quebec (1944-1960). Second, the tenure of most of these parties has been associated with strong leaders: Tommy Douglas (Saskatchewan's CCF); Leslie Frost, John Robarts, and William Davis (Ontario's Conservatives) and Maurice Duplessis (Quebec's Union Nationale). Third, Alberta parties are not as kooky as their detractors have alleged. Recent work on Social Credit under Aberhart, for example, has demonstrated how much the party shared with the CCF, farm and labour movements of the day. Social Credit under E.C. Manning, who was premier from 1943 to 1968, jettisoned virtually all of its distinctive ideological baggage and became an efficient conservative administration. Alberta's political parties and their leaders have, it is true, articulated rebuttals to the "national" consensus as defined by Ottawa, Ontario, and Quebec (for example, on the National Energy Program and more recently on policies such as multiculturalism and bilingualism), but these rebuttals are not completely unreasonable. Fourthly, Albertans are neither as homogeneous nor as lemming-like as political folklore likes to pretend. Aberhart swept into office in 1935, but had to battle to win again in 1940. E.C. Manning racked up impressive majorities, but almost lost the 1955 election. In the 1986 and 1989 provincial elections, the Conservatives steadily lost support to the New Democrats and the Liberals.

Nonetheless, Alberta's political system does have distinctive features. While other provinces have elected governments and leaders for long periods, none have kept their rulers in office for quite as long as Albertans have. While Alberta is far from politically homogeneous, it has clearly tended towards a unique mix of populist and conservative political movements. Finally, while Alberta has had eleven premiers since provincehood in 1905, three of them are outstanding—Aberhart, Manning, and Lougheed. Despite their different personalities, ideologies, and political styles, they have each reflected and articulated something essential about the province's political outlook and practices.

The unique and sharp lines that define Alberta's political life have attracted attempts at explanation, the most famous of which is C.B. Macpherson's claim that Alberta demonstrated the workings of a "quasi-party" system to meet the needs of a society that was politically and economically a subordinate part of a mature capitalist economy.[1] In a normal party system there is some competition among parties that represent different social coalitions and classes. The distinctive feature of Alberta's system, evident well before the 1935 Social Credit victory, was the absence of competitive parties. Macpherson argued that the provincial preference for single, dominant parties was due to two factors: the province's virtual colonial status in relation to central Canada, and its class homogeneity, with a preponderance of farmers. While

Macpherson's description of the style of Alberta politics is penetrating and accurate, his explanation of that style has been widely criticized over the years. Ed Bell's research as outlined in his chapter, "Reconsidering *Democracy in Alberta*," shows that Alberta was a complex heterogeneous society even in the Social Credit period.[2] By the 1960s all observers agreed that the province's class composition was no longer dominated by petit bourgeois commodity producers, and yet the political patterns evident in the 1930s endured. As for Alberta's quasi-colonial status, it is part of western folklore that central Canada exists only to rob the province blind, but despite the strong evidence of "regional alienation," research tends to show that the west is not markedly different in lifestyle than other parts of the country.[3] Its natural resource wealth has given the province a standard of living and political leverage unimaginable a generation ago.

A way around these difficulties is to explain the pattern of provincial politics by reference to political culture. Gurston Dacks, for example, argues that since 1900 the "Alberta consensus" has rested on two pillars: regional alienation and "the inclination of Albertans to relate to provincial politics in terms of the interest they have believed they share in a single dominant commodity rather than in terms of social class or some other form of consciousness." Together these forces produce an artificial homogeneity that persuades Albertans to support their government in its battles with Ottawa.[4] The presence of a "dominant commodity" merely masks the real differences within Alberta's political community, it does not negate them. Dacks speculates that with the decline of the oil and gas industries in the province, the Alberta consensus may evaporate as well, exposing a more conflictual and competitive political process.

Given Alberta's population growth from immigration over the last two generations, the cultural argument can only work if newcomers absorb a pre-existing set of political assumptions and arguments. A political culture like this must have a source and must be transferred across generations. Unless we are willing to accept some "hidden hand," it should also be clear that the culture needs to be actively maintained and transferred; it has no automatic preeminence. The source of Alberta's distinctive political culture is its political system itself, or more precisely, its party system, its discourse on partisanship, its tradition of government dominance of the legislature and the strategic intervention of such leaders as Aberhart, Manning and Lougheed, who reshaped the political culture to meet new circumstances. Albertans have to look somewhere for their cues about politics, they have to listen to arguments about the nature of the political, and they have to see evidence of principles turned into practice in order to believe and to act on that belief. The system of political leadership and the political executive provides these cues. The argument is circular only if the influence of institutions is ignored. As Macpherson pointed out, Alberta's early political experiences reinforced a strong distaste for partisanship.[5] The nonpartisan tradition took root in the territorial period before 1905 because party divisions were considered irrelevant to pressing local concerns and because of the need to maintain a united front against Ottawa in order to wrest provincial status.[6] As L.H. Thomas pointed out, Alberta voters seem to respond to "the man or movement that makes what appears to be a nonpartisan appeal."[7] W.L. Morton also noted the Alberta tradition of nonpartisanship:

> The second [historical feature of western politics] is the apolitical, or even anti-political, character of its public life. The development began in the assertion of the sectional needs of the West; it found fullest expression in Alberta through Social Credit as a medium of expression of religious fundamentalism, sectionalism, and the sense of novelty, of the possibility of new beginnings.[8]

Nonpartisanship was evident even in the very partisan period of Liberal government from 1905 to 1921. It found its first unambiguous expression, however, in the United Farmers of Alberta (UFA) government that swept to power in 1921. Nonpartisanship was not mere talk; it translated into specific forms of political practice, the most important of which were extensive community-based political organization of the dominant party and plebiscitary decision-making. William Aberhart himself came to Alberta in 1910 and experienced the nonpartisan tradition directly under UFA governments. He and his Social Credit colleagues were inexperienced parliamentarians (Aberhart did not speak publicly in the Alberta legislature until 1939) and so naturally turned to UFA practices and political discourse as models which they could refashion to meet their own needs. E.C. Manning came to Alberta to attend Aberhart's Bible Institute, and so had to absorb Alberta's political culture and practices under the UFA as well. He carried that tradition on brilliantly for twenty-five consecutive years as premier. Peter Lougheed, in turn, came to political maturity under Manning's Social Credit government, and absorbed and refashioned its political style for the needs of a new, urbanized Alberta.

This chapter makes several simple arguments. Class and colonialism are important to understanding the origins of Alberta's tradition of non-partisanship, but these origins had to be institutionalized somehow in order to preserve their influence. The political culture and discourse of nonpartisanship gradually congealed into a set of political practices and institutions that provided new and old Albertans with a portrait of "what made sense" and what seemed right in political life. Political leaders and their parties were expected to "rise above and reach beyond" petty squabbles, to represent the essential interests of the province for its internal needs and its external relations. There is nothing mechanical about this process, however. The refashioning of the nonpartisan tradition and the redesign of nonpartisan practices requires leadership, a capacity to sense instinctively the patterns of accepted discourse and the creative, even artistic, ways in which they may be modified to suit different interests and agendas. As well, nonpartisanship should not be taken literally. As a discourse and as a practice, it masks the partisan use of power to serve some interests at the expense of others. But it resonates so deeply in the Alberta political psyche that, paradoxically, the pursuit and maintenance of power must somehow appear disinterested and impartial.

Territorial Government to Social Credit, 1888-1935

The achievement of provincial status in 1905 was the culmination of twenty years of territorial political struggle. Until 1888, the Northwest Territories were governed by the Lieutenant Governor and a territorial council comprising both elected and appointed members. In 1885, F.W.G. Haultain, a recent British immigrant to the Territories, was elected to the council. His was a consistent voice demanding responsible government from Ottawa and he rapidly emerged as the council's leader. He later became the Territorial Premier.

In 1888 the territorial council was converted to a legislative assembly,[9] and the Lieutenant Government selected an "advisory council" on financial matters drawn from the assembly. The council was clearly a quasi-cabinet, but under Haultain's leadership chaffed against Ottawa's tight control over its grants to the Territories (virtually the only source of Territorial revenue). Haultain resigned from the advisory council in

1889 to protest its powerlessness. This caused two years of legislative paralysis, as new advisory councils were appointed by the Lieutenant Governor only to be censured and defeated by Haultain's group.[10] Amendments to the Northwest Territories Act in 1891 met these objections in part by reducing the Lieutenant Governor's powers and expanding the legislature's powers. The role and appointment of the advisory council was left vague, however, and so the legislature decided to appoint its own "executive committee" with Haultain as chair. A year later Haultain succeeded in persuading the federal government to transfer its grants as a lump sum to be administered and dispersed by the Northwest Territories.[11] This achievement was capped with the 1897 amendments to the Northwest Territories Act that finally granted responsible government. The Lieutenant Governor was to act only on the advice of a cabinet that enjoyed the confidence of the legislature.

The next obvious evolutionary phase was provincial status. By the turn of the century the area was growing rapidly because of immigration, and without provincial status the territories lacked independent powers of taxation to raise necessary revenues. Haultain began his formal campaign for provincial status in 1900 with a speech to the legislature that was then conveyed to Ottawa (in the tradition of grievance "letters to Ottawa" from the preresponsible government days). Even at this stage, party divisions were assiduously avoided in the territorial legislature. While differences of opinion and interest certainly existed, and sometimes coincided with party lines, the territorial priorities at the time were so overwhelmingly clear and in almost all cases involved maintaining a solid front against Ottawa, that a political practice of nonpartisanship grew quickly and naturally. It was more than a practice, however, and Haultain felt that partisanship was responsible for most of the irrationalities of politics. "He did not totally condemn party politics, but he believed it was unnecessary at the municipal and provincial levels of government and that Canadians had too much of it at the federal level."[12]

As it turned out, Haultain allowed himself to be drawn into, and eventually became the victim of, the very partisanship that he despised. His dream was for "one big province" consisting of both present-day Alberta and Saskatchewan. This coincided roughly with the existing territorial boundaries, and Haultain thought that the current administration in Regina worked perfectly well without having to be reproduced and duplicated for two provinces. One large province would also provide a better economic and political power base for the emerging west. Haultain sensed that the federal Liberals under Laurier were less sympathetic to this project than were the Borden Conservatives, and so urged people to vote Tory in the 1904 federal election. As well, he allowed himself to be identified with the newly emerging territorial Conservative party. Laurier won the 1904 election and within a year introduced legislation to create not one big province, but two. As well, the federal government decided to impose requirements for separate schools on the two provinces and to retain ownership and control over natural resources. Lieutenant Governors with clear Liberal affiliations were appointed in the two new provinces, and they in turn appointed interim Liberal administrations who then had the advantage of incumbency in the 1905 elections. Not surprisingly, Liberals were returned in both provinces.

The snub to Haultain was astonishing, given his dominance of Territorial politics for the previous twenty years. He decided to fight the Saskatchewan election, but not as a Tory against Liberals. He articulated his suspicion of party divisions in his farewell speech to his old constituents of Fort Macleod before leaving for Saskatchewan:

> As for myself, I stand for no-party government, regardless of what any political party or both political parties may decide. The welfare and interests of this great western country are more important than the success or convenience of any political party.[13]

Instead, he headed a loose "provincial rights" party protesting the terms of provincial status, and particularly the separate schools provisions. Haultain was irritated by the federal imposition of requirements in an area of clear provincial jurisdiction, but was concerned as well that the heterogeneity of the region's population demanded uniform institutions and education into citizenship. The issue was too arcane for the first campaign of a new province, and Haultain won only 9 seats to the Liberals' 16. He left politics to become the provincial Chief Justice, but the legacy of nonpartisanship and suspicion of mainline political parties remained a strong force in Alberta provincial politics after 1905.[14]

The first premier of Alberta was A.C. Rutherford. He had run and lost in his first election for the territorial legislature in 1896, but won in 1898 on a platform supporting Haultain.[15] While his affiliations were Liberal (he joined the party in 1900), he ran as an independent supporter of Haultain in the 1902 election (arguing in favour of two provinces rather than one). Rutherford became the first leader of the provincial Liberal party at its founding convention in 1905, and on 2 September Lieutenant Governor Bulyea (a former member of the territorial assembly and a Liberal) called on him to form an interim provincial government leading up to elections. The Liberals enjoyed the advantages of incumbency, and were faced by Conservatives led by R.B. Bennett, then a Calgary lawyer. Bennett made a fine target because of his CPR connections, and most Albertans "could find some reason for disliking the great corporation."[16] It was a rout; the Liberals took 23 of 25 seats. They were to remain in power for sixteen years, when they were discarded as ignominiously as the Tories had been in Alberta's first provincial election.

Alberta's first cabinet had only five members. Rutherford was premier, treasurer, and minister of education, establishing a pattern of dominant leadership that would continue through to the Lougheed years. Rutherford dominated in this period more through his energy and zeal than through any great love or loyalty from the party, but his party's dominance of the legislature made his own personal dominance of the government more assured. Rutherford was never as nonpartisan as Haultain had aspired to be. While he shared Haultain's resistance to separate schools on the grounds that a uniform educational system was necessary to build a coherent society on the frontier,[17] he made sure that the provincial university was located in his own riding of Strathcona, across the river from Edmonton which, much to the chagrin of Calgary, was chosen as the provincial capital. But like most of his preautonomy colleagues, Rutherford had absorbed a political rhetoric of nonpartisanship, and his 1909 election campaign echoed Haultain's attack on faction and party. In his own address to his constituents in Strathcona, Rutherford appealed to them "for the elimination of selfish and partisan considerations. I appeal to you not as Liberals or Conservatives, but as Albertans. The Province must stand before the party."[18] Rutherford's Liberal colleagues were not pleased with this nonpartisan ploy, though the election results mollified their discomfort: 37 Liberals, 2 Conservatives, 1 Independent and 1 Socialist.

The 1909 election was the zenith of Rutherford's career. Shortly afterwards he became embroiled in a railway scandal that one authority has called a "critical event" in the province's history.[19] At the time, a key provincial priority was building an efficient transportation system, and every town wanted rail service. A great deal of provincial government energy went into negotiating agreements with railway companies for approvals and support. In 1910 the Conservative opposition successfully pressed the case of the Alberta and Great Waterways Railway, alleging both stupidity and impropriety among ministers in their dealings with the railway. The essence of the scandal was that the cabinet had furnished generous bond guarantees to a company that it knew nothing about and which met virtually none of its promises regarding the construction of the railway. At the very least, the case suggested ministerial incompetence; at worst, ministerial corruption. A Royal Commission was appointed, and its report documented the cabinet's incompetence but found no direct evidence of corruption. The scandal remained in the public eye for years because the provincial government tried to claim over $7 million in bond proceeds as its own to be transferred to provincial accounts from private banks.[20]

Rutherford was directly implicated in the scandal, and was deposed as premier and leader of the party in 1910 shortly after it came to public light. The federal Liberals had pulled the strings to position the provincial party in 1905 to capture the government, and once again intervened in 1910 to deal with the railway crisis. With their support and encouragement, Rutherford and the cabinet colleagues who supported him were ousted, and Arthur L. Sifton, who resigned as the Chief Justice of the Province, assumed the premiership and leadership of the party in May 1910.[21] Sifton's Liberal credentials were impeccable, but his position as chief justice gave the veneer of impartiality and propriety that the government needed to cleanse itself of the allegations surrounding the railway scandal. The party had to "rise above and reach beyond" for its new leader, and Sifton proved a capable and dominant leader for three successive elections. The Alberta and Great Waterways crisis had, however, subtly changed the nature of political discourse in the province. It reinforced Albertan suspicion of monopolistic business interests, banks and eastern political institutions. It also reinforced, in Sifton's own person, a provincial preference for leaders and governments somehow above the fray. It undermined what faith there had been in the old line parties, and injected a new and eventually powerful line of division within the legislature. Rutherford, while out of the cabinet, was still nominally a Liberal and remained in the legislature with a small group of supporters. After 1910, the legislature was split between the Sifton Liberals, the Rutherford Liberals, and Conservatives, divided by their "degree of resistance to the centralizing tendencies of a long-entrenched and powerful federal government."[22] In the 1913 election, while Rutherford ran as a Liberal, he openly attacked Sifton's policy of trying to get the Alberta and Great Waterways Railway bond money from the banks, and offered to campaign for the Conservatives. At one point during his own nominating meeting, he rejected the party label and called himself an independent. While he lost his seat, his biographer sees a lingering effect in his sad decline from prominence:

> Rutherford's frustrated political career helped to set Alberta on a unique political course. As a political leader, Rutherford was essentially an Ontario-bred, non-partisan, provincial nationalist, and as such he set himself—and Alberta—on a collision course with the fiercely partisan and centralist preoccupations of the Laurier regime.[23]

The Liberals under Sifton won both the 1913 and 1917 provincial elections, but were increasingly driven by policies and issues originating in movements outside of their own party, such as prohibition, women's suffrage, and especially farm and other policies pressed by the newly formed United Farmers of Alberta. The UFA influence over the Liberals was evident in the 1913 campaign, for example, in the government's pre-election passage of the Direct Legislation Act which provided for initiation or approval of legislation by electors. The UFA had passed a resolution calling for this in January 1913,[24] and while officially neutral in the campaign, recommended to its members that they vote for the government because the Conservatives were more under the control of the "money power" than the Liberals.

While the UFA stayed out of the 1917 election as well, the Liberals had to contend with the newly formed Non-Partisan League, led by William Irvine. The League originated in the United States and managed to win the North Dakota state legislature in 1916, the same year that Irvine helped establish it in Alberta. Its key platform point resonated with the traditional discourse of Alberta politics: "To overcome partisanship by the election of a truly people's government and the establishment of a business administration instead of a party administration."[25] The Non-Partisan League won only two seats in the 1917 election (one of which was Louise McKinney's, a prohibitionist and suffragette, the first woman to be elected to any Canadian legislature). After the Liberal victory, Sifton resigned as premier and went to Ottawa to join the Union government. His departure precipitated the demise of the Liberal party in Alberta. Sifton's strong personality, and his appeal as the "nonpartisan" from above who had come to cleanse the party had held the Liberals together through two elections. But the earlier split between Rutherford and Sifton was now compounded by another: between Liberals who supported the Union government in Ottawa consisting of Liberals and Tories, and those who followed Laurier in his rejection of the Union scheme.[26] Charles Stewart took on the premiership, but had virtually no impact on Liberal fortunes.

The UFA, under the leadership of Henry Wise Wood, had eschewed direct political participation. It was an organization designed to press the interests of farmers and farmers only, on the principle of what it called "group government."[27] Borrowing the theories of Herbert Spencer, Wise Wood argued that history was evolutionary (not revolutionary as the socialists held) and that the principle of co-operation among classes would eventually triumph over competition. Its model form of government required that each major group in society send delegates to an assembly to negotiate with the delegates of other occupational or industrial groups. Any decisions would have to be ratified by the group's members in a form of direct democracy. Traditional political parties by their nature had to aggregate interests to win legislative power. Moreover, the traditional parties were interested in suppressing, not extending democracy, because in practice they were dominated by elite interests.

This was a primitive social and political theory, but it had certain practical consequences. The UFA under Wise Wood's leadership had no desire to enter politics in the traditional way because to do so would have transformed it from a movement to a party. The UFA preferred to pressure incumbent (Liberal) governments on farmers' interests. This began to unravel in 1919 because of the growing severity of the post-World War I depression and the influence within the UFA of the Non-Partisan League, which had no qualms about fighting elections (the UFA and the Non-Partisan League informally amalgamated in 1919). That year the UFA reluctantly decided to allow candidates in the election, but left the decision up to UFA locals in the constituencies. This was a significant move, since the UFA had a vast network of locals throughout the province, a species of proto-constituency associations unrivalled by the traditional parties. The UFA fought its first campaign in the Cochrane by-election in 1919 against an incumbent Liberal, and after a fierce contest, won the seat. This marked the end of the fuzzy detente that had characterized UFA-Liberal relations for close to a decade.

The UFA swept the 1921 provincial and federal elections in Alberta, winning 39 of 57 provincial seats (the Liberals captured only 14) and 10 of 12 federal seats.[28] The provincial campaign was peculiar by any standard. The UFA had won 39 seats without having established a separate party with its own leader. Not surprisingly, without a real party or leader it had little in the way of a provincial platform. Indeed, it won power while insisting that it opposed "partyism" with its caucus secrecy and cabinet domination, endorsing instead direct democracy and independent voting by MLAs. The natural choice for leader was Henry Wise Wood, president of the UFA, but he declined ostensibly because of worries that his American birth and upbringing would offend the electorate. Herbert Greenfield (himself English-born), a 52-year-old farmer long active in UFA affairs, became premier.

The UFA came into power as a movement against politics, and its more radical and committed wing tried at first to resist the larger institutional logic of the parliamentary system. The first UFA caucus, for example, spent some of its first meetings debating its own structure and relation to the traditional party system. Greenfield was challenged to include Liberals in the UFA cabinet, and to encourage sufficient co-operation that the very idea of an "official opposition" would be extinguished.[29] John Brownlee, the party's solicitor and future premier, encouraged a more "pragmatic" approach in what would be the first of a series of small steps towards orthodoxy. To do anything more would have required a revolutionary fervour the party lacked. It slowly inched its way into routine politics with cabinet leadership and caucus solidarity. In practice, however, the UFA was, like all Alberta governments before and after, relatively independent of the legislature as an institution. It enjoyed sufficient dominance that its rule was the rule of party and state, not party through the legislative process. With its promise of a new democratic utopia tarnished by practicalities, the UFA went into the election of 1926 like most incumbent governments and defended its record. The mid-1920s had been economically kind to Alberta, and the UFA had some significant achievements (e.g., the Alberta Wheat Pool) to its credit. Herbert Greenfield had resigned under pressure from the party in 1925 and been replaced with the UFA's former solicitor and Attorney-General, John E. Brownlee. Brownlee led the party to victory in the 1926 election, and again (with a reduced majority), in 1930.

Brownlee was a lawyer in charge of a farmers' movement, and that very anomaly had persuaded the UFA to select Greenfield as its leader in 1921. In a caucus of farmers without any parliamentary experience, however, Brownlee quickly emerged as the dominant figure, eclipsing even the premier. While he reinforced the party's more conservative tendencies, and urged it to reconcile itself to parliamentary practices, he did not ignore the movement's nonpartisan inspiration. In the 1926 election he urged the electors to remain free of "partyism." The traditional parties were dominated by Ottawa and forced to sacrifice provincial interests. Moreover, the party system divided people into two camps. "If there is one thing that I rejoice in," he said, "it is to be able to stand here with a clean conscience and say that our effort has been to organize on a basis of freedom to select men absolutely regardless of their political affiliations."[30] He was far from a prairie firebrand and orator, however. Cautious and conservative, he irritated the more radical wing of the movement by opposing the extension of social programmes like old age pensions. Nonetheless, he quickly established his dominance over the party and the larger movement.[31] Cabinet ministers were expected to be routine administrators, while Brownlee made the larger strategic decisions. "Cabinet meetings were not really decision making sessions but rather opportunities to discuss decisions at which Brownlee had already arrived."[32] He had the reputation of living out of his briefcase, working ceaselessly (and somewhat humourlessly) for the public good. The opposition dubbed the UFA caucus after 1926 as the "Brownleeites." His success in having jurisdiction over natural resources finally turned over to the province in 1930 increased his stature greatly and assured victory in the provincial election that year.[33]

Brownlee's premiership was not without controversy. He was fiscally conservative, and had to fight constantly against demands within his party and the province for then radical social welfare schemes. Despite these difficulties he might have retained power for another twenty years had it not been for a sensational scandal in 1933, when his former secretary charged him with seduction and forced sexual relations. The court ruled against Brownlee in 1934 (the verdict was upheld on appeal to the Judicial Committee in 1940) and he resigned in disgrace, to be replaced by R.G. Reid.[34] The UFA may conceivably have been able to withstand the Brownlee scandal, but it had a much bigger worry on the threshold of the 1935 provincial election: William Aberhart and the Social Credit movement.

Much more has been written about William Aberhart than any other premier of Alberta.[35] He was born in Ontario, and in 1910, at the age of thirty-one and married, moved with his family to Calgary where he had been offered a teaching position. Within a year he was given a principalship, and in 1915 he became principal of the newly organized Crescent Heights High School in Calgary. He remained principal there until becoming premier in 1935. The most detailed biographical portrait of Aberhart shows a intensely religious and energetic man who was almost maniacally busy with his work, his community and his ministry.[36] His intellectual style was inflexible, given to rote learning with a strong dose of authoritarianism. He could also be a great raconteur and social companion, and his religious preaching honed his flair for story telling and public speaking. William Aberhart was anything but ordinary.[37] Even before his political career, Aberhart was the sort of man people either liked or disliked intensely.

Aberhart was a fundamentalist Christian with a particular interest in the literal meaning of the Bible.[38] He preached at a Baptist church for the first few years after his arrival in Calgary, but in 1918 established the inter-denominational Calgary Prophetic Bible Conference. In 1925, with some misgivings, he agreed to do weekly religious radio broadcasts. Soon he was being beamed into Saskatchewan, Manitoba, British Columbia and some American states.[39] Until 1932 the broadcasts were exclusively religious, though as the Depression deepened after 1929 there were inevitable references to the growing destitution and unemployment. In 1932, however, Aberhart stumbled across the writings of Major C.H. Douglas, an Englishman, on the theory of social credit. Douglas was not an economist by training, and his ideas were ridiculed by most of the economics profession. He argued that the depression was due not to the incapacity of the industrial system (indeed, even in the early 1930s it was clear that there was more than adequate productive capacity to meet people's needs) but to insufficient purchasing power. At the economic level, Douglas's theory called for government stimulation of consumption through the issuing of "social credit" (Aberhart's famous $25 per month). The failures of the economic system were variously blamed on the mechanisms of capitalism itself or the self-interest of financiers and capitalists. Douglas also expressed distaste for the traditional party system which in his view corrupted the productive potential of the industrial system with political self-interest. He advocated a greater role for "experts" in the policy process, relegating elected officials to a more general steering function.

William Aberhart was an enthusiastic if undisciplined convert to social credit. The ideology's anti-capitalist tone, its attacks on bankers and rich, heartless industrialists, and its promise of social credit dividends or monthly cheques were predictably popular in the middle of the depression. But Aberhart also instinctively built on several key Albertan political traditions. The first was constituency organization and populism, twin forces that had sustained the UFA's early successes. Aberhart's radio broadcasts gave him the technological capacity to be heard in virtually every living room in the province. In late 1932 he began to mix social credit ideas in with his religious programming. His Bible Institute and radio programs rested on an infrastructure of religious study groups that were easily transformed into social credit study groups and the sinews of a political movement by 1935. Just before the election, for example, there were 63 active study groups in Calgary alone.[40]

Another powerful and resonant characteristic of social credit as Aberhart described it was its nonpartisanship. Aberhart did not even run in the 1935 election (like the UFA in 1921, Social Credit was elected as the government without a formal "leader"). Social Credit was to be above the competitive fray of the political system, and institute a government, as one 1933 newspaper account had it, that would "function for the benefit of all the citizens instead of favouring privileged classes, whether manufacturers, producers, or bankers."[41] Until January 1935 social credit was simply a movement urging the traditional parties, particularly the UFA government, to adopt its principles. Aberhart appeared before the legislature's Agricultural Committee in 1934, with Major Douglas, to press the case for social credit, and he tried but failed to get the endorsement of the UFA. On 1 December the *Alberta Social Credit Chronicle* announced that in the face of this refusal, social credit would in some manner (but *not* as a political party!) contest the 1935 provincial election. Aberhart called for the study groups to submit the names of "100 honest men." In the words of the *Chronicle*: "Reliable, honorable, bribe-proof businessmen who have definitely laid aside their party politic affiliations will be asked to represent Social Credit in every constituency."[42] As Aberhart said in one of his pre-election broadcasts: "The Alberta Social Credit League is the organization behind this broadcast. It is against party politics and holds no party affiliation."[43] The nonpartisan appeal worked in a very partisan way: the Social Credit party of Alberta, formed only months before the 1935 election, won 56 of 63 seats. The Liberals elected 5 members, and the Conservatives 2. The UFA was completely erased.

Nonpartisanship from Aberhart to Getty

As its leader and founder, Aberhart dominated the Social Credit party
and government for its first few years. Within two years, however, he
had to face down insurgency from radical elements within his own movement. The Social Credit platform had been nothing if not ambitious. It
had called for a complete overhaul of the monetary system, banks, the
redistribution of income, a $25 a month "social credit dividend" to every
household in Alberta, price controls, medicare and state control over
industry. The $25 dividend was a remarkable promise at a time when
a dozen eggs cost a nickle and a good roast went for $0.75.[44] Moreover,
Aberhart had promised to implement the Social Credit platform within
eighteen months of being elected, only to discover on taking office that
the province was on the verge of bankruptcy. Aberhart had been repudi-
ated by the Douglas organization in London before the 1935 election,
and after it Douglas refused Aberhart's urgent pleas for specific advice
on the implementation of social credit in Alberta. Patience among his
more ideological followers was wearing thin by 1937, and in the face of
a party revolt Aberhart agreed to pass the Alberta Social Credit Act. Two
British advisors were brought to Edmonton to assist the newly established Social Credit Board (comprised of five MLAs appointed for ten
years). All Social Credit MLAs, including cabinet members, had to sign
an "Agreement of Association" to subordinate themselves to Board.[45]
The Board and its commission of experts were the source of much of
the social credit legislation that eventually was disallowed by Ottawa
on constitutional grounds.[46]

By the time Aberhart died in 1943 Social Credit was on the threshold of
becoming just another conservative party. The early populism and grassroots democracy of the movement, built on study groups, had been replaced by tight cabinet control.[47] Its economic agenda of radical financial
reform had been disallowed by Ottawa and the courts, and made largely
irrelevant by wartime prosperity. Fortunately, despite its parliamentary
inexperience and exotic ideology, Social Credit proved to be a reasonably
competent government in other respects, and was re-elected in 1940 with
a reduced majority. While Ottawa-bashing had not figured in the 1935
election, Aberhart relied on it increasingly as Social Credit legislation
was struck down by "the east." Its submission to the Rowell-Sirois Commission in 1938, entitled *The Case for Alberta*, listed the usual grievances
and signalled a resuscitation of a hoary western political theme.[48]

After Aberhart's death, his disciple and protege E.C. Manning became leader and premier. Manning had come to Alberta to study at Aberhart's Bible Institute and was its first graduate. While studying there, he boarded with the Aberharts, and after his graduation helped Aberhart in his ministry. When Aberhart turned to Social Credit, so did Manning, and the two then spent their 1934 summer vacation travelling across the province and speaking in towns and villages. After the 1935 election victory, Manning was appointed to Aberhart's eight-man cabinet as Provincial Secretary, which at the age of 26 made him the youngest cabinet minister in the British empire.[49] Manning had none of the fire or eccentricity that made Aberhart so imposing a figure. His style was more reserved and placid, but it masked a remarkably astute Albertan politician. Manning succeeded in transforming the Social Credit party in several important ways. First, despite a half-hearted and final attempt to implement social credit monetary theory in the 1946 Alberta Bill of Rights Act,[50] Manning firmly disassociated the party from the radical social credit movement. By the middle of the war, Major Douglas and his followers had degenerated into anti-semitism and conspiracy theories of global cabals of financiers, and Manning found this personally repugnant and politically crippling. Second, he redefined the party's policies to exclude its early, radical proposals and succeeded in identifying socialism, not capitalism, as the threat against which Social Credit would defend the people of Alberta.[51] Whereas Aberhart had railed against the "50 big shots" who ran the country, Manning built alliances with the business classes, particularly American oil companies.[52]

Manning was an exceedingly skillful politician, winning seven consecutive provincial elections between 1944 and 1967. During the height of the Cold War he repeatedly identified socialism as the external threat.[53] His entente with the oil companies was geared to building a free enterprise climate in the province, and generous leases with low royalty rates were granted to counteract what Manning perceived to be Alberta's disadvantages in the international oil production market. Manning projected a nonpartisan image as a devoutly religious man who kept up Aberhart's tradition of weekly religious radio broadcasts (at the time of his retirement, Manning was still the host of "Canada's National Back to the Bible Hour"). He only faltered once, in 1955, when opposition charges of government corruption reduced Social Credit to 40 per cent of the vote and 37 seats (versus 24 seats for the opposition). After that election Manning established a Royal Commission to investigate the corruption charges, and he also took up some of the opposition's proposals, such as larger fiscal transfers to municipalities.[54] The result was that in the 1959 election Manning and the Social Credit party won 61 of 65 seats.

Alberta had a curiously apolitical public life in the later Manning years; as one writer put it, the multi-party system fell into a "twenty-year coma."[55] The legislature met for only six or seven weeks each year, and the party caucus virtually never met when the legislature was not sitting. The cabinet and E.C. Manning made the key decisions, which then could be easily passed in the legislature dominated by the party.[56] It was the Social Credit party under Manning that started a practice (adopted later by Peter Lougheed) of "cabinet tours" across the province, apparently to show the people that this was their government. Before he retired in 1968, Manning twice tried to "rise above and reach beyond" partisan politics. The first was in a white paper he presented to the legislature in 1967 on Human Resources Development. This document tried to articulate his blend of free enterprise and social policy ideas—which he called "social conservatism" as an alternative to the current ideological choices:

> This paper is non-partisan . . . . If the time and energy, presently spent in political manoeuvering for partisan advantage, were instead channelled into a supreme and constructive effort to solve the problems and meet the challenges confronting our nation, Canadians would not only be happier but infinitely further ahead.[57]

The White Paper was paralleled by a book Manning published in 1967 entitled *Political Realignment*, which called for a new national political alignment of the Social Credit and Progressive Conservatives against the Liberals and the NDP. While this clearly had a partisan purpose, its key arguments depended on rising above traditional partisanship at the two ends of the political spectrum.

The key to Alberta leadership politics since 1905 had been nonpartisanship. The spectacular victories of the UFA in 1921 and Social Credit in 1935 had been supported by the twin pillars of extensive constituency based organization and the appearance or veneer of being disdainful of routine political competition. These were precisely the weapons that Peter Lougheed brought to bear in 1965-1971 in his successful strategy of capturing the provincial government. Lougheed decided to enter provincial politics in 1964 by seeking the leadership of the nearly dead Conservative party. The leadership convention was held in 1965, and

Lougheed won handily, though Manning's ascendancy in the province was so strong that it seemed like a dubious triumph. After winning the leadership, Lougheed concluded that "the organization had to be built at the constituency level. No party had done this since 1945."[58] Lougheed's nonpartisan approach to winning power was reinforced when he visited Duff Roblin, the Conservative Premier of Manitoba, who advised him to look for the best candidates irrespective of party affiliation. "Lougheed became convinced that 'the more non political, the more apolitical a person is, the better chance he has of winning.' "[59]

The 1967 election provided the opportunity to put these principles into practice. The Conservatives targeted their appeal to younger, urban Albertans, and managed to capture 26 per cent of the provincial vote and elected six MLAs, including Lougheed himself. Lougheed had carefully refrained from attacking Manning personally, given the premier's enormous personal popularity. The Tories ran a positive campaign, with several innovations. One was the filming of a TV documentary on Lougheed. Another was the adoption of NDP door-to-door campaigning.[60] Once in opposition, Lougheed perpetuated the nonpartisan, apolitical theme in advocating some relaxation of party discipline to allow MLAs occasionally to vote against party policy.[61] This was an echo of Alberta's traditional political discourse on democracy, but Lougheed's actions belied his words. He worked tirelessly to strengthen his party's organization and position in the legislature. He was helped by Manning's resignation in 1968 and replacement by the lacklustre Harry Strom as premier.[62] Strom did not have a strong leadership image, was soft-spoken and seemed shy, in sharp and unfavourable contrast to both E.C. Manning and Peter Lougheed.[63] Strom did not perform well on television, while Lougheed had worked hard to make it his medium. In an interesting parallel with Aberhart, Lougheed built his political success on a new technology that his opponents either ignored or misunderstood. In the 1971 provincial election, Strom appeared on radio but not television,[64] whereas the Tories spent 85 per cent of their campaign funds on TV advertising.[65] The strategy worked and as shown in the Savage-Hughes and Taras chapter, "The Media and Politics in Alberta," television remained an essential political medium for the Conservatives. Lougheed's Conservatives won power with 49 seats; Social Credit was reduced to 25 and the NDP received 1. A post-election survey showed extraordinarily high levels of support for Lougheed.[66]

Lougheed had not won on personal appeal alone. The party's platform in 1971 called for greater provincial government efforts to diversify the province's economy, and many of the key policy initiatives undertaken over the next fifteen years were in support of this goal.[67] These initiatives, along with the government's interpretation of the logic of non-partisan leadership, led to important changes to the machinery of executive government in Alberta. On assuming power, for example, Lougheed discovered that the Social Credit cabinets of Manning and Strom had kept no minutes or agendas. The only records of executive council decisions were orders-in-council.[68] Lougheed re-organized the council machinery so that it functioned more efficiently but also with tighter control and more secrecy than had been characteristic of the Social Credit era.[69] He also introduced a much larger cabinet of 22 members, almost half of his entire caucus. This was coupled with changes in the senior levels of the bureaucracy, where 70 per cent of deputy ministers in the first term were replaced.[70]

Lougheed became a master of nonpartisan leadership, but he had several advantages. First, his time in office coincided with unprecedented provincial prosperity. Albertans consequently enjoyed some of the highest levels of government services and the lowest level of taxation in the country, a politically appealing combination. Second, he had to defend that prosperity in series of bitter federal-provincial fights over energy policy after the first OPEC price surge in 1973. Having a Liberal government headed by Pierre Trudeau as his federal adversary for all but two and a half years of his premiership, Lougheed had ample opportunity to project himself as the defender of all Albertans against a rapacious central government. The formula worked exceedingly well, and Lougheed won lop-sided victories in 1975, 1979, and 1982, usually without much mention of the provincial opposition parties at all. The victories created another problem, however. Most political leaders have to worry about the legislature because they face some opposition there; in Lougheed's era the legislature was secure and therefore politically irrelevant. As leader, his problem was to keep his caucus together and to ensure close and direct contact with the people. Under Lougheed, therefore, every government member was to serve on a task force, study group or committee. Policy conferences were held every fall, and the caucus met daily when the legislature was sitting. The meetings sometimes were lengthy, and even when the legislature was not sitting, caucus would come together once a month or as vital issues arose. Lougheed organized the caucus into three different types of committees: standing committees (e.g., economic affairs, utilities, health and social services), ad hoc committees on special issues such as native rights, and task forces.[71]

The concomitant of a strong cabinet and vigorous, if disciplined, caucus, was a weak legislature. Between 1971 and 1979 only two private members bills were passed by the legislature of Alberta.[72] The Alberta Heritage Savings Trust Fund, established in 1976, was and is under direct cabinet control and the legislature's oversight powers are anaemic.[73] The quasi-public firms of the Lougheed era, most notably the Alberta Energy Corporation and Pacific Western Airlines (PWA), were a mix of private and public ownership that put them in a grey zone outside of detailed legislative review.[74] None of this was troubling to the Tories, since their dominance of the legislature made it largely irrelevant. The real debates and discussions over policy took place in caucus; the real decisions were made in cabinet. Peter Lougheed dominated both, but ensured that there was genuine debate and, on lesser issues, caucus control and sometimes veto over policy.[75] It is unquestionable, however, that Lougheed had a firm grip on the party. In the 1982 election, for example, the party's proposals to spend Heritage Fund money, the Mortgage Interest Reduction Plan, and the Small Business and Farm Interest Shielding Plan were largely Lougheed's ideas.[76] He ensured his personal influence over the party by maintaining "separate networks of contacts in various communities, working them tirelessly on the telephone to consult, stroke and reassure."[77]

Lougheed's successor and current premier is Don Getty, who served in Lougheed's cabinet in the 1970s but then retired to pursue business interests. He was the party establishment's candidate, favoured by Lougheed, party officials and much of the caucus. Despite this support, Getty failed to win a first ballot victory at the leadership convention in 1985, throwing some doubt on his support among the grassroots.[78] These doubts were reinforced by the party's performance in the 1986 election, where the opposition won 22 out of 83 seats. Six cabinet ministers were defeated. Unlike his predecessor, Getty was not able to blame a Liberal administration in Ottawa for the province's troubles, but lack of support among Tory voters themselves reduced the turnout and gave an opening to the provincial Liberals and NDP. The premier's travails continued with the call of a snap election in 1989. Tory electoral support dropped from 51 per cent to 44 per cent, even though the party captured 59 seats. The premier lost his own Edmonton seat, however, and had to win another in a by-election.

Getty's stumbling performance was a surprise to some given his reasonably good record as cabinet minister and his apprenticeship to Peter Lougheed. Getty has maintained most of the mechanisms of the political executive designed by Lougheed, principally the Premier's Office and the Executive Council Office. The Premier's Office consists of an executive director, a director of policy research, a director of the Premier's Office in Calgary, a communications office, and the Premier's executive assistant. The executive director is responsible for security, protocol, executive air travel, and relations with the Prime Minister's Office and the party. The Executive Council is the cabinet and its committees, of which there are seven standing policy committees and five standing operating committees. The premier chairs Council as well as two policy committees: the Committee on Priorities, Finance and Coordination and the Committee on Agriculture and Rural Economy. As in the Lougheed days the caucus meets daily when the legislature is sitting. There are ten caucus committees, and government MLAs must sit on at least two committees. All cabinet decisions are discussed in caucus, and the premier has insisted on a "buddy system" wherein each minister is responsible for immediately reporting cabinet discussions to a designated MLA (in some cases two).

Ironically, this system was established by a strong, dominant premier at the head of a party that itself dominated the legislature. It is the executive structure of nonpartisan leadership, the type that aspires to represent the entire population, to speak for the entire province against some (usually external) adversary. This style of leadership has so far eluded Premier Getty, despite attempts to champion a Triple-E Senate against Ottawa and more recently to pose as the leader of the western provinces in negotiating a post-Meech Lake constitutional agreement. In contrast to Manning and Lougheed, Getty's ersatz nonpartisan pose makes him an easy target in an increasingly partisan provincial political climate with strong Liberal and New Democratic opposition parties.

Conclusion

There can be no question of Alberta's distinctive political practice. It has been ruled for long periods by fringe parties (the UFA and Social Credit), it has a strong tradition of protest against the central government and "eastern interests," it seems to have a preference for direct forms of democracy, and it has entrusted itself to dominant leaders. This chapter began with the review of the prevailing theories of Alberta's exceptionalism. The three conventional explanations—Alberta's class structure, its colonial position vis-a-vis the east, and its political culture—are not convincing. In examining the history of political leadership in this province, it is clear that in addition to the characteristics mentioned above, Alberta has a strong identification with a nonpartisan tradition of politics. Every important leader since 1905 has adopted this formula and the practices that flow from it.

Nonpartisan politics sounds like an oxymoron. A glance at the UFA, Social Credit, and Lougheed Conservatives reveals a fairly clear meaning, however. The tradition is one that rejects superficial divisions of the electorate into classes or groups and politics built on their competition. Instead, while it recognizes the economic and social differences that exist in the province, the nonpartisan discourse yearns for leaders and governments that serve the people as a whole, that rise above their differences to serve fundamental needs. The roots of this mentality are doubtless in the semi-colonial situation that the territories found themselves in before 1905, and the circumstances of provincehood after that. But once the discourse was established, it nurtured every major political movement and leader that Alberta ever produced. Haultain, Rutherford, Sifton, Irvine, Wise Wood, Aberhart, Manning and Lougheed stand in an unbroken line of Alberta politicians who instinctively seek to frame their appeals in terms that are above and beyond the shrill partisanship of normal politics. By 1921 the requirements for success in this appeal were clear. Leaders, in order to appear detached and nonpartisan, had to be uncorruptable and dedicated. Brownlee's sex scandal would have destroyed his political career in any case, but was devastating to the UFA as it faced the teachers and preachers that led Social Credit in 1935. Ernest Manning's personal popularity was nutured by a general respect for his moral character. Peter Lougheed was the object of a few charges of impropriety, but always rectified them quickly.

Another key element in the formula is organization. The party that aspires to be ''nonpartisan'' must establish direct links with the electorate. Every major party in Alberta has built its organization at the constituency level and has circumvented the legislature to maintain its connection. The techniques have varied from forms of direct democracy to open access to ministers, but the principle is the same. One result of this practice is a weak legislature, since one-party dominance ensures the leader's dominance, which in turn ensures that decisions are made by the leader and cabinet and simply ratified by the legislature.

There is nothing inevitable about this formula or this tradition. It might conceivably disappear to be replaced by more traditional forms of party competition. But the roots of nonpartisanship run deep in Alberta's political discourse and practice. While the specific form of non-partisan politics has to be reinvented in each area, it is a valuable resource to those leaders who can use it wisely and well. William Aberhart tapped it to build Social Credit, and Peter Lougheed tapped it to destroy Social Credit. There is little sign that Don Getty has the personality to call forth its power, but he faces several obstacles as well.

The first obstacle is the absence of a Liberal administration in Ottawa. Peter Lougheed enjoyed tremendous popularity for his staunch defence of Alberta's interests, particularly against the 1980 National Energy Program. The Tory administration in Ottawa not only dismantled the NEP, but has placed western cabinet ministers such as Don Mazankowski and Joe Clark in key positions. Fortunately, there is such a deep Albertan reservoir of ill-will towards Ottawa, no matter what the political stripe of the government, that Getty has managed to capitalize on "defending" Albertans against, for example, the GST. A second problem is that the erosion of the government's legislative dominance over the last two elections makes the opposition much more visible and relevant than in the Lougheed era. Opposition attacks have astutely concentrated on two themes: the government's apparent cosiness with special business interests and allegations that the premier has used public office for personal gain. These are serious charges in any regime, but particularly in Alberta with its expectation that leaders and governments are nonpartisan. Getty's personal style is less austere and driven than Manning's or Lougheed's were, and so he lacks that quality of severity and discipline that makes nonpartisan claims plausible.

A third problem is the province's troubled economy. Layoffs, high unemployment, increased taxes and public service cuts have set the stage for widespread public dissatisfaction and open squabbling between business, labour and professional groups. Ironically, this disgruntlement has created a fourth problem for the Getty government that simultaneously demonstrates the continuing strength of the nonpartisan ideal. The Reform Party of Canada is a typical Albertan phenomenon: it calls for more genuine grassroots democracy and expresses distrust of government in general and of Ottawa in particular. While it has decided not to run provincially, it is a political movement that may yet upset the provincial Tories. Preston Manning's rhetoric is an uncanny echo of traditional Albertan appeals to rise above the old partisanship of incumbent parties and interests.

The emergence of the Reform party suggests that Alberta may be preparing for one of its epochal political shifts. It is an odd coincidence that Alberta's provincial premiers seem to come in threes. The pattern has been first to win power with a strong leader who obliterates the preceding government, maintain that power under a competent successor, and finally lose office with the third leader. This happened to the Liberals (Rutherford, Sifton, Stewart), the UFA (Greenfield, Brownlee, Reid), and Social Credit (Aberhart, Manning, Strom). This pattern may be more than mere coincidence. It may reflect the turbulence of a political system that tries to combine the exercise of power with the discourse of nonpartisanship. The inevitable tension at the heart of this formula makes the demand for nonpartisanship more plausible than its practice, gives credibility to apolitical movements ''outside'' of the system, and eventually undermines those movements once they achieve power. The provincial Tories have failed to articulate a fresh version of Alberta's nonpartisan discourse, and have been challenged by the Reform party on their own ground. If history does repeat itself, Don Getty may yet step aside to make way for Alberta's third and last Conservative premier.

NOTES

1. C.B. Macpherson, *Democracy in Alberta: Social Credit and the Party System* (Toronto: University of Toronto Press, 1953).

2. For a thorough treatment of the entire Social Credit period, see Alvin Finkel, *The Social Credit Phenomenon in Alberta* (Toronto: University of Toronto Press, 1989), chap. 1.

3. Roger Gibbins, ''Western Alienation,'' in *The Prairie West: Historical Readings*, 1st ed., Douglas R. Francis and Howard Palmer, eds. (Edmonton: Pica Pica Press, 1985), p. 608.

4. Gurston Dacks, ''From Consensus to Competition: Social Democracy and Political Culture in Alberta,'' in *Socialism and Democracy in Alberta: Essays in Honour of Grant Notley*, Larry Pratt, ed. (Edmonton: NeWest Press, 1986), p. 187.

5. Howard Palmer with Tamara Palmer, *Alberta: A New History* (Edmonton: Hurtig, 1990), p. 136.

6. J. William Brennan, "The 'Autonomy Question' and the Creation of Alberta and Saskatchewan, 1905," in *The Prairie West: Historical Readings*, 1st ed., Douglas R. Francis and Howard Palmer, eds. (Edmonton: Pica Pica Press, 1985), pp. 364-65.

7. L.G. Thomas, *The Liberal Party in Alberta: A History of Politics in the Province of Alberta 1905-1921* (Toronto: University of Toronto Press, 1959), p. 172. The tradition was reinforced by the social gospel movement at the turn of the century. As Allen notes, "To speak of such a politics, a politics beyond the strife of partisan context, was to speak the language of the progressives of the farm and labour movements." Richard Allen, *The Social Passion: Religion and Social Reform in Canada 1914-28* (Toronto: University of Toronto Press, 1973), p. 200.

8. W.L. Morton, "A Century of Plain and Parkland," in *The Prairie West: Historical Readings*, 1st ed., Douglas R. Francis and Howard Palmer, eds. (Edmonton: Pica Pica Press, 1985), p. 33.

9. Grant MacEwan, *Frederick Haultain: Frontier Statesman of the Canadian Northwest* (Saskatoon: Western Producer Prairie Books, 1985), p. 46.

10. Ibid., pp. 53-56.

11. Ibid., p. 68.

12. Ibid., p. 140.

13. Ibid., p. 158.

14. Thomas, *The Liberal Party in Alberta*, p. 23.

15. D.R. Babcock, *Alexander Cameron Rutherford: A Gentleman of Strathcona* (Calgary: The Friends of Rutherford House and The University of Calgary Press, 1989), p. 10.

16. Thomas, *The Liberal Party in Alberta*, p. 27.

17. Babcock, *Alexander Cameron Rutherford*, pp. 35-36. This was one reason he moved as early as he did (1906) for the establishment of a nondenominational provincial university. He hoped it would pre-empt denominational ones.

18. Babcock, *Alexander Cameron Rutherford*, p. 42. Rutherford's remarks were published in the *Strathcona Plaindealer*.

19. Thomas, *The Liberal Party in Alberta*, p. 58.

20. The banks refused and the case made its way through the courts up to the Judicial Committee of the Privy Council in 1913, which decided in the banks' favour. This not only reinforced Albertan resentment of banks and eastern institutions, but it also affected provincial finances, which had counted on receiving the $7 million.

21. Thomas, *The Liberal Party in Alberta*, p. 58.

22. Ibid., p. 116.

23. Babcock, *Alexander Cameron Rutherford*, p. 73.

24. Thomas, *The Liberal Party in Alberta*, p. 136.

25. Anthony Mardiros, *William Irvine: The Life of a Prairie Radical* (Toronto: James Lorimer and Company, 1979), p. 57. Indeed, the power of discourse is shown in an intriguing parallel between the position taken by the American Non-Partisan League in World I and the Aberhart Social Credit position taken in World War II. Both urged a conscription of wealth before a conscription of men for the war effort.

26. Thomas, *The Liberal Party in Alberta*, p. 181.

27. Macpherson, *Democracy in Alberta*, chaps. 2 and 3, is still the most lucid and penetrating discussions of UFA theory and practice. See also William Kirby Rolph, *Henry Wise Wood of Alberta* (Toronto: University of Toronto Press, 1950).

28. Palmer and Palmer, *Alberta: A New History*, p. 196; Thomas, *The Liberal Party in Alberta*, p. 204.

29. Franklin Lloyd Foster, *John Edward Brownlee: A Biography* (Ph.D. Dissertation, Queen's University, Kingston, 1981), pp. 137-36.

30. Ibid., p. 287.

31. Ibid., p. 304.

32. Ibid., p. 345.

33. Palmer and Palmer, *Alberta: A New History*, pp. 216-17.

34. Brownlee maintained his innocence to the end, and there is no conclusive proof as to who was lying. See James H. Gray, *Talk to My Lawyer!: Great Stories of Southern Alberta's Bar and Bench* (Edmonton: Hurtig, 1987), chap. 7; Thomas Thorner and G.N. Reddekopp, "A Question of Seduction: The Case of *Macmillan v. Brownlee*," *Alberta Law Review* 22 (1982): 447-74.

35. Among the best sources are Macpherson, *Democracy in Alberta*; John A. Irving, *The Social Credit Movement in Alberta* (Toronto: University of Toronto Press, 1959); Finkel, *The Social Credit Phenomenon in Alberta*; David R. Elliott and Iris Miller, *Bible Bill: A Biography of William Aberhart* (Edmonton: Reidmore Books, 1987). L.P.V. Johnson and Ola J. MacNutt, *Aberhart of Alberta* (Edmonton: Co-op Press, 1970) is hagiographical, but contains some interesting appendices with Social Credit pamphlets and some of Aberhart's radio broadcasts.

36. Elliott and Miller, *Bible Bill*.

37. Elliott and Miller, *Bible Bill*, p. 19 for how busy Aberhart was in 1929.

38. For a discussion of Aberhart's religious views and inspiration, see Elliott and Miller, *Bible Bill*, chap. 4.

39. Johnson and MacNutt, *Aberhart of Alberta*, p. 64.

40. Johnson and MacNutt, *Aberhart of Alberta*, pp. 107-10. On the importance of organization to social credit, see Finkel, *The Social Credit Phenomonon in Alberta*, p. 47; Elliott and Miller, *Bible Bill*, p. 168.
41. *Calgary Herald*, February 1933; as quoted in Johnson and MacNutt, *Aberhart of Alberta*, p. 105.
42. Johnson and MacNutt, *Aberhart of Alberta*, pp. 124-25.
43. Elliott and Miller, *Bible Bill*, p. 157.
44. Carlo Caldarola, "The Social Credit in Alberta, 1935-1971," in *Society and Politics in Alberta: Research Papers*, Carlo Caldarola, ed. (Toronto: Methuen, 1979), p. 38.
45. Johnson and MacNutt, *Aberhart of Alberta*, pp. 169-72.
46. The classic discussion of this is J.R. Mallory, *Social Credit and the Federal Power in Canada* (Toronto: University of Toronto Press, 1954).
47. Johnson and MacNutt, *Aberhart of Alberta*, p. 178; also Finkel, *The Social Credit Phenomenon in Alberta*, p. 72.
48. For excerpts, see L.H. Thomas, ed., *William Aberhart and Social Credit in Alberta* (Toronto: Copp-Clark, 1977). As early as 1911, the Liberal MLA for Lloydminster published a book entitled *Canada and Her Colonies or Home Rule for Alberta*.
49. James A. MacGregor, *A History of Alberta* (Edmonton: Hurtig, 1981), p. 267.
50. David G. Wood, *The Lougheed Legacy* (Toronto: Key Porter Books, 1985), p. 23. The Act would have established a Board of Credit Commissioners to license chartered banks. It was disallowed.
51. John J. Barr, *The Dynasty: The Rise and Fall of Social Credit in Alberta* (Toronto: McClelland and Stewart, 1974), pp. 121-22.
52. Palmer and Palmer, *Alberta: A New History*, p. 289; Finkel, *The Social Credit Phenomenon in Alberta*, pp. 83-86.
53. John Richards and Larry Pratt, *Prairie Capitalism: Power and Influence in the New West* (Toronto: McClelland and Stewart, 1979), p. 81.
54. Finkel, *The Social Credit Phenomenon in Alberta*, pp. 129-34.
55. Barr, *The Dynasty*, p. 149.
56. Wood, *The Lougheed Legacy*, p. 25.
57. Quoted in Finkel, *The Social Credit Phenomenon in Alberta*, p. 159.
58. Wood, *The Lougheed Legacy*, p. 47. Also see Allan Hustak, *Peter Lougheed* (Toronto: McCelland and Stewart, 1979), pp. 72-73 for Lougheed's early recognition of the importance of organization at the constituency level.
59. Ibid., p. 73.
60. Ibid., p. 99.
61. Ibid., p. 118.
62. On Strom's assumption of leadership and his record as premier, see Barr, *The Dynasty*, chaps. 10-13.

63. David K. Elton and Arthur M. Goddard, "The Conservative Takeover, 1971," in *Society and Politics in Alberta: Research Papers*, Carlo Caldarola, ed. (Toronto: Methuen, 1979), p. 53.

64. Wood, *The Lougheed Legacy*, pp. 71-73.

65. Ron Chalmers, "Insults to Democracy During the Lougheed Era," in *Socialism and Democracy in Albera: Essays in Honour of Grant Notley*, Larry Pratt, ed. (Edmonton: NeWest Press, 1986), p. 133.

66. Elton and Goddard, "The Conservative Takeover, 1971," p. 59.

67. See Wood, *The Lougheed Legacy*, chapter 7 for a discussion of the range of policy initiatives and chapter 8 for a review of the "energy wars."

68. Wood, *The Lougheed Legacy*, p. 86.

69. Allan Tupper, "Opportunity and Constraint: Grant Notley and the Modern State," in *Socialism and Democracy in Alberta: Essays in Honour of Grant Notley*, Larry Pratt, ed. (Edmonton: NeWest Press, 1986), p. 95.

70. Hustak, *Peter Lougheed*, p. 140.

71. Wood, *The Lougheed Legacy*, p. 188-90.

72. Hustak, *Peter Lougheed*, p. 242.

73. L.R. Pratt and A. Tupper, "The Politics of Accountability: Executive Discretion and Democratic Control," *Canadian Public Policy* 6 (1980): 254-64.

74. Tupper, "Opportunity and Constraint: Grant Notley and the Modern State," p. 96.

75. Andrew Nikiforuk, Sheila Pratt and Don Wanagas, *Running on Empty: Alberta After the Boom* (Edmonton: NeWest Press, 1987), pp. 91-101.

76. Wood, *The Lougheed Legacy*, p. 195.

77. Nikiforuk et al., *Running on Empty*, p. 96.

78. Ibid., p. 100.

2

The Role of Government

Allan Tupper, Larry Pratt and Ian Urquhart

The Alberta government's economic, political and social roles are deeply controversial. Despite the rhetorical commitment of successive Progressive Conservative governments to laissez-faire principles, the modern, interventionist Alberta government, through its expenditure, taxation and regulatory policies, exerts a pervasive influence. Neither recent events nor possible future political and economic developments suggest a radical reduction in the provincial government's roles.

This chapter's objective is to highlight some of the basic political questions about government's role in Alberta. In this context, the approach is deliberately selective. The focus on financial institutions, forestry development, the public finances and public accountability is designed to raise questions and to highlight broader characteristics of provincial politics not to provide detailed accounts of the substance of policy. The conclusion raises another general question—will a change in the partisanship of the Alberta government exert a substantial influence on the content of public policy? Put differently, does party matter?

An important theme dominates this essay. Government activity in Alberta is powerfully shaped by several features of the province's economic landscape. Alberta's chronic economic instability, its dependence on primary resource production and its acute vulnerability to external forces, both economic and political, exert an extraordinary influence on government. The related desire of elites to escape the vagaries of a "boom and bust" economy through government sponsored programs of economic diversification and stimulus adds further controversy.

Persistent economic instability and dependence on resource production contribute a unique dimension to Alberta government activity and to the broader pattern of provincial politics. But our analysis cautions us against interpreting the contemporary Alberta experience as uniformily unique. In common with other liberal democracies, Alberta policy making is characterized by a complex interplay between interest groups, powerful bureaucracies, media commentators and vote seeking politicians. Like other modern democracies, Alberta politics has spawned politically active and sophisticated environmental, women's and aboriginal people's movements. And as our analysis shows, declining resource revenues have compelled the province to rely more heavily on personal taxation as a source of provincial revenue. Questions about the burden of taxation and the beneficiaries of public expenditures, shunted into the background during the affluent 1970s, now loom large in the province's political discourse. Declining revenues and mounting debts have also forced recent Alberta governments, like their counterparts in Canada and abroad, to restrict public expenditures in politically controversial areas and to incur voter wrath as the quality of public services declines. Such questions as the ethical conduct of public officials, citizen involvement in policy-making and access to government information are now assuming greater political prominence. In these and other areas, Alberta's political agenda is becoming similar to that prevailing elsewhere. Seen in this light, one may ask whether Alberta is still a province "pas comme les autres."

The Politics of Instability

In the early 1980s, about a decade after Peter Lougheed's Progressive Conservatives took power in Alberta, the economy was battered by a succession of external shocks that revealed the province's continuing vulnerability to federal energy policies, the volatility in energy and agricultural markets, rapid technological change, and other forces well beyond regional control. After years of fostering public expectations about economic diversification, the Lougheed government was confronted with the rising costs of Alberta's economic instability in the face of perverse policy-making in Ottawa and sudden shifts in the international petroleum economy. After 1981, Alberta's economy plunged into a major downturn "notable for its sharpness and persistence,"[1] and the years of record growth and easy money abruptly ended.

Peter Lougheed's Conservatives had pursued a number of interventionist "province-building" policies during the 1970s boom.[2] Some of these policies attained their goals, but others—for instance, the implicit policy of using permissive regulations as a way of assisting the growth of Alberta-based financial institutions; or the extension of additional concessions and subsidies to an already-overheated oil and natural gas sector—created serious difficulties for Alberta policy-makers in the years after the boom. Lougheed's province-building strategy unravelled amidst the virtual collapse of the western Canadian economy after 1981, but that did not mean that the government's intervention in the economy had ended; in some ways, the Alberta government chose, or perhaps was driven by necessity, to become even more interventionist, though in different ways and for different motives, in the difficult decade since the boom ended. By the early 1990s, the pattern of government involvement looked more reactive and makeshift than in the 1970s, it became (with a few exceptions) ad hoc rather than planned, it seemed to be driven more by external circumstance than by design. Yet the current pattern is hardly one of retreat to laissez-faire. In fact, after Pierre Trudeau's Liberal government unveiled its controversial National Energy Program in late 1980, the Alberta government, first under Lougheed and then Don Getty, engaged in a costly, protracted struggle to smooth out the cycles of the unstable economy, while at the same pursuing its avowed economic strategy into new areas such as northern forestry development and pulp mills—projects that involve large and politically risky packages of government financial assistance deemed necessary to secure the needed capital investments from the multinational forestry companies. And, simultaneously, the provincial Conservative government tried to protect its eroding political base by compensating many of those interest groups and individuals who took imprudent decisions or became overextended (with assistance in some cases from what a judicial inquiry called "the wilful refusal of the regulators to act effectively"[3]), and then claimed the right to have their losses indemnified by the public treasury when the economy collapsed. Legitimate or not, such claims could only be satisfied at the expense of other constituencies, typically those without the resources or political clout to threaten the ruling Conservatives. So-called "rent-seeking" activity—the competition by politically influential groups and institutions to shelter themselves from market forces or the impact of government cutbacks—now comprises a very large but mostly unstudied sector of the political economy of Alberta.[4]

The source of the continuity linking the economic policies of the early Lougheed years to those of the Lougheed and Getty governments after 1981 is found in the highly cyclical and unstable nature of the Alberta economy itself. The economy is more unstable than that of other Canadian provinces, and the responsiveness of its key economic aggregates—personal income, employment, net migration of population—to unexpected shocks is much greater than is, say, Ontario's.[5] Only Saskatchewan and British Columbia begin to approach Alberta in comparative measurements of economic instability. The revenue base of the Alberta government has also been so closely tied to the fortunes of the energy industry that its expenditures and programs have experienced the same vulnerability, as for example following the 1986 collapse in world oil prices when provincial revenues fell by 30 per cent. (Since that event, up to 50,000 jobs are estimated to have disappeared from the Alberta oil and gas industry). A good argument could be made that the need to mitigate this basic instability, to smooth out the boom/bust cycles of a resource-dependent economy has been the central priority of Alberta's economic policy, not just since 1981, but for many decades. Moreover, there is no reason to doubt that the same instability will continue to constrain provincial policy-makers in years to come, no matter which party holds power. Without discounting the explanatory value of such variables as leadership, party ideology, federal-provincial relations, or class position, we believe these have less analytic power in the interpretation of the policies and interventions of the provincial government than does the unpredictable and extreme variability of Alberta's economy.

Instability and Policy

In a recent study of the Alberta economy, Robert Mansell and Michael Percy devised indexes of regional provincial economic instability for a number of measures: personal income, per capita personal income, employment, population, and output.[6] Their analysis, which is based on data covering 1961 to 1985, shows that Alberta's economy is the most unstable in Canada and that regardless of the variable used, the province exhibits much greater variability than the country as a whole or any of the other provinces; indeed, Alberta's economy appears to be considerably less stable than that of Texas or Oklahoma, the two American states whose economic base most resembles Alberta's.

The unavoidable conclusion is that Alberta's economic instability is indeed a very serious problem. Regardless of the variable used, the province tends to exhibit much greater variability than does the country as a whole and, indeed, than does any other province. Moreover, it is evident that, although the 1982-85 experience accounts for a substantial portion of the unusually large measures of instability, the problem is not limited to this period.[7]

They found that Alberta's primary industries—agriculture and oil and natural gas—are especially variable and that many other sectors—construction, manufacturing, transportation, finance, insurance and real estate—are also subject to wide swings because of their close links to the energy industries. Until its growth was curtailed in 1981-82 by the National Energy Program and by the impact of high interest rates and weakening world prices, Alberta's oil and gas sector led the boom in investment in the province, attracting capital and labour from other areas and enhancing economic specialization. Although Alberta took some measures to dampen the energy boom, many of its policies reinforced the emphasis on oil and natural gas and thus encouraged expectations of further sharp increases in energy prices. Massive energy projects such as the $12 billion Alsands project only made sense if these expectations were correct; and, in the event, they were not. Since 1982, world energy markets have been in disarray because of surplus productive capacity, falling oil and gas prices, and the restructuring of the petroleum industry. The instability of world prices discouraged investment (as did the National Energy Program and high interest rates) and Alberta's boom had been largely driven by new investment. The combined impact of the collapse of Alberta's energy megaprojects and the flight of rigs and exploration dollars on other areas of the economy—construction, finance, real estate—was devastating.

Alberta's specialization in energy was not necessarily the wrong economic strategy, but the early 1980s and the sudden fall in world oil prices in 1986 revealed that the provincial economy and the government's thinking had become rigidly linked to the future of a single commodity. A strategy of specialization requires some capacity to adjust to changing conditions, a capacity to be flexible as well as prudent. In retrospect, it should have been clear to private-sector and public-sector decision-makers that the high oil prices of the 1970s would bring on new supplies and discourage demand for energy, resulting in falling prices; but neither the oil companies nor the federal and Alberta governments believed this would happen. Irrational psychology was at work here: "In practice we have tacitly agreed, as a rule," noted John Maynard Keynes, "to fall back on what is, in truth, a convention. The essence of this convention—though it does not, of course, work out quite so simply—lies in assuming that the existing state of affairs will continue indefinitely."[8]

The Lougheed government continued to operate on this assumption well into the 1980s. Its 1984 White Paper on an industrial and science strategy acknowledged that the boom was over and stressed the need for economic diversification; yet it also described the oil and gas industries as the "engine of growth" of the economy, and it painted an unbelievably rosy picture of some sectors—e.g., financial institutions—that were, in fact, very close to collapse. On the latter question, the White Paper was part of an elaborate effort by the province to keep the public and the media from learning what the government's regulators knew: that the steep decline in real estate values throughout Western Canada had already rendered insolvent most of the region's locally-owned banks, mortgage companies and financial investment houses. Alberta's credit unions were in the throes of crisis by 1984. The statement of government confidence in local financial entities was undoubtedly intended to reassure small investors and to prevent a panic, but the reassurance also encouraged new investors to put their money into technically-bankrupt institutions and provided them a strong legal case for compensation from all taxpayers when the inevitable happened.

It is possible to mistake good fortune for competence. It is possible to exaggerate a government's independence because we only get rare insights into the lobbying process in Alberta. After the traumatic failure of the Principal Group in 1987, the judicial inquiry into the affair headed by William Code went deeply into the relationship between this family-controlled, Alberta-based institution and the Alberta government. Code discovered an appalling record of inadequate regulation, ministerial interference in the administration of the statute governing investment firms, and a pattern of high-level lobbying—involving Premiers Lougheed and Getty and many members of cabinet—by Principal's owners and management to block amendments to legislation or to prevent the regulators from pulling the companies' licenses after they were insolvent. The Code Report reveals that the Lougheed/Getty cabinets were especially keen to preserve local financial institutions which they had nurtured in the 1970s and that ministers went to considerable lengths a decade later to prevent the government's own regulators from enforcing the law and protecting small investors. The policy, said Code, derived from "a general Government desire to preserve Alberta-based financial institutions and public confidence in them."[9] Although he was not implicated in the inquiry's damning judgement, this policy was of course Lougheed's. The government's "province-building" strategy meant close alliances between it and the larger pools of Alberta capital, and these alliances were maintained, it would seem, at the political level, where over-zealous "negative thinking and consumer-protective personalities"—as the owner of Principal described the regulators—could be controlled. But a government that links itself to the fortunes of particular businessmen and uses a lax regulatory system to build up industries makes itself a hostage to these same groups.

A broader point merits attention. Ironically, these locally-based capitalists, having received preference on political grounds, may also be the ones which are hardest to regulate. The problem arose in the Principal affair because of the government's long-standing distrust of banks and financial institutions based in Central Canada—a distrust it shared with earlier administrations of Social Credit and the United Farmers of Alberta. The distrust is understandable but the economic provincialism to which it gives rise is costly and risky. Social Credit established the Treasury Branches for much the same reason that the Lougheed Conservatives fostered Alberta-based financial entities. In each case the politicians were gravely threatened by failures and scandals associated with the dubious operations of these homespun institutions. For the depositors and contract-holders who have placed their savings in these entities are also voters and a financial fiasco can present the government with a choice between an expensive bailout or electoral defeat. A prudent government would be less impressed with "Alberta-first" rhetoric about the ownership of financial assets and more determined to regulate this complex industry in an impartial manner.

The Quest for Diversification

An abiding theme in modern Alberta politics is the need to diversify the provincial economy. But while the province's political discourse has long stressed this theme, clear discussion of diversification is elusive for several reasons. First, no dominant definition has emerged. Protagonists often employ different concepts of diversification and the best means of achieving it. As Michael Percy and Robert Mansell note in their discussion of Alberta's recent economic performance:

> . . . there is no clear definition of "diversification". It could mean expansion in the range of products produced by industries in the province; vertical integration and additional upgrading of primary products within the province; diversification of the markets for the existing range of commodities produced in the province; or the introduction of new industries that exhibit either less variance than do the province's basic industries, or negative covariance with them (counter cyclical behaviour), or both.[10]

A second question asks whether the provincial economy has been diversified and if so how? Here the evidence is mixed and subject to competing interpretations. Percy and Mansell point to the emergence of a substantial provincial petrochemical industry, some growth in the production of manufactured goods, an expansion of the service sector and efforts by large Alberta firms to broaden the range of their goods and services and to sell these in new markets. But their overall conclusion is that Alberta's economy remains dominated by the traditional pillars of oil, natural gas and agricultural production. A third perennial question is the role of public policy in generating diversification. Have provincial policies prompted economic transformations or do they primarily result from secular changes in the domestic and international economies? In turn, what sorts of policies best promote diversification? Should the state sponsor an "industrial policy" and thereby support certain industries or should government merely create a climate conducive to private sector expansion?

The achievement of economic diversification remains a basic policy goal of Alberta's Progressive Conservative government. But its pursuit of diversification has been a twin-edged sword and a source of serious political contradictions. The Conservatives, and especially Peter Lougheed, saw the vision of a more stable economy as the basis of the party's appeal to Alberta's growing urban electorate. Accordingly, the Tories stressed their political and managerial capacity to engineer diversification and to transform the provincial economy. Particularly through the 1970s, public expectations were consciously raised as the Tories solidified their electoral base. But contradictions emerged even before the economic turmoil of the 1980s. Lougheed's Tories soon learned that having popularized diversification, they would ultimately be held accountable for its accomplishment. More interestingly, having championed diversification, the government also learned that a series of ideological, economic and political roadblocks stood in its way. And by 1984 in his last major policy pronouncement, Lougheed stressed his commitment to diversification but claimed that his vision had been misunderstood.[11] Oil and gas were the mainstays of the provincial economy—diversification was merely an effort to "broaden" the economic base not to "artificially change" it. As dramatic boom changed to distressing bust, the government tried to douse the flames of public enthusiasm it had itself fanned.

Like its predecessors, Premier Getty's governments raised the banner of economic diversification. But in Alberta's changed economic environment of the late 1980s and early 1990s, the politics of diversification had changed substantially. A key task for Getty has been to stabilize the province's economic and financial situation after the traumas of the early and mid-1980s. Alberta's dream of becoming a major financial centre was shattered and the province's finances were in disarray as oil and gas revenues declined precipitously while demands for public expenditure grew. Rather predictably, the Tories were denounced for not having diversified the economy during the boom. The Getty government faced its detractors with a deficit-ridden Treasury and, unlike the Lougheed governments, was therefore less able to develop political and economic strategies based on substantial expenditures. To make matters worse, Getty faced the politically difficult task of paying the bills for a spate of failed industrial development and financial initiatives, the most notable being the Principal financial conglomerate and the Gainers' meatpacking plant in Edmonton. Particularly controversial has been the government's use of loan guarantees and grants to private businesses. Such a policy is attacked from the right as a wasteful and misguided intrusion into the marketplace and by the provincial New Democrats as a pathetic effort to maintain private profit at public expense. The Alberta Heritage Savings Trust Fund, whose role it was both to promote diversification and to protect provincial revenues from wild swings, is apparently unable to perform either function effectively. By the mid 1980s, Alberta's much discussed development strategy, which less than a decade ago was often advanced as a prototype for other provinces, was in tatters.

Forestry Development in the 1990s: Old Wine in Old Bottles?

The Getty government struggled with economic decline but it also embarked on a major economic development initiative. Northern Alberta's forests, long neglected by provincial policy makers, unexpectedly became the site of an unprecedented state-sponsored expansion of the province's pulp and paper industry. As Table 2.1 reveals, at least $4 billion of forestry-related capital investment is either planned or committed in the province.[12] Most of the expansion is linked with the construction of several new "mega" pulp mills notably Daishowa Canada's pulp complex at Peace River, Alberta-Pacific Forest Industries (Al-Pac) proposed mill at Athabasca and significant developments by Procter and Gamble, Alberta Energy Company and Weldwood of Canada. In its negotiations with such companies, the province entered into Forest Management Agreements granting the recipient firms exclusive, long-term access to vast wilderness areas. The Al-Pac and Daishowa leases, for example, permit access to areas of 61,000 and 40,710 square kilometres respectively. Such data are put in context by noting that the surface area of New Brunswick is 73,346 square kilometres.

The Getty government espoused the need for an active governmental presence in the economy. Accordingly, the provincial government has been a major catalyst for the forestry boom. It aggressively pursued potential investors, trumpeted the province's pro-business climate and stressed its determination to develop new pulp facilities. But the province's role was not limited to that of mere promoter. As Table 2.1 reveals, it also undertook substantial financial and infrastructure commitments, the total cost of which is $1.35 billion. For example, the Al-Pac project received a provincial loan of $250 million and $75 million for roads, raillines and other infrastructure while the Weldwood mill was backed by a $285 million loan guarantee. The Daishowa undertaking at Peace River required $65 million of provincially funded infrastructure. The province's entrepreneurial and financial roles with their emphasis on rapid forestry development under private auspices now rest uneasily with its traditional forestry management duties and its increasingly important function as guardian of the environment.

Alberta's forestry boom is a classic case of state-driven industrial development in the sense that its roots lie within government. Prior to 1986, governments never defined forestry as a major sector of the provincial economy and the industry's potential as a source of economic growth

TABLE 2.1   Capital Investment in Alberta's Forest Industry in $Millions*

	1987-1990 Committed/Spent	Committed** Expansions
Pulp & Paper	3 800	1 300
Solid Wood	150	125
Panel Products	125	100
Total	4 075	1 525

* $1 CDN = $0.86 U.S.
** Two major uncommitted timber areas exist which could potentially add another $11.5 billion of capital investment.

Government Financial Assistance in $Millions*

	Pulp & Paper	Other	Total
Loan Guarantees	615	15	630
Debentures	525	25	650
Infrastructures	170	—	170
Total	1 310	40	1 350

* $1 CDN = $0.86 U.S.
SOURCE: J.A. Brennan, E.R. Rolley, *Forest development strategies—Recent experiences: Alberta, Canada and Tasmania, Australia*, March 17-20, 1991.

was certainly not a subject of widespread public discussion.[13] Ernest Manning's Social Credit governments undertook only modest development initiatives in the 1950s and 1960s. The Lougheed Tories launched no major forestry projects and, in contrast to the oil and gas industries, maintained Social Credit's laissez-faire approach to forestry. The 1984 White Paper mentioned forestry as a sector with economic promise but only in passing and in context with a range of other development possibilities.

The government's policy of forestry development originated within the bureaucracy—from professional foresters in the old Department of Energy and Natural Resources—during the process leading to the 1984 White Paper. A confidential internal study argued that forestry development would stimulate and diversify the Alberta economy, but such development was constrained by: high freight rates and lack of access to tidewater; inadequate roads and rail infrastructure; financing problems; lack of research into the utilization of aspen (hardwood); and the threat of American protectionism. The bureaucracy recommended a broad and expensive policy of government-sponsored research, infrastructure improvements, and financial incentives to encourage the development of world-scale forest product facilities. At an early date in preparing this strategy, it was agreed to target Japan as both an investor and a key market; Japanese firms were cash-rich and Alberta wanted to diversify its trade links.

Premier Getty, not Premier Lougheed, gave the forestry strategy the political support it required. Lougheed had no interest in forestry and, perhaps, very little awareness of the resource's potential. It did not fit his conception of diversification: Lougheed was interested in high technology. Getty had more interest in the forestry proposal and he got strong support from a trusted cabinet colleague, Don Sparrow. By 1986, when the government announced its $435 million Alberta Forest Industries Development Initiatives, the provincial economy was in the doldrums, oil prices were dropping, and very little new construction or engineering work was underway in Alberta. Getty was under great pressure to stimulate the economy by announcing new projects and activity. Economic stimulation and electoral politics, rather than long-term diversification, were the primary motives; and yet the province used diversification as its rationale.

The aggressive marketing of Alberta's forests was undertaken by civil servants when in 1986 a new office—the Forest Industry Development Division of the Department of Forestry, Lands and Wildlife—was set up. Officers from this division, armed with videos and expensive brochures, flew to Japan, South Korea, Taiwan and the United States to attract foreign capital. They stressed Alberta's political stability, its strong "work ethic," its record of labour stability (compared to BC or Quebec) and the primarily nonunionized nature of Alberta's forest industries. They promised cheap and abundant energy, low delivered wood costs, and long-term security of tenure over immense tracts of forests. They also offered loan guarantees, debentures and improved infrastructure. A clear conclusion thus emerges—the Getty government's forestry strategy was undertaken prior to any serious public debate about its economic, social or political consequences. As Andrew Nikiforuk and Ed Struzik argue:

"The biggest land rush since the opening of the West ended in December, 1988, before most Canadians knew it had begun."[14]

Such terms as industrial and diversification "strategies" imply a degree of planning, a sense of purpose in public policy and widely accepted economic and political rationales. In practice, what politicians identify as a strategy may be little more than an amalgam of guesses and questionable economic and political assumptions. The latter characterization is a more apt description of Alberta's forest strategy than the former one.

The Getty government has never issued a comprehensive forestry policy statement. It is thus necessary to piece together the underpinning logic. On the economic side, the emphasis on forestry was justified in terms of world demand for paper products, which was rising when the investments were committed, and Alberta's apparently unique capacity to provide substantial new supplies of timber. On the supply side, the government emphasizes technological advances which make Alberta's bountiful supply of aspen, once described by foresters as a weed, a very valuable resource. In this vein, the premier and senior ministers spoke frequently, but backed by no compelling evidence, about Alberta's new found "natural advantage" in forestry development. Several other arguments buttress the government's aggressive exploitation of Alberta's forests including the very dubious idea that forestry, especially its pulp sector, is a stable industry and one relatively immune from boom and bust. A further idea is that timber, again in contrast to oil and gas, is a renewable resource and hence one that will serve as a long-term backbone of the provincial economy. Moreover, the primary forestry industry, if properly nurtured, will diversify the economy as spinoffs occur in such areas as furniture manufacturing and fine paper production. To the degree that environmental concerns were addressed, the government assumed that the technological and scientific advances, championed by the pulp producers, were effective and that the industry's rapid expansion was thus compatible with environmental protection.

Many of the Getty government's economic assumptions are questionable but a contradiction leaps to the fore. Why, if Alberta enjoys a comparative advantage in forestry development and if the province is uniquely placed as a supplier of timber, was the province compelled to engage in a competitive "fistfight" with other jurisdictions to lure pulp producers to the province with promises of financial assistance and low royalties?[15] Was the province bargaining with the private sector from a position of strength as some of its pronouncements implied or from a position of dependence on major private firms? Was the province reaping maximum benefit from the rapid development of an allegedly valuable resource?

As the Canadian intellectual tradition of political economy powerfully reveals, economic forces will not by themselves produce a governmental response. Governments have autonomy and may respond in different ways to external stimuli. What forces therefore account for the Conservatives' decision to nurture a major forestry industry? A possible argument is that the Conservatives, as a government party, merely presumed that their electorate remained enamoured with the pursuit of a diversified economy and that economic growth remained the prime concern of Albertans. As well, the government in the face of serious economic problems including the collapse of the Principal empire was desperate to reestablish its image of managerial competence. In short, the successful generation of a forestry boom would allow the government to portray itself as a successful economic manager with a mission and a clear sense of direction. The government engineered forestry boom was seen by Premier Getty as a major, albeit very costly, economic stimulus for a shaky provincial economy. The particular form of the forestry strategy with its emphasis on an active role for the state must also be seen in the context of Alberta's political climate in the late 1980s. At this time, the Tories faced stiff competition especially in urban centres from the statist New Democrats and from the reborn provincial Liberals whose vague policies were broadly similar to those of the governing Tories. Under these electoral circumstances, and prior to the rise of the Reform Party and an explicit challenge from the right, the Conservatives were comfortable with an economic strategy that gave evidence of aggressive state action while remaining compatible with their rhetorical preference for the private sector. Finally, the forestry strategy with its emphasis on natural resource development, mega projects and corporate capitalism was familiar territory for the Conservatives. While forestry represented a new dimension for the provincial economy, its political and economic imperatives were congruent with past initiatives and hence probably more attractive to Alberta policy makers than the relatively uncharted waters of "high tech" and secondary industry development. In this vein, W.T. Easterbrook's rhetorical question about the tendency of faltering elites to shore up their positions by relying on once successful strategies is instructive. "Is it not a universal propensity of such elites to seek perpetuation of their leadership by reliance on strategies that in the past have brought them to pre-eminence?''[16]

The Conservatives' approach to forestry development in the late 1980s and early 1990s was broadly similar to its stance on resource developments in the booming 1970s. It therefore ignored significant changes in the pattern of provincial politics in the intervening years. As a result, the forestry developments raised a stormy debate about several difficult questions that had been ignored in the affluent 1970s. A vexing problem was the effectiveness of the provincial government as a negotiator. Many observers argued that the province had not bargained hard enough and that it had unwisely ceded control over vast lands and a valuable resource. Nick Taylor, a Liberal MLA and an oilman, compared the province's approach to the forestry companies to Social Credit's posture toward multinational oil companies after the Leduc strike.[17] The firms were thought to be footloose and to hold all the cards. The government assumed, moreover, that tough bargaining on royalties and environmental protection would drive investors away. As a result of such assumptions, critics maintained that royalties were too low and that the state had underwritten the risks involved. A general skepticism also arose about the need for extensive government financial assistance for the mills. Might they not have proceeded without state assistance? A second source of public concern was the environmental impact of major new pulp mills. Here the Getty government proceeded shakily as it struggled to come to grips with newly organized environmental groups, more politicized and effective spokespersons for aboriginals and demands for evidence about the environmental impact of the mills. The government's perennial response to environmental concerns—that overzealous safeguards would drive investors away—was repeatedly expressed by LeRoy Fjordbotten, the minister of Forestry and the Conservatives' principal advocate of rapid development.[18] But his arguments held little sway with an aggressive environmental movement with the result that the government was forced to pay much more public attention to environmental concerns. An upshot of these events was the spectacle of public disputes between ministers about the environmental consequences of forestry development and the proper government response. Unlike the case of tar sands development, a coalition of environmental, aboriginal, and labour groups now rejects the ''development at all cost'' ethos that characterized provincial policy-making until the mid 1980s. A final theme of the debate concerned, for lack of a more precise term, the ''style'' of provincial policy-making.

In this context, the concerns were the government's penchant for secret negotiations with the forestry companies, its unwillingness to consult publicly with concerned communities and its failure to state precisely the long-term financial, social and environmental costs and benefits. A stinging editorial in the *Calgary Herald* summarized such concerns:

> There is only one thing more astounding than the scale of plans to expand Alberta's forest industry—the secret way they were carried out.

> Without any public discussion the Conservative government committed nearly $1.2 billion to help pulp and paper companies exploit 240,000 square kilometres of virgin forest.

> Without one word of warning, one-third of the province has been thrown open to an industry not known for its clean environmental record.[19]

The Conservatives' traditional modus operandi, to demand maximum autonomy for the political executive to negotiate agreements with private firms, was widely challenged.

Forestry Development and the "New Politics"

What general lessons about the role of government and provincial politics flow from Alberta's forestry boom? How do recent events illuminate our interest in change and continuity? A striking feature of the forestry debate is its exclusively provincial focus. The heart of the discussion remains the economic role of the provincial government, the interests served by rapid development and the environmental impact. Unlike other areas of policy-making, the role of the federal government is not a major issue. In this context, efforts by LeRoy Fjordbotten to condemn the federal government for allegedly demanding stricter environmental controls in Alberta than elsewhere and for apparently favouring development "in the east" fell on deaf ears and never became part of the debate. A provincial agenda has clearly emerged as witnessed by the absence of federal-provincial squabbles in the forestry debate. Rather ironically, a more diversified economy, an economic situation that is at best described as stable and a marked diminution of intergovernmental conflict over resource policy have changed Alberta's politics. In the early 1990s, Albertans are cool to claims that they must present a united front against hostile external forces. Other political cleavages—between rural and urban areas, between men and women and between aboriginal and white populations—have become stronger, more visible and more politicized. In the face of a provincial agenda and a more divided electorate, the Conservatives' traditional attempts to divide Albertans into two warring camps—the "doers" (those in favour of rapid resource development) and the "knockers" (everyone else)—have failed miserably.

A second lesson is the greater complexity and divisiveness of policy-making in the face of a barer Provincial treasury, in the face of the government's determination to eliminate the provincial debt and in the face of cuts to the education, health and welfare budgets. In this environment of restraint, the government is challenged by critics who note the opportunity costs of substantial expenditures on pulp mills. The Alberta Medical Association, for example, questioned the environmental impact of major forestry developments but also asked how the province could justify large expenditures on private sector development when hospitals were being closed and health care workers were being laid off. Unlike the boom years of the 1970s, the government can no longer easily sustain increased expenditures on both development and social services. In the early 1990s, such priorities are competitive rather than complementary and no economic forecast suggests radical changes to provincial finances for the foreseeable future. Like most other democratic jurisdictions, the Alberta government must now justify its tax and expenditure priorities before a skeptical electorate. Who gets what?—arguably the core question in political life—is now defined more clearly for Albertans whose politics, in this sense, increasingly resemble those of other Canadian jurisdictions.

The forestry controversy also points to growing demands for public participation in decision-making. Such demands, which as the Meech Lake debate illustrates are not unique to Alberta, reflect several little understood political trends including the emergence of new interest groups, a growing public awareness of environmental issues and a sharp decrease in deference to political elites. The Alberta Progressive Conservatives long accustomed to weak opposition parties, a servile legislature and limited public accountability are particularly ill at ease with this more demanding policy-making environment. Only the Al-Pac project at Athabasca was subject to formal public hearings and it remains unclear whether the Conservatives grasp the changed milieu. The Al-Pac debate revealed their genuine surprise at the range and intensity of public opposition to secretly negotiated, environmentally controversial pulp mills.

It is simplistic to maintain that problems of public participation in resource policy-making merely reflect the stubbornness of an aging, increasingly rural and often arrogant government. For in the classic tradition of opposition parties guided by the proposition that governments defeat themselves, neither the provincial Liberals nor the New Democrats have much advanced our thinking about diversification, the trade-offs between growth and environmental protection or new forms of public involvement. As the twenty-first century approaches, policy making in Alberta may be conducted in an environment where the party system and political processes have changed less than their underlying social, political and economic foundations.

Boom, Bust, and Provincial Fiscal Policy

Alberta's unstable economy exerts powerful influences on the province's revenues and expenditures. For given the importance of resource royalties to provincial finances, the revenue effects of boom and bust are dramatic. The boom of the 1970s produced a spectacular upsurge in resource revenues. In 1970, Alberta's resource revenues were $233 million. Ten years later the total was $4,657 billion or twenty times the 1970 figure. The 1980s stood in sharp contrast to the preceding decade. Until 1985 petroleum revenues hovered around their 1980 level. In 1986, as the collapse of world petroleum prices turned boom into bust, these revenues plunged precipitously. In 1986 alone resource revenues fell by sixty-three per cent. Although the world price for petroleum recovered during the remainder of the decade, resource revenues were less resilient. By 1989, resource revenues flowing into the province's general revenue fund were only fifty per cent of the 1980 total.[20]

This dramatic rise and fall in resource revenue drove provincial expenditure decisions in the 1970s and 1980s. During the heady days of the 1970s, when Alberta's population mushroomed and all observers presumed petroleum prices were on a permanent upward spiral, government expenditures grew explosively. Between 1970 and 1980, program expenditures rose from $1.104 billion to $6.294 billion.[21] In real per capita terms provincial program spending had grown threefold from 1969 to 1982.[22] This ascent was distinguished by election year peaks and post-election plateaus.

Explosive growth between 1971 and the election year of 1975 was followed by a plateau extending from 1976 to 1978. In 1979, another election year, program expenditures surged ahead again—this time by a whopping 58 per cent. The 1980 and 1981 fiscal years were marked by modest nominal increases in spending. In 1982, as sagging petroleum prices dragged resource revenues down and Albertans headed to the polls, provincial spending surged ahead dramatically. From 1981 to 1982 nominal provincial program expenditures rose by 43 per cent. Incentives for the ailing energy industry accounted for $1.322 billion of a $3.303 billion increase in spending.

The Practice and Politics of Restraint

The spectacular budget increase of 1982 is an exception to the overall record of the 1980s, a decade characterized by Conservative budgetary restraint. Program expenditure growth failed to keep pace with inflation between 1982 and 1989. This feature of provincial fiscal policy was celebrated in the 1991 budget address when the provincial treasurer boasted about the government's success in controlling expenditure growth. Alberta's expenditure management record, he claimed, was second to none. His claim was supported by the fact that provincial increases in program spending averaged only 1.9 per cent annually since 1985/86, well below the average annual inflation rate.[23] While curbing expenditure growth was a prominent feature of the province's overall fiscal record in the 1980s, this general feature masks the fact that the burden of restraint falls more heavily on some functions of government than on others.[24] Six program functions of government suffered ''restriction,'' a mild version of restraint, during the 1980s. Social services, health, resource conservation and development, protection, housing, and regional planning and development all received real increases in spending of varying degrees during the 1980s but much less than in the 1970s.[25] Between 1981 and 1989, social services claimed the largest real spending increases. The depth of the province's economic decline propelled social services spending upwards by 53 per cent in real terms over this period. Health (34%) received the second largest real increase over this span of time. Education, the province's largest single program commitment in 1981/82, experienced a second type of restraint budgeting—"the freeze." It received neither a real increase nor a real decrease in funds over this period. Consequently, by the 1989/90 fiscal year, health had replaced education as the province's most expensive commitment. Four functions of government suffered "retrenchment," dramatic real cuts in funding, between 1981 and 1989: environment (-92%), transportation and utilities (-77%), recreation and culture (-73%), and general government (-49%).

The province's troubled fiscal picture in the 1980s is well captured by the fact that the only item to escape restraint was debt servicing. The costs of servicing the government's burgeoning debt skyrocketed after 1985. In 1981, the costs of servicing the general revenue fund debt amounted to slightly less than $22 million. In the 1989/90 fiscal year these costs rose to $880 million or 7.3 per cent of total provincial expenditures.

What helps us to understand restraint in modern Alberta? One fashionable explanation is to stress the changing ideological environment by emphasizing the "right wing" alternative recently espoused by the Reform party. The recent rise of the right is important, especially for the future, but it cannot easily explain the events of the early and mid 1980s when budget restraint began.

Ideology may partially explain a general commitment to restraint but it is less helpful in accounting for the variety of restraint in Alberta— restriction in some areas, freeze and retrenchment in others. In this context, a promising explanation is found in the outlook of government members regarding what policy areas they feel are personally important and what areas they think are important to the public. Tension exists between these two assessments. When government members were recently asked to give their personal ranking of policy issues, the deficit emerged as their dominant concern. When they were asked instead to offer their perceptions of what issues the public believed were important, education, health, environment and taxation all were close rivals to the deficit.[26] These perceptions probably reveal Albertans' and Canadians' often contradictory attitudes about public spending. Citizens support restraint in principle while often opposing specific program reductions.[27] Recent provincial fiscal policy reveals the impact of such underlying attitudes. For example, the 1991-92 budget speech trumpeted the government's commitment to tough expenditure management—the budgets of over half of the government's departments and agencies would be cut in the 1991-92 fiscal year. In the next breath the budget speech affirmed the government's commitment to the excellence of the province's health care system and pledged to increase health care spending by ten per cent in 1991-92. Similarly, the treasurer announced that spending on primary/secondary education, the environment, and family/community support services delivered by municipalities would rise by more than the provincial inflation rate. By offering Albertans both retrenchment and restriction, the budget tried to satisfy the contradictory majorities found in public opinion.

How might this approach to restraint shape the government's political support? Spending increases of the scale announced in the 1991/92 budget will not likely satisfy those constituencies already disaffected by restraint. The eight per cent increase to the family and community support services program (FCSS), for example, while described by one social worker as "a move in the right direction," did not compensate for the cuts of previous budgets.[28] Nor did this increase do much to improve the situation of the vast majority of people receiving social assistance in the province. As the National Council of Welfare reported, the welfare income for a couple with two children in Alberta rose by less than 0.4 percent between 1986 and 1989.[29] Provincial increases to shelter and food allowances in November 1990 still left Alberta's welfare families struggling to survive on incomes well below the poverty line. Municipalities soon realized that the province's eight per cent increase in spending for FCSS would actually amount to an inconsequential increase. For after the deficits of 1989-90 and 1990-91 were covered, the increase was negligible. In Edmonton, the eight per cent increase amounted to an increase of only 1.6 per cent.

The Tories are also having difficulty shaking the impression that their budgets have led to a deterioration in the provincial health care and education systems. For example, the ten per cent increase in the 1991-92 health budget did little to silence criticism from the public, hospital boards, the United Nurses of Alberta, and both opposition parties that the government is underfunding health and hospital care in the province. With hospital grant increases in 1991 pegged at less than the provincial inflation rate, hospital boards have had little choice but to close beds and layoff hospital staff in order to comply with the government's order that hospital budgets must be balanced. Large layoffs at major hospitals are commonplace as administrators struggle to balance their budgets.

Longtime foes of the government, the United Nurses of Alberta and the Canadian Union of Public Employees, are now joined in their health care campaigns by a loose coalition of senior citizens groups. Bed closures, longer waiting periods for bed space or surgery, layoffs of nurses and changes to health programs for seniors have contributed to and reinforced the public's belief that quality health care is in jeopardy in Alberta.[30] The 1991-92 budget mobilized a number of senior citizens groups to protest the government's financial commitment to health care. The focus of the seniors' attacks is changes to health programs which effectively require the elderly to pay for a greater percentage of their health care bill. Opposition parties warned that the introduction of cost-sharing for seniors marked the end of universality and have seized upon these changes to argue that the treasurer's promise to balance the 1991-92 budget will be fulfilled in part on the backs of senior citizens. Such a backlash against restraint is inevitable in a province whose Conservative governments incessantly claim that they provide superior public services at the lowest rates of tax in the country. In this sense, successive Conservative governments have raised the very expectations they now deem unrealistic.

These criticisms of the government's spending record in the social services and health services areas are fuelled by the belief that the government has not distributed the burden of restraint fairly. As already noted, the government has curtailed social spending while committing substantial public resources to the financing of private sector investments. This contradiction is glaring to many citizens. Between 1985 and 1990, government guaranteed debentures and loans rose from $466 million to $3.2 billion.[31] The government's use of loan guarantees was criticized recently by the Auditor General who concluded that the government is underreporting the amount of money the province might lose on its guarantees—a troubling practice since the government's losses on these guarantees had climbed from $8 million to $115 million over the past five years.

TABLE 2.2   Percentages of General Revenue Fund Derived from
Nonrenewable Resource Revenue, Taxes, and Heritage Fund
Investment Income, By Fiscal Year

	Nonrenewable resource revenue	Taxes	Heritage Fund Income
1971	25.6	34.9	—
1977	50.0	24.8	—
1978	56.0	23.2	—
1979	55.5	20.1	—
1980	50.6	24.1	—
1981	47.0	27.5	—
1982	39.7	24.2	12.2
1983	44.7	20.9	15.8
1984	38.9	25.2	15.6
1985	36.9	26.1	16.9
1986	19.3	32.8	20.1
1987	26.9	34.8	14.3
1988	23.4	39.8	13.8
1989	23.0	39.8	12.8

SOURCE: Alberta, *Public Accounts.*

The Provincial Revenue Picture—Completing the Circle

Several features of the revenue side of the provincial finances are also
noteworthy. The transition from Lougheed to Getty, coinciding as it did
with the collapse of petroleum prices, was accompanied by a sharp reversal in the resource revenue/taxation revenue mix. Table 2.2 illustrates
this reversal well.

Resource revenue accounted for 36.9 per cent of total revenue in the
1985 fiscal year only to fall to 19.3 per cent of total revenue in 1986.
Since the modest post-1986 recovery in world oil prices this percentage
has not risen very much, averaging 23.2 per cent over the 1986-89 fiscal
years. In contrast, the average for the 1982-85 fiscal years was 40.1 per
cent. As energy revenues declined, taxes, personal income tax and health
care premiums, increased both absolutely and relatively. Over the 1982-85

fiscal years, total taxes averaged 28.4 per cent of provincial revenues. Since 1986 they have averaged 35.8 per cent. With taxation now seemingly established firmly as the primary source of government revenues, the resource royalty/taxation mix in the provincial finances has returned to approximate the pre-energy boom distribution.

This is not to suggest that the declining dependence of the provincial treasury on nonrenewable resource revenues has transformed Alberta's revenue mix into the equivalent of other provinces such as Ontario or British Columbia. Clearly, Alberta is much more dependent upon resource revenues and less dependent upon taxation than either of these provinces. In the 1988 fiscal year, for example, taxes accounted for 72.5 per cent of Ontario's revenues and 55.8 per cent of British Columbia's revenues while accounting for only 35.8 per cent of Alberta's.

Table 2.2 suggests that the politics of taxation will be a much more important part of Alberta's political future. The government is running out of alternative revenue sources. One of the last sources to be tapped is the Alberta Heritage Savings Trust Fund. Beginning in the 1983-84 fiscal year, the government began to transfer the fund's investment income into general revenue. In 1987, the government stopped diverting nonrenewable resource revenue into the Heritage Fund. This latter decision in particular has eliminated the ability of the Fund's investment income to play a more significant future role in the provincial revenue picture, a trend suggested by the percentages reported in Table 2.2. This likelihood is strengthened by two recent developments. First, the 1991 budget predicts that by March 31, 1992 the Fund's assets will stand at $12.009 billion, $736 million less than on March 31, 1987. Second, the budget revealed that the government will continue to privatize Heritage Fund assets as it did with Alberta Government Telephones in 1990. According to this intent, any profit made above the book value of the Fund's assets will be transferred to general revenues. As a result, at best, the size of the Fund will remain the same. Privatization is an option open to a government which desperately needs revenue but is reluctant to consider basic changes to the provincial taxation structure.

What does this brief look at provincial fiscal policy tell us about continuity and change in Alberta politics? First, it is clear that Getty is less able to employ Lougheed's strategy of using government spending as a tool to promote the Tories' re-election. As Lougheed once explained, his government, armed with abundant monies, followed a very deliberate four-year political budgeting cycle, one where programs generally were introduced on the eve of the next electoral campaign.[32] Getty has moved away from Lougheed's version of political budgeting. In the first election fought by the Progressive Conservatives under Getty's leadership real program spending dropped; it dropped again in the fiscal year preceding the calling of the 1989 provincial election, although the 1989 election campaign featured debate about several costly government expenditure proposals. This change in budgetary policy may reflect Getty's different leadership style. But more obviously, the fiscal position of the province has deteriorated to the point where Lougheed's "political" budgeting cannot be sustained. Part of this deterioration is reflected in the declining importance of resource revenues to the province's finances. The massive revenue surpluses which financed Lougheed's electoral largesse no longer exist and are unlikely to reappear. The second significant element of fiscal deterioration is the dramatic rise in the provincial debt. The Provincial Treasury worries that unless deficits are eliminated, Alberta, like the federal government, will be trapped on a treadmill of chronic deficits where debt interest payments absorb an escalating percentage of provincial revenues.

The Politics of Democracy

Our analysis has so far stressed questions about public finance, forestry development, economic diversification and the management of financial institutions. Our particular concern is the influence of Alberta's chronic economic instability on policy-making in these areas. Our focus now shifts to an important but very different set of policies—those relating to governmental accountability, the ethical conduct of politicians and the political management of the civil service.

Debates about the quality of democratic life are not new to Alberta. The growth of government in the Lougheed years, the development of quasi-public institutions like the Alberta Energy Company and the active governmental pursuit of economic diversification led to an expansion of the cabinet's power. Alberta's opposition parties, especially the New Democrats in the 1970s, often worried about the growing imbalance between the executive and the legislature, the lack of public accountability and an excess of secrecy in provincial administration. But their concerns for more open government never engaged the public's imagination during the boom years and are best interpreted as efforts to challenge the electorally dominant Conservatives. For the New Democrats, a focus on accountability was perhaps their only option given the broad similarity between theirs and the Tory vision of economic development under the aegis of an interventionist provincial administration. And rather obviously, a small, badly outnumbered legislative opposition is prone to highlight its lonely role as critic of a powerful cabinet.[33]

But in the early 1990s, questions about the quality of democracy in Alberta are much more widely debated. As noted earlier, Alberta's environmental movement, like its counterparts elsewhere in the democratic world, stresses the need for greater public participation in policy-making and administration. Greater partisan competition and the advent of larger, more aggressive legislative oppositions have also contributed to more careful scrutiny of the government. As well, Alberta's politics are certainly not immune from broader regional and national debates about the quality of democracy. The resurgence, under the Reform party's banner, of traditional populist appeals for direct democracy have expanded the agenda. The Meech Lake debate also stressed the inadequacies of elite dominated policy-making and raised difficult questions about how constitution-making and politics generally can be made more democratic. The Charter of Rights and Freedoms has forged new groups and interests who reject paternalistic government and whose political actions reveal little deference to authority. Moreover, political sociology and the more impressionistic insights of the modern media stress a restless electorate, one increasingly skeptical of established elite practices and one with limited commitment to political parties. Such developments suggest that the democratic quality of political decision-making will remain an important part of Alberta's political agenda for the foreseeable future. The provincial debate is now driven by forces that transcend the simple dynamic between the government and its legislative opposition.

Information and Ethics: The Continuing Controversy

An insightful area of investigation into political change in Alberta is the specific debate about "conflict of interest" and the more general problem of ethical political conduct. The roots of contemporary controversy lie in Peter Lougheed's "development strategy" of the early 1970s which saw the provincial government as a leader in economic development initiatives but in concert with the province's bureaucratic, professional and corporate elites. This strategy demanded a strong political executive and fostered a fusion between political and economic elites. Such interactions raised serious questions about the possible links between political office and personal gain and Premier Lougheed responded with a set of guidelines for ministers in 1973.[34] These guidelines together with several clauses of the Legislative Assembly Act remained the heart of Alberta's conflict of interest regime until 1991. In a general way they spelled out and tried to limit some of the more obvious tensions between a person's private life and her pursuit of public duties. But the guidelines were never given statutory force, their interpretation and enforcement were the premier's prerogative and they omitted a range of controversial behaviour including the "post employment" dealings of ministers and senior civil servants. As a result, allegations of unethical behaviour abound in Alberta politics, the most recent major example being a prolonged debate about Premier Getty's dealings with oil and real estate interests.

Continuing uncertainty about the adequacy of extant provincial policy led Getty to appoint a task force to examine the issue. Headed by Mr. Justice Edward Wachowich of the Provincial Court of Alberta, an investigatory tribunal called for an overhaul of Alberta's conflict of interest regime.[35] Among other things, it recommended the appointment of an Ethics Commissioner to investigate allegations of wrongdoing, the passage of a strong statute and a broader definition of inappropriate practices. While such proposals are important, it is the report's premises that are particularly significant as they represent a serious challenge to the status quo. In particular, the Wachowich report demolished a pillar of the Conservatives' defence of the status quo—that provincial elections are appropriate arbiters of politicians' ethical behaviour. The absurdity of the notion that re-election signified public acceptance of existing political morality was firmly, albeit politely, pointed out. The Wachowich report also stressed that political and bureaucratic conduct, to be deemed acceptable, must avoid even the appearance of wrongdoing. Finally, the report undercut another basic Conservative defence of weak guidelines— that a strong law would deter able people, particularly from the private sector, from entering public life. The government surprised its critics in 1991 and passed a comprehensive piece of legislation that applies to MLAs and ministers and calls for the establishment of an Ethics

Commissioner. The 1992 Speech From the Throne promises comparable legislation for senior civil servants.

Another area of continuing controversy is the government's views about administrative secrecy. Since 1991, the Conservatives have repeatedly rejected opposition calls for "Freedom of Information" legislation along the lines of the federal statute and those prevailing in several other provinces and many other democracies. Debate about more open government was part of Alberta's political agenda through the boom years of the 1970s. But the debate was conducted by and between elites in the context of the classic partisan interaction between government and opposition. The "ins" opposed the "outs" demands. But in the late 1980s, open government has become a broader issue as interest groups, environmentalists and aboriginal peoples, for example, realize that information is a vital political resource. They have come to link changes in political processes with the pursuit of substantive policy goals. Critics of the forestry boom argue that effective public participation in policy development and administration demands access to information and early involvement in decision-making. Their struggle is partly against a process that allows controversial deals to be struck without public input and whose precise contents remain shrouded in secrecy. Similarly, the acquisition of the Gainers meatpacking plant in Edmonton remains controversial as the government refuses to release the "master" agreement.

Alberta's tradition of one-party dominance, "businesslike" governments and weak legislative oppositions has won it a reputation as a province where political accountability is particularly weak. Whether such a reputation is justified, especially when compared with circumstances in other provinces where electoral competition has been more vigorous, is unclear. The complex modern state has challenged the integrity of democratic institutions and practices in countries with very different patterns of economic organization and political competition. This having been said, certain characteristics of modern Alberta politics suggest that more open politics will be slow to emerge. First the need for a strong political executive unfettered by demands for public input, legislative oversight or the release of information is a hallmark of the Conservatives' development strategy and in their view a necessary condition of effective public policy. Such ideas are central to the Conservatives' "style" as witnessed by the forestry development strategy which rests on secret negotiations between the government and firms. Social democrats have opposed such practices but so too have some conservatives who see greater limits on cabinet discretion as an opportunity to restrain the government's interventionist tendencies. The point is that debates about political accountability in modern Alberta, far from being lofty discourses about democratic governance, are at heart controversies about the ends pursued by governments. A further obstacle to reform is the Tories' hardening view about the inherent correctness of their policies and their approach to politics. Here the issue is one-party dominance in its temporal sense. Long standing governments often come to see their ideas as the only correct ones with the result that internally generated reform is unlikely. The Getty government is likely to resist innovations through simple inertia with the result that reforms may require a change of government.

This having been said, the Conservatives again caught their critics off guard when in March 1992, in the face of persistent opposition demands, they announced plans to pass Access to Information legislation. The details of the proposed law, and hence its precise impact, are not known at time of writing. But if Alberta's experience with such legislation is like that of other Canadian jurisdictions, it is likely that the statute will modestly improve public accountability without altering dramatically the balance of power or relations between the opposition, the government and the civil service. Viewed in this light, one may legitimately ask why the Conservatives were so reluctant to pass legislation whose impact on their freedom of action is unlikely to be great.

A change of government is probably a necessary condition for substantial democratic reforms to occur, but is it a sufficient one? No crystal balls are available but caution is urged for several reasons. First, long standing opposition parties, when finally given a chance to govern, often become champions of policies and practices that they once denounced. Various "imperatives" of government are employed as rationales for their departure from the democratic ideals they espoused from the opposition benches. And in the Alberta context, it is difficult to discern precisely the commitment of either the Liberals or the New Democrats to democratic reform. Neither seems poised to advance a clear alternative.

Moreover, the Conservatives' commitment to freedom of information and conflict of interest legislation in 1991 and 1992, however belated or insincere, remove key and long standing elements from the opposition parties' critiques of the Tories political *modus operandi*. These recent government initiatives have therefore removed another important difference in the public positions of Alberta's three major parties. Whether the voters are impressed by the Conservatives' new found enthusiasm for democratic ideals remains unclear.

The Government and the Civil Service

The public service is a badly neglected institution in the study of Alberta politics. A thorough examination of the public bureaucracy is beyond our reach in this short essay but some comments are important as the government-civil service relationship, like other aspects of provincial politics, is changing rapidly. A potentially adversarial relationship between the government and its employees was patched over during the boom years of the 1970s. But the economic traumas of the 1980s and the government's related emphasis on expenditure cuts and deficit reduction politicized latent tensions and made the management of a large, unionized public sector work force a major political problem.

A particularly contentious issue is public sector industrial relations where the Conservatives steadfastly maintain that no public employee should have a legal right to strike.[36] Rather, compulsory arbitration is the best way to harmonize the interests of public employees with the broader public interest. This total prohibition of public sector strikes rests uneasily with both the public sector unions and the Alberta New Democrats. But the issue of public sector industrial relations remained muted until the early 1980s when in a series of moves the provincial government became more aggressive in its efforts to cut expenditures. A particularly controversial action was an amendment to the Public Sector Employee Relations Act in 1983 which instructed arbitrators to consider provincial fiscal policy as a factor in their deliberations. Public sector unions argued that arbitration, far from being a neutral process, was biased in favour of the government. Such changes, the government's desire to limit wage increases and deteriorating working conditions led Alberta's nurses and more recently provincial social workers to engage in bitter illegal strikes which particularly in the former case seemed to enjoy public support.

As we enter the 1990s, the Alberta public service as an institution is the object of explicit Conservative policies. Significant layoffs are occurring, privatization is widely discussed and shrinking budgets make industrial relations problematic. A nascent, yet controversial policy of administrative decentralization, which involves the transfer of public

employees from Edmonton to smaller communities, has driven a further wedge between the government and its employees.

Several important lessons flow from the increasingly fractious relationship between the government and its employees. First, the now
openly conflictual relationship between the Alberta government and its
bureaucracy is a further consequence of the deterioration of the province's
fiscal and economic position. Like most other democratic jurisdictions,
the government of Alberta must now make decisions that involve trade-
offs between competing values, that unleash conflicts of interest and that
evoke serious political controversies. Like other governments, it now
faces substantial opposition from its own workforce as it pursues a restraint agenda. In this sense, Alberta's economic decline has made provincial politics much like those prevailing elsewhere. Second, the political
management of the public service poses serious contradictions for the
governing Conservatives and for that matter for Alberta's opposition parties. For the Tories, civil service layoffs, privatization and decentralization have heightened conflict between the party's conservative, rural faction and its once dominant, now weakened, urban wing. Ministers from
both Edmonton and Calgary have publicly worried about the economic
and political impact of administrative decentralization and have even
stated that the province's public sector industrial relations legislation
deserves an overhaul. Their challenge to their party's traditional opposition to legal public sector strikes reflects their anxieties about the
Tories' ascendant rural wing and about their own declining urban electoral prospects. And while the partisan behaviour of civil servants
remains the subject of scholarly controversy, Edmonton with its large
number of public sector employees will likely remain cool to Conservative appeals. The Conservatives' contemporary agenda, with its emphasis on deficit reduction and public sector cutbacks, challenges an important component of the Alberta labour force. Alberta's public service has
recently been offered little by its Tory masters. But once again, we must
ask whether a change of government will alter the situation radically.
The Liberals, for example, are broadly supportive of public sector cutbacks and fiscal restraint. And while the New Democrats are committed to an expanded public sector and reformed industrial relations, the
recent experiences of an NDP government in Manitoba and the Parti Quebecois attest to the frosty relationship that may develop between social
democratic governments and their civil servants under the pressures of
fiscal restraint. Finally, we note the emergence of the public sector unions

and some public employees, notably nurses, as advocates, not merely of better working conditions for their members, but also of increased public expenditures on social services, health and education. For example, the nurses and social workers, while on illegal strikes, focussed their public appeals on questions about provincial funding per se and on the government's apparent preference for economic development at the expense of education, health and welfare. Their appeals were overtly political. Public employees and their traditionally conservative unions are slowly emerging as interest groups within the Alberta state.

Conclusion

Our theme has been the impact of economic instability on the activities of the government of Alberta. Our conclusion leaves this idea and ponders how a change in government might alter the role of the provincial government. In this vein, an interesting political consequence of long-term one-party dominance emerges. As one-party dominance persists, critics of the government, buoyed by the rhetoric of opposition parties, often assume that a change of government will bring significant changes to all aspects of political life. But will it? Will a change of government alter, for example, the economic realities faced by Alberta decision-makers or the limits imposed by federalism?

Such questions plunge us into a complex controversy which focusses on the importance of partisanship and local factors as compared with broad economic and social forces in shaping government activity. Seen from one angle, all democratic governments can be said to face, and to respond similarly to, broad economic, social and political constraints. But in a different light and employing different criteria, we can stress the distinctiveness of particular parties and the importance of political institutions and personalities.

In probing such issues in Alberta, we will assume that for the 1990s the economy will be relatively stable. That is, we will witness neither pronounced booms nor serious downturns. In this context, what sort of policies might we expect from a Liberal provincial government? The Liberals, like the governing Conservatives, emphasize fiscal restraint, balanced budgets and predictably, economic diversification. They stress the virtues of free enterprise and market forces but also acknowledge a commitment to an active role for government in shaping economic forces. The Liberals now stress the need for greater "democracy" as evidenced by their interest in "Access to Information" laws and ethical conduct in government. And like the Conservatives, they countenance the maintenance of the provincial "welfare state" but argue that they will not launch major new programs. The Liberals also want to do a better job of putting money in the pockets of those "most in need." In short, the Liberals present themselves as a pro-business alternative to the Conservatives and as a party that sees itself as bringing new blood, not major new policy initiatives, to government. The Liberals stress their capacity for "better management" of the status quo.

And what of the Alberta New Democrats whose mild brand of democratic socialism permits, indeed encourages, substantial private sector activity? One area of difference between the parties is the New Democrats commitment to greater public spending on health, education and welfare and its greater skepticism about the virtues of balanced budgets, privatization and expenditure restraint. The New Democrats also allude to the need for serious tax reform but no blueprint is available and the depth of the party's commitment remains unclear. And they express interest in the well-being of such groups as women, aboriginal peoples and gays, all of whom are at loggerheads with the government and all of whom seek either better protection of their rights or expanded programs in such areas as affirmative action and pay equity. The further reform of provincial labour relations legislation in both the public and private sectors is a priority. Like their major opponents, they are committed to economic diversification but rather imprecisely, through an expanded role for the state. Seen in this light, a New Democrat government would advance some innovations through an expanded public sector but would mount no major challenge to the nature of government activity in the province.

Our tentative argument is therefore that a change in government would not significantly alter the state's role in Alberta. While deeply critical of the Conservatives, both the Liberals and the New Democrats offer a broadly similar program of public priorities. All three parties accept the need for government intervention, a welfare state, substantial public expenditures on education and economic infrastructure, economic diversification and stricter environmental controls. None offers a compelling vision of how to end the province's persistent economic instability or how over the longer term, and in the absence of major tax reform, to reduce the Treasury's dependence on resource royalties.

A last interesting prospect is the possible emergence of new parties, notably the Reform party. The Reformers have so far declared themselves against an immediate entry into provincial politics. But the door remains open and the following possibility therefore requires some consideration. Bearing in mind that future federal and provincial general elections will probably be held quite close together, either a disappointing or a surprisingly strong federal performance by the Reform party will probably encourage a plunge into the provincial arena where the Reformers have long been optimistic about their electoral prospects. Such a scenario sees the quick emergence of a strong, avowedly anti-statist party. Under these circumstances, numerous possibilities arise. For example, both the Liberals and the Conservatives might shift to the right in an effort to undercut the Reformers. But such a move would open up new possibilities for the New Democrats whose ranks might be swollen by those who saw themselves as progressive Liberals. And if the Conservative vote held, a minority government could result with important implications for the content of policy. Finally, would a Reform government quickly abandon its anti-statism and adopt many of the orthodoxies it now detests? No clear answer emerges to this question. But even a cursory review of the experiences of the United Farmers of Alberta and Social Credit reveals the rapid deradicalization of these populist movements.

NOTES

1. Robert L. Mansell and Michael B. Percy, *Strength in Adversity: A Study of the Alberta Economy* (Edmonton: The University of Alberta Press, 1990), p. 1.

2. See John Richards and Larry Pratt, *Prairie Capitalism: Power and Influence in the New West* (Toronto: McClelland and Stewart, 1979), chaps. 7 and 9.

3. From the final report of the Inspector, William E. Code, QC, into the Principal affair. Court of Queen's Bench of Alberta, 18 July 1989, p. 330. Hereafter cited as Code Report.

4. On the theory and practice of rent-seeking, see Anne O. Kreuger, "The Political Economy of the Rent-Seeking Society," *The American Economic Review* 64, no. 3 (June 1974): 291-303.

5. See Mansell and Percy, *Strength in Adversity*, pp. 76-77.

6. Ibid., chap. 4.

7. Ibid., chap. 4.

8. J.M. Keynes, *The General Theory of Employment, Interest, and Money* (New York: Harcourt/HBJ, 1964), p. 152.

9. Code Report, p. 413.

10. Mansell and Percy, *Strength in Adversity*, p. 2.

11. For details see Government of Alberta, *White Paper: Proposals for an Industrial and Science Strategy for Albertans, 1985-1990* (Edmonton, July 1984).

12. For a brief, but insightful, overview of Alberta's forestry boom see Andrew Nikiforuk and Ed Struzik, "The Great Forest Sell-Off," *Report on Business Magazine* (November 1989), pp. 57-67.

13. For historical background on Alberta's forestry initiatives see Michael Howlett, "The Forest Industry on the Prairies: Opportunities and Constraints to Future Development," *Prairie Forum* 14, no. 23 (Fall 1989): 233-57.

14. Nikiforuk and Struzik, "The Great Forest Sell-Off," p. 57.

15. See, for example, Premier Getty's remarks in the Alberta Legislative Assembly, Debates, 5 May 1987, p. 1007. (Hereafter referred to as Debates, date, page.)

16. W.T. Easterbrook, *North American Patterns of Growth and Development* (Toronto: University of Toronto Press, 1990), p. 44.

17. Debates, 18 April 1988, pp. 504-5.

18. See, for example, Christopher Donville, "Minister defends proposal for controversial Alberta-Pacific mill," *The Financial Post*, 22 January 1990, p. 3 and Jack Danylchuk and Scott McKeen, "Minister blasts pulp-mill foes," *Edmonton Journal*, 23 September 1990, p. A-1.

19. "Alberta forest out on limb," *Calgary Herald*, 7 March 1989, p. 7.

20. P. Boothe, "Time-Consistent Data for Alberta's Public Finances: 1968-1989," Department of Economics, University of Alberta, Research Paper No. 90-8, October 1990, Table 2, p. 12.

21. Ibid., p. 12.

22. Paul Boothe, "Public Sector Saving and Long-term Fiscal Balance in a Resource-Based Economy: Alberta 1969-1989," Department of Economics, University of Alberta, Research paper no. 90-13, August 1990.

23. Alberta, *1991 Budget Address*, p. 23.

24. For a useful typology of variations of restraint see Allan M. Maslove, Michael J. Prince and G. Bruce Doern, *Federal and Provincial Budgeting* (Toronto: University of Toronto Press, 1986), p. 207.

25. These percentage changes are calculated by using the actual spending reported for the 1981/82-1988/89 fiscal years and the forecast spending for 1989/90 as reported in provincial budget addresses. The inflation rate is the Alberta inflation rate for the 1981-89 calendar years.

26. Mike Nickel, "A Less Than Perfect Process: Media-Politician Relations in Agenda-Setting" (unpublished M.A. Thesis, University of Alberta, 1991), pp. 112-15.

27. Richard Johnston, *Public Opinion and Public Policy in Canada* (Toronto: University of Toronto Press, 1985).

28. Richard Helm, Ross Henderson, and Kathleen Engman, "Opposition calls budget 'misleading'," *Edmonton Journal*, 5 April 1991, p. A-3.

29. "Welfare rates leave thousands impoverished, national study finds,"*Globe and Mail*, 19 December 1990, p. A6.

30. One Angus Reid poll concluded that forty per cent of Albertans believed that health care in the province had deteriorated. See Sherri Aikenhead, "System in the throes of reforms," *Edmonton Journal*, 29 December 1990, p. C3.

31. Alberta, *Budget Address* 1986, p. 40; Alberta, *Budget Address* 1991, p. 42.

32. Allan Tupper and G. Bruce Doern, "Alberta Budgeting in the Lougheed Era," in *Budgeting in the Provinces: Leadership and the Premiers*, Allan M. Maslove, ed. (Toronto: The Institute of Public Administration of Canada, 1989), p. 130.

33. For details see Allan Tupper, "Opportunity and Constraint: Grant Notley and the Modern State" in *Socialism and Democracy in Alberta: Essays in Honour of Grant Notley*, ed., Larry Pratt (Edmonton: NeWest Press, 1986), pp. 88-111.

34. For details of Premier Lougheed's guidelines for ministers see *Debates*, 2 May 1973, pp. 2739-2740. Lougheed views about the conduct of senior public officials are found in *Debates*, 26 May 1975, pp. 159-60.

35. Conflict of Interest Review Panel, *Report on Conflicts of Interest Rules for Cabinet Ministers, Members of the Legislative Assembly and Senior Public Servants* (Edmonton: 1990).

36. For details of the government's position see *Debates*, 10 May 1977, pp. 1245-1249. Concern about the government's steadfast "anti-strike" position was recently expressed by Elaine McCoy the provincial Minister of Labor. For details see Sherri Aikenhead, "Minister ready to debate public servants' right to strike," *Edmonton Journal*, 13 July 1990, p. A-7.

3

Alberta and the National Community

Roger Gibbins

Alberta's place within the Canadian political community is an abiding preoccupation for Albertans that has shaped the political landscape of the province. It finds reflection in patterns of provincial support for national political parties, in the interplay among parties in the provincial arena, and in the attitudes of residents toward a national political process deemed to be at best indifferent to, and at worst hostile to the interests and aspirations of Albertans.

Albertans' preoccupation with their sense of place within the Canadian community leads us to *western alienation*, a sentiment by no means confined to Alberta but which often finds particularly virulent expression within the province. It also leads us to the heart of the constitutional strategies adopted by Alberta governments, strategies which have left their mark on the broader Canadian constitutional landscape. Alberta governments, and particularly those of the last two decades, have pursued two quite different constitutional objectives—the enhancement or at least protection of provincial jurisdiction and the reform of national institutions. Until the early 1980s, the two objectives found expression within a coherent constitutional strategy. In more recent years, however, this strategy has started to unravel as the two objectives have come into conflict with one another. As a consequence, Alberta's stance in the national constitutional arena has become less coherent and therefore less influential. This incoherence reflects not so much a lack of direction by the provincial government as it does both an enduring provincial ambivalence about the national political community, and the impact of political and economic changes within and without Alberta.

Setting the Stage

Alberta has a unique and interesting demographic position within Canada. With just under ten per cent (9.4%) of the national population,[1] Alberta is much smaller than either Ontario or Quebec (with 35.9% and 25.8% of the national population respectively), and significantly smaller than British Columbia, which has 11.4% of the national population. At the same time, Alberta is much larger than the remaining provinces; it has more than twice the population of Manitoba or Saskatchewan, and more than the population of the four Atlantic provinces combined. Alberta is thus the largest of the small provinces and/or the smallest of the big. (In the minds of Albertans, I suspect that the latter image prevails.) It is worth noting in this respect that, should a reformed Senate be based on equal provincial representation, Alberta would be the only province to come up with approximately the same proportion of seats in the Senate that it has in the House of Commons.

The demographic landscape of Alberta has been shaped by successive waves of immigration which have ebbed and flowed in response to the province's vacillating economic fortunes. The first waves came before the Great Depression, and came in response to the opening of the agricultural west. The later waves came after the Second World War, and in fact largely after 1973, and were in response to the province's new found energy wealth. The mobility of the Alberta population has an important consequence during times of economic recession and depression. Just as people flood into the province during boom conditions, they tend to leave again during times of bust. Therefore, and at least since the end of the Depression, Alberta has been largely spared high unemployment rates when economic conditions are bad; the unemployed leave, and the burden of unemployment is shifted to other provinces.

Alberta's share of the national population has grown in recent decades, but has grown less than the omnipresent boosterism of provincial residents might suggest. As Table 3.1 shows, a noticeable demographic transformation occurred between the 1971 and 1981 census, as Alberta's share of the national, regional and prairie populations increased significantly. With population growth fueled by the prosperity of the energy industry, Alberta's population also increased significantly relative to the populations of BC, Ontario, and Quebec. However, Table 3.1 also shows that this demographic transformation was brought up short by the collapse of the energy boom and concomitant recession in the early 1980s. Only

TABLE 3.1   Demographic Transformation of Alberta

	1971	1981	1986
Alberta's % of the national population	7.5	9.2	9.4
Alberta's % of the prairie population	46.0	52.9	53.3
Alberta's % of 4 western provinces	28.4	32.1	32.3
Alberta's % of BC's population	74.5	81.6	82.2
Alberta's % of Ontario's population	21.1	25.9	26.1
Alberta's % of Quebec's population	27.0	34.8	36.3

very modest change occurred between 1981 and 1986, and little change is expected when the 1991 census figures are released.

These demographic dynamics feed into constitutional politics in a number of ways. During the 1970s and early 1980s they contributed to the sense of frustration and even exasperation that infused political life in the province. Alberta seemed to be on the move, people and money were pouring in, and yet Albertans could not secure what was thought to be their rightful place in the national sun. The flow of political power into the province was not seen to be commensurate with the intake of population and money. In the mid to late 1980s, and into the early 1990s, a more static demographic situation tempered constitutional ambitions. The belief prevailing in the late 1970s, that the country's centres of economic and political power were moving inexorably westward, was dealt a crippling blow by the economic downturn of the mid 1980s.

The underlying demographic instability of the province is related to economic instability, which in turn helps shape the dynamics of constitutional politics. Alberta's prosperity rests not on its abundant endowment of natural resources, but rather on the state of international markets for those resources. International resource markets suffer from instability and uncertainty, and thus the provincial economy rollercoasters its way through cycles of boom and bust. As a consequence, Alberta politics have been driven by the quest for economic stability and security. Provincially, this has meant an ongoing search for economic diversification, the creation of the Alberta Heritage Savings Trust Fund, and a wide array of social programs and educational opportunities to stem the periodic tides of out-migration, and to enable daughters and sons to stay within the province.[2] Federally, it has meant a search for greater security with respect to ownership of the provincial resource base, and greater provincial influence on the levels of the national government which shape trade and macro-economic policies. Thus the quest for economic security has found expression in the search both for constitutional guarantees which would protect the province's natural resources from external exploitation and for institutional reform.

Western Alienation

Economic discontent within Alberta, and within the broader western region, provides the foundation upon which the political superstructure of western alienation has been constructed. In an earlier work, I defined western alienation as follows:

> Western alienation is best seen as a *political ideology* of regional discontent. [It] embodies a socially shared set of interrelated beliefs with some degree of cultural embodiment and intellectual articulation, with a recognized history and constituency, and with recognized spokesmen and carriers of the creed. Western alienation encompasses a sense of political, economic and, to a lesser extent, cultural estrangement from the Canadian heartland.[3]

It is important to note that the dominant theme of western alienation, the belief that the West is always outgunned in national politics and as a consequence has been subjected to varying degrees of economic exploitation by central Canada, enjoys both deep historical roots and contemporary nourishment. Thus the national tariff policy of 1879, the 1980 National Energy Program, the insensitivities of eastern financial institutions during the Depression, and the 1986 decision to award the CF-18 maintenance contract to a Montreal firm[4] are all woven together into a seamless web of regional protest.

It is also important to note that western alienation is central to the regional identity of Albertans. It is the cloak or costume that Albertans slip on when they want to position themselves with respect to the national community; they learn its tenets as they emerge from the egg, and seldom lose the faith no matter where in Canada they might come to live. In this respect, then, western alienation is also central to the political culture which both shapes and reflects political behaviour in the province. Admittedly, some readers may consider it inappropriate to use the regional term western alienation to describe the essence of the political culture in Alberta. After all, Alberta is not the West, the province's economic and demographic profile is unique, and political developments within the province are often unrelated to those in the neighbouring provinces of British Columbia and Saskatchewan. Moreover, Alberta governments have been emphatic in their rejection of regional visions of Canada; provincial and not regional equality has been the constitutional touchstone of Alberta governments. (The Alberta government categorically rejected the 1991 recommendation of the Beaudoin-Edwards Committee[5] that the constitutional amending formula be changed from provincial to regional vetoes.) Yet, appropriately or not, Albertans have incorporated ''the West'' into their political culture; the province has been inflated to become synonymous with the West in political discourse, something that does little to endear Albertans to other western Canadians.

Western alienation in Alberta is not symptomatic of political disengagement or apathy. To the contrary, it has been the source of a good deal of political energy as Albertans have fashioned imaginative political responses to their regional complaints. The United Farmers of Alberta, the proponents of Social Credit monetary theory, Bert Brown and the Committee for a Triple-E Senate, and the Reform Party of Canada may be or have been tilting at windmills, but they are tilting nonetheless. Indeed, it is the engaged nature of western alienation that carries Alberta discontent onto the national political stage, and into the centre of Canada's ongoing constitutional debate.

The Constitutional Debate

Alberta's initial constitutional objectives sprang directly from the province's terms of entry into Confederation. When Alberta became a province in 1905, control over its natural resources remained with the Parliament of Canada. Thus the overriding constitutional objective was to acquire ownership of those resources, and to do so under the same terms and conditions enjoyed by other provinces. The passage of the 1930 Natural Resources Transfer Act secured this first and primordial constitutional objective.

The next set of constitutional objectives started to take shape in the late 1960s and early 1970s as Canada began to search for a new constitutional definition of Quebec's place in Canada. This stage in the constitutional process coincided with important changes within Alberta; the energy boom of the early 1970s was well underway, and an aggressive Progressive Conservative government had been elected in 1971 to end 35 years of Social Credit rule. By themselves, these changes would not have been sufficient to open up a national constitutional debate. However, once that debate had been opened up by the Quiet Revolution and separatist threat in Quebec, Alberta was well-positioned to be an active player. In a sense, the Alberta government and its new premier, Peter Lougheed, surfed adroitly on the constitutional waves generated by the nationalist movement in Quebec.

Alberta's constitutional objectives in the 1970s were primarily defensive in character. Throughout the first three terms of Peter Lougheed's government, the provincial government sought to shore up provincial ownership and jurisdictional control of natural resources, and to ward off any incursions by the federal government, and by implication "central Canada," into the natural resource field. As Alberta sought both an expansion of provincial control and a reduction in federal intervention, it found a ready ally in Quebec. Thus despite the fact that the Alberta *public* was never much in tune with, and certainly not supportive of Quebec's constitutional agenda, that agenda found a receptive audience within the Alberta government and particularly within the Department of Federal and Intergovernmental Affairs. Given that constitutional politics in the pre-Meech period were somewhat removed from public scrutiny and participation, the discrepancy between the constitutional perspectives of the Alberta government and public did not become problematic until the premiership of Don Getty. The mythological "redneck" Albertans may have complained about Quebec in the bars and hockey rinks but, behind the scenes, their government used the nationalist movement in Quebec as a source of leverage for its own and not dissimilar constitutional objectives.

The Alberta government's defensive constitutional strategy enjoyed a good measure of success in the negotiations leading up to the Constitution Act, 1982. The inclusion of section 92A in the 1982 Act clarified and to a degree further protected Alberta's control over natural resources. Section 92A(1) states that:

In each province, the legislature may exclusively make laws in relation to (a) exploration for non-renewable natural resources in the province; (b) development, conservation and management of non-renewable natural resources and forestry resources in the province, including laws in relation to the rate of primary production therefrom; and (c) development, conservation and management of sites and facilities in the province for the generation and production of electrical energy.

Section 92A (2) states that "in each province, the legislature may make laws in relation to the export from the province to another part of Canada of the primary production from nonrenewable natural resources and forestry resources in the province and the production from facilities in the province for the generation of electrical energy, but such laws may not authorize or provide for discrimination in prices or in supplies exported to another part of Canada." While both clauses apply to all provinces, they are of particular importance to Alberta in the aftermath of the 1980-81 energy wars between Alberta and the federal government. Their inclusion in the 1982 Constitution Act was an unequivocal albeit shared achievement for the Alberta government.

The Alberta government also played a major role in crafting the various amending formulae built into the 1982 Constitution Act. It was here that the government made substantial progress with respect not only to the protection of provincial resources, but also with respect to the *constitutional enshrinement of provincial equality*. The general amending formula in section 38 (1)—Parliament plus seven of the ten provinces having in aggregate at least fifty per cent of the population of all provinces—recognizes the equality of the provinces by denying any single province the power of veto. Section 41 grants each and every province a veto over changes to "(a) the office of the Queen, the Governor General and the Lieutenant Governor of a province; (b) the right of a province to a number of members in the House of Commons not less than the number of Senators by which the province is entitled to be represented at the time this Part comes into force; (c) subject to section 43, the use of English or the French language; (d) the composition of the Supreme Court of Canada; and (e) an amendment to this part [changes to the amending formula itself]." Section 38 (2 and 3) of the general amending formula gives provinces the right to opt out of any constitutional amendment "that derogates from the legislative powers, the proprietary rights or any other rights or privileges of the legislature or government of a province . . . ." Thus the other provinces can not gang up on Alberta through the general amending formula to strip the province of its ownership or jurisdictional control over natural resources.

The Alberta government had every right to be pleased with the provisions of the 1982 Constitution Act, for the new constitution provided both substantive protection for Alberta interests and recognition of provincial equality. At the same time, the defensive posture of the provincial government also meant that no progress was made with respect to the reform of national parliamentary institutions. Admittedly, it is by no means clear that progress could have been made in this respect no matter what stance was adopted by the Alberta government; it takes more than Alberta's enthusiasm to move the national political process. Nevertheless, the much more difficult task of institutional reform was passed on to Premier Getty and the negotiations surrounding the Meech Lake Accord.

Perhaps the point to stress is that the 1982 Constitution Act brought to a successful conclusion Alberta's campaign to provide additional constitutional protection for provincial resource ownership. Indeed, Alberta secured more from the 1982 Act, with respect to economic protection, than did Quebec with respect to cultural protection. In any event, the stage was set for the second and more difficult act in the constitutional drama—the reform of national institutions, and more specifically the Senate.

Alberta's early initiatives with respect to Senate reform were very much in keeping with a stronger role for *provincial governments* in the national legislative process, and were thus compatible in spirit with the quest for greater jurisdictional control and a more decentralized federal state. The Senate reform proposals embedded in the 1982 Alberta position paper *A Provincially-Appointed Senate: A New Federalism for Canada* envisioned a provincially-appointed Senate, or "House of the Provinces," that would give provincial governments considerable influence in areas of federal legislative jurisdiction.[6] Federal legislation which impinged on provincial responsibilities and interests would have to win the approval of provincial government delegations before becoming law. Provincial governments would become the regional watchdogs in Ottawa, looking over the shoulder of MPs to ensure that they kept regional interests in mind. The goal, then, was to expand provincial government input into national decision-making while at the same time further restricting national input into provincial decision-making. In this respect, the Alberta proposal would have created a substantially decentralized federal state in which provincial governments would be autonomous in their own domain and significant players in the federal legislative domain.

Even though this version of Senate reform appeared to be compatible with Quebec's province-centred constitutional agenda, it did not elicit any enthusiastic response from the Quebec government.[7] Yet Quebec's support was critical because Alberta alone could not drive the constitutional debate. Alberta had to ride the wave for constitutional reform generated by Quebec's discontent, and then transform that wave into support for institutional reform which Quebec itself did not support. The dilemma was acute and perhaps unsolvable. When Alberta moved from a focus on the federal-provincial division of powers to a focus on parliamentary reform, the constitutional alliance with Quebec began to evaporate. The constitutional alliance deteriorated even further as the Alberta vision of Senate reform was radically altered in the early 1980s.

The origins of the Alberta government's current enthusiasm for an elected Senate, and more specifically for an elected, equal and effective Senate, are not to be found in the government itself. In the early 1980s, the provincial government was still wedded to a House of the Provinces model, and the Special Select Committee on Senate Reform established by the Lougheed government in 1983 was designed to explore and promote that alternative. However, the government lost control of the reform agenda when presentation after presentation in public hearings supported the Triple-E model, which had been aggressively promoted by the Canada West Foundation and the Committee for a Triple-E Senate, and when no public enthusiasm was uncovered for a provincially appointed Senate. Thus the Committee ended up supporting a Senate reform model that was contrary to the style and practice of the Lougheed government, a model in which elected Senators would likely eclipse provincial premiers on the national stage. Whereas the role of regional representation had been fulfilled by provincial premiers during the heydays of executive federalism which marked the Lougheed governments, a Triple-E Senate would remove this role from provincial premiers and place it in the hands of elected Senators within the national legislative process. Ironically and inadvertently, the strongly provincialist Alberta government found itself leading the fight for Senate reform which would diminish the role of provincial governments and premiers in Canadian political life.

By taking the Senate reform issue to the people, the Select Committee forged a link between public attitudes towards constitutional reform and the constitutional position of the Alberta government, a link that has since been strengthened by Premier Getty's stalwart support for an elected Senate and by the 1989 "election" of the late Senator Stan Waters. In the past, the very absence of any such linkage enabled the Alberta and Quebec governments to pursue a common constitutional agenda. However, the Alberta debate over the Meech Lake Accord illustrated how complicated constitutional politics can be when the linkage is in place. The provincial government found itself supporting the Accord when polls in the province suggested that public support stood at less than ten per cent, and when public support for the "distinct society" cornerstone of the Accord was negligible. Electoral support for the government was damaged as a consequence, and the continued viability of the Alberta-Quebec constitutional alliance was placed in serious jeopardy. Indeed, the common interest between the two provinces has all but evaporated as Alberta has become the constitutional pointman for a Senate reform model that is unacceptable to Quebec. The Quebec government has no interest in elected Senators who would challenge the right of the Quebec premier and National Assembly to speak for Quebec, no interest in equal provincial representation, and no interest in the revitalization of national institutions that is implied by an "effective Senate." Thus Alberta and Quebec are now pursuing quite divergent and likely irreconcilable constitutional agendas. If this development is problematic for Quebec, it is even more problematic for Alberta. Quebec, by playing the threat of independence, may be able to move the constitutional process on its own accord, but Alberta cannot.

The Partisan Dynamics of Constitutional Politics

Alberta's constitutional politics, and the broader quest for a comfortable sense of place within the national political community, have been thoroughly entangled with partisan politics. In itself, this is not surprising, and indeed we should not expect anything else in a province where constitutional politics are so deeply embedded in the political culture. However, the entanglement has been greater than has been the case in

either Saskatchewan, in which a rough and ready constitutional consensus has prevailed, or in British Columbia where constitutional politics
have been largely unconnected to the dynamics of provincial party competition. In this sense, Alberta appears much like the "Quebec of English
Canada."[8]

The entanglement of constitutional and partisan politics has been
complicated by a number of unique or at the very least distinctive features
of electoral politics in Alberta. Although these features are discussed at
greater length in Keith Archer's chapter, "Voting Behavior and Political
Dominance in Alberta, 1971-1991," they are important enough for the
present argument to merit a brief discussion. We might note, for example,
the penchant that Albertans have for backing losing political parties on the
national scene. Since Alberta became a province, Albertans have elected
a majority of their MPs to the winning side of the House of Commons on
only seven of 24 occasions: 1908, 1917, 1958, 1962, 1979, 1984, and 1988.
To the extent that constitutional politics have traditionally been dominated by governments rather than by legislatures more broadly defined,
Albertans have not been well positioned in the constitutional process.

Albertans have not only tended to vote against the winning party, but
have also gone through long periods of support for third parties lacking
any significant national presence. In 1921, Albertans joined a regional
surge to the Progressive party by electing eleven Progressive MPs. What
set the province apart, however, was not this initial enthusiasm for the
Progressives, which was shared across the prairie West and rural Ontario,
but the persistence of Progressive support. In 1925, only 24 Progressives
were elected, of whom 9 came from Alberta. In 1926, 20 were elected,
including 11 from Alberta, and in 1930 only 12 were elected, of whom
9 came from Alberta. The Progressives were born regionally, but came
home to die in Alberta. Then, in 1935, Alberta voters began sending Social
Credit MPs to Ottawa: 15 in 1935, 10 in 1940, 13 in 1945, 10 in 1949,
11 in 1953, and 13 in 1957. The point to stress in this chronology is that
Alberta's support for third-party MPs was much more than a reflection
of western alienation. It was also a cause, in that third-party support
tended to isolate Albertans from the national political process. Because
there were not enough Alberta MPs, the relatively small handful of
Progressive and Socred MPs could be and were ignored. Alberta became
little more than a curiosity, the freak show in the national political
circus. By electing Social Credit MPs, Albertans drifted to the margins
of national political life.

TABLE 3.2   Federal Progressive Conservative Support in Alberta

Federal Election	Total Alberta seats	PC Alberta seats	Alberta PC seats as a % of total PC seats
1958	17	17	8.2
1962	17	15	12.9
1963	17	14	14.7
1965	17	15	15.5
1968	19	15	20.8
1972	19	19	17.8
1974	19	19	20.0
1979	21	21	15.4
1980	21	21	20.3
1984	21	21	10.0
1988	26	25	14.8

In the critical election of 1958, Albertans threw their support behind Progressive Conservative John Diefenbaker, who took all 17 Alberta seats and swept the country. Alberta was thus briefly part of the national mainstream. When support for both Diefenbaker and the Conservatives began to wane across the country, Albertans remained steadfast in their Tory support. As Table 3.2 shows, this support gave Alberta MPs considerable clout within the national Progressive Conservative party. By remaining grimly loyal to the Conservatives through a sustained period of Liberal national dominance, Albertans were able to regionalize the Conservative party, and transform it into a vehicle for western discontent. The cost, however, was considerable as Alberta was shut out of the caucus and cabinet of the governing Liberals. When the Conservatives swept back into national office in 1984, Albertan MPs were finally on the right side of the House, and Harvie Andre, Joe Clark, and Don Mazankowski had positions of substantial influence within the federal cabinet. Yet again, there was a cost as Alberta MPs found their influence within the national Conservative party greatly reduced. Hence the irony; Alberta MPs traded a regionalized national party for national office, but in so doing lost the capacity to express clearly a regional perspective on the national political stage. In effect, the Reform party today may have picked up the expressive torch of regional discontent that the Conservatives dropped in their successful bid for national power.

During the period of Liberal dominance in Ottawa that stretched almost unbroken from 1965 to 1984, monolithic Conservative support in Alberta allowed the federal Liberals, and to some degree the government of Canada, to write off Alberta. After all, the Liberals had no seats to lose in Alberta, and little prospect of improvement. To the extent that this period was also an intensive one for constitutional politics, the partisan isolation of Albertans from the federal government reinforced the defensive stance of the provincial government in constitutional negotiations. Federal constitutional initiatives were viewed with a great deal of suspicion because they came from a Liberal government, and provincial critiques of federal proposals were intensified in part by the partisan rift between the Alberta and federal governments. While this is not to suggest that partisanship dominated the constitutional arena, it did shade the strategies and reactions of the Alberta government during a period when Albertans lacked any effective voice within the national government, and thus had to rely exclusively on the provincial government.

All of this changed dramatically when the Progressive Conservative government led by Brian Mulroney was elected in 1984. When the next round of the constitutional process opened with the negotiations surrounding the Meech Lake Accord, Albertans were well represented within the national government, and Conservative governments were in office in both Ottawa and Edmonton. Not surprisingly, then, the Alberta government was very much onside with the federal government with respect to the Meech Lake Accord, as initially were all other provincial governments, and Premier Getty was one of the Accord's most enthusiastic supporters. However, it was not only the partisan dynamics which had changed; the Meech Lake debate and Premier Getty's leadership of the Triple-E Senate crusade brought the Alberta public into the constitutional fray. Therefore peace on the partisan front was coupled with growing public antagonism to the constitutional positions of Quebec, the federal government and, necessarily, the government of Alberta. With the federal and Alberta governments lined up solidly behind Quebec's agenda, disgruntled Albertans began to look for a new partisan champion for their own constitutional aspirations. That champion emerged in 1987 with the creation of the Reform Party of Canada (RPC) and the selection of Preston Manning as the new party's leader.

It is worth noting, incidentally, that the involvement of the Alberta public in the constitutional debate has not parochialized that debate. A careful reading of the public's participation in the debate over the Meech Lake Accord suggests that Albertans share a common constitutional agenda and perspective with most Canadians outside Quebec, that their views are far from idiosyncratic. Although there is little doubt that Senate reform plays a greater role in the constitutional perspective of the Alberta public than it does elsewhere in Canada outside Quebec, this reflects little more than the symbolic centrality of Senate reform in the traditional rubric of western alienation. In some important respects, it might even be argued that the Alberta public is more in line with the broader patterns of constitutional thought outside Quebec than is the provincial government.

The rise of the RPC marks an important transition in the political leadership of western alienation, and an important transformation in constitutional dynamics. During the years of the Trudeau Liberals, leadership was emphatically provided by the Alberta government, and was backstopped by Alberta Progressive Conservative MPs who wielded a good deal of weight within the federal Tory caucus. Then, when the Mulroney Conservatives assumed federal office in 1984, and when Peter Lougheed retired to be replaced by Don Getty, a leadership vacuum began to emerge. At the very least, it was difficult for a Conservative premier to fight hammer and tongs with a Conservative prime minister. Whereas the constitutional politics of Peter Lougheed were thoroughly entangled with conventional tactics of Ottawa-bashing, Getty found himself sharing a common party label with a very unpopular federal leader. Ottawa-bashing was more difficult and, when practised, often seemed contrived and theatrical. More fundamentally, the provincial and federal governments shared a constitutional position that enjoyed little public support in Alberta. Thus in the late 1980s and early 1990s, leadership of the western constitutional agenda slipped from Tory hands both federally and provincially, and the Reform party moved in to fill the vacuum.

The Reform party provides an effective advocate for the traditional interest that Albertans have had in the reform of national institutions. In fact, the RPC provides a more effective voice than the Alberta government could ever provide, given that governmental support is inevitably tempered by the realization that a reformed Senate along the lines of the Triple-E model would undercut the national role of provincial governments and premiers. It should also be noted, however, that the RPC constrains the constitutional position and strategies of the Alberta government. The threat that the RPC might enter provincial politics and thus challenge the provincial Conservatives on their own turf means that the current government must be cautious in its support for federal constitutional initiatives. The Alberta government can no longer play the helpful fixer role that it played in the Meech Lake Accord, coming to the aid of the federal Conservatives and government in their time of need. The looming presence of the RPC makes any Quebec-Alberta constitutional alliance, or even any Ottawa-Alberta alliance, much more problematic. Moreover, now that the genie of public participation has been released from the constitutional bottle, it will be increasingly difficult for the Alberta government to pursue, as it did in the past, a constitutional strategy and alliance at odds with public opinion.

Conclusion

Over the past thirty years, the major constitutional challenge to the Canadian federal state has come from the nationalist movement in Quebec. At the very least, Quebec politicians have sought a fundamental realignment in the federal division of powers; at the extreme, they have sought the dismemberment of the Canadian federal state and the creation of an independent Quebec. While neither goal has yet been accomplished, there is little question that Quebec's aspirations have dominated the constitutional arena and have provided the major incentive, and indeed imperative, for constitutional reform. This domination has in turn obscured and to a degree negated Alberta's ongoing challenge to the constitutional and institutional status quo.

From the early institutional radicalism of the United Farmers of Alberta and the economic radicalism of Social Credit through the Senate reformers of the last decade and the Reform Party of Canada, Albertans have again and again challenged the constitutional and institutional organization of Canadian political life. What is striking, however, is that the Alberta challenge has had little if any impact on the national scene. The national preoccupation with Quebec has been so pervasive and so complete that Alberta initiatives for *institutional reform* have gone all but unnoticed. While Alberta's interest in *the protection and extension of provincial powers* certainly had an impact on the framing of the 1982 Constitution Act, and also found reflection in the ill-fated Meech Lake Accord, this may do little more than expose a basic truth. When Alberta's constitutional aspirations have been in line with those of Quebec,

Alberta's weight has been felt. When those aspirations have been at odds with Quebec's, Alberta's ability to influence the national political process has been negligible.

This discrepancy is best illustrated by the recent Alberta Senate reform initiative which has been supported by the provincial government, the Committee for a Triple-E Senate, the Calgary-based Canada West Foundation, the Reform Party of Canada and, if the polls are to be believed, by a vast majority of Albertans. In the fall of 1989, this initiative was brought into focus by Canada's first Senate election, in which Albertans went to the polls to select the individual that Premier Don Getty would recommend to Prime Minister Mulroney for appointment to the Senate. At the time, there was a strong expectation among Senate reformers that the Alberta election would set into motion similar elections across the country, and that Alberta would lead the country towards substantive Senate reform. In fact, nothing happened, or at least has happened to date. The Alberta initiative was not picked up, and the Meech Lake Accord debacle makes it unlikely that the Alberta election will even provide a precedent for future Alberta appointments to the Senate.

Again, the lesson seems clear. Alberta is able to have an impact on national political life when the province is in tandem with the constitutional aspirations of Quebec, something that is most likely to occur when constitutional politics are confined to intergovernmental negotiations and are not exposed to public debate. However, when Alberta's aspirations diverge from those of Quebec, something that is likely to happen when the Alberta public becomes engaged in constitutional politics, Alberta's influence diminishes in direct proportion to the degree of divergence, and the province retreats toward the margins of Canadian political life. In effect, Alberta's influence has been dependent upon that of Quebec, a conclusion that has interesting implications should Quebec decide to withdraw from the Canadian federal state.

Since the early 1960s, Quebecers have shared a "national project," a collective ambition to establish a greater degree of control over their economic, cultural and political life. While there has been a lively debate about how far this project should be carried—can it be realized within the constraints of a renewed federalism or does its fulfillment require a sovereign Quebec state?—there has been general agreement about the centrality of the Quebec government to that project. During this same period, Albertans have also shared a common political project, although it has less clearly articulated ends and has experienced little consensus as to means. The essence of that project has been to end the province's marginalization, to move Alberta into the Canadian economic, cultural and *political* mainstreams. Albertans want to get off the bench and into the game.

This project has enjoyed its greatest success in the economic realm where the combination of abundant natural resources and favourable global markets has given Albertans one of the country's highest levels of per capita wealth. Indeed, during the late 1980s, it appeared that Alberta would capture such a large proportion of the nation's wealth that the federal structures of the Canadian state would be threatened. However, the collapse of world oil prices, a national and international recession, and the National Energy Program rapidly deflated Alberta's economic balloon. In retrospect, the 1980s have demonstrated the persistent vulnerability of the provincial economy to external markets, the resultant instability of that economy, and the elusive nature of economic diversification. While Albertans have escaped marginalization on the economic front, they have not seen their province established as the cornerstone of the Canadian economy.

Escape from marginalization has been more difficult to realize on the political front. Little if any headway has been made on Alberta's quest for institutional reform; although Senate reform is now on the federal government's constitutional agenda, its attainment is far from certain. The province's steadfast support for the federal Progressive Conservatives has led less to provincial influence within that party than it has to the subordination of the Alberta agenda to the party's electoral and constitutional preoccupations with Quebec.

The Alberta government has now nailed its colours to the mast of the Triple-E Senate, and to the underlying principle of provincial constitutional equality. Neither is likely to be acceptable to Quebec or Ontario. Thus we have a classic western show-down. Will Albertans and their provincial government succeed in the quest for Senate reform, if not necessarily to the extent of a full Triple E? Or will the provincial government and the Senate reformers get shot down, western alienation flare up in even more intense forms, and a new gunslinger (Preston Manning and the RPC) be brought in for one more try? Or will there be time for one more try?

NOTES

1. The demographic data are taken from the 1986 census.
2. For a detailed and insightful discussion, see John Richards and Larry Pratt, *Prairie Capitalism: Power and Influence in the New West* (Toronto: McClelland and Stewart, 1979).
3. Roger Gibbins, *Prairie Politics and Society: Regionalism in Decline* (Toronto: Butterworths, 1980), p. 169.
4. For a discussion of this decision, see Robert M. Campbell and Les Pal, *The Real Worlds of Canadian Politics* (Peterborough: Broadview Press, 1989), Chapter 1.
5. Hon. Gerald Beaudoin, Senator, and Jim Edwards, M.P., *The Process for Amending the Constitution of Canada*, Report of the Special Joint Committee of the Senate and the House of Commons, 20 June 1991.
6. The House of the Provinces is conceptually similar to the Council of the Federation proposed in the federal government's 1991 constitutional package, *Shaping Canada's Future Together*. The powers of the proposed Council, however, would extend only to federal legislation in areas of provincial jurisdiction, and to federal legislation affecting the economic union.
7. One year later, however, the Quebec Liberal Party's Beige Paper advanced a similar model.
8. See Doreen Barrie, "Alberta, the 'Quebec' of English Canada," in Roger Gibbins, Keith Archer and Stan Drabek, eds., *Canadian Political Life: An Alberta Perspective* (Dubuque: Kendall-Hunt, 1990), pp. 211-18.

4

Reconsidering
Democracy in Alberta

Edward Bell

C.B. Macpherson's *Democracy in Alberta*[1] met with much critical acclaim upon its publication in 1953. One reviewer announced that it "belongs among the best books yet written by Canadian social scientists."[2] Two decades later it was described as "the best political analysis in the Marxist tradition undertaken in Canada,"[3] and "the best historical explanation of the rise of political movements in Alberta."[4] In a commemorative essay following the author's death in 1987, *Democracy in Alberta* was referred to as "a classic account of the contradictions of the petit-bourgeoisie in liberal societies."[5] It has recently been translated into Japanese.

The accolades earned by Macpherson attest to the fact that *Democracy in Alberta* is the most influential book on Alberta politics ever written. It is generally considered to be a standard reference work for the two socio-political movements it analyzes: the United Farmers of Alberta (UFA) and Social Credit. The book also contains some important generalizations about prairie politics and society that continue to inform discussions of these issues today, some four decades after it was originally published. Since the theoretical positions on class and politics taken by Macpherson are said to have general applications, scholars still look to *Democracy in Alberta* to understand political events in other times and jurisdictions.

Democracy in Alberta is a continuing influence on analyses of Alberta society and has contributed to our understanding of Alberta politics, both past and present. This chapter will critically evaluate the central concepts and theses of the book, and in particular Macpherson's "quasi-party'' idea and his portrayal of the role of social class in Alberta. Although *Democracy in Alberta* has been hugely influential, its central assertions rest on infirm and even utopian foundations.

The Issue and Its Explanation

Macpherson claims that ''a new and persistent species of democratic government,'' one which is *''sui generis,''* developed in Alberta with the advent of the United Farmers and Social Credit movements. These groups, which came to power in 1921 and 1935 respectively, are said to have rejected ''the orthodox party system'' in favour of what the author terms the ''quasi-party system.''[6] This departure from the ''ordinary'' party system is the focus of Macpherson's inquiry.

The quasi-party system is defined first in terms of what it is *not* and then in terms of what it *is*. The quasi-party system, Macpherson writes, is not an orthodox party system since ''Government has not been conducted, nor have policies been decided, by continual competition between two main parties for the support of the majority of the electorate.'' He states that from 1921 to 1935, ''no party other than the UFA had any significant existence in provincial politics,'' while from 1935 until ''the present [1962],'' Social Credit ''has held virtually the same monopoly position.''[7] Nor did the two movements comprise part of an orthodox system having third parties, Macpherson claims, as neither the UFA nor Social Credit were ever ''third,'' nor did they go from being third to become one of two major parties; both arose suddenly and nearly displaced all others. The quasi-party system is also said to be unorthodox in the sense that it does not bear a resemblance to the multi-party systems of continental Europe.

Macpherson adds that the quasi-party system is not a nonparty system like that sometimes found in city governments. The two movements were political parties having identifiable party programs for which they tried to gain public support, although their programs included measures to transcend the party system. The quasi-party system is not a one-party system either because ''Other parties, although much reduced, continued to operate and to elect candidates in at least some constituencies.''[8] In sum, Macpherson holds that the quasi-party system is not a non-, one-, two-, three- or multi-party system, and that it is not likely to become one of these other systems.

As for what the quasi-party system *is*, it is said to resemble the ordinary party system in that it involves a recognizable political machine which is opposed, to some extent, by other political machines. It also resembles a nonparty system since administrative concerns tend to outweigh any claims to policy formation. Finally, Macpherson holds that the quasi-party system is similar to a one-party system insofar as party activists maintain that parties per se are not desirable and that a general will exists among the populace.[9]

The quasi-party system can take two forms. One is instructed delegate democracy, which had a short life in the early UFA movement but was "genuinely democratic." The second form, which came into being through the Social Credit party, is plebiscitarian democracy, a system which is "at best an illusory democracy." Macpherson claims that "in reaction against the apparent failure of delegate democracy, [Albertans] swung to what is in fact the other extreme . . .—the plebiscitary democracy in which the people give up their right of decision, criticism, and proposal, in return for the promise that everything will be done to implement the general will."[10]

What caused the deviation from the orthodox party system? The quasi-party system is said to have resulted from "two characteristics, not found together in any of the . . . [nonprairie] provinces . . . ."[11]

> One was their relatively homogeneous class composition, the other was their quasi-colonial status. The former seemed to make a party system unnecessary, the latter led to a positive aversion to party. The absence of any serious opposition of class interests within the province meant that alternate parties were not needed either to express or to moderate a perennial conflict of interests. There was apparently, therefore, no positive basis for an alternate-party system.[12]

But the quasi-party system, like both movements' economic radicalism, is said to have certain "limits." These limits, which form an abiding theme not only in *Democracy in Alberta* but also in Macpherson's subsequent writings on the nature of democracy in capitalist societies, are created by the acceptance of property rights. For Macpherson, the "leaders of both [the UFA and Social Credit] movements were prepared to fight against the quasi-colonial economic subordination of their people, but not to do anything which would undermine the sanctity of property rights." The leaders were not alone in their views on property,

Macpherson contends, as "the limits of the leaders' radicalism were not fundamentally much narrower than the limits of their supporters' radicalism."[13]

Macpherson's assertion that respect for property rights was a crucial limiting factor in the UFA and Social Credit stems from his portrayal of these organizations as movements of the petite bourgeoisie (independent farmers and other self-employed people). Their large numbers account for the aforementioned "relatively homogeneous" class structure, one of the two factors he identifies as giving rise to the quasi-party system. Macpherson characterizes Alberta in this era as a "society of independent producers."[14]

Taking a Marxian view of the petite bourgeoisie, Macpherson maintains that unlike the working class and bourgeoisie, members of this class characteristically possesses "a false consciousness of society and themselves," and have "a delusive understanding of the nature of society, of the economy, and of their own place in it." In times of hardship, the petite bourgeoisie is "liable to be taken in by delusive schemes." Most importantly, being in possession of productive property and having a "consciousness of themselves as entrepreneurs," they will not tolerate the violation of property rights, not even those of the bourgeoisie.[15]

In his analysis of Alberta politics, Macpherson embarks on an effort, however subtle, to show that civilization's ascent to greater heights could begin with the abandonment of property rights. He claims that:

> The limits of *petit-bourgeois* liberalism were reached in the early 1930's with the U.F.A.'s failure to implement the popular will when it had come into conflict with property institutions.[16] There was no question then of the people returning to the orthodox liberalism of the old party system; that would have been to submit again to the outside forces the havoc of whose operations they were determined to resist. On the other hand, as independent producers they were not greatly interested in any socialist transformation of society or socialist vision of democracy. The remaining possibility was some other form of *petit-bourgeois* democracy. The only forms left were various kinds of plebiscitary schemes.[17]

Macpherson claims that no party seeking to promote the interests of the petite bourgeoisie can go beyond the limits of delegate democracy "unless indeed it is prepared and able to do away with the capitalist basis of the whole economy. And once the limits are reached . . . there is no way to hold office but by something approaching a plebiscitarian system."[18] Hence Macpherson implies that there is a higher democracy, presumably socialist democracy, which is obtainable only by abolishing capitalism and which, therefore, is unthinkable for the petite bourgeoisie.

This dilemma—the existence of a higher democracy and the steadfast rejection of it arising from petit-bourgeois false consciousness—is at the heart of Macpherson's explanation of the erratic nature of Alberta politics. The petite bourgeoisie institutes some form of quasi-party system to fight its exploitation by the central Canadian bourgeoisie, but this brings no satisfaction because it never entails a rejection of capitalist relations of production, the root cause of the petite bourgeoisie's suffering. Only the terms of trade dictated by the "quasi-colonial" relationship with central Canada are contested. It is in this sense that agrarian revolt "has occasioned some inconvenience to eastern interests, but nothing serious so far, for the western farmers' consciousness of themselves as entrepreneurs has kept them and their politicians from unduly radical behaviour . . . . The agrarian consciousness is thus at once hostile to and acquiescent in the established order."[19] Hence for Macpherson, the prairie agrarian petite bourgeoisie is like an adolescent who constantly quarrels with his parents but is terrified of leaving home—and great are the undiscovered glories that freedom would bring.

Macpherson's view of the role of class in capitalist societies in general bears an important relationship to his implied solution to the problems of democracy in Alberta. He states that the "concept of class which finds the significant determinant of social and political behaviour in the ability or inability to dispose of labour—one's own and others'— . . . may be thought to remain the most penetrating basis of classification for the understanding of political behaviour."[20] In Macpherson's analysis class is not only the most important source of division in capitalist society; it is the *only* division having fundamental consequences for democracy.

According to Macpherson, there are two main functions of the party system in mature capitalist societies. One is to moderate and contain class conflict, the other to prevent arbitrary rule. Since the petite bourgeoisie accepts "the basic tenets of capitalist enterprise," it too must create a democratic system which moderates class conflict.[21]

In seeing how these ideas are woven into his theory of democracy, one is struck by Macpherson's utopianism. A society without class divisions, he suggests, would not need a party system to moderate class conflict because with no classes or only one class, there can be no class conflict. Furthermore, he is not convinced that arbitrary government would be a concern in a society without class divisions, as in such a society the needs of the populace and the needs of the state would be one and the same.

> Whether the party system is needed in a less class-divided society for the prevention of arbitrary government is not so clear. The need of a party system for this purpose in *any* society can be shown if it is assumed that there is always a natural conflict between the government and the people. It may be said, however, that the more homogeneous a society is, the less likely is the government to be regarded as a natural enemy. At the theoretical extreme of a society without class division, and with popular franchise, the people would regard the state's purposes as their own and the party system would not be required for the maintenance of democracy. Only in such a society is it possible to think of a general will sustaining a democracy without alternate parties. This, of course, is the meaning of the claim made by Soviet Russia and the ''new democracies'' of eastern Europe for their systems as true democracy. With this claim we are not here concerned, for it is appropriate only to a society where class divisions in the Marxist sense have been or are being eliminated by the elimination of capitalist relations of production.[22]

The foregoing, then, provides a synopsis of the phenomena Macpherson is trying to explain and how he proposes to explain them. In brief, Macpherson claims that a unique system of democracy arose in Alberta because of the province's relatively homogeneous (petit-bourgeois) class structure and its colonial relationship with central Canada. The new party system precludes any challenge to bourgeois property rights, a challenge that would ultimately solve the problems of the region, because of the deficiencies inherent in petit-bourgeois class consciousness.

MacPherson's Arguments Assessed

The problems with Macpherson's analysis begin with his failure to establish that what he is trying to explain actually existed. He assumes that a new species of government, something which is *sui generis*, had arisen in Alberta. But had it?

Did Macpherson's "Quasi-Party System" Ever Exist in Alberta?

In a critique of *Democracy in Alberta* published in 1954, S.M. Lipset argues that no significant deviation from the party system occurred. "The fact is," Lipset writes, "that turnover in office is not the normal pattern in democratic politics . . . . [M]any state and city governments in the U.S. and Australia remain almost permanently with one party." Lipset also observes that the large legislative majorities obtained in Alberta since 1921 do not, as Macpherson implies, reflect near unanimity of political opinion in the province since the winning party rarely received more than 55 per cent of the popular vote.[23] He suggests that the opposition vote was fragmented among several parties, and that since Alberta was a "fairly homogeneous" community where divisions of opinion were similar in every constituency, the single member plurality system allowed the dominant party to take a large percentage of the seats without a proportionate share of the popular vote. (Keith Archer's chapter,"Voting Behavior and Political Dominance in Alberta, 1971-1991," examines this point in some detail.) Lipset further claims that under these conditions, a small change in the percentage of the popular vote can cause a major change in the number of seats won by each party. He also argues that there is "no single answer to the problems of [a] class that everyone or even most people in the class need accept," suggesting that there can be differences of opinion on class issues even in societies with homogeneous class structures. He concludes as well that, *contra* Macpherson, class division is not the sole basis of the party system.[24]

The issue of the uniqueness of the Alberta case as compared to other Canadian provinces has been researched by Peter McCormick. He found that with regard to the governing party's longevity of tenure, Alberta is by no means unique as "Canadian politics at both the provincial and federal level tends very much toward long periods of one-party dominance."[25] Nor is it unique in terms of the percentage of the popular vote won by the governing party. From 1905 to 1979 the winning party in Alberta provincial elections received an average 51.1 per cent of the vote which, compared to other provinces, is "quite ordinary and average." McCormick found the Alberta situation to be unusual in one respect: the percentage of the seats in the legislature obtained by the winning party. From 1945 to 1979, the winning party obtained on average

84.6 per cent of the seats, compared to 69.7 per cent for all provincial governments.[26]

In rebutting Lipset, Macpherson concedes that the former's argument about the loose relationship between the percentage of the popular vote and the amount of seats won has some merit, but that it cannot completely explain the Alberta situation. Admitting Lipset's assertion about the division of opinion in homogeneous constituencies, Macpherson claims that one would expect to find frequent changes of government under these conditions because a small change in opinion would have a drastic change on the number of seats won. "But what has to be explained," he writes, "is the unusually infrequent change of government . . . . Homogeneous constituencies set up a presumption of unusual instability . . . ."[27]

But Macpherson's rejoinder does not resolve the issue. First of all, he chooses to ignore Lipset's valid point that changes of government in Alberta have *not* been "unusually infrequent." Macpherson persists in demanding an explanation for this nonfact. Secondly, his presumption that homogeneous constituencies in general are prone to frequent changes of government, an assertion made without evidence, flies in the face of the position taken in *Democracy in Alberta* that the province's allegedly homogeneous class composition "seemed to make a party system unnecessary," and that class-homogeneous societies in general would not even need party systems.

Macpherson further addresses Lipset's critique by arguing that the quasi-party system differs from the orthodox system not only with regard to the size of legislative majorities, which he concedes is an unreliable indicator of public sentiment. The quasi-party system also differs "partly on the suddenness with which each of the two reform movements captured power, partly on the persistence of government majorities, partly on the absence (during most of the whole period) of any opposition party which attempted to get the support of the majority of the electorate as a whole."[28]

Again Macpherson's remarks show that a crucial weakness of his position is that he does not demonstrate that what he is trying to explain— the quasi-party system as he has defined it—actually existed in Alberta. Did the UFA and Social Credit really take power more "suddenly" than political movements in nonprairie provinces or in jurisdictions outside Canada having orthodox party systems? The reader is given no definition of "sudden" or any evidence indicating that the assertion is true.

As for the persistence of government majorities, we have seen from McCormick's study that this does not distinguish the Alberta experience from that of other Canadian provinces. Macpherson has simply reasserted his mistaken assumption about Alberta's uniqueness on this score.

His last point that there were no opposition parties seeking the support of the majority of the electorate for most of the period in question, is very important as it illustrates how the political scene in the province is portrayed in *Democracy in Alberta*. The reader gets the distinct impression that only one party of any consequence exists at a given time in Alberta, and that it governs virtually unchallenged by other parties. Yet even a cursory glance at Alberta election records shows that this too is plainly false. In fact it is false for *every election* between 1921, when the quasi-party system is said to have come into existence, and 1955, when Macpherson's rebuttal was written. One or more opposition parties contested a majority of legislative seats in each of these elections. Moreover, in five of these elections *two* opposition parties did so, and in two elections, *three* opposition parties contested a majority of seats.[29] What actually happens in Alberta has been aptly summarized by McCormick:

> It is not that Albertans vote unusually heavily for a single party, or that they give unusually few votes to opposition parties, but that they scatter their opposition vote in such a fashion that each opposition party suffers heavily from the punitive effects of the single-member electoral system. *The problem is not that Alberta has too few parties, but that it has too many.* [emphasis added][30]

That key elements of the quasi-party system are either contradicted by empirical evidence or not substantiated by such evidence brings into doubt other characteristics of the system which is said to have existed in Alberta. For example, since there was healthy electoral competition between the governing party and opposition parties, it is doubtful that, contrary to the "quasi-party" notion, administrative concerns necessarily outweighed policy formation in the general political discourse in the province. Certain obvious cases come to mind that illustrate this point. For example, the election of 1935, which brought Social Credit to power, was largely a contest fought by advocates of fundamentally different economic *policies*: social credit, democratic socialism, and the orthodox economics of the period. Significantly, only a slight majority of voters chose the first option.[31] The 1940s saw pitched battles between Social Crediters and CCFers, two groups which advocated very different policies. Ideological battles in later years were not as tumultuous as those in the 1930s and 1940s, but nowhere does Macpherson demonstrate that the substance of political debate in Alberta was appreciably different from that in other provinces. Also, what consitutes "policy" as opposed to "administration" is not spelled out by Macpherson. It is important to clarify this point, as some Marxists would argue that any measure that does not contribute to the abolition of capitalism is simply a measure to administer capitalism. Those taking this position maintain that *all* non-socialist governments are concerned primarily with "administration."

The empirical contradictions can also be related to other characteristics of the quasi-party system. For example, it is true that the official ideologies of both the UFA and Social Credit initially advocated transcending the party system but, as Macpherson points out, the experience of governing the province soon led these parties to discard the idea. In practice, great efforts were made to sustain both groups *as parties*, and before long even the nonparty theories were abandoned. That short-lived efforts were made to transcend the party system is significant in itself; but, as the electoral data reveal, the actual practice of democracy in Alberta involved substantial competition between parties.

In his debate with Lipset, Macpherson also responds to criticisms about his position on the relationship between class division and the party system. In so doing, Macpherson switches from the role of beleaguered counsel for the defence of *Democracy in Alberta* to its chief prosecutor. Lipset has attributed to him certain views which are "too silly for anyone to hold." The idea of class unanimity in politics, including the choosing of parties, is "ridiculous" and "the opposite of the view expressly stated in my book . . . . The quasi-party system which I find in Alberta . . . is explicitly not a one-party system."[32]

The quasi-party system is certainly not defined as a one-party system, but Macpherson neglects to add that it is not said to be a two-, three- or multi-party system either. And although no one would accuse Macpherson of asserting that literally *all* members of a class necessarily have the same party preference, he clearly suggests that a *preponderance* does. This is implied in his arguments that the province's class homogeneity "seemed to make a party system unnecessary," and that the "absence of any serious opposition of class interests within the province meant that alternate parties were not needed either to express or to moderate

a perennial conflict of interests. There was apparently, therefore, no positive basis for an alternate-party system."

Macpherson replies to Lipset's point that there is no single answer
to the problems of a particular class by agreeing with him whole-
heartedly. He points out that his book even proposes an explanation as
to why "western Canadian farmers have oscillated between different
answers to the problems of their class."[33] But here again Macpherson
is evading the issue. In *Democracy in Alberta* the agrarian petite bourgeoisie is portrayed as vacillating between different political solutions,
but vacillating *en masse*. An example is the author's assertion that this
class "swung" to the plebiscitarian democracy of Social Credit after the
"limits" of the UFA's delegate democracy had been reached.[34] There is
no suggestion that agrarians were or could have been divided about the
adequacy of either of the two "petit-bourgeois" parties or the quasi-party
system itself.

The Issue of Class Homogeneity in Alberta

Democracy in Alberta has other serious shortcomings. One is that it
dwells almost exclusively on the position of the petite bourgeoisie, in
particular independent farmers. But Macpherson's own figures indicate
that the agrarian petite bourgeoisie comprised only 39 per cent of the
work force in Alberta in 1931. Adding the nonagrarian segment of this
class raises this figure to 46 per cent. By contrast, wage and salary earners,
including both agrarian and nonagrarian segments, comprised appproxi-
mately 50 per cent of the work force at that time.[35] Since wage and salary
earners actually outnumbered the petite bourgeoisie even in 1931, it is
a considerable exaggeration to describe Alberta as "a society of independent producers," or as having had a "relatively homogeneous" class composition, as Macpherson does.[36] This observation has some rather important implications for Macpherson's arguments because class homogeneity
is advanced as one of two necessary conditions creating the quasi-party
system.

Even in the 1962 edition of *Democracy in Alberta*, Macpherson clings
to the idea that the province continues to have a "relatively homogeneous," predominantly petit-bourgeois class composition. He states that
the preponderance of the petite bourgeoisie is decreasing, but that this
decrease is not yet "decisive."[37] Yet even by 1951, two years before the

first edition of the book appeared, the size of the agrarian petite bourgeoisie had shrunk to 30 per cent of the male work force; the total petite bourgeoisie represented only 39 per cent of the occupational structure. And by 1961, a year before the second edition was released, the agrarian petite bourgeoisie was a mere 19 per cent of the male work force; the total petite bourgeoisie was 28 per cent.[38] Obviously, it is difficult to see how the "preponderance" of this class prolonged the existence of the quasi-party system in Alberta. Although the 1961 census was not available when the second edition came out, it was no secret that Alberta's nonagricultural labour force had been growing rapidly in the previous ten years. Surely an acknowledgement of this, and its implications for his analysis, would have been appropriate. In the Preface to the second edition, however, Macpherson writes that "The analysis is not of the sort which needs continually to be brought up to date; it deals with fundamental limiting and directing forces which have not seriously changed."[39]

For all the emphasis Macpherson puts on the link between the petite bourgeoisie and support for Social Credit, he does not provide any evidence that this class actually embraced the movement in proportionately larger numbers than members of other classes.[40] Moreover, Macpherson is inconsistent in the identification of class homogeneity as one of the two causal factors required to produce the quasi-party system.[41] At two points in the book, in the Preface to the first edition and in the final two pages of the last chapter, petit-bourgeois *attitudes* replace petit-bourgeois *class homogeneity* as the first of the two preconditions. This allows Macpherson to predict that a quasi-party system will develop in Canada at the federal level. The "independent-producer assumptions about the nature of society are very widespread in Canada," he suggests; and as matters progress in North America, Canada's relationship with the United States "approximates the quasi-colonial," which provides the second of the two conditions.[42] Thus Macpherson openly contradicts himself, for in Chapter One he goes to considerable lengths in attempting to demonstrate that Alberta had a significantly different class structure from that of the nonprairie provinces and Canada as a whole by virtue of its large petit-bourgeois population. He concludes his comparison of the various class structures by stating that the proportion of the petite bourgeoisie in Alberta is "sufficiently different from the prevalent proportion in Canada as a whole . . . that we should not be surprised to find some difference in political behaviour."[43] But if the necessary attitudes already exist throughout the country, what difference does the class composition make? And what can be the meaning of his statement that "Common relationship to the disposal of labour still tends to give the members of each class, so defined, an outlook and set of assumptions distinct from those of other classes"?[44]

The West's "Quasi-Colonial" Relationship with Central Canada

A cardinal point in *Democracy in Alberta* is that the two movements in question were, first and foremost, "against eastern imperialism."[45] The West's "quasi-colonial" relationship with central Canada is cited by Macpherson as the second of the two conditions creating the quasi-party system. The issue of the exploitation of the West by central Canada is a complex one, and no attempt will be made to assess it here.[46] However, it is useful to consider what the supporters of the two movements in question thought about the matter.

The UFA, and the larger Progressive movement of which it was a part, certainly argued that the West was being economically and politically exploited by central Canada. However, the place of regional exploitation in the Social Credit ideology was very different. Tellingly, although Macpherson cites the viewpoints of political economists on the matter of the West's position in Confederation, he does not provide statements from Social Credit leader William Aberhart or any of his followers on this issue. There is good reason for this for, unlike the United Farmers before them, members of the Social Credit movement had very little to say about the protective tariff, free trade, freight rates or western exploitation in general. The movement was much more concerned with generating public support for the implementation of social credit than addressing regional grievances as such. Aberhart even went so far as to say that "in no way should the introduction of this system [of social credit] be allowed to interfere with the relationship between Alberta and Canada or any of the other provinces."[47] Granted, considerable animosity toward the federal government arose after the disallowance of social credit legislation in the late 1930s, but a strong case can be made that the movement was not founded for the purpose of fighting "eastern imperialism." Macpherson's contention that anti-imperialism was Social Credit's *raison d'être* overlooks the fact that social credit ideology maintains that there are fundamental problems with the economic system as a whole.

Social credit was offered as a policy that could solve the *world's* economic problems, not simply as one which would protect the West against regional exploitation.

An examination of the ideology of the chief rival for Social Credit in its early years, the Co-operative Commonwealth Federation (CCF), supports the position advanced here that there were important differences between the Depression-era movements and the Progressives.[48] The CCF came into being at roughly the same time as Social Credit, namely in the early years of the Depression, and offered solutions for the same problems as its rival. Like Social Crediters, CCF followers did not see regional issues as being at the heart of the Depression dilemma. Macpherson claims that the "protective tariff has been the fundamental federal imposition by which they [western farmers] have seen themselves victimized."[49] Yet the CCF's *Regina Manifesto* of 1932 states that, although the "strangling of our export trade by insane protectionist policies must be brought to an end," the "old controversies between free traders and protectionists are now *largely obsolete*" [emphasis added].[50] With the onset of the Depression, as Craven and Traves put it, "[d]ivisions between free traders and protectionists were subordinated to the struggle between socialism and capitalism."[51] Thus the CCF, like Social Credit, believed that the ultimate cause of the crisis was not regional exploitation brought about by inappropriate capitalist trading policies, but something much more universal.

The foregoing discussion of the role of anti-imperialism in the Social Credit and CCF movements should not be construed as saying that anti-central Canadian feelings were absent on the prairies in the 1930s, or that the region was not being exploited. The contention is that these movements, unlike the Progressive movement which came before them, did not see regional exploitation as a principal cause of the malaise on the prairies. They believed that something much more fundamental was involved, and that only the restructuring of the economy along social credit or democratic socialist lines could solve the problem.

Macpherson's implication that Social Credit was essentially objecting to the exploitation of a lesser-developed capitalist region by a more fully developed one stems from his belief that the petite bourgeoisie is incapable of comprehending its real position in advanced capitalism, and that it is opposed to any fundamental change to this system.

Macpherson's Adherence to the Petit-Bourgeois Conservatism Thesis

Macpherson's analysis of Alberta's political history is based on what he calls the "classic pattern of the *petit-bourgeois* class"[52] which assumes that in all advanced capitalist societies such people think and behave in a confused, conservative, or reactionary manner. Although it is beyond the scope of this chapter to challenge this general theory, suffice it to say that its popularity is not commensurate with the state of the evidence advanced in support of it. According to A.J.P. Taylor,

> . . . all experience shows that revolutions come from those who are economically independent, not from factory workers. Very few revolutionary leaders have done manual work, and those who did soon abandoned it for political activities. The factory worker wants higher wages and better conditions, not a revolution. It is the man on his own who wants to remake society, and moreover he can happily defy those in power without economic risk. In old England the village cobbler was always the radical and the Dissenter. After all, the lord of the manor had to have his boots made and mended, whatever the cobbler's political opinions. The independent craftsman, like the intellectual, cannot be dismissed from his job. His skill protects him from the penalties which society imposes on the—conformist.[53]

While Taylor's statement does not constitute a refutation of the petit-bourgeois conservatism thesis, it does provide some plausible grounds for doubt. Taking the case at hand, we may wonder if the prairie agrarian petite bourgeoisie really was a staunch defender of property rights, as Macpherson contends. In reviewing the larger corpus of Macpherson's writings on democracy, K.R. Minogue weighs Macpherson's view that the defence of private property has been a persistent problem for thinkers throughout the modern era. Minogue finds this view to be considerably exaggerated, and suggests that "Macpherson tends to project this exaggeration back through the centuries. *His* problem [property] is everybody's problem."[54] One wonders whether in *Democracy in Alberta* Macpherson's problem is projected onto the petite bourgeoisie. Were property rights, especially those of central Canadian bankers and industrialists, really an overriding concern for the agrarian petite bourgeoisie at this time? Would the violation of bourgeois property really have been perceived as a threat to the petite bourgeoisie's very existence, as Macpherson suggests?

Contrary to the position taken in *Democracy in Alberta*, it is not self-evident that the agrarian petite bourgeoisie would have an unshakable faith in "the basic tenets of capitalist enterprise," especially during a prolonged depression. As one writer put it,

> "Why should *we* worry about property rights?" the farmers ask when you suggest that they are striking at the fundamental economic structure . . . .
>
> When your farm is covered with mortgages, your cattle tied up with a barnyard loan, your machinery attached by a chattel mortgage, your previous year's taxes unpaid, and your coming crop covered by a seed lien—and then you get no crop—you fail to see just what it is you may lose with the collapse of capitalism.[55]

A cursory review of the history of this period also casts doubt on the petit-bourgeois conservatism thesis. While the UFA and Social Credit were not Marxist/Leninist movements, neither were they staunch defenders of property. In fact, before the 1935 provincial election the Edmonton Chamber of Commerce stated that the Social Credit party "threatens the ultimate mortgaging or confiscation of all private property."[56] The movement's stated position on this matter in 1933 was that it would support individual property rights "where possible."[57] Although this is not the place to discuss Social Credit's views on property in detail, it is fair to say that the movement in the Aberhart era did not bestow property rights with "sanctity," as Macpherson puts it.

A more obvious illustration of the agrarian petite bourgeoisie's willingness to violate bourgeois property rights can be found in the history of the CCF. This is a messy business which Macpherson does not address. There are passing references to the CCF in *Democracy in Alberta*, but no explanation of how an ostensibly socialist movement could have become so popular on the prairies, forming the government in Saskatchewan in 1944 and achieving considerable popular support in Alberta as well.[58] Although his book was not intended to be about the CCF, one would think that such a glaring counter-example to his statements regarding the petite bourgeoisie and property would warrant at least a brief comment.

The stock answer to this dilemma is that the CCF was not socialist and was not perceived to be socialist. While there is no consensus concerning the definition of the word "socialism," it is a fact that in the 1930s and 1940s the CCF advocated the socialization of large sections of Canadian industry and finance, and proposed that "planning" replace the largely unregulated market as the driving force of the economy. This would make the CCF at least as socialist as say, the British Labour Party. There is a striking incongruence, therefore, between agrarian petit-bourgeois support for the CCF and Macpherson's portrayal of this class as one wedded to the sanctity of property rights.

One may wish to argue in opposition to this view that the petite bourgeoisie's support for the CCF did not entail a desire to see capitalism torn asunder. But this argument can be made with equal force for the working class' endorsement of the party, or for workers' support for social democratic parties the world over. The idea that the working class is a revolutionary or potentially revolutionary class, while the petite bourgeoisie is irretrievably reactionary, is not buttressed by a history of Marxist-socialist militancy on the part of a substantial proportion of the working class in capitalist societies. The Canadian working class in the 1930s and 1940s, for example, was not throwing its weight behind a "real" socialist party when a substantial proportion of the prairie agrarian petite bourgeoisie was settling for the CCF.

Macpherson's Vision of the Future of Democracy in Canada

Democracy in Alberta ends, predicably, in an ominous way. After suggesting that the quasi-party system is the wave of the future in Canadian national politics, the book's final sentences read:

> The only requirement for [the quasi-party system's] indefinite continuance is the continuance of a degree of economic expansion which can accommodate the aspirations of those who have become disillusioned with the orthodox party system. The quasi-party system may thus be considered either the final stage in the deterioration of the capitalist democratic tradition, or a way of saving what can be saved of liberal-democracy from the threatening encroachment of a one-party state.[59]

Although the closing message is ambiguous, the general mood is one of impending doom or cataclysm. Whatever form it may take, democracy under capitalism in Canada is becoming grossly inadequate to meet the needs of its citizens. Deliverance is possible but will not be immediate, as capitalist economic expansion will mollify Canadians, delude us about ultimate realities, and prevent us from achieving true democracy, just as it has done in Alberta for decades.

This brings us to a final important point. Suppose the people of Alberta had abandoned their "false consciousness" and taken the course tacitly advised by Macpherson. Although he is reluctant to state in explicit terms what "true consciousness" entails, he provides some rather strong intimations that the abolition of capitalism would result from it. But he provides no guidance as to how this could have been accomplished or, more importantly, what the consequences would have been. No arguments are presented that would convince readers that the moral and economic failure that resulted from the other experiments of this kind would not have been repeated in Canada. Moreover, as the history of countries in which capitalist relations of production have been eradicated has shown, his claim that the elimination of capitalism creates a unity of interests between the people and the state is highly questionable, if not positively utopian.

Conclusions

Macpherson set out to explain what he perceived to be a unique system of democracy in Alberta. To explain it he relied on Marxian interpretations of class and class division, in particular the Marxian portrayal of the petite bourgeoisie, as well as the traditional arguments regarding the economic exploitation of western Canada by the central provinces.

A core problem with Macpherson's analysis is his unquestioned assumption that Alberta's party system was unique in the ways he believed it to be. He maintains that the province had a party system that was unusual with regard to the level of public support for the governing party, the persistence of government majorities, the propensity of opposition parties to seek province-wide support, and the ability of new movements to come to power suddenly. However, it has been argued here that Alberta was very much like other Canadian provinces with regard to the first three of these characteristics, and that the fourth is an unfounded assertion. Other weaknesses in Macpherson's characterization of Alberta politics are noted, including his contention that administrative concerns outweighed policy matters and that efforts to transcend parties were an enduring characteristic of the theory and practice of democracy in the four decades analyzed by the book. In sum, a fatal weakness of *Democracy in Alberta* is Macpherson's failure to demonstrate Alberta's electoral uniqueness; in other words, he does not demonstrate that the much discussed "quasi-party system" existed.

A second major weakness involves one of his causal variables: petit-bourgeois class homogeneity. The existence of this too is rejected on empirical grounds, even for the inter-war years. Moreover, class homogeneity is not consistently posited as a causal variable. I also contend that his other causal variable, the "quasi-colonial" relationship, may be problematic in analyzing Depression politics in that the movements of this era may have been primarily concerned with correcting what they viewed as problems with the economic system as a whole rather than addressing purely regional grievances.

Also to be considered is the "classic pattern of the *petit-bourgeois* class," which Macpherson presents as an accurate depiction of this class' outlooks and behaviours. The foregoing has shown that this portrayal of the petite bourgeoisie is open to serious challenge. Finally, we have seen that underlying Macpherson's analysis is the rather dubious assumption that the abolition of capitalism would solve some of the most persistent problems of democracy, in particular those associated with conflicts of interest between the populace and the state.

One may wonder whether, given all its faults, *Democracy in Alberta* has contributed at all to our understanding of Alberta politics. This writer thinks that it has. Although many of its bold statements were misguided, they sent scholars searching for the ways in which Alberta politics were different from those of other provinces. As a result, it is now recognized by researchers in the field that Alberta has had unusually large government majorities, and that this has occurred because the single member plurality system often does not permit a vigorous but fragmented opposition to translate its share of the popular vote into seats in the legislature. The identification of such characteristics has stemmed largely from attempts to assess Macpherson's work. Similarly, the importance Macpherson placed on class structures and class issues has inspired many researchers to take a close look at such matters in analyzing Alberta politics. Finally, his identification of regional alienation as an important aspect of western Canadian politics, although somewhat misleading in his account of Social Credit, has certainly sensitized many observers to its influence in Alberta. If analysts of contemporary Alberta politics examine the issue of the province's uniqueness, the role of class, and the influence of regional alienation with the same passion that Macpherson did for the era he examined, Canadian scholarship will be the better for it.

Acknowledgements

The author gratefully acknowledges the financial assistance received from the Calgary Institute for the Humanities and SSHRC (Award #456-90-0018) while writing this chapter. Harvey Rich, Richard Ogmundson, Thomas Flanagan, Richard Hamilton and Allan Tupper provided valuable comments on an earlier draft.

NOTES

1. C.B. Macpherson, *Democracy in Alberta: Social Credit and the Party System*, second edition (Toronto: University of Toronto Press, 1962). The first edition of 1953 bore the subtitle *The Theory and Practice of a Quasi-party System*. Aside from some minor changes, the text of the second edition is identical to that of the first.

2. Norman Ward, review of *Democracy in Alberta*, *Canadian Historical Review* 36, no. 1 (March 1955): 61.

3. Leo Panitch, "The role and nature of the Canadian state," in *The Canadian State: Political Economy and Political Power*, Leo Panitch, ed. (Toronto: University of Toronto Press, 1977), p. 10.

4. J.A. Long and F.Q. Quo, "One Party Dominance," in *Canadian Provincial Politics*, Martin Robin, ed. (Scarborough: Prentice-Hall, 1972), p. 24.

5. Daniel Drache and Arthur Kroker, "C.B. Macpherson: 1911-1987," *Canadian Journal of Political and Social Theory* 11, no. 3 (1987): 100.

6. Macpherson, *Democracy in Alberta*, pp. xi, 239.

7. Ibid., pp. 237, 4.

8. Ibid., p. 238.

9. The quasi-party system is defined in ibid., pp. 237-39.

10. Ibid., pp. 247, 233.

11. Ibid., p. 21. Macpherson claims that in the other two prairie provinces, political parties "did not follow the normal pattern," and that "a regular

alternate-party system" did not develop there. Ibid., pp. 4-5. An examination of the history of Saskatchewan and Manitoba, he claims, "would probably show that the [quasi-party] system has been in effect there for some time already, although in a slightly different form." Ibid., p. 248.

12. Ibid., p. 21.

13. Ibid., p. 220.

14. Ibid., p. 220.

15. Ibid., pp. 225-26, 247, 229. For discussions of the Marxian treatment of the petite bourgeoisie and the adoption of this position by non-Marxist writers, see Richard F. Hamilton, *Restraining Myths* (Toronto: John Wiley & Sons, 1975), Chapter 2; and Edward Bell, "The petite bourgeoisie and Social Credit: A reconsideration," *Canadian Journal of Sociology* 14, no. 1 (Winter 1989): 46-47.

16. Macpherson believes that in the early 1930s, "popular sovereignty would have produced a direct attack on vested property rights." Macpherson, *Democracy in Alberta*, p. 232. This comment contradicts his previously quoted statement that "the limits of the leaders' radicalism were not fundamentally much narrower than the limits of their supporters' radicalism."

17. Ibid., p. 233.

18. Ibid., p. 236.

19. Ibid., p. 229.

20. Ibid., p. 225. Macpherson adds the following disclaimer, which makes his proposition virtually unfalsifiable: "This does not necessarily mean that the members of a class, so defined, are sufficiently conscious of a class interest to act mainly in terms of it in making political choices. Nor need it mean that their outlook and assumptions are a conscious reflection of class position or needs as an outside observer or historian might see them." Ibid.

21. Ibid., pp. xii, 239-46.

22. Ibid., p. 245.

23. *Democracy in Alberta* reports only the number of seats won in Alberta elections. No accounts of the popular vote are given.

24. Seymour Martin Lipset, "Democracy in Alberta," *Canadian Forum* 34, no. 406 (November 1954): 176-77.

25. Similarly, it has been argued that one-party dominance can occur without either of Macpherson's causal variables present. See Maurice Pinard, *The Rise of a Third Party: A Study in Crisis Politics* (Montreal: McGill-Queen's University Press, 1975), pp. 66-71.

26. Peter McCormick, "Voting Behaviour in Alberta: The Quasi-Party System Revisited," *Journal of Canadian Studies* 15, no. 3 (Fall 1980): 87-88, 90. McCormick's inclusion of the years 1971-1979, the first eight years of Conservative rule in Alberta, does not skew the results toward greater similarity

with other provinces. In the three provincial elections in this period, the Conservatives took an average of 55.5 per cent of the popular vote and 83.7 per cent of all seats. Government of Alberta, *A Report on Alberta Elections: 1905-1982* (Edmonton: Office of the Chief Electoral Officer, 1983), pp. 17-18.

27. C.B. Macpherson, "Democracy in Alberta: A Reply," *Canadian Forum* 34, no. 408 (January 1955): 223.
28. Ibid.
29. Government of Alberta, *A Report on Alberta Elections*, pp. 11-15.
30. McCormick, "Voting Behaviour in Alberta," p. 91.
31. Social Credit received 54 per cent of the popular vote, the Liberals 23, the UFA 11, the Conservatives 6 and Labor 2. Government of Alberta, *A Report on Alberta Elections*, p. 13.
32. Macpherson, "Democracy in Alberta: A Reply," p. 224.
33. Ibid. In his rebuttal Macpherson also invokes the disclaimer quoted in note 21 above.
34. Macpherson, *Democracy in Alberta*, p. 233.
35. Ibid., pp. 15-19.
36. For a fuller discussion of this issue see Bell, "Social Credit and the petite bourgeoisie," pp. 48-52.
37. Macpherson, *Democracy in Alberta*, p. 236.
38. Government of Canada, *Census of Canada 1951* 4, Labour Force (Ottawa: Queen's Printer, 1953), pp. 3-13; Government of Canada, *Census of Canada 1961* 3, Part 2, Labour Force, Bulletin 3.2-9 (Ottawa: Queen's Printer, 1963), pp. 9-168; my calculations. The male work force, as opposed to the total work force, is cited here to avoid complications arising from spouses being classifed as members of different social classes. For these years only a small percentage of women worked full-time outside the home.
39. Macpherson, *Democracy in Alberta*, p. x.
40. For a fuller discussion of this issue, see Bell, "The petite bourgeoisie and Social Credit," pp. 45-54, and Edward Bell, "Class Voting in the First Alberta Social Credit Election," *Canadian Journal of Political Science* 23, no. 3 (September 1990): 520-21.
41. At one point these two factors are referred to as "specific conditions." Macpherson, *Democracy in Alberta*, p. 246.
42. Ibid., p. 249. Macpherson's assertion that Canada's relationship with the United States is becoming "quasi-colonial" is inconsistent with his definition of this term. Contrary to statements made by many commentators, "quasi-colonial" is not intended to mean that the prairie economy was not fully "dependent" on central Canada. "Quasi" is used to indicate that the "typical prairie producer" had not been "reduced to the status of a wage-earner dependent on employment," that is, that such producers were

petit-bourgeois, unlike in other colonies. Ibid., p. 10. (One may wonder why the term "quasi" was chosen to indicate this.) However, since the vast majority of working Canadians were wage and salary earners when Macpherson's book was published, the use of the term "quasi-colonial" is by definition inappropriate in the context of Canada's relationship to the United States.

43. Ibid., p. 20.

44. Ibid., p. 225.

45. Ibid., p. 220.

46. See Kenneth H. Norrie, "Some Comments on Prairie Economic Alienation," in *Society and Politcs in Alberta*, Carlo Caldarola, ed. (Toronto: Methuen, 1979), pp. 131-42 for a critical assessment of the standard arguments on this issue.

47. William Aberhart, *Social Credit Manual; Social Credit as applied to the Province of Alberta* (Calgary, 1935), p. 5.

48. For a similar argument, see W.L. Morton, *The Progressive Party in Canada* (Toronto: University of Toronto Press, 1950), p. 287.

49. Macpherson, *Democracy in Alberta*, p. 9.

50. Section 5. The *Regina Manifesto* is reprinted in Walter D. Young, *The Anatomy of a Party: the National CCF 1932-61* (Toronto: University of Toronto Press, 1969), pp. 304-13.

51. Paul Craven and Tom Traves, "The Class Politics of the National Policy, 1872-1933," *Journal of Canadian Studies* 14, no. 3 (Fall 1979): 36.

52. Macpherson, *Democracy in Alberta*, p. 224.

53. A.J.P. Taylor, "Introduction," in *The Communist Manifesto*, K. Marx and F. Engels (Markham: Penguin Books, 1967), pp. 20-21. Marx and Engels themselves observed that it is difficult to win proletarian support for socialist revolutions. In 1845, Engels gave a series of lectures at Elberfeld in which he outlined what his proposed communist society would look like. After the third meeting he wrote to Marx that "All of Elberfeld and Barmen, from the monied aristocracy to *small shopkeepers*, were represented, the proletariat being the only exception." [emphasis added] Friedrich Engels, "Speeches in Elberfeld," in *Collected Works*, K. Marx and F. Engels (New York: International Publishers, 1975) Volume 4, p. 697, n. 91.

54. K.R. Minogue, "Humanist Democracy: The Political Thought of C.B. Macpherson," *Canadian Journal of Political Science* 9, no. 3 (September 1976): 388.

55. Datus C. Smith, Jr., "North Dakota Seeks a Demagogue," *New Republic* 53, no. 1035 (3 October 1934): 205; quoted in S.M. Lipset, *Agrarian Socialism* (Berkeley: University of California Press, 1971), p. 155.

56. Edmonton Chamber of Commerce, pamphlet, "The Dangers of Aberhart's Social Credit Proposals" (Edmonton: 1935), p. 2.

57. William Aberhart, pamphlet, "The Douglas System of Economics; 'Credit Power for Democracy'," (Calgary: 1933), p. 8.

58. In the Alberta provincial election of 1944, the CCF took 25 per cent of the popular vote (but only 2 of 57 seats). The Labour Progessive (Communist) Party received 4 per cent of the vote, bringing to 29 per cent the total popular vote for socialist-oriented parties in the province. Government of Alberta, *A Report on Alberta Elections*, p. 14.

59. MacPherson, *Democracy in Alberta*, pp. 249-50.

5

Voting Behaviour and Political Dominance in Alberta, 1971-1991

Keith Archer

The Alberta party system over the last two decades has given the appearance of overwhelming stability and one-party dominance. Reaching farther into Alberta's political history, one-party dominance appears as a recurring pattern of party politics. This pattern has led many analysts to try explaining Alberta's "exceptionalism," and to focus on those aspects of Alberta politics and society which are unique.

The distribution of legislative seats in Alberta is produced by two separate processes—individual voting decisions (which may include abstaining from voting) and the aggregation of the votes through the electoral system. To understand elections in Alberta one must examine the behaviour of *individuals* and the workings of the *electoral system*. When this dual focus is used to examine the "Tory era" in Alberta, we find that Alberta is not an "exceptional" case. Furthermore, the evidence suggests that the "Tory era" has three separate and distinct periods: the rise of the Conservatives to legislative dominance; the period of one-party dominance; and the emergence of a competitive party system. This chapter first develops the analytical framework, and then applies it to the "Tory era" in Alberta.

The Determinants of Voting

Canada's party system has been called a system of *stable dealignment*.[1] The term, stable dealignment, developed to describe parties at the national level, implies a political system whose electorate has flexible rather than stable partisan ties and whose individual voters feel relatively unconstrained about switching their votes and their partisan self-images from one election to the next. It also implies that this relative fluidity in partisan preferences among the electorate is itself not changing—that partisan flexibility (i.e., dealignment) is a stable, continuing characteristic of Canadian politics. Systems of stable dealignment may also experience periods of temporary alignment when a confluence of factors combine to overcome the movement and change endemic in the system.

A number of factors have been said to account for partisan flexibility in Canada, of which two are particularly important. First, one's partisan attachment is usually limited to a psychological commitment to a party. Very few Canadians actually belong to political parties, carry party cards, pay membership dues, attend party gatherings or benefit from patronage appointments.[2] In addition and in contrast to the situation in the United States where citizens publicly declare their partisanship when registering to vote, enumeration in Canada does not include registering one's party affiliation.

Flexibility in partisanship has also been widely ascribed to the relative weakness of sociodemographic determinants of voting. That is, knowing a voter's social class—even if one readily uses a class self-image—or religion, gender, level of education or other indicators of social position in general, indicates little about voting preferences. Considerable controversy continues over why that is the case among Canadian voters,[3] but such debates occur in a broad consensus that sociodemographic factors carry little stock in explaining Canadian partisan allegiance.[4]

Research on the psychology of voting has pointed consistently to three types of factors which bear on the voting decision: attitudes towards the political parties, the issues, and the party leaders. Rather than being a long-term stabilizing force on the electorate which influences the vote as well as influencing attitudes towards leaders and issues, partisanship in Canada is much more likely to change with changes in the vote. There is no Canadian analogue to the American phenomenon of ''Democrats for Reagan.'' Voters supporting Mulroney usually think of themselves as Conservatives and, if they come to support Jean Chrétien, will think of themselves as Liberals. Thus, partisanship represents one's current party preference rather than a long-standing voting intention.

The short-term nature of partisanship in Canada is further reinforced by federalism and by the tendency of Canadians to hold a split identification—to identify with different parties at different levels of government. The relative separation and compartmentalization of federal and provincial partisan politics provides an opportunity for the development of distinctive party systems at the national and provincial levels, as the Alberta case powerfully illustrates. Federalism thus also provides for a further weakening of the long-term stabilizing dimension of partisanship.

Not all Albertans approach general elections without any partisan predispositions. On the contrary, most Albertans will admit to feeling closer to one of the parties than to the others. For many voters this attachment is strong and stable, and may even be consistent at the federal and provincial level. However, in Canada such voters comprise only one-third of the electorate, and in Alberta they comprise less than one-half.[5] Among the remainder, partisanship and voting patterns are more flexible. Those with a flexible partisanship provide parties with support contingent upon such short-term factors as campaign issues and/or attitudes towards the party leaders. Although parties may be relatively successful in marshalling support based on short-term factors, those same factors by their very nature infuse the political system with a dynamic property and with opportunities for change.

Research on voting at the national level in Canada consistently demonstrates the importance of attitudes towards party leaders. To a considerable extent, the television coverage of election campaigns personalizes the contest as one between the leaders of the major parties. The parties have responded in kind by placing an increasing emphasis on their leader, and on his or her "team." Thus, the party leaders have become political commodities who are packaged so as to elicit the trust and confidence of the electorate, not so much for *what* they are saying as for the *image* they are able to project. Admittedly, it is possible for parties to win an election without a popular leader, and to lose an election with a leader who is personally popular; leadership presents no magic formula for electoral success. Nonetheless, attitudes towards party leaders remain one of the major forces of voter mobilization. And, with many flexible partisans in the electorate, the number of voters who are strongly affected by short-term forces is always high. Leadership has played a very important role in partisan politics in contemporary Alberta.

Parties' appeals to voters, and voters' response to parties, also are affected by the issues of an electoral campaign. For issues to play a role in individual voting decisions, they must be salient and the parties must be identified with different positions on the issues. Furthermore, for the issue to affect the outcome of an election, opinion must be skewed in favour of one party over another. Research on national elections indicates that parties have not consistently mobilized the electorate behind political issues. Indeed, issues are rarely able to meet the three conditions of salience, linkage to parties, and skewness.[6] Consequently, it is often difficult to discern a government's policy mandate following a general election.[7] For much of the 1970s and early 1980s, circumstances in Alberta provided the governing Conservatives with an ideal environment which met all three conditions for issue voting. More recently, the collapse in energy prices, and the increase in taxes and the government debt, have created a less favourable issue environment in Alberta, making more difficult the Conservative government's quest for the support of flexible partisans.

The Electoral System

While the factors of partisanship, issue attitudes, and feelings about party leaders combine to determine individual voting patterns, their effect is less direct on seat distribution in the legislative assembly. Legislative seat distribution is affected by three factors distinct from the voting decision of the electorate: the electoral system, the competitiveness of each electoral district, and the shape of the voting public. It is commonplace to describe the outcome of an election according to the distribution of legislative seats. Doing so, however, can provide a highly distorted representation of public support for the government. Two familiar examples, both from the national level of government, help illustrate the problem of focusing on seat distribution. In the 1979 federal election, the Trudeau Liberals were defeated by Joe Clark's Conservatives, and Clark became prime minister with a minority government. Yet the Liberals received 40 per cent and the Conservatives only 36 per cent of the popular vote. Something happened to transform the Conservatives' lower vote percentage into a higher seat count, and that ''something'' was the effect of the electoral system. Similarly, the 1988 federal election campaign was widely perceived as a test of support for the Free Trade Agreement negotiated by the Conservative government. Party positions were unusually clear; the agreement was supported by the Conservatives and opposed by the Liberals and New Democrats. In the election, the

Conservatives won 43 per cent of the vote compared to a combined Liberal and New Democrat total of 52 per cent, but the Conservatives won a strong majority government and the Free Trade Agreement was ratified. Voting matters in Canada, but voting occurs within a particular institutional and legal context.

All democratic political systems have an electoral system, and all electoral systems contain biases. In Canada, and in Alberta, we use a single member constituency, plurality electoral system with simple preference voting. The biases of the electoral system are well known.[8] Perhaps most importantly, it over-rewards winning parties and often transforms a plurality of votes into a majority of seats. Parties whose support is highly concentrated in geographical areas are also rewarded, whereas those with broad but diffuse support often are penalized. At the national level, the NDP has always been penalized by the electoral system, whereas the governing party (either Liberal or Conservative) and regional parties, such as Social Credit, have been rewarded.

Closely related to the confounding effects of the electoral system is the degree of competitiveness of each of the legislative districts. In general, the greater the number of competitive parties in a constituency, the greater will be the electoral distortion. For example, in a constituency with three competitive parties dividing the vote relatively evenly, one need obtain only a third of the vote, plus one, for a victory. Looked at another way, two-thirds of the voters could support losing candidates. Because of the distortions that may result from the degree of competitiveness of constituencies, it is the case that great swings may take place in legislative seats with relatively modest aggregate shifts in party support. Constituencies which lack electoral competitiveness can experience substantial and dramatic shifts in aggregate level of support for the parties, while at the same time experiencing little or no change in the distribution of legislative seats. Alberta has experienced both of these phenomena over the past two decades, although the province now exhibits a number of highly competitive constituencies. As a result, the likelihood of dramatic swings in seat distribution following the next several elections has been strongly enhanced.

The third factor affecting seat distribution is the "shape" of the electorate. At each election there are important changes in the composition of the voting public. The most obvious change is voter replacement, in which older voters permanently leave the electorate through death or disability and are replaced by the newly enfranchised who may be either those first coming of voting age or those gaining voting rights in the province by migrating from elsewhere in Canada or by immigrating from outside Canada and gaining citizenship. If the new groups entering the electorate hold partisan views that differ from those leaving, then change can occur despite the underlying stability of the permanent electorate. During a four-year period between elections, as many as 12 to 15 per cent of the electorate may be new voters.

Added to this are the changes taking place as some of those eligible to vote move into and out of the electorate. At each election, some voters who cast a ballot previously will choose to refrain from voting, whereas others who missed the last election will rejoin the active electorate. Many reasons account for voters abstaining from voting or rejoining the electorate including, most importantly, an evaluation of the government's performance, and the credibility and desirability of the political alternatives. Research at the national level, where the turnout fluctuates very little from one election to the next, has found that about 12 to 13 per cent of voters are part of the transient electorate, with relatively equal numbers leaving or re-entering at each election.[9] In Alberta, which has seen turnout as high as 72 per cent and as low as 47 per cent in the period since 1971, the importance of transient voters has been much more pronounced.

The modern Alberta party system can best be understood by focussing on two separate processes—the determinants of individual voting and the determinants of legislative seat distribution. This analysis now applies this framework to three distinct stages in the development of the modern party system: 1967-1971, when the Conservatives rose to legislative dominance; 1971-1985, when a one-party dominant system prevailed; and 1985-present, which reveals the collapse of Conservative hegemony and the emergence of a competitive party system.

The Rise of the Conservatives, 1967-1971

The modern Conservatives' rise to political dominance in Alberta began inauspiciously. The 1967 provincial election produced an outcome which typified electoral politics in the province over the preceding three decades. Premier Ernest Manning led the Social Credit party to its seventh consecutive victory since his rise to leadership in 1943 and to the party's ninth consecutive victory since its inception in 1935. Once again, the government dominated the legislature, receiving for the sixth time under Manning at least 85 per cent of all seats. The Socreds received only 45 per cent of the votes, but that was not unusual. They had twice previously failed to obtain 50 per cent of the vote and had never received more than 56 per cent. Thus, support for the Social Credit party always looked much stronger from the vantage point of the legislature than it did when one examined popular support. However, because of several changes which occurred around the 1967 election, because of the nature of partisan choice in Canada, and because of the nature of seat distribution, this election ushered in a period of substantial change.

Perhaps the greatest change was in the way in which partisan politics was delivered to voters. The 1960s marked the beginning of the period in which television became the major transmitter of political and campaign information—the 1967 campaign was also the first occasion in which a televised leadership debate took place during a provincial election campaign in Alberta.[10] The Social Credit party owed its very origin to the evangelical radio broadcasts of William "Bible Bill" Aberhart, a tradition continued by Ernest Manning who remained host of "Canada's National Back to the Bible Hour" throughout his tenure as premier.[11] The electronic media had long played an important role in Alberta politics but a critical change was the shift from radio to television.

The Progressive Conservative party had been a moribund organization at the provincial level for some years. At the national level, self-styled prairie populist John Diefenbaker had been highly successful in appealing to supporters in western Canada, beginning with his initial minority government victory in 1957, and particularly with his landslide 1958 victory. From 1958 until Diefenbaker's last election as party leader in 1965, Albertans elected Conservatives to fill at least 14 of their 17 seats in the House of Commons. National Conservative support, however, did not transfer automatically into the provincial realm, but instead illustrated the importance of split partisan identification in Canada. Although support for the provincial Conservatives surged from 9.2 per cent in 1955 to 23.9 per cent in 1959, it fell to 12.7 per cent in the 1963 election.

When the Conservatives held a leadership convention in 1966, they were poorly organized, poorly financed, and without strong prospects. They chose Peter Lougheed as their leader and found in him a well-connected, ambitious, and successful young lawyer and businessman.[12] Many commentators have referred to Lougheed's projection of a Kennedy-like image, an image of youthful dynamism coupled with political commitment and conviction, an image that projects well on television.

The Conservatives' new leader was tested the following year. Going into the 1967 election, the Socreds held 60 of 63 seats, compared to two for the Liberals and one Independent. In the election Social Credit lost 10 per cent of the vote, dropping from 55 to 45 per cent, but retained 85 per cent of the legislative seats. The Liberals also dropped, from 20 to 11 per cent of the vote, but gained a seat. Some of the moving vote was captured by the New Democrats who increased their vote from 9.5 to 16 per cent but failed to elect a single member. The biggest gain was made by the Conservatives, who doubled their vote to 26 per cent and thereby elected six members to the legislature. The latter group, which included Lougheed, was of critical importance because the Conservatives became the official opposition, and Lougheed the opposition leader. The party thus had a forum.

Within a year and a half of the election, another major change occurred. Premier Manning resigned the party leadership and his seat in the legislature. The Social Credit convention chose Harry Strom, a member of Manning's cabinet, as party leader. However, in contrast to Manning's forceful personality and articulate, outspoken manner, Strom was soft-spoken and uncomfortable in the public glare.[13] Compared to Lougheed, Strom appeared bland and faded, and projected an image that had worn thin through the passage of time. It was an image that inspired a sense of nostalgia for past glories rather than a sense of confidence or clear future direction.

The contrasting leadership images were crucial in differentiating the Conservatives from Social Credit precisely because so little else was different. During the 1971 election campaign both the Socreds and Conservatives promised greater government assistance to homeowners and pensioners, and both were committed to providing funds for urban transportation.[14] In addition, the Conservatives attacked the government's environmental policies and called for economic relief to municipalities through a new funding formula for education. The Socreds, in turn, promised greater spending in the areas noted but for the most part relied on their past record as the best measure of their administrative competence and political priorities.[15] Neither the New Democrats, who were fighting the election under new leader Grant Notley, nor the Liberals under the leadership of Robert Russell, figured prominently in the campaign. Throughout the interelection period Lougheed and the Conservatives had successfully used their position in the legislature (which had increased by four seats to ten through two by-election victories—including the seat vacated by Manning—and two defections, one Liberal and one Independent) to present themselves as the real opposition and the only viable alternative to the government. The Tories had skilfully introduced private members bills and presented alternative legislation during debate to create and maintain the perception that they were a government-in-waiting.[16]

The results of the 1971 election, as well as all elections since 1967, appear in Table 5.1. A profound change was evident in the legislature following the 1971 election. Social Credit, which had won 55 of 65 seats in 1967, was reduced to 25 seats in a legislature that had expanded to 75 seats. Conservative seats jumped from six in 1967 to 49, or about two-thirds of all legislative seats. Notley won the lone seat for the New Democrats. Thus, in a few short years the Conservative party went from an electoral also-ran without a single seat in the legislature to a government with a strong majority.

This change occurred for several reasons. Most important was the effect of leadership. Public opinion surveys conducted at the time of the election indicated that, taken as a whole, voters held positive evaluations of the Social Credit and Conservative parties, and negative attitudes towards the Liberals and NDP. Furthermore, attitudes towards Lougheed were significantly more positive than for the Conservative party as a whole, whereas voters liked Strom less than they liked the Social Credit party. Positive attitudes towards Lougheed far outstripped those for any other party leader.[17] During the course of the campaign, the Conservatives reinforced and highlighted the importance of leadership while downplaying their policy differences with the government. In short, they focussed on style and leadership, a strategy that maximized their support.

The nature of seat distributions also had a profound effect on the Conservatives' legislative standing. Note that voter support for the Socreds dropped only slightly from 44.6 to 41.1 per cent of the votes. Indeed, an increase in the size of the electorate (through the lowering of the voting age to 18, immigration, and natural increase) and an increased turnout from 63 to 72 per cent resulted in more people actually voting Social Credit in 1971 than in 1967. However, a major change occurred in the voting patterns of those not supporting the government. Conservative voting showed a 20-point increase, from 26.0 to 46.4 per cent, and most

TABLE 5.1 Alberta Provincial Election Results, 1967-1989*

PARTY	1967		1971		1975		ELECTION YEAR 1979		1982		1986		1989	
	%vote	seats	%vote	seats	%vote	seats	%vote	seats	%vote	seats	%vote	seats	%vote	seats
Progressive Conservative	26.0	6	46.4	49	62.7	69	57.4	74	62.3	75	51.4	61	44.3	59
New Democrat	16.0	0	11.4	1	12.9	1	15.8	1	18.8	2	29.2	16	26.3	16
Liberal	10.8	3	1.0	0	5.0	0	6.2	0	1.8	0	12.2	4	28.7	8
Social Credit	44.6	55	41.1	25	18.2	4	19.9	4	8.0	0	—	—	0.5	0
Other	2.6	1	0.1	0	1.3	1	0.8	0	16.3	2	7.1	2	0.3	0
Total Seats		65		75		75		79		79		83		83
Percentage Turnout	63.0%		72.0%		59.6%		58.7%		66.0%		47.3%		53.6%	
Total Votes Cast	498,341		639,862		590,170		710,963		944,936		713,654		829,189	

*SOURCE: Alberta, *The Report of the Chief Electoral Officer on the General Election of the Twentieth Legislative Assembly*, Tuesday, November 2nd, 1982, p. 12; Alberta, *The Report of the Chief Electoral Officer on the General Election of the Twenty-First Legislative Assembly*, Thursday, May 8th, 1986, Appendix C; and Alberta, *The Report of the Chief Electoral Officer on the General Election of the Twenty-Second Legislative Assembly*, Monday, March 20th, 1989.

of this increase was at the expense of the remaining opposition parties. The Liberal vote collapsed from 10.8 to 1.0 per cent, the NDP shrank from 16.0 to 11.4 per cent, and voting for all other parties effectively disappeared. Thus, previous voters for opposition parties were more likely to support the Conservative party in 1971, as were those who came of voting age in this period, those newly arrived in the province, and those who had abstained from voting in 1967.[18] There was also a geographic basis to the voting patterns, with urban residents disproportionately supporting the Conservatives, and rural residents, especially in the south, supporting Social Credit.[19] The Conservative victory was thus one which relied heavily on positive leadership images, on demographic changes in the electorate, and on the highly distorting effects of the electoral system. The weak ties of partisanship in Canada required that if the party were to remain in office, it would have to rely on Lougheed's leadership performance, on the favourable development of political issues, or both. The party was able to get superior performance from both.

The Maintenance of a One-party Dominant System, 1971-1985

The 1971 election provided the Social Credit party with a new experience— that of official opposition. The party proved ill-suited to the task, which in turn was highly beneficial to the governing Conservatives. Soon after the election defeat, Harry Strom resigned from the Social Credit leadership and was replaced by Werner Schmidt, a leader without a seat in the legislature and without legislative experience. Schmidt, a controversial choice for leader, was further compromised by his defeat in a Calgary by-election shortly after his selection as leader. He was able to maintain his grip on the party leadership only after committing himself to resigning if he was unsuccessful in winning a seat in the next general election. At a remarkable risk to the health of their party, the Social Credit caucus accepted the offer. Thus for the inter-election period after 1971, the Social Credit party was led first by Strom, who led his party to the first defeat in its history, and then by Schmidt who was unable to win a seat in the legislature. Although some of the broader changes taking place in the province, such as the dramatic growth in the size of Edmonton and Calgary, a large increase in the number of white collar workers, and the growing importance of oil and gas development, all eroded the agrarian base of the Social Credit party,[20] the absence of effective leadership at this critical juncture prevented the party from developing an image of competence, and an ability to adjust to the changes. When the Socreds were unable to find major policy differences between themselves and the government, their fate was sealed.

The Conservative government began to employ actively the provincial state for the development of the provincial economy while at the same time employing the rhetoric of free-market capitalism.[21] The key to this strategy lay in the fortuitous quadrupling of the price for oil in 1973, resulting from the actions of the OPEC oil cartel. With the further doubling of the price of oil in 1979, it is difficult to exaggerate the magnitude of the economic adjustments which took place across the industrialized world throughout the 1970s and early 1980s. As Alberta was Canada's major producer of oil and natural gas, and given the constitutional division of powers in which substantial control over natural resources is retained by the provinces, it fell to the provincial government to oversee and direct this new energy environment.

Over the next decade the actions of the provincial government came to be known as the "Alberta first" policy, the major components of which have been well documented elsewhere.[22] Among the major initiatives undertaken by the Lougheed Conservatives were "dramatic increases in oil and natural gas royalties; greater controls over energy pricing, marketing and utilization; the acquisition of a regional airline (PWA); the creation of the Alberta Energy Company; heavily assisting in tar sands development; the channeling of excess oil revenues into the Alberta Heritage Savings and Trust Fund, and many others."[23] Time and again the government's province-building strategy led it into direct conflict with the federal government, a conflict from which the provincial Conservatives extracted substantial political benefit. The Conservatives identified themselves as the defenders of Alberta's interests in natural resource development, and identified the federal government in Ottawa as their real opposition. In addition, the massive increase in the flow of resource revenues into the provincial treasury enabled the Conservatives to decrease provincial income taxes to the lowest rate in the country, to eschew a retail sales tax, and to undertake substantial expansion in program expenditures.

The remaining opposition parties found themselves in the unenviable position of competing against a government with a strong and popular leader, and one which had taken a highly popular position on the issue of resource development. To the extent that the government was successful in identifying the federal government as the real opposition, the provincial opposition parties became even more marginalized.

In 1974, the Liberal party chose as its leader a Calgary oilman, Nick Taylor, who had twice previously been unsuccessful in gaining election. At this time, the Liberals suffered from guilt by association. During most of the period of Conservative provincial dominance, the federal government was controlled by the Pierre Trudeau Liberals, a party that was portrayed as depriving Albertans of their rightful resource rents. Such was the animosity that developed towards the federal government that in 1977 the provincial Liberal party formally separated itself from the national wing of the party.[24] The Alberta Liberals attacked the provincial government's emphasis on nonrenewable resources, arguing instead for an economy based on renewable resources and research and development.[25] However, the party's electoral strategy remained focussed on Nick Taylor, a curious decision given that the electorate felt far more warmly towards Lougheed than towards Taylor.[26]

The New Democratic position was more promising than that of the Liberals and Social Credit, but far from that of the Conservatives. The NDP leader, Grant Notley, was able to consistently win his seat in the legislature, ensuring that the party maintained at least a modicum of credibility as well as a forum from which to put forward a vision of the province that was at variance with the government's. On economic policy, New Democrats found themselves in agreement with many of the major thrusts of government policy—particularly the active use of the provincial government to facilitate and guide the development of the province's economy. However, they differed from the government's economic policy with respect to their support of the nationalization of the province's private power companies and their critique of the government's secrecy and general lack of accountability.[27] The NDP focussed their efforts on those policies where they differed substantially from the government, including such social policies as increased support for child care, comprehensive dental care, province-wide pharmacare and greater aid to small business and farmers.[28] However, in view of the massive legislative dominance of the Conservatives, the continuing popularity of Premier Lougheed, and the continuing strength of the government on short-term issues, the NDP also highlighted Notley's role as an alternative voice to the government in the legislature. It attempted to cast itself as the "real opposition" in Alberta politics. The strategy was intended to secure a base for the party from which it could expand when conditions proved more favourable.

Elections during the 1975-1985 period developed a familiar pattern. The Conservative party obtained between 57 and 63 per cent of the votes and well over 90 per cent of the seats. In 1975 only six opposition members were elected, which declined to five in 1979 and four in 1982. The Conservatives' dominant position was undisputed. Under the first-past-the-post electoral system, greater than 50 per cent of the vote usually produces an electoral landslide, an effect which was surely corroborated in Alberta elections of this period. As the government's relations with Ottawa became increasingly strained, and as the Alberta government portrayed itself as the protector of the province's resource wealth and Ottawa as its prime opponent, the electorate responded by supporting the "Lougheed team" at rates approaching or exceeding 60 per cent. The electoral system did the rest.

The disarray surrounding the leadership and policies of the Social Credit party—which eventually degenerated into farce[29]—led to its decline into irrelevance. The Social Credit vote was halved from 41 per cent to 18 per cent in 1975, where it remained through the 1979 election. Social Credit was able to win four seats in each of 1975 and 1979, and remained the official opposition. Werner Schmidt resigned as leader after failing to win a seat in 1975, and the party executive appointed one of the four elected members, Bob Clark, as leader. After failing to increase the party's standing in 1979, Clark resigned and was replaced through a convention by Rod Sykes, a former mayor of Calgary. Once again, Social Credit was led by someone without a seat in the legislature. When a seat became available through Clark's resignation, Sykes decided not to run, opting instead to seek a Calgary seat in the next general election. To the surprise of most observers, Clark's former Olds-Didsbury seat was won by Gordon Kessler of the separatist Western Canada Concept (WCC) party. Within a month of the by-election, Sykes resigned as leader and the three remaining Social Credit MLAs issued a statement confirming the death of the party. Some activists attempted to revive the party later that year, but their efforts were for naught. In the general election of 1982, Social Credit received less than one percent of the votes and no seats.

In the midst of the collapse of Social Credit and the continuing dominance of the Conservatives, the NDP was able to strengthen its claim as the real opposition to the government. Its proportion of the vote rose slowly but steadily from 12.9 per cent in 1975 to 18.8 per cent in

1982. It achieved something of a breakthrough in 1982 by electing a second MLA, Ray Martin, to join Grant Notley in the legislature. Following the 1982 election the NDP was designated the official opposition, which strengthened its position in the legislature. With almost 20 per cent of the vote, however, the NDP was at the point at which the electoral system can be highly distorting and punishing. Although the party had established itself in the north and in Edmonton as an alternative to government, it was unable to parlay that support into substantially more legislative seats.

At the other end of the political spectrum, the continual squabbling between the federal and provincial governments over oil and gas, together with concerns over the size of federal and provincial governments, led to the establishment of several western separatist parties. Chief among them was WestFed, led by Elmer Knutson, and the Western Canada Concept. The WCC entered electoral politics with a bang by winning the Olds-Didsbury by-election in 1982, and incidentally marking the final death knell for Social Credit. Later that year WestFed was absorbed by the WCC, and MLA Gordon Kessler was elected party leader. Separatist candidates, particularly from the WCC, contested almost all constituencies in 1982 but, although they won close to 15 per cent of the vote, they failed to elect any candidates. With the retirement of Trudeau from office in 1984, the election of the Progressive Conservatives at the national level later that year, the dramatic drop in the price of oil, and the rapid dismantling of the National Energy Program (NEP), many of the issues that gave rise to the separatist parties in the early 1980s disappeared. As their raison d'etre disappeared, so too did the separatist parties. However, the re-emergence of some of these same concerns at the end of the 1980s has bolstered the Reform party.

The provincial Liberal party remained an also-ran throughout the period of Conservative dominance. Despite its organizational separation from the national Liberal party, its association in the public mind with the Trudeau Liberals clearly had a powerful negative impact on the fortunes of the provincial Liberals. The party continued to focus its energy and attention on leader Nick Taylor, whose personal appeal proved insufficient to gain him or any other Liberal a seat in the legislature. By 1982 the Liberals could field only 29 candidates for the 79 legislative seats. Taylor's leadership came under criticism on several occasions during his tenure, especially at the party's convention in 1985. Although Taylor was then able to stave off a leadership review, his victory came at a price—thereafter a leadership review would automatically take place two years after the next election.[30]

From 1971 to 1985, Peter Lougheed's Conservatives enjoyed one of the clearest periods of legislative dominance in Canadian history. That dominance was produced by the confluence of popular leadership and an ideal issue environment. It also reflected distortions of the electoral system. Together, these factors gave the Lougheed Conservatives the appearance of an impenetrable fortress, but this appearance was deceiving. The relative weakness of long-term partisan attachments produces almost continual opportunities for political instability and change. As the conditions which lead to short-term voter allegiances change, substantial changes in voting outcomes may occur. These changes may be hidden and distorted by the electoral system, which may then give the misleading appearance of stability. However, once the magnitude of change among voters reaches a critical juncture, dramatic shifts in legislative seats occur. The third period in contemporary Alberta politics is marked by such dramatic change.

The Emergence of a Competitive Party System, 1985-?

The Conservative party faced two major setbacks in the mid-1980s, the combined effects of which have been to loosen its hold on the Alberta electorate. The first setback was the collapse in the world price for oil, which fell from $44 per barrel in 1981 to $10 a barrel in June 1986.[31] This price collapse had several crucial effects including a slowdown in exploration and development, corporate streamlining which caused higher unemployment among both blue collar and white collar workers, and a depression of the provincial government finances, which until that time had relied on oil revenues for over 50 per cent of general revenues. The election of a federal Conservative government with strong Alberta representation, and the dismantling of the NEP, removed Ottawa as the provincial government's villain, thereby leading to the emergence of a *provincial* political agenda.

The second Tory setback was Peter Lougheed's resignation in 1985. For much of his term as Premier, the Conservatives ran election campaigns focussed squarely on Lougheed. He had been actively involved in all major areas of policy.[32] Throughout his tenure, the Conservatives experienced a high rate of voluntary retirement, with as many as 42 per cent of Conservative MLAs choosing not to seek reelection,[33] a fact which may be explained by the tight grip which Lougheed maintained over the caucus and over the government. For many voters, Peter Lougheed was the Conservative party, and the change in leadership led many to question their continuing support for the party.

Lougheed announced his resignation in July 1985, and a leadership convention was held during Thanksgiving weekend. The widely acknowledged front-runner and heir-apparent was Don Getty, a businessman and former athlete who had been elected with Lougheed in 1967, and who had served as Minister of Intergovernmental Affairs and then Energy until his retirement from office in 1979. Getty support was allegedly so strong that no senior ministers entered the contest. Instead, Getty was challenged for the leadership by Julian Koziak, an Edmonton MLA and Minister of Municipal Affairs, and by Ron Ghitter, a Calgary lawyer and former MLA. The contests for selecting convention delegates used the unfortunate mechanism of allowing individuals to purchase a party membership at the selection meeting itself. This procedure encouraged the contestants to sign up as many new party members as they could and to have the new recruits vote as a bloc for the candidates' slate of delegates. The result was that delegate selection meetings in the major cities featured the candidates recruiting busloads of "instant Tories" from senior citizens centres and ethnic community halls. This technique proved highly divisive in the party and had the further effect of tarnishing the image of the candidates. Although Don Getty won on the second ballot, he emerged from the convention less popular than when the contest began.[34]

The contrast between Lougheed's and Getty's leadership has been stark. Lougheed was an activist premier, sometimes described as a workaholic, given to holding cabinet meeting on Sunday mornings and referred to, with both praise and derision, as "King Peter."[35] Getty, by contrast, is an avuncular leader, willing to delegate decision-making power to individual cabinet members, often caught off-guard by major political events such as the collapse of the Principal Group and of the Northlands and Canadian Commercial banks, and who, during his premiership, continued to make liberal use of his vacation retreat in California. Getty's style has generated neither enthusiasm nor widespread confidence.

Within seven months of his selection as party leader, and immediately following the introduction of his government's first budget, Getty called an election for 8 May 1986. The budget projected a deficit of $2.1

billion, which included a four per cent funding increase for hospitals, municipalities, schools and universities, and a 77 percent increase for agriculture.[36] The continuing downturn in the oil industry was treated as a temporary problem and the deficit was forecast to be eliminated by 1991. The Conservatives were running on their record of administrative and political competence over the preceding decade and a half.

The New Democrats had undergone a major change since the 1982 election. Party leader Grant Notley, who had been the party's sole MLA from 1971 to 1982, who had led the party since 1968, and who was leader of the opposition following the 1982 election, died tragically in a plane accident in October 1984. Notley was replaced as leader by Ray Martin, the other NDP MLA, at a convention in November. The by-election to fill Notley's former seat in Spirit River-Fairview was a closely contested race featuring seven candidates, with the NDP's Jim Gurnett holding the seat by a narrow margin. The Spirit River-Fairview victory enabled the New Democrats to retain the status of official opposition for the remainder of the twentieth legislature.

The change in leadership had little effect on public attitudes towards the NDP. Ray Martin shares many of the weaknesses and some of the strengths of Notley. Neither has provided a fiery or dynamic leadership. Notley's major contribution was in providing reasoned and measured critiques of the government's initiatives, and in providing the organizational talents necessary to build the party and to recruit candidates. Martin has been able to project, at best, moderate competence, at least he has not alienated those who for policy reasons might vote NDP. But he has not been able to lead a stampede to the NDP based on his personal charisma. Instead, the party's strategy under Martin has been to take advantage of the years of preparation in positioning itself as the real opposition at a time when the government was facing less favourable circumstances.

The Liberal party had changed little internally prior to the 1986 election, and Nick Taylor had fended off several challenges to retain the leadership. The major change for the party occurred at the national level, with the retirement of Trudeau and the subsequent defeat of the Liberal government in 1984. Voter dissatisfaction with the federal government therefore no longer spilled over into the provincial arena. The party was able to recruit several dynamic, high-profile candidates and their hopes rested on winning a small number of targetted ridings.[37] The two MLAs from the Representative party (i.e., the two surviving Socred MLAs) were expected to do well, but only because of their personal following. The remaining candidates from the separatist parties were expected to show poorly.

The data in Table 5.1 indicate the magnitude of change which occurred in 1986. The Conservatives' support declined 11 percentage points to 51.4 per cent. In addition, support for the Representative and separatist parties was more than halved to 7.1 per cent. Substantial gains were made by the New Democrats, who increased 10 percentage points to 29.2 per cent, and by the Liberals, who also jumped 10 points to 12.2 per cent of the vote. However, when parties receive 50 per cent or more of the vote in an election contested by three or more parties, the result is usually a landslide in legislative seats. Such was the case in 1986. The Conservatives won 61 seats (73 per cent), albeit down from 75 seats in 1982 and despite an increase in the size of the legislature to 83 seats. Faced with only four opposition members in 1982, the government now found itself facing a 22 member opposition, 16 of whom were New Democrats, four Liberals and two Representatives. Ironically, the NDP lost the Spirit River-Fairview seat which it had held since 1971, but retained Ray Martin's seat in Edmonton Norwood and added 15 other seats for its strongest performance ever. NDP support was strongly clustered in Edmonton (11 seats) and the north, although it also won two seats in Calgary. The Liberals finally elected their leader, Nick Taylor, who was joined by three other Liberal MLAs, one from Calgary and two from Edmonton.

The election results held good and bad news for each of the major parties. Conservatives could take solace from the fact that despite a leadership change and an unhealthy economy, they still managed to get a majority of the vote and an overwhelming majority in the legislature. The New Democrats could celebrate their success in finally achieving at least a partial electoral breakthrough by polling almost 30 per cent of the vote and firmly establishing their position as the major opposition party. They now had a large enough caucus to share responsibility for criticizing the government and for offering an alternative agenda. The Liberals could also celebrate a breakthrough of sorts. For the first time since the Conservatives' rise to power, they had elected members to the legislature. They too now had a forum from which to challenge the government.

But the celebrations by each party gave way to the sobering dynamic which underlay the election. The major change between 1982 and 1986 was in the number of Albertans who decided not to vote. Turnout dropped from 66.0 to 47.3 per cent, the lowest turnout rate on record in Alberta.

Furthermore, the decline came almost solely at the expense of the Conservatives. For example, the number of Conservative voters declined by over 220,000 from 588,000 to 367,000. In addition, the separatist parties and independents lost over 140,000 votes, falling from 154,000 to 14,000. The Liberals and New Democrats were able to pick up some of those disenchanted with the government or minor parties. The New Democrats, for example, increased their vote by 30,000 to 209,000, while Liberal support jumped from 70,000 to 87,000. Nonetheless, far more voters dissatisfied with the Conservatives and disenchanted with the separatists registered their protest by staying home. For the NDP and Liberals the question was why were they not able to attract more of the disaffected vote? Although the natural fluidity of partisan allegiances enabled short-term Conservative partisans to move, they generally abstained from voting.

During the inter-election period the parties drew their own lessons from the 1986 experience and used them in setting a course for the next election. Data from 1989 suggest that only the Liberals understood the message. The Getty government continued to experience difficulties on the economic front. The price of oil remained at a level which made mega-project developments highly risky, but various projects continued to receive support from the premier. The declining value of resource rents as a component of the government's revenues (from almost 40 per cent in 1984-85 to less than 25 per cent in 1988-89) together with a decline in Heritage Fund investment income, meant that the government had to cut the growth in expenditures, continue to run large deficits, or raise taxes.[38] They chose to do all three and none was popular. The government also attempted to increase its voter appeal by attacking the federal government in an effort to capitalize on the residual alienation which is a basic component of the political beliefs of Albertans.[39] The Getty government attacked first on the issue of the PGRT, a federal tax based on sales rather than profit and therefore resembling a royalty. The federal government relented and removed the tax, although some have questioned whether the decision was indeed a response to pressures from Getty's government.[40] The second attack came on the issue of Senate reform. Dissatisfaction with policies emerging from the Conservative federal government led an increasing number of Albertans to believe that their interests could be adequately represented only through a major reform in the institutions of the national government. These sentiments coalesced in support for the "Triple-E" Senate proposal, a Senate consisting of an equal number of elected members from each province with effective legislative powers.

In a curious way, the issue of Senate reform became enmeshed with perceptions of Getty's leadership abilities. Getty's image did not benefit from the issue. Although the Premier was able to get some changes in Senate appointments written into the ill-fated Meech Lake Accord, many critics nonetheless argued that Getty had inadvertently made the realization of a Triple-E Senate more difficult if not impossible by endorsing the Accord.[41]

The New Democrats steered a moderate course following the 1989 election. Although some in the party quietly questioned Martin's leadership abilities, there were no overt challenges to his leadership. The party actively criticized the government's labour legislation, concerns with this having crystallized around the deeply controversial strike at the Gainers meatpacking plant in Edmonton. However, and despite the problems which continued to plague the province, the NDP chose not to engage in a far-ranging debate over alternative economic strategies. The NDP's attack, lacking a consistent vision of an alternative economic strategy for the province, focussed more on social than economic policy. Under a regime of fiscal restraint, the party found itself working for the maintenance rather than expansion of social programs, but without providing a detailed prescription for alleviating the chronic budget deficits. The party also attacked the government's administrative record, charging that the province suffered from neglect coupled with incompetence.

The NDP faced serious problems in attempting to increase its support. The experience of 1986 suggested that voters disenchanted with the government were likely to stay home unless convinced to move towards another party. Neither Ray Martin nor the party's policy agenda possessed sufficient pull to bring large numbers of disenchanted voters over to the NDP. Although the NDP are widely regarded as having a long-standing concern with social welfare policies, they were unable to demonstrate how those policies could be protected and strengthened during times of fiscal restraint. On the one issue, administrative competence, where the government was particularly vulnerable, the NDP itself had precious little experience by which to offer a contrast.

The Liberals had committed themselves to reviewing the leadership of Nick Taylor two years after the provincial election. That review led to a leadership convention held Thanksgiving weekend, 1988. The contest drew three contestants—Nick Taylor, who had led the party since 1974 and who first won a seat in the legislature in 1986; MLA Grant Mitchell, a former civil servant and former vice-president of the Principal Group; and Laurence Decore, the mayor of Edmonton. Decore won the leadership of the party and immediately developed the Liberal platform of administrative competence and fiscal responsibility. An able and articulate orator, Decore assumed the leadership of a party with significant financial problems. For example, in 1987 the Liberals raised only $160,000 compared to $493,000 for the New Democrats and $1.5 million for the Conservatives.[42] The Liberals were hoping for a period of time to strengthen their organization before facing the additional burden of financing a general election campaign.

Their wish for time was not granted. Several factors, all of them negative, led Getty to call an early election. Decore had brought a more compelling and vigorous leadership to the Liberal party, and more time would allow him to establish his credibility beyond Edmonton and to strengthen the party's finances. In addition, rising interest rates were leading to further economic problems and perhaps a recession. Meanwhile, the report of the Code Inquiry into the collapse of the Principal Group empire, which was expected to be harshly critical of the government, was due for release in the summer. Therefore, following a speech from the throne in which the government announced it would hold the first-ever election for a Senator as a step toward the Triple-E Senate, Premier Getty called an election for 20 March 1989, less than three years into the government's mandate.

The results of the election indicated a further fracturing of the Conservatives' hold on political allegiances in Alberta, but once again the changes were less evident in the legislature. The Conservatives lost a further 7 per cent of the vote, dropping to 44.3 per cent. As if to add insult to injury, Premier Getty suffered personal defeat in his Edmonton riding. The minor parties and independents all but disappeared, declining from 7.1 to 0.3 percent of the vote. In addition, the New Democrats made no gains in the face of significant losses by the government and indeed dropped three per cent of the vote to 26.3 per cent. The big winners in the election were the Liberals who more than doubled their vote to 28.7 per cent, and thereby surpassed the New Democrats in popular support. The Liberal gain was even more remarkable considering that the party ran an austere campaign, spending only $374,000 compared to $1.2 million for the New Democrats and $1.9 million for the Conservatives.[43]

Fiscal conservatism was the lynchpin of the Liberals' campaign, a theme which was graphically illustrated by Decore raising aloft his wallet in decrying the fiscal extravagance of the government.

Significant changes in voting patterns were again masked by the electoral system. The Conservatives' legislative contingent was reduced by two seats to 59, and they retained 71 per cent of the seats. The New Democrats were able to retain their total of 16 seats, 11 of which were in Edmonton and two in Calgary. The Liberals' vote increase produced only eight urban legislative seats, winning four in Edmonton and three in Calgary. To a very considerable extent, the Conservatives lost their electoral support in the large cities, the base from which they had made their initial breakthrough in 1967 and 1971. The party was increasingly relying on small town and rural support to maintain itself in power. This image was reinforced when Getty decided to maintain the leadership and then won a by-election in the rural riding of Stetler.

As in 1986, turnout in 1989 was low at 53.6 per cent. This figure suggests that while many voters were disenchanted with the Conservatives, they still were not prepared to support either of the opposition parties. For example, Conservative voters remained remarkably stable in absolute numbers, with 367,000 voters supporting the party in 1986 and 1989. The New Democrats experienced a very modest increase from 209,000 to 218,000, a disappointing result given the government's unpopularity. The Liberals made substantial gains, moving from 87,000 to 238,000 voters and thus capturing many of those who left the electorate in 1986.[44] And yet three quarters of a million voters chose not to vote in 1989, a sobering figure for all the parties and a measure of the instability that remains in Alberta politics.

Although the Conservatives continue to enjoy a dominant position in the legislature, it is a position built on an increasingly unstable foundation. Continuing fiscal difficulties and uninspiring leadership have taken the party near the point at which the electoral system will begin working against them. A divided opposition presents some benefit to the Conservatives, but a popular vote in the high 30 to low 40 per cent range produces highly unstable results in legislative seat distribution. Whether the party is able to forestall a further decline, and to reestablish itself as the dominant party, appears highly unlikely.

Conclusion

Partisan instability is a characteristic feature of individual voting patterns in Canada and in Alberta. Through a combination of short-term leader and issue effects, the Conservatives under Peter Lougheed secured the support of a substantial majority of voters. In turn, strong voter support was transformed via the electoral system into legislative dominance. But from the mid-1980s onward, the party has experienced weaker leadership and less favourable issue conditions. Consequently, its electoral support has waned but, through the vagaries of the electoral system, the Conservative party has managed to suffer voter decline without a similar legislative decline. However, it is now approaching the point at which further erosion in popular support will prove costly in legislative seats.

The distribution of voter support in Alberta has become very unstable. The instability can be seen in the changing proportion of votes received by the major parties but also in the dramatic decrease in voter turnout. With almost half the electorate choosing not to vote in recent provincial elections, there appears to be a void which is not being filled by any of the three major parties. A party which is able to appeal to the large numbers of disaffected voters in the province will become a major force on the provincial scene.

Changes in party competition which have occurred at the national level are likely to have a strong effect on Alberta provincial politics during the 1990s. The resentment and dissatisfaction directed by many Albertans toward the Trudeau Liberal government in the 1970s and early 1980s created a surge in support for the Conservative party. For many Albertans, the election of a national Conservative government in 1984 was a signal event for a new national agenda which included a larger role for the West in Confederation. However, and despite the presence of Albertans in the highest ranks of the Mulroney government, many Albertans have found that the Conservative government has the same orientation toward "central Canada" as did the Liberals. Perhaps because they had placed such high expectations on the Conservatives, the government is viewed by Albertans with a remarkable degree of contempt and hostility.

The political void at the national level has been filled by the Reform Party of Canada, created at a Winnipeg convention in 1987. Led by the folksy Preston Manning, son of former Socred Premier Ernest Manning, the Reform party offers a platform based on three major pillars: institutional reform of the central government; fiscal responsibility; and opposition to bilingualism, multiculturalism and "special status" for Quebec.[45] The party has experienced a meteoric rise in support. A Gallup poll conducted in April 1991 found that 16 per cent of Canadians and 43 per cent of Prairie residents supported the party. The Reform party's 1991 decision to expand east of Manitoba will provide it with an opportunity to increase further its support.[46]

The Reform party's performance in the national arena has a bearing on provincial politics in several ways. Most importantly, the decline in support for the federal Conservatives has been mirrored provincially, and the greatest support for Reform is among Albertans. However, the Reform party is committed to pursuing national politics, and it has delayed indefinitely a decision to run candidates provincially. Thus, it is paradoxical that the most popular party in Alberta is refusing to run provincial candidates. The decision of Reform not to run provincially has created considerable uncertainty in provincial politics. Reform has used its support in opinion polls and the spectre of its possible entry into provincial politics as a direct challenge to the existing parties, particularly the governing Conservatives, to adopt Reform's policy initiatives. The Conservative party has responded to the changing partisan forces within the province, and to the presence of Reform, by formally severing its links with the national Conservative party and by adopting some of the Reform party's positions including balancing the provincial budget for fiscal 1991-92. Nonetheless, opinion polls suggest that Reform's increased support in Alberta is mainly at the expense of the provincial Conservatives, and that there has not been a similar collapse in support for the Liberals and New Democrats.

Although the future of electoral politics in Alberta is highly uncertain, several factors relating to party politics should be borne in mind. Legislative domination is not a natural state of affairs in Alberta even though certain features of the system lend themselves to domination. Federalism, especially "executive federalism," encourages provincial leaders to cast themselves as the defenders of the provincial interest against Ottawa, and there are times when such a posture is compelling. In addition, a province whose economy centres on a few commodities is more likely to experience issue voting when that commodity is threatened. If one party is able to identify itself with that issue, it can be well rewarded at the polls. And, of course, the electoral system, under conditions of strong support for a given party, tends towards legislative domination. It is thus not at all inconceivable that a party, Conservative or otherwise, may once again dominate the Alberta legislature.

Yet maintaining such a dominant position will be far more problematic in the future. Changes in election laws have resulted in parties being much better financed today as compared to the period when Lougheed came to power. Opposition parties will therefore be able to purchase media time in getting their message across. As well, political issues and leadership are by their very nature transitory. Leadership sentiments usually are not passed from one party leader to the next, and the issue agenda remains volatile, often changing according to factors beyond the control of parties. The emergence of new parties, and the advent of new leaders and issues will ensure that party support remains volatile.

NOTES

1. Lawrence LeDuc, "Canada: The Politics of Stable Dealignment," in *Electoral Change in Advanced Industrial Democracies*, Russell Dalton, Scott Flanagan and Paul Allen Beck, eds. (Princeton: Princeton University Press, 1984), pp. 402-24.

2. Those areas of the country in which patronage retains an important role in civil service employment, such as on Prince Edward Island, tend to evince more enduring partisan attachments.

3. Compare Robert Alford, *Party and Society: The Anglo-American Democracies* (Chicago: Rand-McNally, 1963); M. Janine Brodie and Jane Jenson, *Crisis, Challenge and Change: Party and Class in Canada Revisited* (Ottawa: Carleton University Press, 1988).

4. Lawrence LeDuc, Harold Clarke, Jane Jenson and Jon Pammett, "Partisan Instability in Canada: Evidence from a New Panel Study," *American Political Science Review* 78 (1984): 470-83.

5. Harold Clarke, Jane Jenson, Lawrence LeDuc and Jon Pammett, *Political Choice in Canada* (Toronto: McGraw-Hill Ryerson, 1979).

6. Keith Archer and Marquis Johnson, "Inflation, Unemployment and Canadian Federal Voting Behaviour," *Canadian Journal of Political Science* 21, no. 3 (September 1988): 569-84.

7. Harold Clarke, Jane Jenson, Lawrence LeDuc and Jon Pammett, *Absent Mandate* (Toronto: Gage, 1990).

8. Alan C. Cairns, "The Electoral System and the Party System in Canada, 1921-65," *Canadian Journal of Political Science* 1 (1968): 55-80; F. Leslie

Seidle, "The Canadian Electoral System and Proposals for Its Reform," in *Canadian Parties in Transition: Discourse, Organization, Representation*, Alain G. Gagnon and A. Brian Tanguay, eds. (Toronto: Nelson, 1989), pp. 249-69.

9. Clarke et al., *Absent Mandate*, pp. 130-31.

10. Alvin Finkel, *The Social Credit Phenomenon in Alberta* (Toronto: University of Toronto Press, 1989).

11. Ibid., p. 141.

12. Andrew Nikiforuk, Sheila Pratt and Don Wanagas, *Running on Empty: Alberta After the Boom* (Edmonton: NeWest Press, 1987).

13. David K. Elton and Arthur M. Goddard, "The Conservative Takeover, 1971-," in *Society and Politics in Alberta: Research Papers*, Carlo Caldarola, ed. (Toronto: Methuen, 1979), pp. 52-53.

14. Finkel, *The Social Credit*, p. 189.

15. Marion McKenna, "Alberta," in *The Canadian Annual Review of Politics and Public Affairs, 1971*, John Saywell, ed. (Toronto: University of Toronto Press, 1972), pp. 214-15.

16. McKenna, "Alberta," p. 207.

17. Elton and Goddard, "The Conservative Takeover," p. 60.

18. Ibid., p. 55.

19. Thomas Flanagan, "Ethnic Voting in Alberta Provincial Elections, 1921-1975," in *Society and Politics in Alberta: Research Papers*, Carlo Caldarola, ed. (Toronto: Methuen, 1979), pp. 319-20.

20. John Richards and Larry Pratt, *Prairie Capitalism: Power and Influence in the New West* (Toronto: McClelland and Stewart, 1979).

21. Allan Tupper, "Opportunity and Constraint: Grant Notley and the Modern State," in *Socialism and Democracy: Essays in Honour of Grant Notley*, Larry Pratt, ed. (Edmonton: NeWest Press, 1986), p. 99.

22. John Richards and Larry Pratt, *Prairie Capitalism: Power and Influence in the New West* (Toronto: McClelland and Stewart, 1979).

23. Larry Pratt, "The Political Economy of Province Building: Alberta's Development Strategy, 1971-1981," in *Essays on the Political Economy of Alberta*, David Leadbeater, ed. (Toronto: New Hogtown Press, 1984), p. 206.

24. David Elton, "Alberta," in *The Canadian Annual Review of Politics and Public Affairs, 1977*, John Saywell, ed. (Toronto: University of Toronto Press, 1978), p. 225.

25. David Elton, "Alberta," in *The Canadian Annual Review of Politics and Public Affairs, 1975*, John Saywell, ed. (Toronto: University of Toronto Press, 1976), p. 217-18.

26. Elton and Goddard, "The Conservative Takeover," p. 66.

27. Tupper, "Opportunity and Constraint," pp. 88-111.

28. Elton, "Alberta," in *The Canadian Annual Review of Politics and Public Affairs, 1975*; David Elton, "Alberta," in *The Canadian Annual Review of Politics and Public Affairs, 1979*, R.B. Byers, ed. (Toronto: University of Toronto Press, 1981); Peter McCormick, "Alberta," in *The Canadian Annual Review of Politics and Public Affairs, 1982*, R.B. Byers, ed. (Toronto: University of Toronto Press, 1984).

29. McCormick, "Alberta," 1984.

30. Peter McCormick, "Alberta," in *The Canadian Annual Review of Politics and Public Affairs, 1985*, R.B. Byers, ed. (Toronto: University of Toronto Press, 1988), p. 378.

31. Nikiforuk et al., *Running on Empty*, p. 227.

32. Ibid.

33. Elton, "Alberta," 1981, p. 371.

34. Keith Archer and Margaret Hunziker, "Leadership Selection in Alberta: The 1985 Progressive Conservative Leadership Convention," in *Parties and Leaders in the Canadian Provinces*, R.K. Carty, Lynda Erickson and Donald E. Blake, eds. (Toronto: HBJ Holt, 1991).

35. Nikiforuk et al., *Running on Empty*, pp. 116-17.

36. Peter McCormick, "Alberta," in *The Canadian Annual Review of Politics and Public Affairs, 1986*, R.B. Byers, ed. (Toronto: University of Toronto Press, 1990), p. 327.

37. Ibid.

38. Mark Dickerson and Stan Drabek, "Provincial Revenues and Expenditures in Alberta: The Boom and Bust Cycle," in *Canadian Political Life: An Alberta Perspective*, Roger Gibbins, Keith Archer and Stan Drabek, eds. (Dubuque, Iowa: Kendall-Hunt, 1990), pp. 135-44.

39. Roger Gibbins, "Western Alienation and the Alberta Political Culture," in *Society and Politics in Alberta: Research Papers*, Carlo Caldarola, ed. (Toronto: Methuen, 1979).

40. Nikiforuk et al., *Running on Empty*, pp. 65-69.

41. For a further elaboration of this issue, see the Peter Meekison and Roger Gibbins contributions to this volume.

42. Alberta, Chief Electoral Officer, *Annual Report on the Election Finances and Contributions Disclosure Act, 1985*, Appendix B.

43. Alberta, Chief Electoral Officer, *Annual Report on the Election Finances and Contributions Disclosure Act, 1989*, Part 2, Appendix D.

44. *A Guide to Alberta's Legislature* (Edmonton: Alberta Teachers' Association, 1989), p. 8.

45. Therese Arsenault, "The Reform Party of Canada: The Secret of Its 'Success'," presented at the Annual Meeting of the Canadian Political Science Association, Queen's University, Kingston, Ontario, June 2-4, 1991.

46. For a good description of the factors underlying Reform's support, and of the change from a "Western" to an "English Canadian" orientation, see ibid.

6

The Legislature

Frederick C. Engelmann

On the face of it, the province of Alberta has a legislature *comme les autres*. It has one house and follows, in form and physical structure of the chamber, the Westminster model. It passes the budget and all provincial statutes, and the premier and his cabinet are responsible to it.

Since Alberta has had, in C.B. Macpherson's now immortal formulation, a quasi-party system over most of its history, the province has been deprived of the traditional Canadian interplay of government and opposition. Only once, in 1971, has a legislative opposition become the government. Of the discarded parties, the Liberals spent most of seven decades in suspended animation, the United Farmers of Alberta disappeared, and Social Credit remained a numerous opposition for four years only. During the first eight decades of provincehood, it would have been a distortion to claim that the Alberta Legislative Assembly had been the breeding ground of oppositions or the seat of alternating governments and oppositions.

With the exception of blips, like the relatively large Liberal caucus elected in 1955, the Legislative Assembly has been marked by continuity: an overwhelming government majority. If there had been any kind of *Hansard* prior to 1972, we could no doubt call it an overbearing majority, legislating with but little debate.

The long-standing, overwhelming majority of government over opposition has deprived the Alberta Legislative Assembly, in whole or in part, of some crucial qualities of legislatures under the Westminster model of responsible government. Under the Westminster model, the legislature cannot normally dislodge the government, but it can hold it publicly accountable for policies and their administration. The most visible part of enforcing this public accountability is a question period which is entirely an opposition show. Another is a public accounts committee which is dominated by the opposition. The opposition must have at least some means to investigate the political administration and the behaviour of government legislators. The Speaker, whether (preferably) elected or appointed, must be, and be seen to be, impartial. Finally, opposition parties must be part of the legislative process not only in plenary debate, but also through active participation in studying committees. But the Alberta Legislative Assembly does fall short of the requirements of the Westminster model.

The elections of 1986 and 1989 have brought a real change to this quasi-party system. The emergence of first one, then a second, opposition party with sizeable caucuses, backed now by a majority of voters, signifies a major change in Alberta politics. Unless the Reform party not only goes provincial but also gains the overwhelming support of urban as well as rural Alberta voters, the quasi-party system is either a thing of the past or at least in long-term abeyance.

The only place where political change has been registered on the seating chart, but hardly in fact, is the Alberta Legislative Assembly. Here, continuity prevails. Will change come or be prevented in the foreseeable future?[1] A statute binding the Electoral Boundaries Commission, though passed in principle by the Court of Appeal in Alberta, was certainly drafted with the intent of keeping the present government in office by overrepresenting its rural majorities. It is an effort to ensure that Albertans will continue to have a quasi-party legislature, with all this implies for imperfect responsible government.

An imperious speakership presides over a body in which members of the opposition are permitted to become privy to some of the government's policy schemes and some of its proposed expenditures. "Some" because many expenditures and many policies are never revealed to the opposition until they have become facts and then they remain unknown to the public unless they are discovered by opposition researchers or by investigative journalists, a rare species in Alberta. And, once such policies or expenditures are discovered, the only follow-ups are opposition questions in the legislature, which often are not answered at all or, if they are, in a more overbearing than illuminating manner, with the Speaker sometimes trying to discourage the questioner. Moreover, if wrongdoing by a member of the cabinet or the government caucus is alleged, the matter normally is closed as an unsubstantiated insinuation.

Estimates of a government department are usually dealt with in one brief evening session, during which opposition members can at best select a couple of items about which they may receive a satisfactory answer. Statutes are presented to the opposition usually only days before second reading debate. Unlike other sizeable provinces, there are no policy committees. Committee discussion takes place in what is normally a brief session of the Committee of the Whole. When there is a fuller committee debate, as on the Legislative Redistribution Act of 1990, the government caucus decides which of the opposition's points raised in debate will be responded to. Meanwhile, the Alberta media remain silent on very many matters that are raised in debate.

Such policy as is ever discussed freely is discussed by Cabinet and by legislative committees. These legislative policy committees, however, are not committees of the legislature at all, but committees of the governing caucus which are as secret as cabinet. Since they have existed since 1975 only, they have throughout been committees of the Progressive Conservative caucus. Other matters of policy are decided when Cabinet approves a department's "request for decision," and financed by Lieutenant-Governor's ("special") warrants. Neither the opposition nor the public learn of them until after the fact.

The procedures and practices result in a usually uninformed opposition being confronted by a partially informed government caucus and, of course, an informed Cabinet. The Lougheed reforms of 1975 were instituted for a body with only six (later five and four) opposition members. They are out of place for an assembly with an opposition that represents 55 per cent of the electorate. Neither the opposition in·the province nor the members they elected can hold the government accountable in a meaningful way. The governing party has no plans to remedy this situation, in which the government caucus takes on many of the legislative functions. Instead, it attempts to keep itself in office through manipulating a mandated legislative redistribution.

The confluence of judicial enforcement of section 3 of the Charter of Rights and Freedoms with only slight changes in party support may still change Alberta's legislature to something more frequently found in the rest of Canada before too long. Until then, Albertans will enjoy the continuity of their quasi-party legislature.

History: Le plus ça change . . .

For the first 16 years of Confederation, Alberta's legislature had all the traditional trappings. Except for the end of the period, the assembly consisted of Liberals and Conservatives. The Liberals were always in charge, with the Conservatives the—not very hopeful—"government in waiting."

Agrarian discontent, arising from the First World War, changed what had been traditional about Alberta politics. In 1921, the United Farmers of Alberta (UFA), though behind the Liberals in popular vote, obtained a secure majority in the legislature. The party followed Henry Wise Wood's notion of "group government." Its members were to remain subordinated to their voters; they were urged to sign undated "recall agreements." Later, under the strong leadership of John Brownlee, the UFA became a more traditional party, maintaining a solid legislative majority. The UFA did not survive the Great Depression. When it faced the voters in 1935, it was reduced to 11 per cent of the vote and no seats.

The 1935 election brought about executive domination of the legislature. In that election, 54 per cent of the votes and 89 per cent of the seats were captured by one man, William Aberhart. I say "one man" because the leader of the just born Social Credit movement had personally selected every single one of its 63 candidates.[2] Aberhart's leadership weakened soon and he died eight years later, but the pattern of 1935 has persisted for at least 39 of the years since 1944. Executive domination was practised with virtuosity by two of Canada's strongest political personae, Ernest Manning (1944-69) and Peter Lougheed (1971-85). In the ten elections these two leaders fought as incumbents, the combined opposition only once gained more than 15 per cent of the assembly seats (35 per cent in 1955). Their re-election was always a foregone conclusion and the opposition, a few times down to three, four or five members, was never a "government in waiting." Until 1986, the Legislative Assembly had no chance to outgrow its quasi-party character. It was not only dominated by one party, but very much by one person—Manning and later Lougheed.

The election of 1982, Peter Lougheed's last, showed a fair amount of NDP strength in Edmonton, but a ruthless Progressive Conservative campaign kept them down to two seats (one in Edmonton and Grant Notley, the leader's, northern rural seat). Don Getty's first general election, in 1986, still gave Progressive Conservatives 51 per cent of the vote, but now there was an opposition of 16 New Democrats, four Liberals and two Representatives (erstwhile Social Crediters). Less than three years later, in March, 1989, Getty's effort to reduce the opposition sharply in an early election misfired. Getty lost his seat, and his party's vote was down to 44 per cent. New Democrats went down from 29 to 26 per cent, while Liberals went up sharply from 12 to 29 per cent. The Edmonton concentration paid off for the New Democrats, electing 16 members to the Liberals' eight. This virtual equality of the two opposition parties was the only good news for the Progressive Conservatives.

In the Legislative Assembly, the years from 1986 to 1989 were only a marginal success for the New Democrats. Their caucus of 16 was only somewhat more effective than Grant Notley alone, or the Grant Notley-Ray Martin duo after 1982, had been. Even with a weaker leader the Progressive Conservatives monopolized the agenda of the legislature. The election of 1989 brought no fundamental change: a three-party system, yes; but still a quasi-party legislature, run tightly by the Speaker, with a closely guarded monopoly of information for the governing side, and opposition participation definitely restricted to opposing.

Structure

The Legislative Assembly of Alberta derives its authority from the Legislative Assembly Act.[3] The Speaker is the Assembly's presiding officer and he is also the head of its administrative structure. Until 1987, his precincts were highly restricted; his authority ended at the door of the legislative chamber. The incumbent in 1991, Dr. David Carter, was able to persuade Premier Donald Getty to relinquish control over the entire building to him, removing an Albertan anomaly.

In the 86 years since Confederation, Alberta has had nine Speakers of whom six have had substantial terms. The record among the long-serving incumbents is held by the Social Credit Speaker Peter Dawson, who served from 1937 to 1963. Whenever there was a change in party, the speakership changed. During the rural decades of the province, the Speakers came from rural areas. Since 1963, incumbents have come from the major cities: Arthur J. Dixon (1963-72) Calgary, Gerard J. Amerongen (1972-86) Edmonton, David J. Carter (1986-) Calgary.

Nearly twice as many members—17—have served as Deputy Speaker and Chairman of Committees, two longer than ten years. The incumbent in 1991, Stan Schumacher represents Drumheller and is a former MP; he has served since 1989.

Only the last two Speakers have been recorded in *Hansard*. The record shows two different personalities under two different circumstances. Amerongen presided over an assembly that revealed its quasi-party nature in form as well as in fact. The only sizeable opposition he presided over was the—in every way—"outgoing" Social Credit caucus of 25 members (1971-75); only four of them retained their seats in 1975. One must of course add to them the late NDP leader Grant Notley, according to many the only effective opposition from 1971 to his death in 1984. Amerongen adhered strictly to the rules but his fairness was generally recognized. He was active in involving the Assembly in external and international activities.

David Carter presides over an assembly the membership of which reflects the newly competitive Alberta politics. In addition, his tasks were multiplied once he became the first "landlord" of the Legislature Building. In this role, he is criticized by members of the press gallery for restricting access to MLAs, particularly to ministers. In presiding, Carter often goes out of his way to make it difficult for opposition members to ask questions. Some of his interruptions are thought to be personally improper by opposition members and members of the press gallery. When questions, or his interruptions, make for an unruly chamber, he occasionally threatens to discontinue question period. In 1987, he provoked a crisis over the use of French in the Legislature. French was finally legalized, for oral use, on 6 July 1988.[4]

Probably the most serious criticism of Carter developed in April, 1990, in connection with the so-called Zarusky affair. Steve Zarusky (PC, Redwater-Andrew) was accused by Stan Woloshyn (ND, Stony Plain) of having pressured the town council of Smoky Lake to locate a chicken processing plant on land in which Zarusky had a financial interest. Premier Getty defended Zarusky, whose answer to the charges was withheld from the opposition and the public by the Speaker until the intervention by Pam Barrett (ND, Edmonton-Highlands) brought an apology from Carter. Despite considerable evidence, the Speaker declared later that "Business activities of members outside this House are outside the scope of privilege and the jurisdiction of the Speaker,"[5] and that he found no evidence that Zarusky, who claimed he no longer owned the land, had intended to deceive the Assembly. The Premier then decided that Woloshyn's allegation had been "completely unsubstantiated."[6] After the New Democrats produced evidence on tape of Zarusky's continued ownership and conflict of interest, the Speaker declared further questions on the matter out of order. The Speaker was roundly criticized by *Calgary Herald* columnist Don Braid for avoiding questions of ethics and not questioning the complete lack of conflict-of-interest rules in the Assembly.[7]

On 26 November 1990, the Assembly reconvened after the *Globe and Mail* ran a long interview with Premier Getty about dealing with oil properties while in office. Since the province at that time had a commission report on conflict of interest (already available during the Zarusky affair), but as yet no legislation, the Premier received a number of questions about the propriety of his dealings and about the promised conflict-of-interest legislation. Carter tried to curb these questions and to shield the Premier. Again, the episode is held up by opposition and press as an example of partiality displayed by Carter.

On 27 March 1991, Carter had six injured workers arrested (not just ejected) for shouting from the gallery; Speaker's arrest had not been exercised since 1930. While it was announced that the Speaker does not comment on his rulings, others did. The *Edmonton Journal* of 1 April editorialized on Carter's "heavy hand," saying that he approached his job in a manner for the wrong century.[8] Later in 1991, Carter sued the *Calgary Herald* for allegedly libeling him in criticizing his conduct in office.

Alberta is one of the few provinces in which the legislature does not have autonomous control over its finances. Estimates are submitted to the Priorities Committee of cabinet. Alberta therefore does not have the more usual "board of internal economy." Its estimates originate in the Special Standing Committee on Members' Services, which is chaired by the Speaker. Of its eleven members, two are New Democrats and one is a Liberal. For several years, a member of cabinet (in 1991, Ken Kowalski) has been one of the seven government members. The Committee is ruled, with an iron hand, by its Associate Chairman, Bob Bogle, PC MLA for Taber-Warner. Bogle, once the highly controversial Minister of Social Services and Community Health, enjoys his position as the Assembly's strongest back-bencher. He is also chairman of the Standing Committee on Legislative Offices and he was, from 1989 to 1990, chairman of the Select Special Committee on Electoral Boundaries. This made him, in 1990, the person in de facto charge of the Legislature and its other offices—the Auditor General, the Ombudsman and the Office of the Chief Electoral Officer—and, in that year, the man with the most power over the Alberta electorate, justifying, for 1989-90, combined payments of salary, expenses, and minister's pension of $144,484, the highest for a private member.[9] Then, and possibly now, there were very few persons in Alberta with greater real political power.

The Members' Services Committee has full power over the Legislative Internship Program and research allowances to the three party caucuses. The Legislative Internship Program, which under Speaker Amerongen had ten interns selected annually by Alberta's three universities, has degenerated to a four-intern program, of which two serve the government party and one each of the opposition parties. The universities have lost all influence over the program, which no longer has any academic content. In 1987, the Members' Services Committee abolished the highly useful Legislative Research Service. These measures are intended to keep the Assembly a quasi-party institution by reducing the opposition parties' means of gathering information.

The Members' Services Committee sets indemnities and basic tax-free allowances for members and additional salaries for ministers and members holding Assembly or caucus offices.[10] Before 1986, these pay items were set by the Assembly; in 1986, a complex but automatic yearly cost-of-living increase was added. Since 1989, the pay items are decided by the Members' Services Committee without the necessity of further legislation. In 1989, the committee decided that, in addition to government and official opposition, any party with at least four seats and five per cent of the popular vote was to be a "recognized opposition party." The Committee also decided that, in future, members' salaries were to be set automatically at 55 per cent of the salary of a provincial judge.

Before deciding this, on 28 August 1989, the committee increased the basic indemnity paid to MLAs by 30.2 per cent and their tax-free allowance by 29.7 per cent, retroactive to April 1, 1989. These massive increases, which raised a storm of protest, brought the indemnity to $38,335 and the tax-exempt allowance to $19,167. Had the entire income been subject to taxation, the "take-home pay" would amount to be taxable salary of about $65,000. In addition, there are benefits, travelling expenses, and fees (available primarily for government private members) for Board and Commission members.

The quasi-party nature of the Assembly is best shown by the exalted position of the government caucus.[11] The caucus was put in that position in 1975 when Premier Lougheed found himself with a caucus of 69 members. The caucus is of course a secret body, but Lougheed was sufficiently proud of his creation, the caucus structure of 1975, to reveal it rather fully to academics. Changes since Premier Getty's accession appear not to have been formal ones. What is different now seems to be little more than the change from the compulsive, controlling Lougheed, one of the strongest premiers in Canadian history, to Getty, who has a laid-back style.

The Progressive Conservative caucus meets under the chairmanship of the premier. The chief whip is deputy caucus leader. Under Lougheed at least, the house leader usually presented the agenda. The Speaker definitely does not attend during sessions; there seem to be exceptions in out-of-session meetings. Caucus meets prior to each sitting of the Assembly, under Lougheed for 45 minutes, every Thursday morning during sessions, and occasionally in the evening; it meets for two days each month when the Assembly is not in session.

Until 1975, the Lougheed caucus operated by consensus. With the much enlarged caucus of 1975, Lougheed believed that it would strengthen both him and the caucus if votes were taken, and there have been frequent votes since then. Lougheed interpreted the votes, and he often told caucus that he would require a two-thirds vote if the caucus was to be committed to a policy or to a course of action; no one was permitted to abstain. Attendance was and is compulsory. Only illness or absence from Edmonton on authorized business are accepted as excuses.

While cabinet members have attended since 1975, Lougheed seated them interspersed with backbenchers in alphabetical order. In fact, caucus prides itself on having no one who could be called a "backbencher," only ministers and "private members." Lougheed often helped his desired decision along by determining the order of speaking. Beyond that, he tried to influence the outcome only when he had very strong feelings on an issue. The example he liked to use was the provincial relief of mortgage interest payments in 1982. Lougheed's overriding concern was to have every member feel as a full participant. To that end he had occasional periods of open discussion without set agenda. Usually, however, caucus meetings had a highly structured agenda.

The only nonmembers of caucus authorized to attend are designated staff members from the premier's office (four under Lougheed). They are called upon to assist more often under Getty, as Lougheed was so well briefed that he needed them rarely. Once there is a caucus decision, absolute discipline is expected. Not only dissent but even abstentions—for reasons of conscience or constituency interest—must be cleared with caucus. Tom Sindlinger, the one member who opposed caucus on an important issue, opposition to Trudeau's constitutional plans, was expelled from caucus and not re-elected. Because the purpose of caucus is to assure predictable behaviour in the chamber, the chief and assistant whips are, next to the leader, the most important persons in caucus.

New Democrats and Liberals have regular caucus meetings also. Because of their relatively small sizes, each member is an opposition critic. The average performance of the critics is good—in the case of a couple of Liberals and several New Democrats very good. In general, it appears that the New Democrats have the better disciplined caucus.

There is little question that the Lougheed caucus reforms were justified when Progressive Conservatives held more than 90 per cent of the seats. At that time, with the exception of several effective opposition critics, the PC caucus was indeed the Assembly. But this view can no longer be maintained with a combined opposition of 27 then 29 per cent of the seats. To persist in giving the government caucus a monopoly of policy committee work and government information continues a quasi-party system which no longer reflects the politics of Alberta society.

Members

Who are the persons who have sat in Alberta's legislature?[12] It is not surprising that, during the first two generations of provincehood (1905-67), only 19 per cent of those elected were native Albertans. Ontario, with 31 per cent, was the most common birthplace. Twenty-one per cent were born outside of Canada: 12 per cent in the United States and 9 per cent in the United Kingdom. By 1991, the situation had changed thoroughly. Native Albertans comprised 71 per cent of the members, while only 11 per cent were born in Ontario, and 11 per cent in the two neighbouring provinces. In 1991 there are now only two foreign-born members: one in the United States, and one in Germany.

Very little has changed in regard to length of service of sitting members. Forty-seven per cent of the 1905-67 group sat for up to five years. The legislative longevity of 26 members then was six to ten years, while it was 11 to 15 years for 17 per cent, 16 to 20 years for 5 per cent, 21 to 25 years for 3 per cent, and longer for 2 per cent. At the beginning of 1991, one member had just been elected in a by-election, while 27 per cent had served up to two years, and 40 per cent from three to five years. Twelve per cent had served from six to ten years, 10 per cent from eleven to fifteen years, 11 per cent from sixteen to twenty years and one member, Ray Speaker (formerly Social Credit, then PC, Little Bow), since the election of 1963. Longevity was considerably greater prior to the election of 1986, which brought a turnover of 47 per cent of the seats.

Of the 1905-67 group, 33 per cent were in business, 32 per cent farmers and ranchers, 12 per cent lawyers and 11 per cent teachers. As of 1991, there has been a slight professionalization: 18 per cent were teachers, 12 per cent lawyers and 16 per cent came from various professions. Members from the business community had declined to 24 per cent, those from agriculture to 20 per cent. Five per cent are best classified as professional politicians.

The educational attainment of members has increased somewhat. Of the 1905-67 group, 37 per cent were university graduates, 13 per cent had some post-secondary education and an additional 17 per cent were high school graduates. In 1991, 59 per cent held university degrees, of whom 58 per cent held some graduate or professional degree; an additional 16 per cent had some post-secondary education. It is not known whether all of the remaining 25 per cent had finished high school. Of the 1905-67 group, a surprising 35 per cent with university degrees had obtained theirs from the University of Alberta. Twenty-three per cent of their degrees were from Ontario universities, 15 per cent from the United States and 7 per cent from the United Kingdom. In 1991, 65 per cent of members with university degrees held them from Alberta institutions, 10 per cent from Ontario and 12 per cent from the two neighbouring provinces, 4 per cent from other Canadian institutions, 6 per cent from the United States and 2 per cent from the United Kingdom.

Previous political experience, 36 per cent for the 1905-67 group, is now down to 27 per cent. Twenty-five per cent of the 1991 members had municipal government experience, three of them as city mayors. Peter Elzinga and Stan Schumacher are former members of the House of Commons.

Of the 1905-67 group, 51 per cent were United Church or Presbyterian, 12 per cent Anglican and 10 per cent Roman Catholic. In 1991, 77 per cent still stated a religious preference. It was (in per centages of the total MLAs) 22 per cent United Church, 18 per cent Anglican, 16 per cent Roman Catholic, 8 per cent Lutheran, 7 per cent other Protestant, 4 per cent Mormon, 1 per cent Ukrainian Catholic, and 1 per cent Orthodox.

As of early 1992, visible minorities are restricted to three members claiming Aboriginal ancestry. About five sixths of the members are of West, North, and Central European parentage.

Women have a long but, on balance, sparse history in the Alberta legislature. As early as 1917, two women were elected, Louise McKinney and Roberta McAdams, each to serve only one term. The 1921 election brought into the Assembly two of Alberta's "famous five" women, Nellie McClung and Mary Irene Parlby; the latter was Alberta's first female cabinet member. Of the women elected by Social Credit, Cornelia Wood served for 23 years. Of the 11 female members who sat in the 1905-67 period, four were housewives. Of the others, two each were teachers and nurses and one each an author, a telegraph operator and an industrial employee. The Honourable Helen Hunley, who had served in the Lougheed cabinet 1971-79, was the first woman to serve as Alberta's lieutenant-governor.

As of early 1992, 13 women (16 per cent of the members) sit in the Assembly. Only three are cabinet members (Nancy Betkowski, Shirley McClellan and Elaine McCoy); there had been five in 1986. Two women are house leaders, respectively, of the New Democrats and the Liberals (Pam Barrett and Bettie Hewes). One of the women is a lawyer, two are farmers, two are businesswomen, three are teachers, one is a nurse, two are other professionals, and two are professional politicians.

Operations

A look at history tells us that the Alberta legislature has been more active under the United Farmers and the Progressive Conservatives than it had been under the Liberals and Social Credit.[13] So far, the Progressive Conservatives (since 1972) have held an average of 324 sittings in five legislative periods, the United Farmers (1922-35), 290 sittings in three periods. The Liberals (1906-21) were far behind, with an average of 199 sittings in three legislative periods. Last was Social Credit (1936-71), with an average of 185 sittings for nine periods. Legislative activity certainly has not kept pace with the growth of Alberta's population or government. In 85 years, the population multiplied, roughly, 25 times; the budget, in nominal terms and again roughly, 800 times.

Has the Assembly sat more since there is a sizeable opposition? Here, we have, for comparison, only one, and a rather short, full legislative period since the election of 1986. A fair comparison between PC legislative periods is to compare the first and second sessions of the Assembly after the elections of 1975, 1979, and 1982 with the first and second sessions after the elections of 1986 and 1989. We note an increase in activity from 1975-76, 1979-80, and 1983-84 to 1986-88 and 1989-90, from an average of 170 to one of 206 sittings. This increase becomes less impressive when we note that it was a decrease from the days of the ineffectual Social Credit opposition. In 1972-73, there had been 238 sittings. The number of sittings, therefore, hardly demonstrates that Alberta has left the era of the quasi-party legislature.

That the business of the Assembly is dominated by the executive is endemic to the Westminster model and therefore deserves brief mention only. Private members are important in the Progressive Conservative caucus, but hardly in the legislative process. Private members' bills are officially designated "public Bill other than a government Bill."[14] They may be moved by any member but must be examined by the Speaker. After first reading, they are dropped to the bottom of the list of private members' bills and must work their way up to second reading; in fact, a caucus may move some of them up. In the order of business, they rank lowest,[15] after government motions, government bills and orders, private bills, and motions other than government motions.

Private members may move Motions for Returns, normally asking for the release of documents. About one-half are accepted by the government; if they are not, the member may have such a motion debated briefly, but no information will be released. In matters requiring more information than is available for oral answers, a member may place a written question on the order paper. Only about one-third are answered.

Speeches in the Assembly are limited to 30 minutes,[16] except for 40 minutes for speeches on amendments to more than one statute. Ninety-minute speeches are allowed to the premier, the leader of the opposition, the mover of the budget, and the mover of amendments to more than one statute.

Alberta's press gallery had, as of early 1991, 42 members. In 1986, it was second in size to that of Quebec.[17] Of the current members, 27 represent the print media and 15, radio and television. Television was admitted to the chamber in 1972, the first legislative year of the Lougheed government. Traditionally, only the Speech from the Throne, the budget speech, and question periods have been televised. In 1986, Speaker Carter ejected camera crews after a question period. After negotiations, the televising of all public sessions was allowed. In fact, however, only question period is televised. Even the print media pay little attention to proceedings outside of question period. The opposition parties, who are primarily interested in the reporting of proceedings, find it difficult to get much attention in the press. However, the columns of Don Wanagas (*Edmonton Sun*), Don Braid (*Calgary Herald*), and Mark Lisac (*Edmonton Journal*) contain interesting items about the Assembly with fair frequency. All tend to be critical of the government's performance in the Assembly and, occasionally, of the Speaker. Before 1986, camera positions facing the opposition were hardly used; since then, speakers of all parties have been shown full face. Access to members inside the Legislature Building by all media is restricted rather narrowly, more so since the building is controlled by Speaker Carter.

For the budget year 1990-91, the Assembly voted close to $21 million for its support,[18] an increase of 12.5 per cent over the previous year (but only of 4.8 per cent over the actual expenditures). This is well below the 29.3 per cent increase for 1986-87, which then was the largest in Canada.[19] The total actual expenditures for the Assembly, for 1989-90, came close to $20 million. For services to members, including constituency offices, the government caucus received over $1.1 million, the official opposition $855,000, the Liberals $449,000.

In addition to the Speaker's Office, the Assembly has the following units: Clerk of the Legislative Assembly; House and Committee Services (under the Clerk Assistant); Information, Reference, and Coordination Services (under the Legislative Librarian); Legal Services (the Parliamentary Counsel); Ceremonial and Security Services (the Sergeant-at-Arms); Reporting Services (Alberta *Hansard*); Administrative Services; Personnel Services; and Information Systems Services (electronic data processing). There are 47 full-time positions, and there was, in early 1991, 209 full-time equivalent employment.[20]

Alberta Hansard is relatively young. In the mid-sixties, Social Credit began to tape proceedings and to record them in mimeographed form. The Lougheed Government introduced a printed *Hansard* in 1972. *Hansard* is unilingual.

Committees

Six provinces have at least a couple of legislative committees specializing in policy areas.[21] Those that do not are Manitoba, New Brunswick, Prince Edward Island and Alberta. And Manitoba, with its hyperdemocratic processes, revealed during the Meech Lake/Elijah Harper crisis—in effect giving a veto to each member—hardly deserves a place on this list.

Of the seven standing committees of the Legislative Assembly of Alberta (the eighth, the Standing Committee on Public Affairs, is merely a manifestation of the Committee of the Whole), two, the Standing Committee on the Alberta Heritage Savings Trust Fund Act and the Standing Committee on Public Accounts, are really control mechanisms. Privileges and Elections, Standing Orders and Printing has among its 20 members four ministers, four New Democrats and two Liberals. It could be important if the Speaker would be more willing to refer questions of privilege to the committee. The Committee on Private Bills has among its 21 members one minister, four New Democrats and two Liberals. The Committee on Legislative Offices has among its nine members two New Democrats and one Liberal. The Standing Committee on Law and Regulations has among its 21 members four New Democrats and two Liberals. The Special Standing Committee on Members' Services is by far the most important Assembly committee (though having crucial household rather than policy functions). Among its 11 members there is one minister as well as two New Democrats and one Liberal.

Since there are no policy committees, once bills pass second reading, they can be discussed only very briefly in the Committee of the Whole Assembly. The Committee of the Whole is headed by the Deputy Speaker in his role as chairman of committees. Its rules are somewhat laxer than those of the Assembly. The Committee of the Whole also sits, for 25 days, as the Committee on Supply. As such, it is supposed to control government departments. However, for some it has no more than about 90 minutes each, and some of this time is taken up by government members making innocuous speeches. Limits on budget debate were adopted in 1982 in adaptation to those of the House of Commons, but in disregard of the fact that in Parliament standing committees examine estimates in detail.

The committee structure shows the quasi-party legislature at its partisan worst, because there also are, under the dome of the Assembly, policy committees. These committees, however, are not committees of the Assembly, but committees of the Progressive Conservative caucus, meeting in secret and without record. Of the 11 caucus committees, nine deal with important policy matters. The caucus committees are: Agriculture and Rural Affairs; Economic Affairs; Irrigation; Education; Forestry and Natural Resources; Health; Social Services; Environment; and Native Affairs. The remaining committees are the Edmonton Caucus and the Calgary Caucus. Caucus members serve on from two to six of these committees. Of the 16 chairmen and vice-chairmen of the policy committees, three are women. The committees on the Environment and on Native Affairs were created in 1989. The Calgary Caucus consists of all members from Calgary: the Speaker, six ministers, and six private members. Because of the lack of private members from Edmonton, and the dearth of private members from the area, the Edmonton Caucus consists of four ministers only.

Caucus committees have two functions. First, they receive and react to policy proposals from cabinet or departments. Premier Lougheed reported that caucus adoption of committee proposals was only about 50 per cent if the proposals were not unanimous. Secondly, since 1979, caucus committees, usually accompanied by the relevant minister, receive and hear delegates from province-wide organizations. The caucus committee chairmen are appointed by the chief whip.

Despite the policy-making role of caucus committees, their members did not consider their legislative role to be very important. In 1985, when they were still able to do research, one legislative intern surveyed 22 private members of the Progressive Conservative caucus.[22] They were asked to rank, in order of importance, these four roles: representative, ombudsman, legislator and partisan. This was the last year of the overwhelming majority, so the by far lowest rank for partisanship was not surprising (16 fourth ranks). The ombudsman role was ranked first (13 first ranks) and the representative role second (nine first ranks). The legislator role ranked only a poor third. The overwhelming importance of ombudsman and representation shows that, while Lougheed clearly wanted to keep his caucus busy with legislation, they might have had enough to do in the first place.

Be this as it may, it is clear that, underlying the caucus committee function, is the notion that any involvement with policy is the clear prerogative of a member of the government caucus. This leaves to opposition members a very occasional speech on second reading, maybe a speech in a brief session of the Committee of the Whole, and the questioning of ministers. Possible reforms will be discussed later. The committee system—policy matters reserved for the PC caucus—is an excellent example of the quasi-party legislature.

Accountability

Overwhelming majorities in the Assembly have, historically, resulted in little accountability in the Alberta Legislative Assembly. Writing two years after the election of 1986, I queried: "It remains . . . a question of speculation whether an opposition of twenty-two members . . . will secure noticeably more accountability than an opposition of four members."[23] In 1992, so far, with an opposition of 24 members, the answer is "no."

The daily oral question period is the principal mechanism by which the opposition attempts to hold the government accountable. It lasts 45 minutes. The Speaker first recognizes the leader of the official opposition for two questions, each with two supplementaries, and then the leader of the Liberals for one question with two supplementaries. Then, question period is open to any member, each with one supplementary. More than in most other legislatures, Progressive Conservatives come up with, if possible, every third question, to make it easier for the ministers and to squander some of the time reserved for criticism.

No matter how diligent the opposition parties' researchers, ministers often have a monopoly of information and they enjoy making the opposition feel it. Even when Grant Notley—often single-handedly—took on Lougheed and his ministers, he had help from a larger number of legislative interns and from the now abolished Legislative Research Service. Also, he had—except for the last few years—less interference from Speaker Amerongen than the two opposition parties have from Speaker Carter, who rules out many questions because of possible conflict with *Beauchesne*—a strict interpretation of whose rules could, in many cases, make questions by opposition members impossible. Since the province often ends up taking people it does business with to court, many questions about provincial business dealings are ruled out because the matter is *sub judice*. *Hansard* also shows that Carter occasionally engages in verbal duels (provided he allows a repartee) with the questioners, thus interfering with the dialogue between questioner and questioned. At its best, question period is one-sided, because the government—and not just the Government of Alberta—has at its disposal the collective wisdom of the provincial bureaucracy. In addition, Alberta continues to eschew a freedom-of-information act,[24] which might work toward equalizing the government-opposition relation.

A compilation by the Legislative Assembly Office,[25] comparing the time consumed by questions in the Third Session of the 21st Legislature (1988) and the First Session of the 22nd Legislature (1989), shows that New Democrats (44 to 46 per cent) and Liberals (30 per cent) used about the same proportion of time in both sessions. However, the Progressive Conservatives gobbled up virtually the entire time share of the defunct Representative party, raising the government share of question time from 14 to 25 per cent (with a caucus declining from 61 to 59 members).

After the 1979 election, when only five opposition members were elected, Patrick O'Callaghan, then publisher of the *Edmonton Journal* and later of the *Calgary Herald*, promised that he would serve as leader of the unofficial opposition. While the Alberta press, and the CBC, like to beard the government now and then, information in the media is sparse, especially outside of question period. Since then, opposition parties have gained the support of 56 per cent of the voters, but much in the Assembly is still stacked against their (proportionately few) representatives. In 1985, a parliamentary intern noted an occasional (she calls it frequent) "feedback cycle":[26] press report—legislative question and government answer—press coverage—more legislative questioning, etc. The cycle would work better if the media did more reporting.

After his opposition experience (1967-71), Peter Lougheed decided that the Standing Committee on Public Accounts was to be chaired by an opposition member. Barry Pashak (ND, Calgary-Forest Lawn) has been committee chairman since 1986. The committee has 21 members: one minister, four New Democrats (including the chairman) and two Liberals.

Lougheed's reform is window-dressing. The committee is dominated by its 15 government members, who caucus prior to meetings. Only ministers can be questioned, no bureaucrats, and there are only three questions to each minister. Government members filibuster much. Before 1990, the chairman was not even allowed to present a report to the Assembly. The committee is authorized to meet only when the Assembly is in session. In 1986, the chairman had persuaded government members to permit year-round meetings of the committee and the questioning of deputy ministers, but both were vetoed by the Members' Services Committee. The chairman's private members' bill to give the committee more powers—including the power to call witnesses—was "talked out" on 21 June 1990. The Public Accounts Committee is thus a toothless tiger. The other accountability committee, the Standing Committee on the Alberta Heritage Savings Trust Fund Act, gives its opposition members little information and thus little opportunity to hold the government accountable.[27]

There is little enough accountability of government for its budget and its legislation. Equally important is that many policies of the government never see the statute book. They are born as "RFDs," a Minister's Request for Decision to Cabinet, which—after internal discussion—often end up as Orders-in-Council. Interestingly, it was RFDs and not bills that were used as illustrations when Peter Lougheed and his ministers lectured on policy-making in Alberta.[28] Opposition parties and media find out about Orders-in-Council through a teletype service made available, without cost, by Alberta Public Affairs. While opposition parties try to catch up with the flow of Orders-in-Council, the media concentrate on drama in the Assembly and lack interest to delve into most of them. The same is true of funds for many of these Orders-in-Council, which are procured, not by the budgetary process, but by Special Warrants, disseminated by the same means as Orders-in-Council, in amounts which recently have grown to about $600 million annually. Most of those are ignored by the media. In 1989, when, because of the unexpected defeat of Premier Getty in Edmonton-Whitemud and a de facto interregnum of several months, Cabinet authorized $4 billion in Special Warrants, there was a quick outcry, but soon everything returned to normal.

The problem of accountability, especially in fiscal matters, has been magnified by the growth of government of Alberta, and by the massive intervention of the Lougheed and Getty governments in Alberta's economy. It is magnified even more as there is increasing evidence of misinvestments and bad loans under Getty.

No doubt the basic handicap for accountability in Alberta is that no one, including the people, seems to be used to it. In 1992, the competition between the two opposition parties seems to be the ideal time to make this lack of accountability a major issue. So far, this simply has not happened. There is a new revelation of mismanagement in many of the question periods, but efforts to get at structural defects in accountability, and not only in fiscal matters, are rare, and never followed up. A Machiavellian explanation would be that both opposition parties are waiting for the time when they can govern with minimal accountability, but this would be unfair. A more appropriate, though not much better, explanation is that these parties also are not used to accountability. A prominent opposition member, when asked why he did not follow up his structural demands, replied that there were more pressing things to do. It is also true that the Conservatives are very jealous of their position in the quasi-party legislature. Every time a structural issue is raised, they attack it with much more vehemence than they normally display.

Redistribution

By statute, legislative redistribution, last done 1983-84, became due after the second election held under the existing scheme, i.e., after the 1989 election. At that time, in *Dixon* v. *A.G. British Columbia*,[29] a Canadian court had just delivered its first judgement on the compatibility of a legislative distribution scheme with section 3 of the Charter of Rights and Freedoms. Mme. Justice McLachlin of the B.C. Supreme Court (now of the Supreme Court of Canada) invalidated that province's scheme because it flew in the face of the requirement of equal weight for votes. While she did not say that absolute numerical equality of constituencies was required, she named the federally allowed variance of ± 25 per cent from the mean as tolerable, and the ± 10 per cent allowed variance in Manitoba as desirable. In August 1989, all three parties represented in the Alberta Legislative Assembly agreed on the striking of the Select Special Committee on Electoral Boundaries, to write new legislation within a twelve months' period prior to the actual process of redistribution by commission. They did so for two reasons: judicial involvement in questions of electoral boundaries was novel, and Alberta's constituencies were about as unequal in population as British Columbia's, giving heavy overrepresentation to many rural areas with strong Conservative majorities. Chairman of the Committee was Bob Bogle (Taber-Warner), vice-chairman of the Members' Services Committee; the vice-chairman was Stockwell Day (Red Deer-North), Whip of the Progressive Conservative Caucus. Additional members were two Conservatives, two New Democrats, and one Liberal. As the Committee's work proceeded, the

Conservative caucus's determination to favour their rural supporters over the more doubtful or downright opposing city dwellers became increasingly obvious.

The Committee heard from experts, including former Electoral Boundaries Commission chairmen, justices Tevie Miller and R.A. Dixon. Barrie Chivers, since December 1991 the New Democrat member for Edmonton-Strathcona, pleaded for heeding Justice McLachlin's opinion. Peter McCormick, a political scientist, warned the committee that the Charter is the law of the land and had to be heeded. The Committee's *Hansard* gives very little evidence that attention was paid to the experts in committee deliberations.

Thirty-nine public hearings were held throughout the province, including seven in Calgary and only four in Edmonton. Even so, rural representatives were heard in urban hearings. Of close to 500 oral and writing witnesses, only 2 per cent were domiciled in Calgary and 4 per cent in Edmonton.

Most witnesses favoured the status quo, or some other form of strong rural representation. Heavy workloads of rural MLAs and the difficulty of seeing rural MLAs in person were predominant points in the submissions. Despite mention of the McLachlin judgement in many of the hearings' introductions, little attention was paid to it during the entire process. Bob Bogle made it a practice to summarize arguments made in favour of rural overrepresentation only. On 12 March, Mike Cardinal (PC, Athabasca-Lac La Biche) moved that the committee delay its report so that additional hearings could be held. The opposition members pointed out that a delay (of about six months) was in violation of the all-party agreement of 16 August 1989. There was a tie vote (government versus opposition), and Chairman Bogle cast his vote for the extension.[30] Stockwell Day, who argued strongly for the extension, did not attend a single one of the ten additional (summer) hearings.

The brief discussion of the Charter in the debate preparing the committee's report reveals that two of the government members of the committee—after one year of committee work—had only a vague notion of Justice McLachlin's opinion and, moreover, of section 3 of the Charter. By 12 October, after at least one long *in camera* session, the committee was in agreement on a five-member (previously seven-member) Redistribution Commission of non-MLAs, with two members appointed by Cabinet, one by the leader of the Opposition (in consultation with the Liberal leader), the Chief Electoral Officer, and a Crown-appointed judge in the chair; two members were to be from rural Alberta. On 23 October, there was agreement on leaving the size of the Assembly at 83, and on using the population of the 1986 census, and not, as hitherto, the enumerated voters, as basis of representation.[31]

That day was decision day. Pam Barrett's (ND, Edmonton-Highlands) motion, that a variance of 10 per cent be the target and 25 per cent the limit on exceptions, was opposed strongly by Stockwell Day and Mike Cardinal; the former maintained that McLachlin had targeted 25 per cent, and the latter that the Charter said nothing about variances and numbers. The Barrett motion was then defeated, four to three, by Bob Bogle's casting vote.[32] It was then that Pat Black (PC, Calgary-Foothills) introduced a complex motion: variance of ± 25 per cent as target; variance of ± 50 per cent permitted for 5 per cent of constituencies; division of the province into 43 single municipality and 40 multi-municipality constituencies. Of the 43, 19 are to be in Calgary, 17 in Edmonton (a gain of one for Calgary, no gain for Edmonton). The 40 multi-municipality constituencies are to include part of three middle-sized cities. They are to include also ridings that are part of "other cities and smaller centres" (soon dubbed "fingers" once most of the Black proposals became law). Criteria for the five per cent ± 50 per cent variance constituencies (four criteria needed to qualify) are: 1. total area 20,000 square kilometres; 2. settled area 15,000 square kilometres; 3. at least 1,000 kilometres of roads; 4. community and diversity of interests; 5. distance from Edmonton 150 kilometres; 6. no population centre over 4,000; 7. dramatic loss of population due to economic factors. After a discussion of less than an hour, the Black motion was passed intact, four to three, again with Bob Bogle's casting vote.[33] It forms the core of the Electoral Boundaries Commission Act of 1990.

The Bogle Committee report was introduced in the Assembly by James Horsman, the Deputy Premier, on 27 November, 1990.[34] He assured the Assembly at the outset "that the legislation will be submitted to the Alberta Court of Appeal by way of a reference." Bill 57, the Electoral Boundaries Commission Act, was formally introduced by Ken Rostad, the Attorney General, on 29 November.[35] It passed second reading, by a vote of 31 to eight, on 4 December.[36] In the committee stage, Bob Bogle suggested that, if the bill failed, an 80-member Assembly, one-half elected according to population, one-half on a regional basis, might be in order.[37] One of the few amendments, sponsored by Bogle, was for the Commission to "take into consideration the Canadian Charter of Rights and

Freedoms."[38] As a special piquanterie, presumably to save the riding of Pincher Creek-Crowsnest (held by Fred Bradley, PC), Bill 57 was given the clause "For the purpose of subsection (2)(e): The Municipality of Crowsnest is not a town."[39] Before the final vote was taken, Barrett summarized the work of the Bogle Committee by saying that " . . . the mind-set that came to dominate was that voter equality was less important than convenience to MLAs."[40] Bill 57 passed the Assembly on 14 December 1990, by a vote of 37 to 18.[41]

On 6 March 1991, the Court of Appeal of Saskatchewan, in a unanimous decision—ruling on a reference of the Attorney General of Saskatchewan—found the Saskatchewan Representation Act, 1989, to be unconstitutional.[42] While this judgment was overturned by the Supreme Court in *Attorney General of Saskatchewan v. Carter* (1991)[43] and the Court of Appeal of Alberta supported the Alberta statute in its judgment in the Alberta reference[44] in November 1991, the Alberta Court was unhappy about the large number of rural seats and promised to keep a watchful eye on Alberta's Legislative Boundaries Commission.

This Commission issued its parliamentary report in December 1991, which, at the time of writing, still has to be submitted to public hearings and legislative action. The dissent of one of the Conservative members, and Mr. Bogle's criticism, make it clear that the Commission, unlike the (majority of the) Bogle Committee, tried to do as equitable a job as the statute permits. Bogle made it clear that the mixed ridings (now called "rurban" or "fingers") were meant to be rural, augmented only by city dwellers on acreages or similar domiciles. The majority of the Commission, wretching no doubt for judicial approval, created one overwhelmingly urban "finger" in Edmonton and a strongly urban one in Calgary. It was also careful with the allowed ± 50 per cent deviating ridings, creating only two, with deviations of only + 25 and 29 per cent.

At the time of writing, there are four possibilities regarding the next election. One is the approval of the Commission report, which would probably pass judicial scrutiny, if tested. The second is an amended Commission report not tested or acceptable to the court. The third is an outcome which would not pass judicial scrutiny, with a scenario similar to that preceding the Saskatchewan election of 1991. The fourth is an early dissolution and an election in the old ridings, in an attempt to prolong not only the Getty government but also its quasi-party legislature.

Reform

It would be unfair to say that there have been no reforms of the Assembly under the Progressive Conservatives; the trouble is that there have been no structural reforms. Early on, Lougheed gave the Assembly *Hansard*, and he introduced television. His only substantial reform was the development of the highly organized Progressive Conservative caucus. Since the caucus is partisan and secret, the reform cannot be said to benefit either the entire Assembly or the public.

So far, the quasi-party nature of the Assembly has prevented structural reform. The governing party wants to keep it that way and seems to understand clearly that any real reform would threaten the system. Ideas for reforms that would matter have therefore come from the opposition parties, which of course are kept out of the policy-making process to a degree much greater than is required by the Westminster model. At the time of writing, the Getty government has promised the establishment of a select special committee to propose reforms. A number of reforms so far bruited about by Liberals and New Democrats (including an ND platform plank as early as 1986) go beyond the Assembly—basic items such as freedom of information (again, promised by the government at the time of writing) and conflict of interest. In part because Premier Getty was, all protestations to the contrary, embarrassed by the *Globe and Mail* revelations, a mild conflict-of-interest legislation was passed in 1991. Implementation began slowly in early 1992 with the appointment as Ethics Commissioner of Robert Clark, a past Social Credit leader.

Since Laurence Decore became Liberal leader, in 1988, he has promoted reforms that definitely involve the Assembly. While he is to be congratulated for a strong stand on freedom of information, conflict of interest, and patronage, his call for the loosening of party discipline in the Assembly is difficult to reconcile with the Westminster model. As the former mayor of Edmonton, he does not see why the Assembly cannot be more like city council, where everyone's ideas have a chance of being realized. It is possible that an increasing number of Canadians consider the parliamentary system counterproductive, and some influential Albertans thought so 70 years ago. There is now evidence that about one fourth of Albertans would countenance some "American" reforms.

On 8 May 1990, Sheldon Chumir (Liberal, Calgary-Buffalo) introduced a private members' motion to "make the Alberta government more open and accountable to Alberta citizens and to the Legislative Assembly . . . .''[45] It included two proposals of special relevance to the Assembly. The one, for reform of the Public Accounts Committee, was similar to a bill introduced by the committee's chairman Barry Pashak (ND, Calgary-Forest Lawn), introduced before but debated after the Chumir motion. Chumir's other proposal called on the government not to introduce legislation without full explanation of purpose or background.[46] The motion was "talked out."

The "Alternative Throne Speech" (14 March 1991) of Ray Martin, the leader of the New Democrats, is for freedom of information and against patronage and conflict of interest. It also comes out against the practice of allowing active MLAs who are former ministers to draw a minister's pension while receiving a legislative salary. This practice came under public attack in late 1991, when the lack of funding of the provincial pension plans was admitted by the Provincial Treasurer.

When the Assembly met in February 1989, Derek Fox (ND, Vegreville) had ready for introduction a private members' bill creating several subject-matter policy committees of the Assembly. Unfortunately, the Assembly was dissolved right after the Speech from the Throne. So far, this or a similar bill has not been (re-)introduced.

Other possible reforms mentioned by opposition members include: several committees on estimates, meeting simultaneously; earlier publication of government bills; review of order-in-council appointments; summoning of committee witnesses by all parties; and the cessation of government domination of the Members' Services and the Public Accounts committees.

Unless one or both opposition parties make structural reform a strong and sustained priority, adapting the Assembly to a multi-party society will have to await a change in government.

Continuity and Change: A Quasi-party Legislature for a Multi-party System

There is something more unequal about the Alberta Legislative Assembly than the ratio between 59 government and 24 opposition members. Government and opposition are about as equal as anywhere in debate, but all that gets debated are the government's finished statutory products. The only members having the benefit of useful committee consideration

are the members of the government caucus. And much of what would
be a statutory product elsewhere never gets debated in the Assembly,
because few of the frequent "requests for decision" submitted by departments to cabinet are submitted to the legislature—most are disseminated
over the ticker-tape as Orders-in-Council, with nothing but the bare text
ever revealed to opposition or public, after the fact. Even the opposition's
show, question period, tends to produce more put-downs by ministers
or the Speaker than answers. Finally, the most time-honoured legislative power, the power of the purse, gives the opposition little effective
control. There is little time for debating estimates, and much of that
is pre-empted by the government. And more than 5 per cent of governmental expenditures are authorized—unbeknownst to the Assembly—
by the Cabinet through Special Warrants or by one minister from lot-
tery funds which, in theory only, belong to the people. In addition, there
is firm government control of the Public Accounts and the Members'
Services committees. All this is continuity—the only change under the
Progressive Conservatives has been an immense growth in the government and slightly more information to the public, through the televising of question period and the printing of *Hansard*.

A break in continuity under the Progressive Conservatives might be
the new conflict-of-interest legislation, once it is fully implemented.
While it could bring a change in the prevailing political climate, it would
not affect the operations of the Legislative Assembly. They could only
be changed by reforms promised in 1992, but at the time of writing, the
scope of possible changes is highly uncertain. In the unlikely event that
the Conservatives, should they lose their legislative majority, would be
permitted by the opposition parties to form a minority government, the
party supporting that government could force changes in the Assembly.
The other at all probable possibility, after the next election, would be
a minority government by either Liberals or New Democrats. Both
parties want change in the Assembly but legislative reform is a high
priority for neither. However, the one of the two parties not forming such
a minority government could almost be relied upon to give Albertans
a legislature with policy committees, more openness, more debate, some
control of the bureaucracy and more fiscal controls. Should the Reform
party enter provincial politics and win, it would likely introduce a few
populist controls. Whether it would open more of the Assembly's activities to its competitors or, for that matter, give more functions to the
legislature, is an open question.

A lively legislature is not part of Alberta's political culture. The person in the street is much less interested in the doings of the Assembly than is the press gallery, but even it thins out or empties as soon as question period is over. Most of the public either sleeps at 11:00 p.m., or it has more exciting things to do than watch question period from 11:00 to 11:45 p.m. on television. Any increasing interest in political competition on the part of Albertans, however, would help impel the government of Alberta, especially under different party control, to allow the state of the Assembly to become more of a public issue than it is now. Such an awakened interest could go a long way toward fulfilling the requirements that make a legislature an effective part of responsible government under the Westminster model. Despite the recent strengthening of the opposition benches, the Legislative Assembly of Alberta is, for the many reasons stated in this chapter, still unable to play this part effectively.

In 1988, I wrote: "As long as the government of Alberta is backed by not only a legislative but also a popular majority, those resisting reform can claim that more than half of Albertans have the Legislative Assembly they want."[47] Since the election of 1989, this claim can no longer be made; opposition support has grown from 49 to 56 per cent. It is one thing to exclude the representatives of a huge minority from more meaningful participation in the legislative process. But now, the members who are hampered in their questioning, debating and controlling functions, the members who enter each session with a great deal of ignorance they cannot reduce, represent two parties with 55 per cent of the popular vote. An attempted gerrymandering process and possibly ineffectual reforms, could still result in maintaining, for the near future at least, lack of effective opposition and control. If the courts do not halt that process, only an alert electorate, sensitized by opposition parties fully awake to their legislative subjugation, can give Albertans the kind of legislature a democratic society deserves.

NOTES

1. The Throne Speech of 19 March 1992 contains the following passage: "In the course of the committee's (Select Special Committee on Constitutional Reform) hearings, many recommendations were made with respect to improving the functioning of this Legislature and making it more respon-

sive to the needs and values of Albertans. My government will propose that a select special committee of the Legislature be established to review how these measures and other reforms may be adopted within the context of the parliamentary system and traditions." (*Alberta Hansard*, 19 March 1992, p. 3). The next day, Speaker Carter announced: "The Chair is pleased that a select special committee will be established with respect to improving the functioning of this Legislature." (Ibid., 20 March 1992, p. 9).

2. John A. Irving, *The Social Credit Movement in Alberta* (Toronto: University of Toronto Press, 1959), pp. 129-31, 141-44, 181-82.

3. Statutes of Alberta, 1983, L-10.1.

4. Statutes of Alberta, 1988, L-7.5.

5. Alberta, Legislative Assembly, *Debates*, 23 April 1990, p. 710. Hereafter cited as *Debates*, date, page.

6. *Debates*, 24 April 1990, p. 743.

7. Don Braid, "Tories chicken out on inquiry," *Calgary Herald*, 24 April 1990.

8. "Mr. Speaker's heavy hand," *Edmonton Journal*, 1 April 1991.

9. Alberta, *Supplementary Information to the Public Accounts, 1989-90*, pp. 1.1, 2.1.

10. For a comprehensive treatment of legislators' salaries, see Alberta Teachers' Association (ATA), *A Guide to Alberta's Twenty-Second Legislature* (Edmonton: Alberta Teachers' Association, 1989), pp. 51-53.

11. Information on the Progressive Conservative caucus is taken from Peter McCormick, "Politics after the Landslide," *Parliamentary Government* 4 (1983), pp. 8-10, and from lectures delivered by the Hon. Peter Lougheed at the University of Alberta, 1986-89.

12. For data from 1905-67 see H.L. Malliah, "A Socio-historical Study of the Legislature of Alberta, 1905-67 (unpublished Ph.D. dissertation, Political Science, University of Alberta, 1970). Recent data are taken from *Canadian Parliamentary Guide* (Ottawa: Normandin; since 1989, Toronto: Info Globe) and from ATA, *A Guide to Alberta's Twenty-Second Legislature*.

13. Most of the information on the Assembly prior to 1986 is taken from John McDonough, *Selected Statistical Measures Pertaining to the Work of the Alberta Legislative Assembly* (Edmonton: Legislative Research Services, 1986). Since the abolition of Legislative Research Services, there is no convenient way of assembling information on the Alberta legislature.

14. Standing Orders of the Legislative Assembly of Alberta, No. 69.

15. Ibid., No. 8.

16. Ibid., No. 29.

17. Robert J. Fleming and Patrick Fafard, eds., *Canadian Legislatures: The 1986 Comparative Study* (Toronto: Office of the Assembly, 1986), pp. 125-126. Unfortunately, this most helpful comparative volume has not appeared since 1987.

18. Alberta, *1990-91 Legislative Assembly Estimates*, p. 9. For actual expenditures for 1989-90, see Alberta, *Public Accounts 1989-90*, p. 3.5.

19. Fleming and Fafard, *Canadian Legislatures*, p. 117.

20. Alberta, *1990-91 Legislative Assembly Estimates*, p. 9.

21. This information has been compiled from the individual chapters in Gary Levy and Graham White, *Provincial and Territorial Legislatures in Canada* (Toronto: University of Toronto Press, 1989).

22. Jean Munn, "Government Private Members in Alberta," unpublished paper, Alberta legislative internship program, 1985, p. 4. Levy and White, *Provincial and Territorial* Legislatures, p. 119.

23. Levy and White, *Provincial and Territorial Legislatures*, p. 119.

24. The Throne Speech of 19 March 1992 promised: "New access to information legislation will be introduced to ensure my government's policy of full disclosure of information is protected in law." *Alberta Hansard*, 19 March 1992, p. 3.

25. Alberta, Legislative Assembly Office, *Annual Report, 1989*, p. 5.

26. Priscilla Schmidt, "Government-Press Relations in Alberta," unpublished paper, Alberta legislative internship program, 1985.

27. Larry Pratt and Allan Tupper's 1980 conclusion still holds: "the record of the government-dominated committee has certainly not been impressive to date" ("The Politics of Accountability: Executive Discretion and Control," *Canadian Public Policy* 6 (1980) Supplement: 263).

28. Lectures by Peter Lougheed, Merv Leitch, and Roy Farran at the University of Alberta, 1985-89.

29. *Dixon v. British Columbia (Attorney General)* (1989), 60 DLR (4th) 445 (B.C.S.C.).

30. Legislative Assembly of Alberta, Select Special Committee on Electoral Boundaries, *Transcript of Meetings*, 28 August 1989 to 6 November 1990.

31. Ibid., p. 923.

32. Ibid., p. 925.

33. Ibid., p. 935.

34. *Debates*, 27 November 1990, p. 2473.

35. Ibid., 29 November 1990, p. 2509.

36. *Debates*, 4 December 1990, p. 2646.

37. Ibid., 6 December 1990, pp. 2702-3.

38. Ibid., 13 December 1990, pp. 2847-48.

39. Statutes of Alberta, 1990, E-4.01.

40. *Debates*, 14 December 1990, p. 2869.

41. Ibid., p. 2877.

42. *Reference Re: Constitutional Questions Act (Sask.)*.

43. [1991] 81 D.L.R. (4th) 16.

44. Appeal #9103-0081-AC.

45. *Debates*, 8 May 1990, p. 1096.
46. *Debates*, 12 March 1990, p. 21; 21 June 1990, pp. 2089-94.
47. Levy and White, *Provincial and Territorial Legislatures*, p. 124.

7

Provincial-Municipal Relations

Jack Masson

Peter Lougheed, Alberta's premier from 1971 to 1985, knew it was important to maintain good political relations with the province's municipalities. He did this by maintaining cordial relationships with municipal politicians, being attentive to the financial needs of municipalities and showing his concern for small and medium sized municipalities. Still, he did not treat municipalities as equals but rather kept them politically and financially subordinate to the provincial government. He was on good terms with municipal political leaders but always made it clear that the relationship was not one of political equality. He provided municipalities with fiscal resources through provincial grant programs but ensured the province controlled and directed how the funds were spent so that municipal policies would complement provincial ones. In the Lougheed government's latter years, municipalities had spending and policy discretion over less than 20 per cent of provincial grants.

When the Conservative leadership passed to Don Getty, the relationship between the province and the municipalities suffered even though Getty favoured giving the municipalities more autonomy. Getty was much less popular with municipal leaders than Lougheed because he had neither his predecessor's political acumen nor the fiscal resources available to placate the municipalities.

Lougheed was concerned about the adverse effects of urbanization. He was perturbed about the deteriorating living conditions in large cities, the worsening of pollution and the increase in crime.[1] It worried him that Edmonton and Calgary were growing rapidly while small towns in Alberta were dying. In an effort to slow the growth of the province's two

TABLE 7.1   Percentage of People Living in Cities and Towns by Year

	1966	1976	1986
Cities and towns	68.5	74.0	78.4
Edmonton and Calgary	48.1	50.7	51.0

Alberta Bureau of Statistics, 1988.

largest cities and to benefit municipalities in the hinterlands, he implemented a policy to decentralize economic activity.

Alberta's municipalities are legally subordinate to the provincial government as is the case of municipalities in all of the provinces. Under the Constitution Act, national and provincial governments have separate spheres of power with local government falling under the purview of the provinces. Thus, constitutionally a province can create, change, and abolish municipalities at will. Nevertheless Alberta's provincial politicians are aware that as the province has urbanized, the urban electorate has become a potent political force. The figures in Table 7.1 show that between 1966 and 1986 the percentage of the province's population residing in towns and cities increased by 10 percent and that by 1986 almost four-fifths of the population lived in larger municipalities with slightly more than half residing in the province's two largest cities.

It did not escape the provincial government's attention that over this same time period the municipalities' administrative apparatus and expenditures grew much faster than their increases in population. Table 7.2 shows that while municipal bureaucracies doubled in size between 1966 and 1986, municipal expenditures increased more than ten-fold. As municipalities grew and became more important, the province met many of their fiscal needs but continued to limit their political power. When the province was financially flush in the 1970s and municipal governments were well funded, the municipalities accepted their subservient political role. But with the economic downturn in the 1980s, the government reduced its fiscal commitment to municipalities which strained the close relationship it had nurtured with them over the years.

Even without resort to its control of finances and its constitutional supremacy, the province has an overwhelming advantage in dealing with municipalities. The provincial government has a well defined political

TABLE 7.2   Municipal Expenditures and Number of Employees for 1966, 1976, and 1986

	1966	1976	1986
No.Municipal Employees	14,421	22,977	29,940
Municipal Expenditures	$342,693,000	$1,963,954,000	$5,618,708,000*

Alberta Bureau of Statistics, 1988.
*average expenditure for 1984 and 1986

structure with public policies formulated by the party in power. In contrast, municipal policies are formulated in nonpartisan political systems in which it is difficult to pinpoint responsibility and which have a distinct middle class bias. With power dispersed, municipal politicians are often unable to muster the political force necessary to deal with the province. Only luck and happenstance have allowed municipal politicians to challenge successfully the provincial government.

Municipal Power and Provincial Decentralization Policy

In its early years, Social Credit was decidedly unsympathetic to the financial plight of cities. Later the party responded to the province's changing demographics, distanced itself from its traditional rural support base and courted the electorate in Edmonton and Calgary. To the chagrin of small town Alberta, in a 1965 speech to the Social Credit Party's faithful, Premier Manning said that "within 10 years, 85 per cent of the population of this province is going to be in Edmonton and Calgary." Nothing could be done about it.[2]

Although Peter Lougheed, then leader of the opposition, was interpreted as the voice of an urban professional class, he was sympathetic to rural Alberta. His wife had her roots in the small community of Hardisty and three of Lougheed's five fellow Tories represented rural constituencies in 1967.[3] Lougheed relied on the advice of Hugh Horner who counseled him on developing policies which would appeal to rural Alberta and erode Social Credit's political support.[4] At the 1970 meeting of the Alberta Association of Municipal Districts and Counties (AAMD&C), Lougheed was warmly received when he argued that if the Conservatives formed the next government, growth would be balanced across the province. Edmonton and Calgary would not be allowed to grow at the expense of rural Alberta.[5] Roy Farran writes that Lougheed's "oft repeated quote was 'better to have four Red Deers than everyone living in Edmonton and Calgary'."[6]

When they came to power in 1971, the Conservatives promised a comprehensive urbanization policy; it was never forthcoming. Nevertheless, Lougheed honoured his commitment to decentralization and the revitalization of small towns. In 1974 he emphasized that one of his government's goals was "to spread the growth on a balanced basis across the province and capitalize upon the potential of the smaller centers."[7] Making a conscious attempt to locate government offices and educational institutions in rural and economically depressed communities, Lougheed established a caucus committee on decentralization which played a lead role in prodding government departments to decentralize to outlying municipalities.

In 1974 the government passed legislation to establish Restricted Development Areas (RDAs) which gave it another tool to control the growth of larger municipalities. The RDAs were used in Edmonton and Calgary to establish an outer ring of land for utility and pipeline right-of-ways, easement ways for other municipal services and transportation routes. It was also envisioned that RDAs would be used to freeze land for park use in urban areas. Ironically, David Russell and William Yurko, representatives of metropolitan ridings, were the architects of the RDA scheme.

Lougheed's commitment to decentralization and balanced economic growth bothered the business community in the big cities but ordinary citizens seemed unconcerned. Therefore, it hardly made a ripple when in 1974 Lougheed announced to the Edmonton Chamber of Commerce that "Edmonton and Calgary . . . are large enough now."[8]

In the early 1970s, decentralization proceeded with little controversy although several times Lougheed singled out Calgary as not being fully behind his programs.[9] Calgary's council voiced its displeasure when the province, without consultation, placed a five-mile wide RDA around the city which stymied an annexation proposal favoured by the administration.[10]

Decentralization became an issue in the Edmonton region when in 1979 the city made a massive annexation bid for the City of St. Albert, the County of Strathcona (including the unincorporated community of Sherwood Park) and significant portions of the County of Parkland and the Municipal District of Sturgeon. A split developed in the party with Edmonton MLAs supporting the city's expansion and MLAs in outlying suburban ridings favoring the status quo. After this episode little was heard of decentralization and the maintenance of viable small communities.

With the onset of the recession in the early 1980s and the rise of pressing economic and fiscal problems, decentralization was placed on the back burner. It is also possible that, after the caucus split in Edmonton, Lougheed was unwilling to further split the party caucus with issues of decentralization. With Don Getty's win in 1986, Lougheed's decentralization policy remained intact but was given low priority. No new decentralization programs were announced and little was heard about it until the spring of 1991 when controversy again occurred.[11]

Big City Expansion and Policies of Conciliation and Compromise

Lougheed's policy on decentralization was counter-balanced by Edmonton and Calgary's desire to expand their boundaries and amalgamate their outlying bedroom communities. With the cities having jousted with the province over expansion since the 1950s, the battle lines had been drawn long before the Progressive Conservatives came to power. Although the two cities' administrations are politically astute, the province through its Local Authorities Board (LAB) and the cabinet holds the upper hand in matters of municipal expansion.

Until 1975 the LAB was the final authority on annexation and amalgamation petitions which could only be initiated by a municipal council, by a majority of the land owners in the affected area, or by the Minister of Municipal Affairs with regard to land in an improvement district. In 1975 the Municipal Government Act was amended to require that LAB decisions be referred to the provincial cabinet for approval. Two years later the Act was again amended so the Lieutenant Governor in Council could annex Crown land to a municipality, improvement district or special area without LAB involvement. In 1978 the Act was again amended to give the cabinet additional power in annexation proceedings.

Besides being able to approve or disapprove a LAB order, the cabinet was given the power to "prescribe conditions" for the adoption of an annexation proposal. In 1981, LAB powers were further weakened when the Act was amended so the Lieutenant Governor in Council had the authority to rule on an annexation and completely by-pass the LAB and its procedures. With these amendments, the cabinet has the final say over municipal expansion and development with the LAB's decision only an interim step in the process. Also important in understanding the government's power is that under the Local Authorities Board Act it is not necessary for a plebiscite to be held in the area to be annexed. Therefore, few are held.

Even though Social Credit was resigned to ever-increasing urbanization, it was committed to "municipal autonomy."[12] The discovery of oil in 1947 was followed by rapid economic expansion and urban growth which caused a financial crisis for the province's towns and cities. The government responded by providing loan assistance programs and establishing district planning commissions. In 1954 it established the McNally Commission to examine and make recommendations for the cities of Edmonton and Calgary on the "financing of school and municipal matters," as well as "the boundaries and the form of local government which will most adequately and equitably provide for the orderly development of school and municipal services."[13] In 1956, the Commission submitted its final report which showed wide variations in the services and tax levels of municipalities in the two regions and argued that a metropolitan area was an economic and social unit that could be "more efficiently and effectively governed by one central municipal authority." On this basis the report concluded "that each metropolitan area would be best governed by enlarging each of the present cities to include its whole metropolitan area." Edmonton was to be enlarged from 107.5 to 290.1 square kilometers (41.5 to 112.02 square miles) and Calgary from 128.2 to 271.4 square kilometers (49.5 to 104.77 square miles).

The recommendations caught the government off-guard. Peter Smith, an urban geographer, writes that "the McNally Commission completely misjudged the will of the Provincial Government and the strength of its attachment to the ideals of local autonomy and self government."[14] The government's position was that "the metropolitan problem" was caused by a lack of fiscal resources. As a consequence, the Commission's recommendations were ignored. Subsequently the government established the Municipal Financing Corporation and grants to Edmonton and Calgary were greatly increased.

Edmonton was particularly unhappy with the provincial government's cool response to McNally's recommendation that the city be allowed to expand almost three-fold. But despite the government's stance, Edmonton expanded from 107.5 to 177.7 square kilometers (41.5 to 68.6 square miles) through piecemeal annexation over the next five years. Then in 1967, in an effort to pressure the provincial government, the city commissioned an economist to conduct a study "in regard to extending the City's boundaries in all directions."[15] His report recommended that the city's size be increased from 222.7 to 756.3 square kilometers (86 to 292 square miles). Since the report was commissioned by the city, the recommendation that a single governmental unit should govern the region was not unexpected. Nor was it surprising that the economist's arguments were based almost entirely on economic considerations. Although the report had its shortcomings, it was well received by almost everyone except the provincial government which pointedly ignored it.

When the Conservatives came to power in 1971, they were not hostile to local government amalgamation as long as its purpose was to strengthen smaller communities. As an example, an act was passed in 1979 amalgamating a number of financially strapped municipalities in the Crowsnest Pass. Shortly thereafter, the government provided "transitional capital assistance" to smooth the amalgamation process. It seems clear that annexation and amalgamation proposals by smaller communities did not concern the Conservatives. Rather it was the province's two largest cities which were monitored and allowed only carefully controlled expansion. In particular, Edmonton, with its aggressive policy of attempting to annex its neighbors, was closely scrutinized and allowed only limited expansion. Calgary was more politically astute and focused its annexation efforts on low density farm land rather than on municipalities with high density housing.

Between 1968 and 1979, Edmonton continued its piecemeal annexation. In March 1979, the city made a bid to the LAB to annex more than 186,800 hectares (467,000 acres) which would increase the city's size from 318.6 to 1813 square kilometers (123 to 700 square miles). The proposal included the City of St. Albert, the unincorporated community of Sherwood Park, the County of Parkland and the Municipal District of Sturgeon. The communities were outraged. Residents of St. Albert and Sherwood Park adamantly opposed amalgamation and held rallies, marched, gathered petitions and wrote letters to their community newspapers and the *Edmonton Journal*. The Edmonton citizenry was uninterested in the proposed expansion although the *Journal* and a number of downtown business people were interested in slowing the regional decentralization of population and industrial activities. They played an active role in the campaign to extend the city's boundaries.

In 1980, the LAB made its decision and awarded Edmonton most of the area it had asked for with the exception of a large block of land to the east of the city in the County of Strathcona. The LAB's order went to cabinet where it was disallowed. Subsequently, a new order was issued which awarded Edmonton 34,000 hectares (86,000 acres). Dissatisfied with the award, Edmonton's mayor vowed the city would continue its attempt to increase its size and less than a year later the city made a bid for 3320 hectares (8300 acres). But then residential construction and the local economy slowed and little thought was given to further annexations.

The governmental reorganization scenario for Calgary was much different than for Edmonton. After the province turned down the McNally Commission recommendation to increase Calgary's size, the city acquired 67.4 square kilometers (26 square miles) in 1956 and then quietly waited until 1961 to bid for an additional 195.5 square kilometers (74.3 square miles). Although the proposal included the amalgamation of Forest Lawn, there was only slight opposition and the LAB awarded the city everything it asked for. In 1963 the city acquired the small community of Montgomery and in 1964 the community of Bowness; in both cases there was limited opposition from community citizen groups and politicians, but the LAB ruled in favour of Calgary. The next annexation occurred in 1971 when property speculators and a large real estate company filed a request for annexation of 170 hectares (419 acres) of farmland to develop low cost housing. Despite protests from the Calgary School Board, concerned about the area's isolation from existing schools, the LAB again ruled for the city. In 1974 Calgary's administrators floated a proposal to annex 514 square kilometers (198.5 square miles) north and south of the city which would almost double the its size. The proposal spawned an anti-annexation group which was concerned about the city's explosive growth and increasing capital debt. Subsequently, the controversial proposal was submitted to the city's electorate who soundly rejected it by almost two to one.

Less than a year after the plebiscite, private developers submitted bids for annexation of land in the same northern and southern sectors. Almost 65 square kilometers (25 square miles) were annexed in 1978. In 1983, the LAB approved the annexation of three land parcels totalling 1800 hectares (4500 acres) which it was estimated would give the city an additional 12-year supply of land for development. Shortly thereafter the city planning department made two massive annexation proposals despite the city's slowing population growth. One proposal, based on outdated population and market analyses, called for the annexation of 329 square kilometers (127 square miles); the other for 241 square kilometers (93 square miles). The latter plan soon became a center of political controversy with a split which developed between city planners and Mayor Ralph Klein and other council members. Preparing for a fall election they had undoubtedly examined the heavy 1974 anti-annexation vote and were responding accordingly. Although the city's planning department adamantly maintained that it was necessary to annex at least 241 square kilometers (93 square miles) to meet future needs for residential and industrial expansion, some members of council and an anti-annexation group, 20th Century Calgary, suggested the city examine other options.

Calgary was unwilling to gamble with untried policies. Rather it modified its 1983 proposal and pursued a policy of territorial expansion which had the whole-hearted support of the city's business community. In 1986 the city announced that it would negotiate with the Municipal Districts of Foothills and Rocky View to annex 256 square kilometers (98.5 square miles) of land in order to have an adequate supply for residential and commercial development. Unlike Edmonton's abrasive stance with its neighbors, Calgary adopted a conciliatory posture and spent two years negotiating agreements with the municipal districts. Finally in 1989, the three municipalities signed an inter-municipal annexation agreement which would give the city 245 square kilometers (95 square miles). With this agreement in hand, Calgary's administration expected the LAB to approve the annexation as a matter of course and was shocked when the amount of land approved for annexation was reduced to 158 square kilometers (61.3 square miles).[16]

While Calgary continued to plan for expansion in the 1980s, little was heard about expansion in Edmonton. Perhaps the city had miscalculated the costs and benefits of annexation and the economic downturn exacerbated the error. In 1979, the city distributed a fact sheet entitled "About the Edmonton Boundaries" which promised that with annexation: "Regional service levels . . . will improve in the outlying areas. This is particularly so for the protection of services such as fire and police."[17] But in 1982 as residential, business and industrial growth halted, the city was unable even to maintain the level of services the annexed areas had enjoyed before they became part of the city. As taxes increased as much as 100 per cent in the annexed areas, the level of services declined.

Several Edmonton council members were critical of the annexation and the shabby treatment meted out to the city's newest residents. In 1983 Jan Reimer complained: "Annexation hasn't benefitted Edmonton at all, we'll be paying years down the road for road maintenance and snow clearance in the new areas."[18] Ed Ewasiuk proposed the city "de-annex" some of the land it had annexed and turn it over to the province or back to its original owners.[19] In 1985 Mayor Laurence Decore said: "We spent hundreds of thousands of dollars on a great big annexation that now appears to be pretty clear we didn't need." Then he qualified himself by saying "but we're just wasting money if we say 'take it back'."[20]

Until Edmonton's affliction with "annexation indigestion," the city was unwilling to restrict its growth to its relatively unpopulated southern sector. The city's politicians seemed to take a perverse pride in being abrasive rather than negotiating with neighboring municipalities on territorial issues.[21] Edmonton's uncompromising stance during the city's 1980-81 annexation battle was not forgotten by the region's municipalities. A decade later "Edmonton baiting" is still found in the St. Albert and Fort Saskatchewan council chambers where there remains a deep rooted resentment against the city.

Most municipalities are politically attuned to the importance of viable and ongoing relationships with their neighbors. Calgary has long had an informal agreement with outlying municipalities that it would not aggressively expand its boundaries if they did not try to attract industry from the city with promises of low property taxes.[22] In the 1980s, Fort Saskatchewan, Medicine Hat, Lloydminster and Lethbridge all recognized the importance of negotiation and compromise. Their annexation proposals raised little conflict. They recognized that by annexing land rather than people, conflict was reduced. Fort Saskatchewan and the County of Strathcona established a "joint planning process" to reach an accommodation over land needed for the city's expansion. In 1981, Medicine Hat entered into protracted annexation negotiations with Improvement District No. 1 which was eventually settled to both parties' satisfaction. In an annexation bid in 1981, the City of Lethbridge established a joint planning committee with the County of Lethbridge. The committee hammered out a number of compromises which were satisfactory to both parties.

Most municipalities are able to negotiate their financial and territorial differences with their neighbors. But there is still a need for a formal mechanism to facilitate municipal cooperation. The LAB fails on this count and as two observers show, municipal conflict is often exacerbated by the LAB process. Using Edmonton as an example, they write:

> . . . the LAB process works reasonably well in dealing with the conventional or typical annexation requests. But the Edmonton application did not fit into this category for it raised other substantial issues not generally dealt with in the conventional annexation hearing . . . . Because the City was, by the nature of the process, the initiator of the annexation application it also became quickly designated as the aggressor by the interveners who emerged as the defenders of the status quo. It was in the interests of the latter, by virtue of the adversarial process which quickly emerged, to smother any attempt to maintain a focus on the wider issues involved.[23]

It is also argued that the quasi-judicial nature of the LAB hearings constrains the parties involved. Plunkett and Lightbody argue that if the province had employed an investigative team from the metropolitan area's municipalities it "would have eliminated the adversarial process . . . and could have provided a means of hearing all parties concerned without resort to tedious cross-examination."

As the provincial economy continues to improve, there will be renewed efforts by municipalities to expand their boundaries and to control area-wide service and financial problems. In all likelihood there will be an increase in inter-municipal conflict. Although a solution might be for the government to revamp the LAB process it is unlikely to do so since it would reopen the question as to whether the government should be furthering urban or rural policies. Moreover, a change in government would not necessarily change the way territorial disputes are resolved between municipalities. The New Democrats would be caught on the proverbial "horns of a dilemma" having to balance concerns with small town grass roots democracy with concerns over equity in the financing of public services for a region. A Liberal Party with Laurence Decore at the helm would be more predictable since during the time he sat on Edmonton's council the city consistently lost out to its suburban neighbors before the LAB. When this is combined with Decore's urban orientation one can safely predict that Decore would make major changes as to how territory is distributed and redistributed at the municipal level and that he would almost certainly favour policies benefitting larger cities.

Grants and Provincial/Municipal Responsibilities

Premier Lougheed held strong views on provincial/municipal power relationships, views which often became policy. In 1972, when asked whether he would consider transferring power from the province to the municipalities, Lougheed replied that it is "not sound policy to transfer jurisdiction or responsibilities to local government if they do not have the fiscal capacity to meet them."[24] Knowing that the key to keeping municipal policy aligned with provincial policy was the control of municipal finances, he was careful to keep the municipalities financially dependent. From 1956 to 1970 Social Credit had allocated from one third to one half of its provincial oil and gas royalties for municipal assistance. Lougheed was critical of Social Credit policy and in government he remained steadfastly opposed to revenue sharing. He was opposed because revenue sharing, which by its very nature has no conditions attached, makes it difficult for the province to control municipal fiscal policy.

But Lougheed was not insensitive to municipal financial needs. Shortly after taking office a five-member committee chaired by MLA Roy Farran was struck and given a mandate to examine provincial and municipal fiscal responsibilities.[25] The committee's report noted Alberta's rapid urbanization and pointed out that the municipalities, with their narrow property tax base, faced a crisis in providing public services. A manifestation of this was a municipal per capita debt of $580.40 in 1970 while the province was debt free. The report argued that by transferring health, social services and a sizeable portion of education to the province, the percentage of the combined provincial/municipal budget financed at the local level would decline from 35 to 30 percent. Homage was paid to decentralization and local autonomy by arguing that changes were necessary to preserve the financial viability of small town Alberta. The report argued:

> To generalize, residential property tax seldom covers the cost of services demanded at a local level and the balance has to come from commercial and industrial development, or it has to come from revenue

sources other than property taxes such as provincial grants. Urban areas therefore compete to obtain more industry, which begets more people, which begets more industry in a perpetual Genesis cycle . . . this equation is one of the many reasons for constant metropolitan growth at the expense of the sparsely-populated rural areas.[26]

On the basis of the report's recommendations, the government passed the Property Tax Reduction Act which made the province responsible for the costs of hospitalization, public health services and a substantial amount of education. On the heels of this act was a provincial program to stabilize the interest on municipal capital loans at eight per cent by making yearly subsidy payments for the debenture rate difference to municipalities. Then during the 1979 provincial election campaign, Lougheed announced the Municipal Debt Reduction Act. Under its provisions each of the province's municipalities and Metis settlements was given a $500 per capita grant either to pay down debenture debt or as an unconditional grant. With $648 million applied to debenture debt and $383 million distributed unconditionally, many municipalities eliminated their long-term debt or established comfortable reserves.

Despite the province's largess, the municipalities remained unhappy insofar as the province's policy increased conditional grants at the expense of unconditional ones. Table 7.3 shows that when the Conservatives came to power in 1971, 48.7 percent of municipal grants were unconditional. This figure jumped to 61 percent in 1972 and then began to slump until it reached 16.7 percent in 1981. Little did municipal politicians know the 1981 grant harkened a provincial policy of having unconditional grants limited to 20 percent or less of total municipal grants.

In 1978, the Alberta Urban Municipalities Association (AUMA) commissioned two University of Alberta professors to examine provincial-municipal relations with a view to improving them. The following year, their report, *The Reform of Municipal-Provincial Relationships in the Province of Alberta*, attracted media attention with the argument: ". . . because it provides greater local autonomy but demands more municipal responsibility, the tax sharing (i.e., a local personal income tax) alternative in conjunction with the selective reduction of conditional grants programs offers the most balanced approach towards correcting the municipal fiscal problem."[28]

The study credited the government with providing adequate funding for the province's municipalities but was critical of fiscal restraints which

TABLE 7.3   Provincial Fiscal Transfers Percentage of Conditional
and Unconditional Grants to Alberta Municipalities by Year[27]

Year	Unconditional Grants	Conditional Grants
1971	48.7	51.3
1972	61.0	39.0
1973	58.2	41.8
1974	34.3	65.7
1975	34.9	65.1
1976	33.8	66.2
1977	31.3	68.7
1978	28.3	71.7
1979	36.0	64.0
1980	26.4	73.6
1981	16.7	83.3
1982	19.2	80.8
1983	17.0	83.0
1984	17.9	82.1
1985	16.1	83.9
1986	16.9	83.1
1987	19.1	80.9
1988	33.9	66.1

Alberta Municipal Affairs, *Minister of Municipal Affairs Conference*, 1988 *Briefing Book*, Table A4.1.3

impaired their policy making and planning. But the report's recommendation on revenue sharing almost guaranteed that the government would ignore its proposals. In April 1979, a report by the Provincial-Municipal Finance Council dealt obliquely with the issues raised by the AUMA report.[29] It argued that revenue sharing would impair the provincial government's fiscal flexibility and "could introduce unnecessary problems and instability in municipal financing." The report defended the government's increasing reliance on conditional grants arguing that, unlike unconditional grants, they recognized "the variation in needs of individual municipalities."

When the government established the Advisory Committee on Provincial Municipal Fiscal Relations in 1981, its members were told by the Minister of Municipal Affairs, "that it would not be useful for them to pursue any proposals for the sharing of either income tax revenue or natural resource revenue."[30] Two days later the minister lost face when he argued that municipalities favoured conditional grants and did not want them "replaced with a straight dollar transfer."[31]

With the onset of the economic downturn in the early 1980s, municipal concerns shifted to the problems posed by major reductions in provincial funding. As the economy weakened, municipal grants were frozen or only marginally increased, a cap was placed on municipal borrowing and the municipal interest subsidization program was terminated. At the same time, municipal councils were confused by a change to the unconditional grant formula which the Minister of Municipal Affairs claimed would "take from the rich and give to the poor."[32] Changing the grant formula so it would reflect a municipality's "relative fiscal capacity" was intended to eliminate grant inequities. Nevertheless, in 1984 not a single "affluent municipality" had its grant reduced under the new formula.

When Don Getty became premier he had already upset a number of AUMA members because, as a Conservative leadership candidate, he refused to attend their annual convention and answer questions. Getty had a position on provincial-municipal relationships but it was not coherent. In an address to the Alberta Association of Municipal Districts and Counties convention, he announced that he was committed to funding municipalities with as few conditions as possible. Shortly thereafter he announced that one level of government should not impose its views on another:

It's the very argument that we have with the federal government, in which the federal government, we've argued, should not, in flowing funds into Alberta, then impose conditions out of Ottawa on the province. Now the argument stands up in the next step: that the province should not impose conditions on municipalities. They are elected. They are representatives of their constituents. If they are doing things that are wrong, their constituents will change it.[33]

Getty was thus committed to local autonomy and "no string" grants but his immediate problem was a weak economy. With operating grants to municipalities, schools and hospitals taking more than 40 per cent of the provincial budget, Getty targeted them for trimming. However, after the Grant Structures Review Committee recommended that municipal unconditional grants should, at a minimum, reflect the annual increase in the consumer price index, unconditional grants were budgeted for a four per cent increase for 1986-87.[34] To honor his public commitments, Getty created the Alberta Municipal Partnership In Local Employment (AMPLE) initiative, an unconditional grant program for municipal job creation and infrastructure rebuilding. Trumpeted as a $500 million grant to municipalities over eight years, $22 million was budgeted for 1987.[35] But in January 1987, municipal councils were devastated when they were informed that basic operating grants for municipalities, hospitals and educational institutions would be reduced by three per cent for 1987-88. Municipal officials criticized such cuts and called for provincial-municipal revenue-sharing. The government announced that 1988 funding for AMPLE grants would be raised to $57.5 million.

In 1988, the government announced a new Alberta Partnership Transfer (APT) program which would amalgamate the Municipal Assistance Grant (the principal unconditional grant for municipalities), the Municipal Police Assistance Grant and the Public Transit Operating Grant, all of which would be rolled into a single cheque and given to a municipality which could then use the money for any purpose. However, the Minister of Municipal Affairs, Dennis Anderson, was quick to point out that "we will continue to identify on the cheque and on the cheque stub the various components which will make up that one grant—in doing so, underlining the priorities of this government . . . ."[36] Several months later Anderson "toyed with" a City of Calgary task force recommending revenue sharing by saying that he was ready to discuss the concept. But he argued that the the city should consider the ramifications of linking its provincial funding to unstable oil prices.

In 1988 the municipalities were disappointed with the province's grants. But this concern was counterbalanced by Getty's position that municipalities should have more discretion in spending and budget making. The importance of Getty's policies to municipalities is shown in Table 7.3 where the percentage of funds allocated for unconditional grants nearly doubled between 1987 and 1988.[37]

Table 7.4 shows the amount of unconditional and selected conditional grants received by municipalities between 1981 and 1989. It illustrates

a provincial fiscal policy which complicated the financial plight of municipalities and made municipal planning difficult. Column I shows the
amount of unconditional provincial grants disbursed to the municipalities in the 1980s. It shows how in the early 1980s the unconditional grant
consistently increased until 1983-84 when it began to fluctuate and hence
cause problems for municipal planning. Unconditional grants are particularly important for municipalities because they allow the cities to
plan and implement unique projects for which no allowance is made
under normal provincial guidelines. Using 1980-81 as the base year and
computing the "real" dollar amounts adjusting for the price index, Table
7.4 shows how in some years (82-83, 83-84, 84-85, 85-86, 88-89) the grant
exceeded inflation but in others (81-82, 86-87, 87-88) it lagged. With
unconditional grants fluctuating from year to year, planning was limited
to a one-year horizon.

The data in Table 7.4 permit a comparison between the government's
treatment of unconditional and conditional grant programs. There are
wide variations in the funding of the conditional grant areas. Column
II shows that provincial funding for the Family and Community Support Services (FCSS) program fluctuated by as much as 30 per cent from
one year to the next. It was difficult for municipal administrators to
develop plans—they also had to contend with grants which contained
no allowance for inflation. Using the formula noted above to calculate
the "real" dollar value of the FCSS grant shows how the grant annually
trailed inflation. As an example, when the grant is adjusted for inflation
for the 1988-89 year, municipalities should have received $43 million
not $29.7 million. An examination of urban municipality transportation
grants in column III and rural transportation grants in column IV shows
inconsistency in funding from year to year. Although there were fluctu-
ations in funding for the three years after 1980-81, the annual grant for
the period is higher in all three years than the adjusted inflation figure.
After 1984, cities annually endured grants that were much less than the
inflation adjusted figure. Particularly dramatic is the disparity between
the government's grant of $122.8 million in 1988-89 and the inflation
adjusted figure of $197 million. Rural municipalities did somewhat bet-
ter than urban ones in both 1985-86 and 1986-87 when their grants were
higher than the inflation figure. Moreover, even when grants were lower
than the inflation adjusted figures, the differences were modest. In
1987-88, the government's grant was $28.9 million while the inflation
adjusted figure was $30 million.

TABLE 7.4   Dollar Amounts of Provincial Unconditional and Selected
Conditional Grants To Municipalities by Year (thousands of dollars)

Year	I Unconditional Assistance (000)	II Family Community Social Services (000)	III Urban Transport (000)	IV County, M.D. Transport (000)	V Library (000)	VI 1981 prices index* (000)
80/81	72389	29045	133161	20954	6579	100.0
81/82	78908	18341	155508	33970	7692	112.0
82/83	107568	22870	210054	35168	9387	120.6
83/84	91364	22869	165678	30407	9731	123.9
84/85	95441	20155	149455	25424	9806	127.9
85/86	97444	24804	153121	29696	10545	132.1
86/87	101362	26282	144524	34129	12126	137.4
87/88	98507	29727	169871	28899	10953	143.1
88/89	112772	31554	122808	27789	10531	148.2

Alberta Public Accounts,1981-1989.
*price index is based on government expenditure for goods and services.
Alberta Economic Accounts, 1988.

When the Alberta economy collapsed in the early 1980s, the province's municipalities suffered more than the provincial government. The province could resort to deficit financing but the municipalities had to balance their accounts each year. While the province had access to income tax revenue, a municipality's primary revenue source was the property tax. More importantly, the province had a broader range of policy options at its disposal. The Progressive Conservatives decided to cut back on grants but to make the policy more palatable the proportion of unconditional grants was increased. Although Premier Getty favours unconditional grants and greater municipal autonomy, it is unclear what the future holds. Both the Liberals and the New Democrats have criticized the Conservatives for refusing to allocate a portion of resource revenues for municipal purposes. But it is unclear whether either opposition party will give the municipalities greater financial autonomy if they win power.

Party Politics and Provincial-Municipal Relations

Alberta politics continue to stress the virtues of nonpartisan local government. Nonpartisanship is still thought to lead to the election of representatives committed to the "public interest" not to narrow, partisan interests. Civic nonpartisanship is rooted in the American municipal reform movement and in the anti-party philosophy of the United Farmers of Alberta and Social Credit parties. Eventually the debate between the proponents of party government and nonpartisan reformers embraced the issue of partisanship's effect on intergovernmental relations. Reformers held that provincial-municipal cooperation suffered when a province and a municipality were governed by political parties of different stripes.

Alberta reformers were determined to prevent the emergence of municipal party politics, although in a few communities a militant labour movement counter-balanced the nonpartisan movement. Early in the century, labour made a concerted effort to capture councils in Edmonton and Calgary where established provincial parties occasionally advanced municipal candidates. However, in Edmonton, Calgary, and Lethbridge, "quasi-parties" (often called associations) were common. They were spawned by a business community fearful of labour's power and determined to instill an ethos of business boosterism at city hall.

The citizenry now seems ambivalent about municipal party politics. A 1977 survey of political attitudes in a Calgary's ward found that only 38 per cent of the respondents agreed with "locally-based political parties contesting local elections." However, in responding to questions about the advantages and disadvantages of party politics most Calgary respondents felt the advantages outweighed the drawbacks.[38] Despite these findings, the 1989 municipal elections yielded no party candidates in Calgary while one association ran candidates in Edmonton.

Linked with the call for nonpartisanship was a demand for at large electoral representation which would make it difficult for parties to organize campaigns. In the early twentieth century, urban parties were powerful because they were well organized at the neighborhood level with "ward heelers" ensuring that people in the neighborhood voted for the party and acting as intermediaries between the local electorate and the administrative and political system. The consequence was councils dominated by working class party members. With the elimination of ward based representation, local parties were undermined and working class council members were often replaced by businessmen and professionals.

With the adoption of at large representation, the business community came to control many councils. For Edmonton it was not until the late 1960s that serious consideration was given to a ward system and then it was only with the shrewd maneuvering by a liberal alderman that the issue was referred to the electorate. After 61.5 per cent of the electorate voted in favour of wards, the council devised four heterogeneous socio-economic strip wards running north to south with three councillors in each. With 65 per cent of the city's population living north of the North Saskatchewan River and 7 of 12 councillors living south of it, strip wards were the only way incumbent councillors could seek re-election in their home ward. The system generated ''safe'' seats for incumbents and disadvantaged working class areas. Middle class areas almost always have a higher voter turnout rate than working class ones. As a consequence, in a heterogeneous strip ward, the middle class almost always elected their candidates to council.

Year after year, Edmonton's council debated the restructuring of ward boundaries. Finally, in 1980 the number of wards was increased to six, each having two members. Even though council agreed the wards were large and cumbersome, the issue languished until 1986 when two council members called for additional reform. Although a 12 single member ward proposal was defeated in 1987, in 1989 council adjusted ward boundaries so their populations would be more equal.

In Calgary there was little concern about the electoral system until 1958 when a pro-business council decided to alter substantially the city's system of proportional representation and mate it with a ward system. Labour agreed to the change believing it would improve its fortunes. It miscalculated for in succeeding elections labour considered itself fortunate when it placed even one member on council. Ward representation was not again an issue until the early 1970s when it became entwined with a demand for greater citizen participation; the mayor established a Standing Policy Committee on Legislation and a Citizens' Open Government Study to determine how citizen input could be incorporated into policy-making. After both bodies recommended a system of 18 single-member wards, council compromised and adopted a system of 14 single member ones.[39]

Until the 1980s the provincial government was little involved in the continuing controversies about municipal representation. During the fracas over Edmonton's ward system the provincial government was unusually quiet, perhaps fearful that a position on municipal representation might raise questions about its own electoral apparatus. It was 1986 before the government became interested in the mechanics of municipal representation and then its concern was with school boards. With more than 50 candidates running at large for nine trustee positions on the Edmonton public school board, 20 per cent of voters for municipal candidates failed to vote for school trustees. For almost three years the Department of Education recommended that the public and separate school boards in Edmonton and Calgary adopt ward systems. Eventually ward representation was adopted by three boards. But it was bitterly opposed by the Edmonton Public School Board since most of its trustees resided in south Edmonton and would have had difficulty being reelected under a ward system. They maintained that a ward system should only be implemented after a plebiscite. Finally, in 1989 the Minister of Education announced that either the Edmonton trustees adopt a ward system or he would impose one. In a political move, the trustees left it up to the Minister and the Department of Education to devise the ward system. Even though the department's system was complicated and confusing, the creation of wards led to an increase in voting for school trustee positions.

Municipal Nonpartisanship and Provincial-Municipal Relations

Without a party system to structure political communication between the province and municipalities, ad hoc systems developed. Shortly after Social Credit's win in 1935, the party decided to run for elective office in the province's larger cities. But this experiment was short-lived. What evolved thereafter was a makeshift system of consultation which advantaged some municipalities and disadvantaged others. Close informal ties evolved between the government and municipal officials in rural Alberta. Representatives of both levels of government shared common political and social values. But the relationship between government members and city politicians was tenuous since they shared few values and were distrustful of one another. Eventually Social Credit realized that it was advantageous to have good relations with all of the province's municipalities. As a result, in the 1950s and 1960s, municipal politicians were often invited to make submissions to cabinet.

After Lougheed came to power the provincial-municipal consultation process was changed and given more structure. The municipal associations were invited to make annual submissions to one of the government's caucus committees. According to the government, this policy was adopted to emphasize the importance of private government members, to manage cabinet ministers' time better and to enable ministers to spend more time on policy formulation. As might be expected, the AUMA was unhappy with this change in policy and asked that it might be allowed to make its annual submission to the cabinet, not a caucus committee.

During the Lougheed years, mayors and council members who were members of opposition provincial parties openly criticized Conservative policies with apparent impunity. One can only surmise that Lougheed had informal political links throughout the province which were used to iron out provincial-municipal problems behind the scenes. After Laurence Decore, a high profile Liberal, was elected Edmonton's mayor in 1983 the Minister of Municipal Affairs said that ''I don't think the question of what his federal political leanings might be has any bearing on his ability to manage the affairs of city hall.''⁴⁰ All the while Conservative cabinet members from Edmonton and Calgary worked closely with city politicians and represented their cities in cabinet. An example of this was the role played by one of Lougheed's key lieutenants, Neil Crawford in the dispute between Alberta Government Telephones and Edmonton Telephones. It was rumored that Crawford, sympathetic to Edmonton Telephones, argued the city's case before cabinet.

Some municipal officials wanted a more structured consultation process. In 1985, the Provincial-Municipal Grant Structure Review Committee released its report which recommended that among other things ''the government develop a mechanism for the coordination of its programs and policies affecting municipalities'' and ''the associations of elected and appointed municipal officials devise a mechanism which would have the mandate to act as a single point of contact for the province to receive municipal input.''⁴¹ Guided by the Grant Structure Committee's recommendation, a Municipal Affairs Caucus Committee was established. The Department of Municipal Affairs also began consulting with the municipal associations on proposed legislation before it was introduced in the legislature.

Premier Getty's relationship with the municipalities has been fractious. Shortly before the Tory's leadership convention in 1985, the party's three leading contenders, Don Getty, Ron Ghitter and Julian Koziak, were invited to participate in the AUMA's annual ''Bear Pit'' session with its sharp question and answer format. Evidently fearing he would be bested by Koziak, the Minister of Municipal Affairs, Getty first equivocated on the invitation and then declined. Many of the AUMA's 1100 delegates were angered by Getty's response.

When Getty took office, the provincial economy and the government's fiscal position were deteriorating. Moreover, Getty seemed uncertain about how to deal with Edmonton where the Tories lost ten seats in the 1986 election. Adding to Getty's quandary was the fact that the city's popular mayor, Laurence Decore, a Liberal, continued to draw political blood with deft jabs at the premier and his programs. Within a short time after taking office, Edmonton Telephones won the "telephone toll war" with Alberta Government Telephones giving the city utility an equitable share of long distance phone revenue. And despite the province's objections, Edmonton Power, the city's other utility, continued to expand its Genessee Power project.

In 1987, when Decore was considering running for the provincial Liberal leadership, relations between he and Getty deteriorated. Decore blamed the Tories for doing little to alleviate the city's high unemployment rate. Decore later accused Edmonton's four Tory MLAs, including Getty, of failing to represent their constituents. Getty lashed back; "We're doing a lot for Edmonton—we're doing a hell of a lot more than city council . . . with the mayor running about the province, the Edmonton caucus really has to represent the city and we are." Decore also criticized the Tory job creation schemes. Again an angry Getty attacked Decore's credibility claiming that his budget had 20 projects targeting $425 million for Edmonton.[42]

By the fall of 1988 Getty was determined to avenge Decore's slights and criticisms. When a press conference was called to announce the relocation of Edmonton's downtown rail yards and an expansion of the Grant MacEwan campus on the vacated lands, only representatives from CN Rail and the community college were present; Decore learned of the impending announcement only hours before. Less than a month later Decore resigned to become the provincial Liberal leader. Council appointed Terry Cavanagh, one of its own members and a Tory, to serve out the mayor's term. In one of his first pronouncements, Cavanagh criticized Decore's relations with the provincial government and, in a slip of the tongue, said the premier's quarrel with Decore had been detrimental to the city's interests.

Edmonton was not the only municipality to suffer the Tories' wrath. In early 1989, the cabinet decided to hold the Western Premiers Con-

ference in Edson on May 25th and 26th. However, with Getty's loss of
his Edmonton seat and the necessity of running a by-election, the conference was postponed. After Edson's New Democrat MLA, Jerry Doyle,
attempted to embarrass the premier during the by-election campaign by
making the conference postponement an issue, the conference was
shifted to Camrose. When Federal and Intergovernmental Affairs Minister
James Horsman was queried about the move, he said that Doyle "brought
it on himself." When asked if the decision was politically motivated
Horsman said, "that's apparent, isn't it?"[43]

Despite these problems, many officials in the provincial and municipal
governments were committed to furthering better relations between the
two levels of government. In 1986 Laurence Decore, in a speech before
the Edmonton Chamber of Commerce, praised Getty for his commitment to open government and recommended that a cabinet level department of city and urban affairs be established.[44] Although the government
did not respond to Decore's suggestion, the Department of Municipal
Affairs was committed to improving provincial-municipal relations and
refining the consultation process between the government and the
municipal associations. When Municipal Affairs began consulting with
the associations it found there was not a single association which
represented the views of all of the province's municipalities. Rather each
association represented a special clientele. The organizations were at odds
with one another. As a consequence, the department received conflicting advice. To remedy this problem, the department proposed that the
associations create an umbrella organization to iron out association differences and to formulate comprehensive proposals. The umbrella group
would meet annually with the Provincial-Municipal Consultation Committee whose membership comprised the premier, the minister of
Municipal Affairs, the Municipal Affairs' caucus committee and other
ministers.

Although the Municipal Affairs proposal was shelved, several of its
components were incorporated into the Provincial-Municipal Premier's
Council which was established in September 1987. Designed to formal-
ize the consultation process between the government and the municipalities, the council comprised the premier, the minister of Municipal
Affairs, four other members, three representatives from the AUMA, three
representatives from the AAMD&C, and one representative from the
Improvement District Association of Alberta. The council has met
irregularly.[45]

With the new council meeting only sporadically, Edmonton alderman Ron Hayter argued that something else needed to be done to improve Edmonton's poor relationship with the province. Decore had resigned as mayor and Cavanagh, a staunch Conservative, was sitting in his chair. But the intergovernmental relations remained unfavourable. In March 1989 Hayter proposed the government create a Tri-Party Edmonton Urban Committee composed of Conservative, Liberal and New Democrat MLAs from the Edmonton region who would consult with City of Edmonton representatives four times a year. After the government dismissed the proposal, MLA Nancy Betkowski explained that "the most effective ongoing and consultative decision-making mechanism would be on a government to government basis." She wrote that it was the "intention of the Edmonton Area Government Caucus to meet on a regular basis with Edmonton City Council to review particular issues between our two governments."[46] Little was heard of these meetings when Terry Cavanagh was mayor although he made much of his Tory connections and his contacts with influential government representatives. Ironically, it was after Jan Reimer, a prominent New Democrat, won the Edmonton mayoralty race in October 1989 that it was reported "council and the four Edmonton-area MLAs emerged from a meeting . . . with smiles and lots of encouraging words about their prospects for working together." They planned to have regularly scheduled meetings.[47]

The Future and Provincial-Municipal Relations

A decade of continuous economic hardship and fiscal restraint for Alberta's municipalities may be ending. There has been some diversification of the economy with the development of a pulp and paper industry, and provincial resource royalties have improved marginally. Municipalities which were economically devastated have seen their revenues stabilize. They are again considering the expansion of some facilities and services, but the future remains very uncertain.

The Conservative government's stance on municipal autonomy and policy making is important. A continued liberalization of municipal grant programs with fewer controls over how funds are spent will allow the Getty government to have good relationships with the municipalities. But if the municipal grants are essentially unconditional, the government will lose a major policy lever over the municipalities.

Equally important is whether Getty has learned from his past dealings with municipal politicians. Several reasons account for the Conservative's electoral losses in Edmonton in 1986 and 1989. But Getty's vendetta with Laurence Decore did little to enhance his image and probably lost him votes. A factor in the Tory's declining political fortune is the inability of Getty's government to work with municipal politicians of different political stripes. In the short run, Getty is able to penalize dissenting municipalities and politicians. Individuals can be snubbed and some grants can be reduced or withheld. But in the long run the two levels of government are interdependent. In an urbanized province, serious political parties need urban electoral support. A party will probably fail if it alienates the electorate by castigating and punishing municipal political leaders. Don Getty's basic political instinct in giving municipalities more discretion in spending and policy may shore up the Conservatives eroding political support. But this support may be lost unless he can deal with municipal politicians who do not embrace all his ideas.

After more than twenty years in office, support for the Progressive Conservatives has declined. Unless the opposition stumbles badly, the governing party will probably change soon. Currently neither the Liberals nor the New Democrats have formulated coherent municipal policies. But such policy coherence may not be necessary since the Progressive Conservatives have governed since 1971 without having formulated a comprehensive plan for provincial-municipal relations.

NOTES

1. Letter from Roy Farran to Jack Masson, 3 December 1990.
2. Alberta, Legislative Assembly, *Debates*, 8 March 1978. Hereafter cited as *Debates*, date, page.
3. The three were Horner, Dowling and Copithorne.
4. Letter from Roy Farran to Jack Masson, 3 December 1990.
5. *Debates*, 23 April 1981, pp. 303-4.
6. Letter from Roy Farran to Jack Masson, 3 December 1990.
7. Premier Peter Lougheed, "Alberta's Industrial Strategy," speech before the Calgary Chamber of Commerce, 6 September 1974.
8. *Edmonton Journal*, 10 November 1974.
9. It particularly rankled Calgary's MLAs that some of the provincial departments in Edmonton were not being decentralized and relocated in Calgary.

10. See Lionel D. Feldman and Katherine A. Graham, "Intergovernmental Relations and Urban Growth: A Canadian View," in *Politics and Government of Urban Canada*, 4th ed., by Lionel D. Feldman, ed. (Toronto: Methuen, 1981), pp. 204-10.

11. In 1988 Getty gave a new twist to decentralization when he responded to a question on declining farm population by saying that "our whole program of decentralization was a manifestation of the government's desire to strengthen the entire agricultural community." *Debates*, 14 April 1988, p. 429.

12. David G. Bettison, John Kenward and Larrie Taylor, *Urban Affairs in Alberta* (Edmonton: Human Resources Research Council of Alberta, 1975), pp. 69-117.

13. Province of Alberta, *Report of the Royal Commission on the Metropolitan Development of Calgary and Edmonton* (Edmonton: January 1956), iv, v.

14. Peter Smith, "Community Aspirations, Territorial Justice and the Metropolitan Form of Edmonton and Calgary," in *Social Geography of Canada*, J. Wreford Watson, ed. (Edinburgh: North British Publishing, 1988), p. 189.

15. Eric Hanson, *The Potential Unification of the Edmonton Metropolitan Area* (City of Edmonton, 1968), p. xii.

16. For a detailed discussion of the 1989 annexation see E.C. Brown, R.M. Miller and B.D. Simpkins, "The City of Calgary's Comprehensive Annexation," *Alberta and Northwest Territories Journal of Planning Practices* 8 (Winter, 1989): 39-78.

17. *Mainstream* (Edmonton), 18 April 1979.

18. *Edmonton Journal*, 30 January 1983.

19. *Edmonton Journal*, 8 March 1983.

20. *Edmonton Journal*, 17 October 1985.

21. An exception was Mayor William Hawrelak who, just before he died in November 1975, was close to negotiating an expansion agreement with the County of Parkland and the Municipal District of Sturgeon.

22. Letter from Roy Farran to Jack Masson 3 December 1990.

23. T.J. Plunkett and J. Lightbody, "Tribunals, Politics, and the Public Interest," *Canadian Public Policy* 8 (Spring, 1982): 207-21.

24. *Debates*, 28 March 1972, pp. 19-24.

25. Province of Alberta, *Task Force on Provincial Municipal Fiscal Arrangements in Alberta* (Edmonton: Queen's Printer, 1972).

26. Ibid., p. 10.

27. Statistics Canada, *Local Government Finance* Catalogue, pp. 68-204.

28. M.L. McMillan and R.H.M. Plain, *The Reform of Municipal-Provincial Fiscal Relationships* (Edmonton: Alberta Urban Municipalities Association, 1979), pp. VI-8-9.

29. Alberta Provincial Municipal Finance Council, *Report of the Provincial-Municipal Finance Council on the Responsibilities and Financing of Local Government in Alberta* (Edmonton: Department of Municipal Affairs, pp. 190-217.

30. *Debates*, 14 October 1981, p. 1077.

31. *Debates*, 16 October 1981, p. 1129.

32. *Municipal Counsellor* (November/December, 1984), p. 13. For details see *Municipal Counsellor* (May/June, 1988), p. 13.

33. *Debates*, 4 May 1988, p. 814.

34. With the 1984 change in the grant formula, 20 municipalities had their grants reduced from the previous year's level, 102 municipalities had their grants frozen and 48 municipalities had increases which were less than the consumer price index.

35. It was a financial sleight of hand which enabled the provincial government to develop its AMPLE program. In 1981 and 1982 the Alberta Municipal Financing Corporation (AMFC) borrowed funds at extremely high rates which it turned around and loaned to municipalities at nine per cent. Much of this municipal borrowing was amortized over 20 to 25 years. In September 1986 the AMFC began refinancing over a two year period some $1.15 billion of debt at lower rates and for five to seven year periods. As Dennis Anderson, Minister of Municipal Affairs, explained, ''This series of AMFC transactions . . . has resulted in savings to the Municipal Debenture Interest Rebate Program, because it is now providing subsidy dollars up to the 12.5 percent rate instead of the rates upward of 17 percent which reigned in earlier years. These are the savings which the government is passing on to municipalities through the AMPLE program.'' *Municipal Counsellor* 34 (January/February, 1989), p. i.

36. *Debates*, 26 April 1988, p. 661.

37. Another important source of funds for municipalities are grants-in-lieu of taxes which they receive from the provincial and federal governments. In 1988 cities received $62,490,743 (2.0 percent of total revenue); towns received $12,565,288 (3.9 percent of total revenue); villages received $1,243,055 (3.2 percent of total revenue).

38. Roger Gibbins, S. Drabek, M.O. Dickerson, and J.T. Woods, ''Attitudinal and Socio-Democratic Determinants of Receptivity to Civic Partisanship,'' paper presented at the annual meeting of the Canadian Political Science Association, University of Western Ontario, London, June, 1978, p. 11.

39. See Stan Drabek, ''The Calgary Ward System,'' unpublished paper prepared for the City of Vancouver Electoral Reform Commission, Calgary, undated.

40. *Edmonton Journal*, 19 October 1983.

41. Government of Alberta, *Grant Structures Review Committee Final Report* (Edmonton: December, 1985), p. i. In 1984 the government proposed that

a Municipal Affairs Caucus Committee be established to serve as one of the primary links between the province and the municipalities with a membership to be composed of caucus members who earlier had served as municipal elected officials.

42. *Edmonton Journal*, 30 March 1988.
43. *Edmonton Journal*, 27 May 1989.
44. *Edmonton Sun*, 16 January 1986.
45. Although the council has not been active, municipal representatives meet with ministers, informally on an on-going basis, on issues affecting them. Also, the tradition continues of Edmonton and Calgary mayors occasionally meeting with the premier.
46. MLA Nancy J. Betkowski, letter to Jack Masson, 6 November 1989.
47. *Edmonton Journal*, 3 November 1989.

8

The Mass Media
and Modern Alberta Politics

*Denise Savage-Hughes
and David Taras*

One of the enduring images of Alberta politics is that of journalists as
the compliant servants of the party in power.[1] Strong and autocratic premiers, the dominance of single parties throughout Alberta's history, and
a public unwilling to tolerate critical assessments of those in power have
produced, it is argued, "booster" journalism. This image stems largely
from Peter Lougheed's 14 years in power—from 1971 to 1985—when
"King Peter," as he was referred to in some circles, seemed to enjoy
unwavering public confidence and the accolades of the media. Hard hit-
ting investigative reporting, combative editorials and the intense questioning and scrutiny of politicians that had become the trademarks of
post-Vietnam and post-Watergate journalism appeared to be absent in
the coverage of Alberta politics. Alberta's political life thus seemed
strangely out of step with attitudes and practices that had become commonplace almost everywhere else in North America.

The image of the press gallery "on bended knee" to the government
is, however, a myth. The relationship between premiers and journalists
has been as fierce, turbulent and antagonistic as anywhere else in the
country. The battle to control the agenda that generally characterizes
the struggle between political leaders and journalists has also played a
significant role in Alberta's politics. The myth of a subservient press is
debunked in this chapter by describing the highly charged nature of
government-press relations under the Liberal, United Farmers of Alberta
(UFA) and Social Credit governments, by analyzing Peter Lougheed's
media strategy and how his actions were often reported critically by the
press, and by evaluating Don Getty's embattled relationship with the

Edmonton press gallery. Our theme is that almost all premiers have had to endure a "media crisis" at least once during their terms of office, a crisis in which the media and not the premiers dictated the agenda. All have suffered the stings of media criticism and have mounted media management campaigns of varying effectiveness.

While Canadian political scientists tend to downplay the significance of the mass media as instruments of power, political leaders have long realized that media coverage can be the daily bread of political survival. The prime ministerships of John Diefenbaker, Joe Clark and John Turner were drastically affected, some might say crippled, by the intensity of negative coverage that their performances and policies received. One of the essential realities of politics is that politicians need to use the mass media in order to get their messages through to the public. Their policies and ideas, indeed the images they wish to convey, must pass through a journalistic filter, a gatekeeping and screening process over which they have little control. Journalists have the power to determine which issues, people and events are important enough to be covered; to decide for how long and in what context politicians will appear or be quoted on television, radio or in the newspapers; and to interpret and question the actions of political leaders. For their part, politicians have developed elaborate media management strategies to gain publicity, to fend it off, and to ensure that media managers and journalists put the best "spin" on the events being reported. Political survival largely depends on winning the media war.[2]

Journalists also have a great deal at stake in their relations with politicians. Political reporting is the cornerstone of most news organizations. Politics receives prominent coverage and often consumes a lion's share of time and space. The careers and reputations of reporters can be made or broken in the hot-house atmosphere of political reporting. Much depends on whether they can cultivate important sources, get interviews, understand and explain the nuances of politics, and gain a following among peers and, more importantly, among readers or viewers. Journalism is a highly competitive profession where pecking orders both within news organizations and in journalism generally are quickly established.

The relationship between politicians and journalists is characterized by conflict and symbiosis.[3] Conflict is endemic because interests are fundamentally at odds. Political leaders wish to convey the impression that the ship of state or their parties are sailing smoothly and that everything is on a steady course. Journalists search for conflict, sensationalism and scandal and know that bad news for politicians often makes good stories for them. Political leaders, or at least those in office, wish to avoid controversy, while journalists thrive on it. Yet even while there is a basic clash in objectives, some cooperation is essential. Politicians need access to the media and reporters need access to newsmakers. The need to cooperate softens the collision of interests. The late Ithiel de Sola Pool once wrote that the "relationship of reporter and politician resembles a bad marriage. They cannot live without each other, nor can they live without hostility."[4] Gary Orren argues that the relationship alternates between "stroking" and "poking."[5] Politicians and journalists in Alberta play by the same rules, use the same strategies of coercion and manipulation, and fight the same battles that politicians and journalists do in other jurisdictions. If anything, the game has been played with greater intensity in Alberta than elsewhere.

From Scandal to Repression: The Party Press in Alberta

Alberta's early history coincided with the era of the party press when newspapers had close ties with political parties and openly proclaimed their partisan allegiance. No clear dividing line was drawn between journalism and politics. Frank Oliver, Prime Minister Wilfrid Laurier's powerful Minister of the Interior from 1905 to 1911, was also the publisher and editor of the *Edmonton Bulletin*.[6] W.A. Buchanan, who founded the *Lethbridge Herald*, was a member of A.C. Rutherford's government and later a Liberal member of Parliament in Ottawa. During the 1920s R.B. Bennett and Senator James Lougheed, Peter Lougheed's grandfather, bought a 49 per cent interest in *The Albertan* in an attempt to wrest control for the Conservatives of the province's leading Liberal newspaper. After much manoeuvering their attempt to gain control failed. *The Albertan*, along with radio station CJCJ, was eventually purchased by Social Credit supporters and the two became the official voices of Aberhart's government; the masthead of *The Albertan* read "A publicly owned newspaper supporting Social Credit principles." During the heyday of the party press, both the *Calgary Herald* and the *Edmonton Journal* were staunch supporters of the Conservative party, reflecting the interests of the province's oil and ranching communities. The Conservative leanings of the two papers remained evident even after they were taken over by the giant Southam newspaper chain.

The brash headlines, sensational reporting, and unbridled partisanship of the party press set the tone for much of Alberta's early history. In fact, the Conservative *Calgary Herald* had a role in breaking the Great Waterways Scandal of 1910 which led to the resignation of Liberal Premier A.C. Rutherford. The paper publicized allegations that prominent Liberals benefited from the sale of bonds that had been issued to finance railway construction. The *Calgary Herald* and the *Edmonton Journal* were also instrumental in the demise of the UFA government. They had been harsh critics of the decision by the United Farmers of Alberta to run as a political party and then became strong opponents of the UFA government. The ferocity of their opposition became evident in the extensive coverage, often four pages a day, given to a sexual misconduct suit brought against Premier John Brownlee by one of his female assistants. A divorce case involving the Minister of Public Works, O.L. McPherson, was also turned into a cause celebre by the newspapers. The controversies that resulted from this sensational reporting did irreparable damage to the UFA government, which was subsequently defeated in 1935.

Although William Aberhart was to some degree propelled to prominence and then power by his popular Bible Institute broadcasts on CFCN, which began in 1925, he showed little sophistication in dealing with journalists.[7] When the *Calgary Herald* ridiculed Social Credit monetary theories and gave cartoonist Stewart Cameron free reign to mock Aberhart (one cartoon depicted Aberhart as a would-be Hitler with his arm raised in a Nazi salute), Aberhart reacted with an iron fist. Aberhart told his radio listeners to cancel their subscriptions, and cartoonist Cameron was forced on at least one occasion to use the fire escape to evade, as he went to and from the *Herald* offices, those who had threatened him.

After Aberhart came to power, both the *Herald* and the *Edmonton Journal* attempted to establish friendlier relations. John Irmie, the *Journal's* publisher, allowed Aberhart to file his own front page stories while attending a dominion-provincial conference in Ottawa. The "entente cordiale," however, quickly broke down. For a time the Premier held daily press conferences and made himself available to be interviewed, but when these efforts failed to produce positive coverage his mood blackened. Reporters from newspapers that Aberhart considered hostile were barred from his news conferences. By 1936 Aberhart advocated licensing as a means of controlling what he called the "mad dog operations" of newspapers. In his broadcasts, he railed against the press as agents of "privilege, lawlessness and gangsterism."[8] *Saturday Night* magazine was banned from the province after it published a picture of Aberhart that he thought was unflattering. Attempts were also made to intimidate reporters. Gallery members believed that their phones were tapped, and one reporter, Fred Kennedy of the *Herald*, thought that his hotel room had been broken into. The Social Credit party also moved directly into the media business by buying *The Albertan* and radio station CJCJ.

In September 1937, Aberhart took draconian action. He introduced the Accurate News and Information Act whose object was to bring the press "under the unchallengeable control of the province."[9] Newspapers were to be licensed; they would be required to publish articles explaining Social Credit policies, and the names of sources would have to be revealed. Aberhart's actions met strong resistance from the province's journalists. *The Albertan* declared its independence from the government and the *Calgary Herald*, the *Edmonton Journal*, and a number of smaller newspapers were awarded a Pulitzer prize for their unrelenting campaign against the legislation. Ultimately the Lieutenant-Governor reserved the bill and it was declared *ultra vires* by the Supreme Court of Canada.

Relations with the press were far more congenial under Aberhart's long-serving successor, Ernest Manning. Although he was premier for close to 25 years, Manning was an intensely private man who rarely made public appearances. Nonetheless, his rigid conservatism, a personal following based on his religious radio broadcasts, and careful management of the public purse gave him wide appeal. The press had little controversy to report from a government that had come to epitomize business as usual.

The Reign of Peter Lougheed:
The King and His Not So Friendly Court

When Peter Lougheed entered provincial politics in 1965 as leader of the moribund Progressive Conservatives, television had become the main vehicle for reaching and galvanizing the public. Although he was at first awkward on television, Lougheed realized that mastering the new medium was essential to political success. With the help of station owner Gordon Love, Lougheed practiced his television delivery during off hours at the studios of CFCN. According to Allan Hustak, it was there that the Conservative leader learned "how to relax in a studio with technicians around, how to shift naturally from camera to camera, how to modulate his voice for the right measure of sincerity, and how to pace his comments to the clock."[10] Lougheed spent heavily on TV advertising during the 1971 election that brought him to power; approximately $80,000 out of a total campaign budget of $120,000 went to buy television ads.[11] Harry Strom, who had taken over the helm from Manning in 1968, was "cold, frowning . . . and unsure" of himself on television. He was no match for the smooth John F. Kennedy style practiced and cultivated by Lougheed.[12] As Howard and Tamara Palmer explain: "It was impossible for Strom to compete as a television personality with a 'big city' lawyer, because rural people had learned through the mass media to expect leaders who are articulate and dynamic."[13]

Lougheed emerged on the political stage when Alberta was experiencing profound social and economic changes. The times were ripe for someone with his slick managerial approach. Indeed, Lougheed came to symbolize the transformation from a predominantly rural to a largely urban society. He also became premier just before the world oil price quadrupled, bringing windfall profits to producers, enriching the province's treasury beyond what anyone had previously imagined, and pitting Alberta against Ottawa in jurisdictional battles over energy. Lougheed was premier during the best of times, and he skillfully spent the windfalls and linked the boom with Tory policies.

Lougheed's political style and relations with the media were carefully managed and choreographed. He was determined to control the agenda, to maintain the tactical advantage, and to avoid being stampeded into action because of adverse publicity or criticism. As Lougheed put it:

> We had a theme in our government and we were so determined that the media will not set the agenda . . . . The media would say this should be the priorities the government has in the next session; pontifications from the *Edmonton Journal* editorial board. I wouldn't pay any attention to that, we would set our own priorities and our own time table . . . . We wouldn't let them push us into a different time table, particularly on what's important . . . . We had to be stubborn and determined to do it . . . . You have to decide what your game plan is and what your program is and then you read the media.

As part of this strategy, Lougheed tightly controlled the timing and flow of government information, and the access given to journalists.

Lougheed's firm grip over his cabinet prevented leaks, and the release of information was centralized through the public affairs bureau that was responsible for all government communication. According to Bill Sass, who reported for the *Edmonton Journal*, "He controlled the flow of information, he controlled the ministers to the point that when a federal budget is read we would literally run and spread out with ten reporters and try to grab individual ministers within minutes of that budget, because ten minutes later they would all tell you the same thing." Most government leaders find it virtually impossible to prevent leaks by cabinet ministers or officials who want to establish their own network with reporters, and to have their version of events or points of view echoed in the media. Indeed, John F. Kennedy once commented that "the Ship of State is the only ship that leaks at the top."[14] Under Lougheed, however, journalists complained about excessive secrecy and about their inability to obtain even basic information. When information was made available it usually came as part of a campaign orchestrated to get out a particular message.

Access to Lougheed was one of the enticements used to reward journalists who were considered favourable to the government. Those who were seen as hostile faced the threat of being punished by being denied access. Journalists who enjoyed access to Lougheed and to ministers and officials had a clear advantage over their rivals; they could cultivate important sources, get leads, and break stories. In the view of Ken Colby, a national parliamentary reporter for CBC-TV during the 1970s, "manipulation of the media really was that simple, friends and enemies, access or not." Colby remembers being denied access, when he was first sent from Ottawa to do a story on the oil industry, because "the CBC was not in the government's good books." The resulting story apparently satisfied Lougheed because Colby was given access after that. According to Gordon Jaremko of the *Calgary Herald*, new reporters who requested an interview with the premier were "checked out" to see whether they were likely to be friendly to the government. Geoff White, a former *Herald* reporter, believes that access was used principally to control the agenda; it was granted sparingly and only when the premier had a specific message he wanted to deliver.

Duncan Thorne of the *Edmonton Journal* remembers being "frozen out" after he wrote an article that criticized Lougheed for not giving enough details about a planned trip to San Francisco; "I was totally frozen out, he wouldn't look at me. I think he did sort of answer my question but the iciness was incredible. He decided that I wasn't worth cultivating any further."

Lougheed and his former press secretaries insist that they treated all gallery members equally. As Lougheed explained his dilemma: "If the word gets around that a journalist is getting an inside track then they get ostracized from the others, so you have got to be pretty even handed, even if it comes to someone you don't like or don't trust." Many of the journalists interviewed for this study believe that treatment was generally even-handed.

Lougheed always attempted to meet journalists under conditions he could control. He preferred the orderliness of news conferences to the pushing and shoving of scrums. Lougheed explained his logic as follows:

> I could do much better at news conferences because I was more in control . . . . In a news conference the person being interviewed is in a much bigger advantage. He's usually sitting down. He's under a controlled environment. His press secretary is acknowledging various people to speak to him . . . . He's able to concentrate on a question and an answer. He can finish that answer before he's interrupted and then go on to the next question. The mistakes that I made and I see often made, I made in a scrum because a question will come out of your left ear and you're not psychologically set for it and it throws you off balance.

Lougheed always came to news conferences well prepared and with a clear message to deliver. He would usually begin by reading a prepared statement, which served the dual purpose of setting the agenda and limiting the amount of time that remained available for questions. Attempts were sometimes made to plant questions with journalists, although one former director of communications denies that reporters were rewarded in any way. Geoff White remembers the "feel" of a Lougheed press conference:

> Questions were often a kind of charade because he often wouldn't answer the question directly. In answering the question he would always revert to his original theme. He repeated over and over throughout the press conference the one or two or three things he wanted people to hear . . . . He brushed aside the critical, scrutinizing role that we had to play; and did it quite effectively.

Ken Colby found that Lougheed's press conferences had a different
texture from the unbridled animosity and adversarial tone that often
characterized Pierre Trudeau's press conferences in Ottawa. The
atmosphere was largely one of cordiality, and Lougheed, while not loved,
had the gallery's grudging respect. As Don Braid described Lougheed's
performance, "Lougheed said exactly what he wanted to say—never
more, never less. He was well prepared. He was never surprised or startled by questions. He was masterful—the best I've ever seen. He was
able and imposing." Colby recalls that even when cornered, Lougheed
could manoeuvre through tough situations with considerable agility. As
Colby remembers: "Lougheed would be effusive in responding if asked
a question he wanted to answer. His response would scream for a hard
follow-up question but if a journalist looked like he was going to ask
a follow-up, Lougheed would move on to someone else before the question could be asked."

Lougheed was careful to avoid situations where his words could be
edited or slanted by reporters. His predilection was for live television
interviews that would run for a predetermined time. One show, "Conversation with the Premier," which ran on CFCN, gave the premier a
congenial setting for expressing his views without having his words lifted
out of context. With print journalists, Lougheed used various devices
to control the interview. Duncan Thorne recalled Lougheed's cleverness
in steering through potentially dangerous waters:

I remember one case where Don Braid and I were interviewing Lougheed at the *Journal*. Whenever we asked any question he didn't like
he would begin shuffling his papers, as if he was about to go. You'd
come in quickly with a very neutral question and he'd calm down.
It was an interesting tactic to keep you from asking anything objec-
tionable.

According to George Oake, Lougheed would not be swayed from his
agenda. As Oake explained, "When I was with Southam News he would
want to get a message out to the eastern papers so he would have you
in to get out that message. And then he was bored with the rest of the
interview because he wasn't going to tell you anything else."

Another Lougheed tactic was to bypass the gallery by dealing directly
with station owners, publishers, and editorial boards. He would have
off-the-record discussions designed to flatter and influence media

managers, to make them feel that they were privy to the government's secrets. Geoff White remembers how effective Lougheed could be in these situations:

> Quite often if the government was developing a complex policy position he wouldn't indicate it to the frontline legislative reporter. He would arrange a meeting with the editorial board of the *Edmonton Journal* and he would outline it there. There was a kind of psychological tactic there, he would have these meetings and the people who were in on them and knew they were not for attribution felt privileged to receive this inside information and quite often after these meetings the editorials would start to come out basically expressing the Lougheed position.

Although the journalists who were interviewed insisted that their stories were not influenced by management, reporters working in the catacombs at the Legislature may have felt uncomfortable knowing that their reporting and opinions might run counter to the consensus that was forming among their senior managers. At times, apprehensive reporters may have felt they had to look over their shoulders to see whether Lougheed was meeting with their superiors, and to determine what their bosses thought of the premier's policies. Their nervousness would have been exacerbated by the fact that Lougheed was quick to phone publishers or station managers to complain about stories that he felt had been unfair, or to explain how a reporter had misconstrued or misunderstood the government's actions.

The overwhelming popularity that the government enjoyed throughout much of its long mandate also conditioned media reporting. This was especially the case when it came to the mood and emotions that surrounded Alberta's energy wars with Ottawa. For much of his tenure in office, Lougheed successfully presented himself as the provincial David single-handedly fighting the federal Goliath. In these circumstances, criticizing Lougheed was often seen as tantamount to attacking Alberta. Lougheed characterized people as being either "doers" or "knockers." Critics were dismissed as "knockers," a viewpoint that seemed to be accepted by many Albertans. Sheila Pratt, formerly the legislative bureau chief for the *Calgary Herald* and now the city editor of the *Edmonton Journal*, describes the psychology that Lougheed had helped to foster:

There was a special culture in Alberta that he sort of built up and promoted, it was sort of like his election slogan; "doers and knockers." You're for him or against him. That becomes a very big factor in how the public perceives the media's reporting and the validity of reporting what you call good news or bad news stories. That's a really significant background to how he and the media interacted. The knockers were people who disagreed with them, so the whole idea of political debate and dissent was not really legitimized . . . . It was almost a kind of . . . loyalty test.

Another critical factor was that the opposition parties had been decapitated by the Conservative hurricane that all but swept the provincial elections in the 1970s. The legislative opposition was pitifully small. As a result, journalists had few opposition voices to turn to for alternative perspectives or for tough criticisms of Lougheed's policies. In the aftermath of the Conservative landslide in the 1979 election, Patrick O'Callaghan, the publisher of the *Edmonton Journal*, took the extraordinary step of writing to the premier to declare that henceforth the *Journal* would act as the official opposition. He then increased the number of *Journal* reporters in the gallery to seven to insure that "even the most minor press release" would come under scrutiny.

Lougheed's shrewd management of the media and the "with us or against us" atmosphere that he engendered were not enough, however, to prevent media crises. At various times Lougheed was caught in a swirl of media controversy, and towards the end of his career in particular his policies received a significant amount of critical coverage. It can be argued, in fact, that Lougheed lost control over the agenda during his last term in office; the agenda was set by the media. Lougheed's own assessment was that his relations with the media were turbulent and often painful. As he expressed it:

I don't think I did have positive relations on three counts. One was when I was very much under the gun involving airline tickets in 1978 and 1979. Secondly, I was always under a lot of criticism, steadily, that I was so called "inaccessible." Thirdly, I guess I was in the middle of the eye of the hurricane. You feel the criticism and you're sensitive to it, particularly if you feel it's unfair.

Don Braid believes that although Lougheed "didn't screw up very often, when he did, we attacked. You won't find any knee-walking sycophancy in our treatment of the airline ticket incident for instance."

Denise Savage-Hughes examined the *Calgary Herald*'s and *Edmonton Journal*'s coverage of Lougheed during his first and last terms in office.[15] Over 60 per cent of articles in the *Journal* and over 40 per cent in the *Herald* reported the premier in a positive manner during his first term in office—31 August 1971 to 27 March 1975. During this period, less than 15 per cent of *Journal* articles and 20 per cent of *Herald* articles were critical of Lougheed. But by Lougheed's last term—3 November 1982 to 27 June 1985—a sea change had occurred. The *Edmonton Journal* had become a persistent critic; almost 40 per cent of the sample contained articles that criticized Lougheed while only 31 per cent were supportive. The percentage of articles in the *Herald* that were critical of the premier rose from 18 per cent during his first term to 30 per cent during his last term.

An argument can be made that Lougheed's fortunes in the media battle-field were linked to the performance of the provincial economy. The rise in international oil prices that took place during Lougheed's first term in office brought an explosion in investment and employment, and gave the premier a strong reputation as an economic manager. Articles about the premier's handling of the economy were reported positively over 60 per cent of the time in the *Journal* and 55 per cent in the *Herald* during his first term in office. Less than 10 per cent of the articles in the two papers were critical of Lougheed's economic policies. Lougheed also received positive coverage when he was defending Alberta's interests in the province's energy battles with Ottawa. When the premier tackled national energy questions he received positive coverage almost 60 per cent of the time in the *Edmonton Journal* and in over 40 per cent of the *Calgary Herald* sample. Only 11 per cent of the *Journal*'s articles and 21 per cent of those in the *Herald* were critical of Lougheed.

But by 1982 boom had turned to bust, and Lougheed was no longer receiving high marks as an economic manager. Stories on the economy during Lougheed's last term in office resulted in negative reporting almost 40 per cent of the time. Only one quarter of the articles on Lougheed's handling of the economy that appeared in the sample from the *Edmonton Journal* were positive. In addition, the public's mood had soured. In September 1984, the "Prairie Napoleon," as Don Wanagas of the *Edmonton Sun* had once described Lougheed, received a chorus of ear-splitting boos when he appeared at centre ice during a hockey game in Edmonton.[16] That booing was echoed to some degree in the negative reporting that Lougheed received from the province's journalists.

Undoubtedly the coverage given Lougheed from 1971 to 1982 contradicts the thesis that Alberta's premiers have been confronted by a critical press. One can argue, however, that the Lougheed years were an aberration; there was unprecedented prosperity, meagre opposition in the Legislature, a perceived threat from Ottawa that allowed Lougheed to mobilize popular sentiment behind him, and a politician unusually skilled at promoting his agenda. But by Lougheed's last term in office relations with the media had normalized. The economy was in recession and some of Lougheed's well worn media management strategies had begun to wear thin. A critical adversarial relationship had again taken hold.

The Wounded Premier: Don Getty's Media War

Don Getty's relationship with the legislative gallery has been harsh and confrontational. While Getty enjoyed a brief honeymoon period with journalists after coming to power in 1986, the man, the times and the changing nature of the gallery made for a different chemistry than was the case under Lougheed. At first, Getty's sincere manner and his "good neighbour next door" friendliness were welcomed by reporters as a change from Lougheed's intimidating and hard driving approach.[17] Getty's espousal of basic values—what one journalist described as "God, football and family"—seemed to make him an Alberta version of Gerry Ford or Ronald Reagan—someone essentially likeable, and hence difficult to attack.[18] He was extremely open with and available to the gallery, sought out journalists to establish personal relationships, and allowed ministers the freedom to speak to reporters. As Don Wanagas remembers, Getty's first days in office contrasted dramatically with the Lougheed governments: "With Getty it was a night and day difference. He was very accessible at first. He would talk about anything at anytime. There were regular press conferences and impromptu scrums that were wide-ranging."

Before long, however, Getty found himself embroiled in a series of media crises. His response was to retreat behind high defensive walls. Part of the media problem was the man himself. Getty was awkward and ill at ease with reporters. He lacked Lougheed's self-assurance and panache and the former premier's intrinsic feel for media relations. He also resisted advice from advisors that he undergo media training, preferring the "real" Don Getty to a more packaged product. As one print journalist put it: "Getty freezes in the middle of the pack. Eighty percent of the reason that we don't have access is because he puts his foot in his mouth. They give him a couple of phrases which he'll repeat. He can't think on his feet in a scrum." Another reporter observed that: "Getty has no real sense of how to play the media. He's hapless. He's alternately too jovial and too abrasive. I almost feel sorry for him." After years in corporate boardrooms Getty seemed unprepared for, even startled by the intensity of the media spotlight.

During the 1986 election, Getty made a number of gaffes that were seized upon by the media. At one point, he stated that Alberta's oil industry might benefit from the nuclear disaster at Chernobyl because nuclear energy would be seen as unsafe. On another occasion he lectured small oil producers, who were experiencing a severe downturn in their fortunes, that they had "just finished the best year ever."[19]

For Don Braid, the symbolic turning point in the relationship between the premier and the gallery occurred in August 1987, at the height of the Principal Affair. Getty was photographed playing golf when his office had said that he was working at home. According to Braid, "That turned it over. After that the fundamental respect crumbled pretty quickly."

Getty was also a victim of the times. Whereas Lougheed presided for the most part over a bountiful economy, and could build and spend almost to his heart's content, Getty took office just as the province's economy was rocked by a steep decline in the price of oil. In 1987 the provincial government raised taxes, imposed deep cuts on hospitals and universities, and eliminated civil service jobs. The provincial debt mushroomed. The collapse of the Principal Group of Companies brought distress to tens of thousands of investors, and led to an inquiry into the government's role. Political fallout from the Principal Affair hung over the premier for months.

Getty's leadership soon created rumblings of dissatisfaction and dissent in the cabinet and the party, which became grist for the gallery's mill. Getty suffered by comparison to Lougheed and memories of the former premier and the confidence of those earlier times still cast a long shadow within the party. The result was a torrent of leaks from Getty's cabinet. As one gallery veteran described the situation, "It was far more difficult to get information in Lougheed's day. The cabinet was locked up tighter than a drum. I could count the times on the fingers of one hand that I got something out of cabinet. Now I need two hands for a single week.''

The 1986 and 1989 elections also produced a strong and vocal opposition in the legislature. Therefore the opposition viewpoint now had to be covered seriously, and opposition leaders vied with the premier to influence how stories were reported. Opposition parties developed their own communications networks and their own sources within the bureaucracy for obtaining information. They would occasionally trade information with journalists.

Dramatic changes had also taken place in the press gallery. There were more newspapers, television and radio stations than in Lougheed's day. In particular the Calgary and Edmonton *Suns*, although founded while Lougheed was still premier, had emerged as major new players. As a consequence reporters felt increased pressure to beat or at least match the competition. Getty also faced a new generation of hungry and hard-nosed journalists who saw it as their duty to question and criticize political leaders. Many had come from or were educated outside the province, had been trained in the cut and thrust of critical journalism, and had little memory of or allegiance to the Lougheed political dynasty. They could not be easily charmed, intimidated or outmanoeuvered.

The 1989 election brought a new crisis, almost a breakdown, in Getty's relationship with the media. The flash point was the press conference that Getty called to announce the election. As he was leaving the room following the press conference, Getty in reference to a column written by Don Wanagas in which he had been accused of being ''a secret seat-belt abuser,'' made what he thought was a humorous remark: ''I may beat my wife, I may whack my kids, but I never abused a seat belt in my life.'' Getty's gaffe became the major news story for days and the TV clip which showed Getty making his remarks was replayed across the country. According to Ashley Geddes of the *Calgary Herald*, the premier ''was literally stunned that we treated his little joke as news. He thought that it was a remark you make between teammates in a locker room. He was stunned, blown away by the fact that we made it controversial.'' From that point on, the media pack was in hot pursuit, questioning the premier at every opportunity, probing statements and policy announcements, and pouncing on every mistake. Getty, who probably expected the election to be a subdued and graceful coronation, appeared rattled by the media assault.

Some reporters believe that revenge was at work. A "bloodlust" against Getty had been building among members of the gallery because of the contemptuous way that they thought they had been treated. As one reporter remembers the gallery's mood: "During the election some press people were reacting to the bad treatment that we'd received. He (Premier Getty) doesn't believe that reporters have emotions, that reporters can get angry. In the election he had to face us. This was a chance to get the guy." Others argue that Getty brought the poor coverage on himself by making blunders that journalists could not ignore. For instance, Getty got confused over whether his interest shielding plan involved loans or grants, and pledged to pave the province's secondary roads within a decade, an outlandish promise given the costs involved and the need for financial restraint. In the view of one of the gallery's leaders, "The adversarial role was stretched about as far as it could go. We literally hounded him on spending. Of course he set himself up for it."

Getty responded by retreating behind a wall of inaccessibility. He was protected by a wedge of security people, a flying V, that cleared the way so that he could leave quickly after speeches. Reporters were sometimes jostled when they attempted to get close to the premier. When Getty did face reporters they were often given only a minute or two to ask questions.

Relations continued to deteriorate after the election. One reporter remembers the bitter atmosphere that prevailed among those close to the premier: "They blamed the media for his [Getty's] loss in Whitemud. Their position was that the media maggots tore him up during the campaign. It was war from then on. It really was. They saw us as the enemy." The Getty government's post-election media strategy was to limit contact with and bypass "enemies" in the gallery, particularly newspaper reporters, and concentrate on television where the message could be controlled more easily and where the premier's athletic looks and sincerity could make a good impression.

Rule number one was to curtail the access enjoyed by reporters. Few requests for interviews were granted, and the Confederation Room of the Legislature, where reporters had routinely met with the premier and ministers after question period, was turned into a lounge. Reporters continued to be excluded from Government House, and thus reporters waiting to talk to Getty or ministers were forced to stand outside for hours, an especially difficult post during the cold of winter. Many announcements and media events took place outside of Edmonton where Getty's strategists believed that he could get favourable local coverage while bypassing the critical gallery reporters. Moreover, reporters were often kept in the dark about the premier's schedule; they sometimes did not know whether he was even in town.

The government also attempted to reach the public directly through paid television and radio ads. After the April 1991 budget, for instance, the Getty government inundated the airwaves with hard-hitting ads boasting that the province had balanced its budget, a claim that many reporters would dispute.

Another tactic in Getty's media management strategy was the old standby of drowning out "bad" news by orchestrating a "good" news event at the same time. In April 1991, for example, the government attempted to bury an announcement by Health Minister Nancy Betkowski that there would be over $20 million in increased health fees and cuts in benefits by scheduling another announcement on the same day by Attorney General Ken Rostad, which pledged new spending to deal with a backlog in the courts.[20] Treasurer Dick Johnston's tough April 1991 budget was delivered during the opening game of a Flames-Oilers "battle of Alberta" Stanley Cup hockey series. Needless to say, the public did not pay much attention to the budget.

The heart of Getty's strategy was to rely on television to get his message across. Given that television reaches the largest audience, and that a story can be told through pictures, special attention could be given to settings and backdrops, and to making the premier look good for the cameras. Television reporters have less room for critical comment, and so the message can be delivered relatively unfiltered. Getty's rehearsed phrases and canned lines would be repeated often enough that TV reporters would include them in their stories. According to one newspaper account, at the Conservative party's annual convention in 1991, everything was done to ensure that the premier spoke under conditions that would produce the best television pictures. Getty's supporters sat in the front rows at the premier's wrap-up news conference and, with the cameras rolling, showered the premier with a standing ovation. Reporters who asked difficult questions were jeered.[21]

Another element in Getty's media strategy has been to build bridges with rural and small town newspapers. The prevailing wisdom is that the premier's fortunes depend on shoring up support among voters in rural areas, the bedrock of the party's popularity. The government has therefore deluged smaller papers with a steady stream of press releases.

One of Getty's communications assistants, Peter Tadman, visited each of the province's 140 rural newspapers in 1991.[22]

Despite Getty's efforts to control the agenda, the premier has been wounded by media crises and harsh criticism. Media reporting has caused the premier considerable anguish. In November 1990, for example, *The Globe and Mail* featured an expose of Getty's financial holdings, in which it insinuated that the premier had a conflict of interest because of investments in oil and natural gas that he made prior to becoming premier. Reacting to the story, Getty complained bitterly about the painful costs of public life, and about the media's indifference. He told *The Globe and Mail*'s Miro Cernetig and Peter Moon,

> I mean you take my point of view. You're in something at great sacrifice, tremendous stress on your family and it's unbelievable. I mean I live with it so I'm used to getting bang, bang, bang. But they don't . . . . But I wonder what the hell, do you folks ever think of the impact you make on a son or a wife or anything like that.[23]

Getty's actions again came under intense scrutiny in June 1991 when he refused to release the itinerary for a trip that he and his wife were taking to New York, London and Paris, a trip he claimed was for government business. He faced a barrage of questions from reporters about the costs of his airline travel and hotel rooms, whom he was meeting and why his wife was accompanying him. The premier saw this as an attempt to make normal public duties seem scandalous. To the reporters who covered the premier, it was a case of holding Getty accountable for spending the taxpayer's money.

Suspicion and rancour continue to plague relations between the premier and the journalists who cover him. Both sides look across barricades that are now built more on conflict than cooperation.

Conclusion

Much research remains to be done on the impact that the mass media have had and continue to have on Alberta politics. For instance, surveys have not been conducted on how members of the Edmonton press gallery or media managers see their responsibilities. The media management strategies of premiers or political parties have not been examined in detail. Scholars have not yet attempted to gauge the ways in which public opinion and voting have been influenced by media coverage, and no study exists on how media crises have affected government thinking and policy-making.

Studies in other jurisdictions suggest that the media have had an enormous impact on almost all aspects of politics. Agenda-setting studies have documented a high correlation between the issues that are given prominence in the media and issues that are seen as important by voters.[24] There is also evidence that media crises can have a dramatic effect on the behavior of decision-makers.[25] A siege mentality can develop in governments that believe that they are under attack by the media; the decision-making circle narrows to include only the handful that can be trusted to keep the government's secrets, thus increasing the likelihood of defective and dysfunctional group dynamics. Those who hold dissenting views or have different ideas about policies will be excluded from decisions. There are also indications that the climate created by adversarial reporting, by investigative journalism, and by news formats that have as their focus two points of view—a pro and a con—make it difficult for governments to build consensus and mobilize opinion behind their policies. In addition, as Joshua Meyrowitz points out, politicians are sometimes judged by superhuman standards that doom them to failure.[26]

The management of media relations has been a central and consuming task for most Alberta premiers. From Rutherford's fall from power, due to revelations in the press, to Aberhart's draconian attempts to silence critics and to Getty's attempts to bypass the gallery, media relations have been instrumental to both success and failure. While Lougheed developed strong TV skills and devised an effective media strategy, he did not sail effortlessly on a calm sea of media reporting. He enjoyed positive coverage during much of his tenure in office, but ultimately faced the same storms of controversy and waves of negative reporting that confronted the other premiers.

The relationship between Alberta's government leaders and journalists conforms to the broader North American pattern. They, like the leaders of other jurisdictions, have had to survive in a bitter sea of scrutiny and criticism that has had important consequences for the practice of democracy.

NOTES

All quotations not footnoted in the section on Lougheed, with the exception of quotes by Don Braid, are derived from Denise Savage-Hughes, ''Peter Lougheed and the Press: A Study of Agenda-Building,'' Masters thesis, University of Calgary, 1990, or from interviews conducted by David Taras in February 1991.

1. Roger Epp, ''The Lougheed Government and the Media: News Management in the Alberta Political Environment,'' *Canadian Journal of Communication* 10 (Spring 1984): 37-65.

2. For an elaboration on this theme see David Taras, *The Newsmakers: The Media's Influence On Canadian Politics* (Toronto: Nelson Canada, 1990).

3. See Michael Grossman and Martha Kumar, *Portraying The President: The White House and the News Media* (Baltimore: The Johns Hopkins University Press, 1981).

4. Quoted in Paul Taylor, *See How They Run* (New York: Alfred A. Knopf, 1990), pp. 255-56.

5. Ibid., p. 256.

6. The early history is covered in Denise Savage-Hughes, ''Peter Lougheed and the Press: A Study of Agenda-Building,'' Masters Thesis, University of Calgary, 1990.

7. See David Elliot and Iris Miller, *Bible Bill: A Biography of William Aberhart* (Edmonton: Reidmore, 1987); and Fred Kennedy, *Alberta Was My Beat: Memoirs of a Western Reporter* (Alberta: The Albertan, 1975).

8. W.H. Kesterton, *A History of Journalism in Canada* (Ottawa: Carleton University Press, 1984), p. 228.

9. C.F. Steele, *Prairie Editor: The Life and Times of Buchanan of Lethbridge* (Toronto: Ryerson Press, 1961), p. 139.

10. Allan Hustak, *Peter Lougheed* (Toronto: McClelland and Stewart, 1979), p. 98.

11. David Wood, *The Lougheed Legacy* (Toronto: Key Porter, 1985), p. 75.

12. J. Barr, *The Dynasty: The Rise and Fall of Social Credit* (Toronto: McClelland and Stewart, 1974), p. 229.

13. Howard and Tamara Palmer, ''The 1971 election and the fall of Social Credit in Alberta,'' *Prairie Forum* 1, no. 2 (1976): 126.

14. Quoted in Taras, p. 81.

15. Savage-Hughes, p. 47.

16. Don Wanagas, ''The Siren Sounds,'' in *Running On Empty: Alberta After The Boom*, Andrew Nikiforuk, Sheila Pratt, and Don Wanagas, eds. (Edmonton: NeWest Press, 1987), p. 24.

17. Sheila Pratt, "The Grip Slips," in *Running On Empty: Alberta After The Boom*, Andrew Nikiforuk, Sheila Pratt, and Don Wanagas, eds. (Edmonton: NeWest Press, 1987), p. 106.

18. Ibid.

19. Ibid., p. 109.

20. Ashley Geddes, "Tories delivering news with Madison Avenue Flair," *The Calgary Herald*, April 14, 1991, p. E6.

21. Ibid.

22. Don Braid, "Premier battles rumors of bias," *The Calgary Herald*, March 5, 1991, p. A2.

23. Premier Getty's interview with Miro Cernetig and Peter Moon of *The Globe and Mail*, November 22, 1990, p. 40.

24. Everett Rogers and James Dearing, "Agenda Setting Research: Where Has It Been, Where Is It Going?" in *Communications Yearbook* 11, James Anderson, ed. (Beverley Hills: Sage, 1988).

25. See Grossman and Kumar, chapter 11.

26. Joshua Meyrowitz, *No Sense Of Place* (New York: Oxford University Press, 1985).

9

The Politics of Gender in Modern Alberta

Linda Trimble

Alberta was at the forefront of the movement toward gender equality during the first wave of feminism. It was the first province to elect a woman to the legislature, the first to appoint women to the cabinet and the bench, and the second to give women the vote (in 1916). Yet in the 1970s, with the revival of feminism as a social movement, Alberta was seen as a laggard compared to other provinces which were creating status of women councils and responding to the recommendations of the Royal Commission on the Status of Women. In 1976 the newly-formed Alberta Status of Women Action Committee (ASWAC) criticized the government of Alberta for "moving very slowly indeed."[1] In 1982, Alberta was called the "most macho of provinces" by a feminist newspaper columnist.[2]

During the Lougheed years (1971-1985), gender equality issues were not featured in the government's policy program. Since 1985, however, the government has introduced an Advisory Council on Women's Issues and its Women's Secretariat has developed a Plan of Action for Women. Clearly the political agenda has changed and "women's issues" are now on it. Gender politics are now salient because of three changes in the political environment: a shift in federal-provincial relations which undermines the standard Alberta government tactic of focusing on external political "enemies"; the apparent end of one-party dominance; and an increased number of women, and feminists, in elite political roles.

The essential goal of feminism is to break down the barriers separating the private sphere of home and family, to which women have been relegated, from the public spheres of business and government, which

219

have been dominated by men. Gender politics include any kind of political action which challenges the division of labour, power, roles and resources between the sexes. As such, gender politics involves feminist politics as well as the activities of those who wish to maintain clear dividing lines between the public and private spheres (antifeminists). To what extent are gender politics in Alberta different from gender politics elsewhere in Canada?

It is difficult to generalize about feminist politics as the movement is broad in scope and politically heterogeneous. But it is possible to argue that feminists in Alberta, as elsewhere, are ambivalent about the state[3] and its ability to help achieve the goals of feminism. Feminists view the state as patriarchal because it is male-dominated and because government action, by controlling reproduction and property ownership, has maintained the separation of public and private spheres.[4] Feminists want gender to be considered in every policy area. They are suspicious of government responses to their demands and see many status of women agencies and policies as methods for marginalizing gender while appearing to be sensitive to "women's issues." For these reasons, even those feminists who see a need to work within mainstream political institutions believe segments of the women's movement must remain independent of the state.[5]

Many contemporary Canadian feminists are alarmed at the growing support for conservative policies and parties. The movement seeks an extension of the social welfare system and active state policies to address women's subordinate economic position. But such measures are antithetical to the political objectives of restraint-minded governments.[6] The women's movement wants universal day care, homemakers pensions, income security for single mothers and elderly women and pay equity—policies which involve expenditures or increased government intervention. Yet federal and provincial governments are attempting to balance budgets and to privatize aspects of social welfare policies. In these endeavours, governments are supported by an antifeminist segment of the women's movement which lobbies for the protection of "motherhood and the family."

These features of gender politics are clearly evident in Alberta, where feminists see the Tory government as neo-conservative and antifeminist. They are disturbed, moreover, by growing support for the Reform party. However, the lack of *rapprochement* between the women's movement and the Alberta government is to some extent based on indigenous factors. The fact that gender equality was not on the Conservative government's political agenda until it proved politically advantageous to respond to the women's movement has fostered a level of distrust which is not found in provinces such as Ontario and Quebec, whose governments appear open to feminist lobbying. Alberta feminists feel marginalized and believe that their interests are not well served by the Minister Responsible for Women's Issues, the Women's Secretariat or the Advisory Council on Women's Issues. Some groups assert that the Lougheed and Getty governments have consciously attempted to demobilize the feminist movement in the province and to depoliticize women's issues.[7] As a result, Alberta women's groups have developed political strategies which bypass mainstream partisan politics. Some have abandoned direct lobbying altogether.

This paper explores the politics of gender by contrasting two phases in recent Alberta history: the Lougheed years (1971-1985), when gender equality was not a significant part of the political agenda; and the Getty years (1985-1991), which are characterized by state articulation of "women's issues." Alberta politics are currently in a state of flux—some analysts are predicting the demise of the Conservatives, an end to one-party dominance and the advent of a new style of politics. I end speculatively with some comments about the future of gender politics in this changing political landscape.

On the Margins: Gender Politics from 1971-1985

In the 1960s and 1970s, Canada experienced considerable social change, relative economic prosperity and a dramatic reawakening of the women's movement. The resurgence of feminist activism was inspired by the realities of women's lives. For single and married women, paid labour outside the home became an economic necessity and many women entered the labour force. As Table 9.1 indicates, Alberta women comprised 26 per cent of the labour force in 1961, with a significant jump to 35 per cent in 1971. The number continues to rise—women now constitute close to half of the paid labour force in the province. However, women in Alberta, like their counterparts elsewhere in Canada, encounter formal and informal barriers to employment along with job segregation and unequal pay. In the 1970s, women working full-time in Alberta earned 59 cents for every dollar men earned.[8] Data for 1988

TABLE 9.1   Women in the Alberta Labour Force, 1961-1989

Year	Females (%)	Males (%)
1961	26	74
1971	35	65
1981	42	58
1989	44	56

SOURCES: Census of Canada and Alberta Women's Secretariat, ''Fact Sheet on Women and Families in Alberta,'' 1990.

show women earning 65 per cent compared to their male counterparts in the province.[9]

Canadian women (increasing numbers of whom were single mothers) found it extremely difficult to conduct ''parallel lives'' —carrying out private duties while working full time in the paid labour force. In 1970, for example, 20 per cent of women with children under fourteen were in the workforce even though licensed, regulated childcare was not readily available.[10] As a result, activists demanded the creation of a federal Royal Commission to determine the barriers to women's equality and to recommend government action. The 1970 Report of the Royal Commission on the Status of Women, which recommended the implementation of child care initiatives, maternity benefits and affirmative action in the civil service, was a catalyst for considerable feminist lobbying.

Alberta was the first province to appoint a committee to respond to the Royal Commission on the Status of Women's recommendations— the Social Credit government created the Citizen's Advisory Board in 1971, just before it was defeated by the Progressive Conservatives. The blossoming women's movement (which, by 1975, included about 75 women's groups)[11] pressured the government to implement the recommendations of the Citizens' Advisory Board which called for better day care, a more equal distribution of marital property, the elimination of gender-role stereotypes in the educational process and the creation of an independent advisory council on the status of women.[12]

The newly elected Tory government approached the status of women recommendations cautiously and was initially reluctant to commit itself to fundamental changes. When questioned about the Advisory Board's report in 1972, Minister Without Portfolio Helen Hunley said:

> Some of these [recommendations] have already been implemented, some of them are in the process of being studied and analyzed at the moment, and some of the recommendations will not be possible because at this point they are not economically feasible . . . .There are some recommendations that perhaps are not socially acceptable at this time.[13]

Opposition MLAs continued to ask about the government's response to the Advisory Board's report but answers were not forthcoming. A status report prepared in 1975 concluded that the Alberta government had fully implemented four of the federal Royal Commission's 49 recommendations directed at provincial governments and had partially implemented 23. The Conservatives had responded adequately to recommendations about education but had largely ignored proposals about marriage and the family.[14]

The Conservatives made a significant move in response to women's groups when they passed the Alberta Bill of Rights in 1972 and the Individual Rights Protection Act in 1973. These laws prohibited discrimination on the basis of sex in public accommodation and services, in tenancy and in employment. In 1974 a Human Rights commission was set up to hear complaints and educate the public about the legislation. Women's groups were pleased with this legal recognition of their rights in the paid labour force but demanded much more of the government. After all, the oil-induced economic boom allowed for the expansion of the state and the promotion of new social and economic policies. New and established groups sought policies to address the informal barriers to women's participation in the public sphere.[15] Feminists wanted increased spending on day care, provisions for paid maternity leave, affirmative action and pay equity in the civil service, improved maintenance enforcement, and enhanced education and job training programs.[16]

Most of these pressures were ignored or deflected by the Conservatives, for four reasons. First, Alberta decision makers, like many Canadians at that time, believed equality would be ensured if formal barriers to women's advancement in the public sphere were removed. The Conservative government felt it had, with a legislative *coup de grace* (the Individual Rights Protection Act), "outlawed discrimination" in the province. Deputy Premier Hugh Horner declared, in 1976, "legally, in this province, men are equal to women, and women are equal to men."[17] The concept of systemic discrimination was not widely understood or accepted and few recognized the importance of subtle, informal impediments to women in business and government.[18]

Secondly, gender equality issues were tangential to the political agenda of the Lougheed government. Alberta political discourse in the 1970s and 1980s focused on the oil and gas industry and related questions about resource pricing and jurisdiction. Although the Conservatives began their mandate by reorganizing the bureaucracy, drafting human rights bills, and writing legislation about mental health treatment, their focus quickly shifted to oil and gas, energy "megaprojects," economic diversification and infrastructure development.

A focus, however myopic, on the politics of oil and gas does not by itself keep feminist demands off the political agenda. An intervening factor is required, and in Alberta this factor has been federalism. The federal government is also involved in the politics of oil and gas because of its control over interprovincial trade and this led to jurisdictional disputes between the two levels of government. Because of these disputes, and because some Albertans feel under-represented in national political institutions, most Albertans have come to "view the dominant issue in provincial politics as an external one—the need to give the provincial government the strongest possible mandate with which to represent Alberta in negotiations with Ottawa."[19] The Conservatives went to the polls in 1975 with the express purpose of seeking a "strong mandate" from the public to continue its battles with Ottawa. The external "enemy" also justified government incursions into the economy and the establishment of the Heritage Savings Trust Fund.

Since the Conservative Party consistently achieved a plurality of votes, and the vagaries of the first-past-the-post electoral system fractured the opposition, the first 15 years of Conservative rule (1971-1986) were characterized by one-party dominance of political office. Moreover, the political culture which supported the Alberta government's focus on external threats disallowed any significant internal political disagreements. During the Lougheed years, the "we're all in this together" mentality was promoted by a premier who considered dissent to be disloyal. For example, the premier's tactic of refusing to acknowledge the existence, much less the activities, of the meagre legislative opposition was well known.

The Lougheed government's responses to feminist demands in the 1970s provide evidence of its reluctance to make room for issues tangential to the well-being of the oil and gas industry, economic diversification, or issues likely to divide Albertans along class or gender lines. In fact the Conservatives had little to gain by responding to the policy demands of the women's movement in the province. Although the feminist movement gained momentum with the creation of several new groups in the early and mid 1970s,[20] gender was not an issue at the polls; whatever diffuse interest in gender equality Alberta women shared was crosscut by ideological, class and demographic differences. Gender was not relevant to party politics.

Finally, throughout the 1970s and into the mid-1980s, feminist ideas and goals were not represented in the legislature and civil service. In this vein, my premise is that since women are more likely to be affected by gender inequality than men, it follows that female political elites are more likely to see gender equality as an important political goal.[21] Tables 9.2 and 9.3 tell the numerical tale: Alberta political parties selected few women candidates and as a result only two women won office in 1971 and 1975 while six were successful in the 1979 and 1982 elections. All the women elected between 1971 and 1986 were Conservatives.

Table 9.2 illustrates the phenomenon Sylvia Bashevkin calls "the more competitive the fewer," which is prevalent throughout Canada.[22] The greater the chance the party has of winning the riding, the less likely it is to nominate a female candidate. Indeed, the Conservative and Social Credit parties each ran only two women candidates in 1971; in the Conservative sweep, both PC women were elected. In subsequent elections the two competitive parties nominated few women even though women were very active in party politics. The Socreds selected one candidate in 1975, three in 1979 and four in 1982. For Conservatives winning the nomination was akin to winning office, yet the party did not use this opportunity to engage in affirmative action for female partisans; it chose only two female candidates in 1975, six in 1979 and six again in 1982. The New Democrats, who entertained slim chances of winning seats, consistently presented 11 to 15 women candidates, roughly 20 per cent of total NDP candidates. Women were often selected as Liberal candidates but the party was a lost cause electorally until 1986. Women comprised thirty per cent of Liberal candidates in 1975, for example. This percentage has declined as the Liberal share of the popular vote has increased.

TABLE 9.2   Woman Candidates in Alberta Provincial Elections,
1917—1989 (Percent of Total Party Candidacies in Parentheses)

Election Year	UFA	Liberal	CCF/NDP	SC	PC	Other*	Total Candidacies
1917	—	0 (0.0)	—	—	0 (0.0)	2	2 (1.8)
1921	2 (4.4)	2 (3.3)	—	—	1 (7.7)	3	8 (5.1)
1926	1 (1.7)	1 (1.9)	—	—	0 (0.0)	—	2 (1.4)
1930	2 (3.9)	0 (0.0)	—	—	0 (0.0)	—	2 (1.4)
1935	—	1 (1.6)	—	2 (3.2)	1 (2.6)	1	5 (2.1)
1940	—	0 (0.0)	2 (5.6)	4 (7.1)	—	1	7 (4.2)
1944	—	—	2 (3.5)	3 (5.3)	—	6	11 (6.0)
1948	—	2 (4.1)	3 (5.9)	2 (3.5)	—	1	8 (4.6)
1952	—	3 (5.5)	1 (2.4)	3 (4.9)	1 (20.0)	—	8 (4.4)
1955	—	3 (5.7)	4 (10.5)	4 (6.5)	1 (3.8)	—	12 (5.9)
1959	—	5 (9.8)	2 (6.3)	4 (6.4)	1 (1.7)	—	12 (5.6)
1963	—	2 (3.6)	4 (7.1)	2 (3.2)	0 (0.0)	—	8 (3.6)
1967	—	2 (4.4)	6 (9.2)	1 (1.5)	1 (4.4)	1	11 (4.7)
1971	—	3 (15.0)	11 (15.7)	2 (2.7)	2 (2.7)	—	18 (7.4)
1975	—	14 (30.4)	13 (17.3)	1 (1.4)	2 (2.7)	3	33 (11.3)
1979	—	20 (25.6)	13 (16.5)	3 (3.8)	6 (7.6)	2	44 (13.2)
1982	—	4 (13.8)	15 (19.0)	4 (17.4)	6 (7.6)	11	40 (11.6)
1986	—	10 (15.9)	18 (21.7)	—	10 (12.0)	13	50 (15.0)
1989	—	16 (19.3)	19 (22.3)	—	12 (14.5)	—	47 (18.6)

SOURCES: Michael Palamarek, *Alberta Women in Politics: A History of Women and Politics in Alberta* (Report for Senator Martha Bielish, December 1989), Appendix A, Appendix B, and p. 140; Alberta, *Report of the Chief Electoral Officer on Alberta Elections, 1905-1982*; Alberta, *The Report of the Chief Electoral Officer on the General Election of the Twenty-First Legislative Assembly, Thursday, May 8th, 1986*; and Alberta, *The Report of the Chief Electoral Officer on the General Election of the Twenty-Second Legislative Assembly, Monday, March 20th, 1989.*

* This category includes independent candidates as well as candidates for fringe parties such as Labour-Socialist, Labour-Progressive, Communist, Western Canada Concept and the Representative Party of Alberta. In 1982, there were 11 such candidates; four running for the Communist Party, four for Western Canada Concept, one for the Alberta Reform Movement, and two independents. In 1986, 13 fringe candidates were women; 5 standing for the Representative Party of Alberta, 3 for the Western Canada Concept, 3 independents, 1 running for the Confederation of Regions and 1 for the Communist Party.

TABLE 9.3   Woman MLAs in Alberta Provincial Elections, 1917—1989

Election Year	Total Seats	Seats Won By Women	Percentage Female MLAs
1917	58	2	3.4%
1921	61	2	3.3%
1926	61	1	1.6%
1930	63	1	1.6%
1935	63	2	3.2%
1940	57	1	1.7%
1944	57	3	5.3%
1948	57	2	3.5%
1952	60	2	3.3%
1955	61	2	3.2%
1959	65	4	6.2%
1963	63	2	3.2%
1967	65	1	1.5%
1971	75	2	2.6%
1975	75	2	2.6%
1979	79	6	7.6%
1982	79	6	7.6%
1986	83	10	12.0%
1989	83	13	15.7%

SOURCES: Michael Palamarek, *Alberta Women in Politics: A History of Women and Politics in Alberta* (Report for Senator Martha Bielish, December 1989), Appendix C, and Alberta, *Report of the Chief Electoral Officer on Alberta Elections, 1905-1982.*

Until quite recently, it has been political suicide for women candidates and office holders to declare themselves as representatives of the women's movement or advocates of gender equality.[23] To align themselves with feminism at election time was to risk being seen as ''single issue'' or ''special interest candidates'' and to discuss ''women's issues'' in the legislature was to risk ridicule. Female elites in Alberta, like their counterparts elsewhere in Canada, did not take such risks. For example, the six Conservative women elected in 1979 said they were not feminists and did not want to ''make waves about women's issues.''[24]

This is not surprising, as gender equality was not featured in their party's legislative agenda. Male members of the opposition, particularly NDP leader Grant Notley and Social Credit leader Bob Clark, occasionally raised status of women issues but the government's response was generally vague or evasive.

Women have not been well represented in elite roles in Canada, especially the position of cabinet minister, which is a key decision-making post in a parliamentary system. When women are appointed to cabinet they are clustered in stereotypically "feminine" policy areas or portfolios dealing with culture, social services, consumer issues and the status of women.[25] The Lougheed government reflected both of these trends. Between 1971 and 1979 it appointed one woman to cabinet, increasing the number to two between 1982 and 1986. These appointments fell into stereotypical gender patterns, although Helen Hunley, who was appointed Minister Without Portfolio responsible for the Women's Bureau in 1971 was promoted to the prestigious position of Solicitor General in 1973. After the 1975 election, Hunley was given the Social Services and Community Health portfolio. Mary LeMessurier served as Minister Responsible for Culture from 1979 to 1985, and Connie Osterman was Minister of Consumer and Corporate Affairs from 1982 to 1986.

In the civil service women were represented by a Women's Bureau which was established in 1966 to collect information on matters of concern to women and to make such information available. The Bureau produced pamphlets about legal rights, maternity leave and labour force regulations. But it did not have the statutory mandate to elicit the demands and concerns of the women's movement and communicate these concerns to government. Moreover, the Bureau had limited resources and only two staff members—a director and a secretary.

Faced with these constraints, yet frustrated with the government's slow response to their demands, feminist activists believed their message would be heard if women were better represented in mainstream politics and if gender-specific structures were created within the government. Lobbying in the late 1970s worked towards these goals but with little success. As a result some groups began to question mainstream pressure tactics and to change their strategy in the 1980s. The evolution of the Alberta Status of Women Action Committee (ASWAC) clearly illustrates this point.

A group of Alberta women created ASWAC in 1975 to act as the liaison between the movement and the government. ASWAC coordinated a series of regional workshops which discussed strategies for change and served as the foundation for a report presented to cabinet in October 1976. The carefully worded document was conciliatory in tone but argued that the Alberta government had been too slow to respond to women's demands. ASWAC acknowledged the Individual Rights Protection Act but urged the formation of government structures designed to address such issues as child care, maternity leave and equal pay. The group called for an independent advisory council on the status of women and a women's secretariat within the bureaucracy which would report to a minister responsible for the status of women. ASWAC stated that such institutions reflected a need for a cooperative approach:

> We are not asking Government alone to shoulder the task of accelerating positive social change. We would expect to assume our fair share of the responsibilities . . . the route to change is one of joint initiatives.[26]

ASWAC members, who admitted to being novices at lobbying, were shocked by the government's response.[27] Hugh Horner, the deputy premier, argued that the Individual Rights Protection Act provided a legal basis for equality. He then dismissed all of the concerns and recommendations of the report by saying:

> We have equality in Alberta. If it was any other way, I, as an elected representative of all of the people of my constituency, could stand before you and agree there is or was need for the Government to create a Ministerial portfolio and a bureaucracy designed especially for a group without rights. To create a Ministership responsible for the Status of Women would be an act of discrimination and an act of discrimination not against men, but against women! Such a Ministership would suggest that women are incapable of looking after themselves and would suggest that they need special protection. My understanding of the aspirations of the women in Alberta is one which indicates to me that they do not want ''special status'' but equality! Further I believe that women can take care of themselves and that they do an excellent job of getting their views across to all segments of society, including government.[28]

When questioned about his government's response to the ASWAC brief Premier Lougheed noted that Horner's comments did not satisfy ASWAC, but he saw no need to further discuss the issue of structural changes; "It's our view that any further discussions aimed at altering our position from an organizational point of view would not be productive."[29]

ASWAC continued to pressure the Tories to move on such issues as day care, matrimonial property, maintenance enforcement, affirmative action and pay equity. Limited reforms were implemented, such as weak day care regulations in 1976, provision for unpaid maternity leave in 1977 and in 1979, legislation ensuring a more equitable distribution of marital property. Because their policy concerns were not readily adopted by the cabinet, feminist activists continued to work towards greater representation in the legislature and civil service. In 1978, ASWAC conducted election clinics and prepared a "Political Involvement Handbook" instructing women about lobbying techniques, the workings of the legislature, and avenues for involvement in party politics.[30] The 1983 Edmonton municipal election featured an "All Women Campaign Committee" in one ward, which attempted, unsuccessfully, to elect a woman to city council.

In 1977 and 1978 opposition parties and women's groups asked the government to change its mind about the creation of an advisory council and a minister responsible for the status of women. By this time, most provincial governments (as well as the federal government) had established councils and mechanisms to co-ordinate policy on women's issues.[31] The government's answer was an unqualified no.[32] The Tories argued that existing arrangements adequately met the need for communication and consultation; they pointed to the Women's Bureau, and the policy of rotating responsibility for women among cabinet ministers.[33] Horner argued that women had full access to cabinet; "I am satisfied that the opportunity afforded to organizations to submit presentations to Cabinet periodically . . . has provided an essential open door to Government."[34]

In 1981, the Social Issues Committee of the Calgary YWCA discovered that cabinet's door was not fully open; the Committee's brief on women in nontraditional jobs had somehow escaped the notice of the Minister of Labour.[35] The committee concluded that women's needs were unlikely to be met without a structure to conduct research and prod government into action, and thus another lobby for the creation of an advisory body began.[36] The Social Issues Committee met with a number of women's groups and formed a steering committee called the Provincial Committee for an Alberta Council on Women's Affairs (the Committee). The quest for a council consumed much of the movement's energy in the early 1980s and involved virtually every women's group in the province including status of women groups, professional groups and shelter associations.[37]

ASWAC ultimately declined to formally support the Committee, which seems rather surprising given its earlier efforts to establish a council. At this point, ASWAC had difficulty with the Committee's recommendations but was also questioning the strategy behind them. ASWAC saw the Coalition's proposal as politically naive because it did not advocate additional ministerial and bureaucratic structures to support the council, and did not adequately ensure council autonomy. As well, ASWAC wondered whether a council would really raise the status of women. In its October 1980 newsletter, ASWAC announced that traditional lobbying was often futile:

> ASWAC has, to a large extent, continued to be a lobby organization. The belief persisted that if enough evidence were gathered, enough statistics collected, enough well thought out, well written briefs were presented, bearing irrefutable evidence about the problems facing women in areas such as education, social services, employment, that the government—SURELY—would acknowledge the problems and work towards the solutions . . . The belief was in vain.[38]

The women's movement had met with little success said ASWAC; why would a council do any better? In fact, ASWAC had changed its strategy and had certainly given up on taking MLAs to lunch. As well as presenting the occasional position paper to the government the group offered services and information directly to women seeking help with child custody, wife battering, sexual assault and employment. ASWAC's new approach to organizing was not atypical. Women's groups in many western industrialized countries engage in ad-hoc political activities[39] such as community action and self-help. Women across Canada, frustrated with the lack of action by governments, set up day care centres, women's centres, and shelters for battered women and children.[40]

ASWAC's cynicism about mainstream political pressure tactics was not unfounded, as it took 14 years of lobbying to establish an Advisory Council. The Tories proved adept at stalling on this issue. In 1983 the

Minister Responsible for Women's Issues, Dick Johnston, said that while between 40 and 50 groups supported the council, the government was still not convinced.[41] In 1984 the opposition tabled a motion to create a council but the government said the "right moment" was not yet at hand. The Conservative party finally seriously entertained the idea in 1985 when leadership hopeful Don Getty wooed Tory women with a promise to establish an advisory body.[42]

At the end of the Lougheed years, feminist groups gave the Conservative government a failing grade for its performance on gender equality issues. In 1985, the last year of the United Nations' Decade for Women, ASWAC criticized the government for moving slowly on the Advisory Council, for failing to fund provincial women's groups, for doing little more than "semantic housecleaning" of statutes in response to the Charter of Rights, for refusing to entertain pay equity and affirmative action legislation, and for being inaccessible to women's organizations.[43] By the time Don Getty assumed the leadership of the party, many women's groups had given up on the government.

The "Women's Issues" Phase: 1986—?

The Conservative government took a remarkably different approach to the politics of gender after the 1986 election. An Advisory Council was created by the passage in 1986 of the Alberta Advisory Council on Women's Issues Act. As well, the Women's Bureau was transformed into a Women's Secretariat with better funding and an enhanced mandate. The Secretariat reports to the Minister Responsible for Women's Issues and is responsible for raising gender equality issues in the bureaucracy and reviewing government policy with women's concerns in mind. By 1989, the "women's" structures were joined by a female minister responsible for Women's Issues, a Plan of Action for Women, several educational initiatives, changes to day care regulations and subsidies and a "Dialogue on Economic Equality for Women."

Gender "made it" onto the political agenda because Alberta women, along with women across Canada, are increasingly aware of their gender-based disadvantages and are mobilizing across class and ideological groupings. Gender became an issue for political parties in the 1984 federal election because pollsters discovered a "gender gap" in voting intentions; "Canadian women appeared to be ready to choose between the parties on the basis of what they were doing for and saying about women, rather than on their positions on regional, religious, developmental or other issues."[44] Subsequent public opinion polls show that Canadian men and women continue to hold different attitudes on policy questions, with women more likely to support an expansion of the social welfare system.[45]

In Alberta gender disparities are illustrated by the fact that the economic situation for women has not improved significantly despite the years of prosperity and women's increased participation in the work force. In 1989, 65 per cent of all working age women in Alberta were in the labour force—a higher rate of participation than in any other province. More than three quarters (78%) of women between the ages of 20 and 44 were in the paid labour force in 1989, indicating significant labour force participation of women with children. Indeed, 61 per cent of Alberta women with preschool age children worked outside the home in 1986. Yet the pay gap has not decreased significantly; the wage gap between men and women was 35 per cent in 1988. And women are still segregated into low-paying job ghettos. In 1989, 58 percent of Alberta women were working in clerical, sales or service occupations.[46]

Changes in women's lives were not politically salient in the 1970s and early 1980s because many Albertans believed their economic well-being would be ensured by a government which "fought the feds" and supported the oil and gas industry. The recession destroyed these hopes and revealed significant class and gender cleavages in Alberta society, divisions the Alberta Tories could no longer easily obscure by pursuing an "anti-Ottawa" strategy. The election of the Conservatives to national office in 1984 eliminated the external scapegoat and focused Albertans' attention on internal problems such as the recession, the decline of the oil industry and labour relations. Unable (or unwilling) to adequately deal with these issues, the provincial Tories appear out of touch particularly since they continue to stress the unity of Alberta society and to downplay economic problems.[47] Attempts to deflect internal conflicts by focusing on Senate reform and on such issues as the family illustrate the Conservatives' inability to adjust to new political and social realities, including the increasing political significance of gender. The significance of gender is illustrated by the growth of women's lobby groups, in 1988 the Women's Secretariat listed 300 women's groups active in the province, an increase of 225 groups since 1974.

In the 1986 and 1989 elections, the Conservative electoral stranglehold weakened and sizeable oppositions were elected. These elections

also significantly increased the representation of women in the legislature. Ten women were elected in 1986 (3 NDP, 1 Liberal, 6 PC) and 13
won seats in 1989 (3 NDP, 2 Liberal, 8 PC). Several were self-declared
feminists. Liberal MLA Bettie Hewes and New Democrats Pam Barrett
and Marie Laing wasted no time in criticizing the Getty government for
its approach to gender equality matters. The three ND women introduced
their legislative colleagues to feminist discourse; for example, Marie
Laing, formerly the executive director of the Edmonton Sexual Assault
Centre, shook up the Legislative Assembly in 1986 when she remarked
that the family is the most dangerous place in society for women and
children.[48] Even a cursory glance at *Hansard* illustrates that gender equality issues have been a source of debate in the legislature since 1986,
indicating that the opposition parties see the Tories as vulnerable in this
area. Liberal and ND attacks on the 1988 budget estimates centred on
gender, as the opposition parties criticized the Tories for spending too
little on the Secretariat, the Council, day care and battered women's
shelters.

That the Conservatives see the necessity of responding to the gender
factor is seen in cabinet appointments and bureaucratic structures. Four
women were appointed to the cabinet in 1986 and 1989. For the most
part the women remain in typically "female" ministries, such as Consumer and Corporate Affairs, Social Services and Career Development
and Employment. But the Getty Conservatives moved Nancy Betkowski,
who served as Minister of Education from 1986 to 1989, to the large and
influential Health portfolio. As well, the Tories appointed a female
minister responsible for Women's Issues. Elaine McCoy, a Calgary lawyer who won in Lougheed's former riding, took on this job in 1987 and
was also given the Labour portfolio in 1989.

McCoy promised to act as an advocate for women[49] but was not automatically welcomed by feminists, for whom distrust of the Conservative government was now deeply ingrained. Women's groups were also
wary of the bureaucratic bodies McCoy presided over in her position as
Minister Responsible for Women's Issues and were particularly critical
of the new Advisory Council. The fifteen members of the Council are
selected by cabinet and its independence from government is thus questioned. Many of the initial appointees had no background in gender equality issues. The fact that the Council reports to the Minister Responsible
for Women's Issues rather than to the cabinet was also challenged.
Finally, as the legislative opposition and women's groups pointed out,

the Council had the mandate to make recommendations to government and to provide information to the public but was not given the authority to conduct research.

What was worse, the Tories appointed Margaret Leahey, a television reporter who had no contacts with the feminist movement and no experience in gender equality issues, as chair of the new Council. Leahey was accused of being a closet Tory. Moreover, she initially refused to identify herself as a feminist, and in one of her first statements to the press advocated the appointment of a ''strong male'' such as Peter Pocklington to the Council.[50] The Council's first report, released in October 1987, was challenged by women's groups. It skirted controversial issues such as pay equity and funding for women's shelters, leading ASWAC to suggest that the Council was afraid of the government.[51] The Council's 1988 recommendations were deemed poorly researched by the Calgary YWCA Social Issues Committee.[52] Alberta women's groups believed the Council was not communicating effectively with them.

Leahey initially defended the Council, but soon became more publicly critical. She said the government was underfunding services for women, such as battered women's shelters, and claimed the minister, Elaine McCoy, was giving orders to Council members and interfering with its independence. Leahey's supporters asserted that McCoy only considered Tory women for vacancies on the Council, an assertion the minister denied.[53] While this very public dispute was not unique to Alberta—indeed, it was reminiscent of the Ontario Status of Women Council's rocky beginning—it did under cut the Conservative government's new strategy for women. Women's groups did not trust the government and believed the Council was not independent enough. The various groups which had lobbied for a Council now demanded that it be restructured and made autonomous. Women's groups also pointed out that the new ''women's'' structures and had not resulted in any concrete policy initiatives. Some Tories began to worry that the absence of a satisfactory policy response to women's demands would hurt them at the polls.[54]

The 1989 election results revealed a significant Conservative decline, particularly in urban ridings, leading the Getty government to respond in a seemingly contradictory fashion in an attempt to win back the cities while holding rural support. This dual focus is reflected in the cabinet. There are several progressive Tories, including relative newcomers like McCoy and Health Minister Nancy Betkowski, who are in favor of "women's issues" policies and support a philosophy best described as liberal feminist. McCoy and Betkowski are pro-choice on abortion; McCoy further asserts the need for policies designed to engage the full participation of women in the paid labour force. But, a different group, including Deputy Premier James Horsman, Treasurer Dick Johnston, Advanced Education Minister John Gogo and Family and Social Services Minister John Oldring, exhibits traditional attitudes about gender roles.[55] The traditionalists, supported by the antifeminist group, the Alberta Federation of Women United for Families (AFWUF), resist feminism and assert the primacy of traditional families and the need to return to "Judeo-Christian ethics."[56]

The "traditional family" approach was emphasized in the 1989 election campaign, during which Getty promised to promote stronger families. Rhetoric about the family is not unique to Alberta, though; the federal Tories also see the family as the cornerstone of society. But Alberta Conservatives have acted on their promises. In 1988 a minister, James Dinning, was appointed to take care of family issues, a move fully supported by AFWUF. The Premier's Council in Support of Alberta Families was constituted in 1989 and it created a provincial holiday called Family Day. To set the new holiday off to a good start, a conference called "Celebrating Alberta's Families" was held and a glossy brochure was mailed to every household. Feminists criticized the agenda of the conference, saying that the topics and speakers illustrated an extremely limited definition of the family. A number of groups, including ASWAC and the Alberta Advisory Council on Women's Issues, issued a press release which condemned the conference for ignoring certain types of families including single parent, refugee and immigrant, native and low-income families.[57]

The government's action to promote "the family," while largely symbolic, led Alberta feminists to question its commitment to "women's issues." The women's movement worries that gender equality issues will be subsumed under so-called family issues. In 1989, for instance, the Chair of the Advisory Council on Women's Issues told the press she believed the government was planning to absorb her Council into the newly announced family council.[58] Her tactic had the desired effect—support for the Council and the Chair was publicly expressed by previous critics such as the NDs, the Liberals, ASWAC and the Social Issues Committee of the YWCA.[59] But it also cost Leahey her job. Four days before her term expired, with no commitment from the cabinet to reappoint her, Leahey resigned, along with several other Council members.[60]

Fears about the future of the Women's Issues Council proved groundless, as Elaine McCoy assured feminist groups the Council would not be disbanded and named an interim Chair, Elva Mertick, from the remaining six Council members. This appointment was applauded by some because of Mertick's work with sexual assault victims but criticized by others because she was once on the executive of a Conservative riding association in Calgary. McCoy subsequently filled the vacancies on the Council, appointing women who pleased the feminist movement and incensed AFWUF.[61] Of the eight appointees, four were clearly tied with the women's movement.

McCoy also revitalized the Secretariat which, under her predecessor, was prevented from using the words "women," "equality" and "equity" in its publications.[62] The Secretariat produced a package of policy proposals called the *Alberta Plan of Action For Women* in July 1989.[63] While containing few specific promises, the plan allowed McCoy to assert the progressive faction's view of women and the family, which recognized "the diversity of family structures" and the need to "promote economic equality for women in the home." Such phrases, vague as they were prompted AFWUF to complain that the traditional family was being undermined. AFWUF also criticized calls for expanded day care subsidies for low income families, demands for better trained day care workers and proposals for more funding for women's shelters.[64]

Alberta feminists believe the Conservatives are reducing social welfare spending under the guise of "providing choices to families" thereby neglecting lower-class women. The government's "women's issues" policies do little to allay these fears. For instance, operating grants to day care centres were discontinued in favor of increased subsidies paid directly to parents, thus "helping families who need it most."[65] However, as day care advocates point out, low income parents may have fewer subsidized spaces to choose from, as day care centres typically set aside the minority of spaces for subsidized families and reserve the rest for full-fee paying parents. As well, parents receiving subsidies have been charged fees above the subsidy amount, to make up for lost operating grants. Most of the other initiatives are educational or directed at middle and upper class women. The 1989-90 measures included: a plan for a mentoring program in the civil service; a pilot project in the high schools designed to encourage girls to enter male-dominated fields of work; a four-week advertising campaign stressing "the varied roles women play in the life of the province"; and education and retraining for nurses.[66] The only action truly applauded by women's groups was the extension of funding for battered women's shelters.

The "women's issues" approach is constrained by certain ideological and political realities within the Conservative party. Given the economic downturn, the Getty government is reluctant to expand the welfare state in response to feminist demands. The Alberta government cannot easily reduce the bureaucracy, balance the budget and deliver new expenditure programs for women. As well, the party emphasizes individual initiative and responsibility and is more likely to "privatize" welfare state initiatives than expand state involvement. This philosophy is apparent in the Conservative policy document entitled "Caring and Responsibility: A Statement of Social Policy for Alberta." This "statement of social policy recognizes the desire of women to live in a humane and dignified manner and reflects *a philosophy that stresses individual initiative, independence, and responsibility.*"[67] Because of this view, the Conservative party will not consider using state intervention to address systemic discrimination.

Because of their free-enterprise philosophy the Tories refuse to advance a pay equity policy. While the issue is impossible to ignore (both opposition parties support pay equity legislation), the Minister Responsible for Women's Issues has defused it by bypassing the feminist movement and speaking to "ordinary Alberta women." Rather than calling for briefs from interest groups and individuals on the topic of economic equality for women, the Women's Secretariat selected, on the basis of "advice from community leaders,"[68] 200 women from across the province to participate in focus-group discussions on women and work. This "dialogue" resulted in a summary document and a vague promise to take concerns expressed by women into account when developing "initiatives to enhance (sic) women's economic equality."[69]

Despite the new government agencies and policies designed to appease the women's movement, Alberta feminists continue to feel that their efforts are undermined by the mainstream political process. Many believe the government has set up gender specific structures to avoid listening to the women's movement. They see the government's neo-conservative strategy as precluding an effective response to the problems experienced by women. In contrast feminists are empowered by independent, grassroots organizing. Feminism is increasingly expressed in nonpolitical channels, as witnessed by the women's spirituality movement and groups which deal with sexuality issues. Feminist cultural events and groups, such as women's film festivals and theatre groups, are flourishing and groups such as ASWAC say they are making progress by working outside of mainstream political structures.[70] They continue to employ such traditional lobbying tactics as presenting briefs to Cabinet, phoning MLAs and contacting the media, but Alberta women's groups are now pursuing their own agendas.

Conclusions

During the Lougheed years the Alberta government believed demands for gender equality were adequately addressed by legal rights. Since gender was not an obvious issue at the polls, there were few political incentives for engaging in a dialogue with feminists or for creating structures which allowed these interests to be represented. Groups such as ASWAC found that their lobbying was unsuccessful as gender equality issues were tangential to the government's agenda and probably peripheral to the political priorities of many Albertans. Because mainstream political action was unsuccessful, groups such as ASWAC developed strategies for grassroots or ad hoc politics in addition to techniques for lobbying the government.[71]

The new political environment in Alberta is characterized by recognition of "women's issues" and reflects the government's attempt to shore up its eroding electoral support by responding to popular demands. But feminists in Alberta question the Conservatives' motives. Many feel their interests are no better represented than during the Lougheed years. Distrust of the state is deeply ingrained in segments of the women's movement; many activists are not willing to trust any government with the feminist project. As one woman put it:

Women must guard against handing over our own business to government. If we were to do so, institutionalization would, beyond a doubt, mean increasing loss of women's control over our own destiny . . . ."[72]

The women's movement recognizes, however, that the inception of competitve electoral politics and the "collapse of consensus"[73] described earlier create new opportunities for feminist organizing. Gender is now on the political agenda. The Conservatives may be headed for electoral defeat and both opposition parties support pay equity, increased funding for services directed at women, and more comprehensive government policies on such issues as violence against women and the feminization of poverty.[74] But should Alberta feminists expect a new and improved gender politics discourse to result from a change in government?

In a word, no. The Alberta women's movement should continue its present strategy, which blends lobbying with grassroots organizing, consciousness raising and service delivery. While it would be tempting to focus considerable effort on electoral politics in the 1990s, independent organizing must remain a priority for four reasons. First, none of the three contending parties—the Conservatives, Liberals and New Democrats—field many female candidates at election time. As Table 9.2 shows, the percentage of female candidates chosen in 1989 ranged from 15 per cent for the Conservatives to 19 per cent for the Liberals and 22 per cent for the NDP. Even if the parties boost the numbers to 30 per cent, we will not likely see women comprising 20 to 25 per cent of the legislators as in Manitoba and Ontario.

Secondly, the three parties are "distressingly similar in their policy positions."[75] All are parties of the centre, including the NDP, which advances a moderate version of social democracy. The New Democrats, however, would likely revise the Individual Rights Protection Act to protect gays and lesbians and implement pay equity legislation. Thirdly, future Alberta governments, regardless of their partisanship, will face serious fiscal problems. They will not have the option of taking a freewheeling approach to government spending. Costly programs desired by the women's movement may not be high priorities. Finally, Alberta party politics are like party politics elsewhere; parties must broker a wide range of interests, some of which oppose feminism. Increased support for the federal Reform party, which espouses the traditional family and prefeminist values, reveals a continuing antifeminist element. The politics of traditionalism may constrain any new government, limiting it to incremental administrative changes, such as increased independence for the Alberta Advisory Council on Women's Issues.

Alberta feminists must not put all of their eggs into the legislative basket. By the same token, they must not overlook mainstream strategies. If women's groups continue to express antipathy towards conventional politics, they may guarantee their own marginalization. Feminists may be ambivalent about the role of the state in achieving their goals.

But they cannot completely bypass conventional routes especially when Alberta politics are volatile and in obvious transition.

Acknowledgement

I would like to acknowledge the special efforts of Judy Davidson, who tirelessly gathered the research material for the paper.

NOTES

1. Alberta Status of Women Action Committee, *Joint Initiatives* (Edmonton: October 1976).

2. Suzanne Zwarun, "Women in Provincial Politics: Alberta," *Chatelaine* 64 (April 1982) pp. 178-90.

3. For the purpose of this paper, I will distinguish between the government and the state. The government refers to members of the ruling party, while the state includes the government, the opposition parties, and the civil service.

4. See Sandra Burt, "Legislators, Women and Public Policy," in *Changing Patterns: Women in Canada*, Sandra Burt, Lorraine Code and Lindsay Dorney, eds. (Toronto: McClelland and Stewart, 1989), pp. 129-55.

5. On the "independence versus partisanship" dilemma, see Sylvia Bashevkin, *Toeing the Lines: Women and Party Politics in English Canada* (Toronto: University of Toronto Press, 1985), chapter one.

6. See Lise Gotell and Janine Brodie, "Women and Parties: More Than an Issue of Numbers," in *Party Politics in Canada*, 6th ed., Hugh Thorburn, ed. (Toronto: Prentice Hall, 1991), pp. 53-67.

7. Telephone interview with Meg Dean of the Alberta Status of Women Action Committee, 5 March 1991.

8. Edmonton Working Women, *Women: Know Your Rights* (Edmonton, 1978), p. 5.

9. Alberta, Women's Secretariat, *Fact Sheet on Women and Families in Alberta* (Edmonton, March 1990).

10. See the *Report of the Royal Commission on the Status of Women* (Ottawa, 1970). In 1984, only 9 percent of children requiring child care were in licensed facilities. See the *Report of the Task Force on Child Care* (Ottawa, 1986), p. 8.

11. Alberta, Women's Bureau, *A Directory of Organizations of Interest to Alberta Women* (Edmonton, 1974). The directory listed 64 groups, but it went to press too early to include several recently formed groups.
12. Alberta, Citizen's Advisory Board, *An Interim Report on the Status of Women in Alberta* (Edmonton, 1972).
13. Alberta, Legislative Assembly *Debates*, 18 May 1972, p. 11. Hereafter cited as *Debates*, date, page.
14. Alberta Human Rights and Civil Liberties Association, *1975 Where Are We Now?* (Report by Stella Bailey et al. assessing the provincial government's implementation of the recommendations of the Royal Commission on the Status of Women), p. ii.
15. Established groups included the local Councils of Women and Women of Unifarm; new feminist groups included the Calgary Status of Women Action Committee and Options for Women, both formed in 1973.
16. See ASWAC, *Joint Initiatives*, for an overview.
17. Hugh Horner, "Comments on Joint Initiatives," Address to the Alberta Status of Women Action Committee, 29 October 1976, p. 2.
18. See Janine Brodine, *Women and Politics in Canada* (Toronto: McGraw Hill, 1985), chapter one.
19. Gurston Dacks, "From Consensus to Competition: Social Democracy and Political Culture in Alberta," in *Socialism and Democracy in Alberta*, Larry Pratt, ed. (Edmonton: NeWest Press, 1986), p. 187.
20. The Alberta Women's Bureau's, *A Directory of Organizations of Interest to Alberta Women* (Edmonton, 1974).
21. Janine Brodie, "The Gender Factor," in *Party Democracy in Canada*, George Perlin, ed. (Scarborough: Prentice-Hall, 1988), pp. 172-87.
22. Bashevkin, *Toeing the Lines*, p. 55.
23. See Bashevkin, *Toeing the Lines*, pp. 89-95, for a description of how female political elites in Canada distance themselves from the women's movement.
24. Zwarun, "Women in Provincial Politics: Alberta," p. 190. Also, see Michael Palamarek, *Alberta Women in Politics*, Report for Senator Martha Bielish (Edmonton, 1989), p. 160.
25. Bashevkin, *Toeing the Lines*, p. 78.
26. Ibid., p. 60.
27. Lorraine Mitchell, "Changing Ways to Change the World: Ten Years of ASWAC" (Edmonton: ASWAC, November 1986), p. 4.
28. Horner, "Comments on Joint Initiatives," p. 3.
29. *Debates*, 1 November 1976, p. 1768.
30. Alberta, Women's Bureau, *Political Involvement Handbook for Alberta Women*, Prepared by ASWAC for the Alberta Women's Bureau (Edmonton, 1978).

31. See ASWAC, *Joint Initiatives*, pp. 30-41.
32. *Debates*, 17 October 1977, p. 1490.
33. This was an ad-hoc arrangement; the portfolio known as Minister Responsible for Women's Issues was not created until 1979.
34. Horner, "Comments on Joint Initiatives," p. 4.
35. Suzanne Zwarun, "Women's Council Is Vitally Needed," *Calgary Herald*, 17 January 1983.
36. Suzanne Zwarun, "Blitz continues quest for provincial women's council," *Calgary Herald*, 14 January 1983.
37. Provincial Committee for an Alberta Council on Women's Affairs, *Fact Sheet*, Edmonton, 6 October 1983.
38. ASWAC Newsletter, Vol. 1, no. 8 (October 1980).
39. This term is used by Vicky Randall, *Women and Politics: An International Perspective*, 2nd ed. (Chicago: University of Chicago Press, 1987), pp. 58-60.
40. See Nancy Adamson et al., *Feminist Organizing for Change: The Contemporary Women's Movement in Canada* (Toronto: Oxford University Press, 1988) p. 40.
41. *Debates*, 25 March 1983, p. 299.
42. Robert Sibley, "'Right moment' awaited for women's council," *Edmonton Journal*, 7 January 1986.
43. Karen Booth, "Province 'Feeble'—Women's Groups," *Edmonton Journal*, 8 March 1985.
44. Janine Brodie, *Women and Politics in Canada* (Toronto: McGraw Hill, 1985), p. 125.
45. See Brodie, "The Gender Factor in National Leadership Conventions."
46. These statistics were taken from the Alberta Women's Secretariat's "Fact Sheet on Women and Families in Alberta" (March 1990).
47. Allan Tupper, "Alberta Politics: The Collapse of Consensus," in *Party Politics in Canada*, 6th ed., Hugh Thorburn, ed. (Toronto: Prentice Hall, 1991), pp. 451-67.
48. "Here Comes the Left," *Alberta Report*, 14 July 1986, p. 6.
49. Kate Harrington, "Elaine McCoy: A Different Approach," *The Newsmagazine* (January/February 1988), pp. 19-20.
50. "Fifteen females in search of issues," *Alberta Report*, 1 December 1986, p. 5.
51. "Trying to Please All the Women," *Alberta Report*, 26 October 1987, pp. 8-9.
52. Calgary YWCA, Social Issues Committee, "Report concerning Recommendations and Activities of the Alberta Advisory Council on Women's Issues" (Calgary, 1988), p. 8.
53. See "Cursing, screaming and yelling," *Alberta Report*, 21 November 1988, p. 10; and Kim McLeod, "Women Seek Answers from Getty," *Edmonton Journal*, 21 February 1989.

54. Don Braid, "Brontosaurus Chorus Is Pleased When McCoy Is Under Fire," *Calgary Herald*, 28 January 1989.

55. See "The Cabinet Erupts in Schisms," *Alberta Report*, 7 March 1988, pp. 5-6 and AFWUF, *The AFWUF Voice*, 8 September 1989. Family and Social Services Minister John Oldring was a guest speaker at AFWUF's 1989 conference. See "Help for the Underprivileged Male," *Alberta Report*, 24 April 1989, p. 24, regarding Gogo.

56. "The New Wave Pounds Feminism," *Alberta Report*, 13 November 1989, p. 36.

57. Alberta Advisory Council on Women's Issues, Press Release, 20 February 1990.

58. Lasha Morningstar and Duncan Thorne, "Future of Women's Council in Doubt," *Edmonton Journal*, 9 March 1989.

59. Both the Calgary Herald and the Edmonton Journal ran editorials in support of the Council, and ASWAC initiated an emergency plan to fight for the Council. See, for example, "Minister says women's group won't get axe," *Calgary Herald*, 29 March 1989.

60. Marilyn Moysa, "With Future in Limbo, Leahey Quits Council," *Edmonton Journal*, 25 March 1989.

61. "Equal Representation???" *AFWUF Voice* 8 (September 1989), p. 6.

62. Elaine McCoy, "Winning More Seats at the Table," Speech given at the University of Alberta, 4 March 1991.

63. Alberta, *Alberta Plan for Action for Women*, July 1989.

64. Alberta, *1989-90 Initiatives: Alberta Plan for Action for Women*, July 1989.

65. Alberta Family and Social Services, *Alberta Day Care Reforms* (Edmonton, July 1990).

66. Alberta, Women's Secretariat. "Update! Alberta Plan of Action for Women," April 1991.

67. Alberta, *1989-90 Initiatives: Alberta Plan of Action for Women*, p. 5.

68. Ed Struzik, "McCoy Defends Pay to Women in Study," *Edmonton Journal*, 20 January 1990.

69. Alberta, Women's Secretariat, *Person to Person: An Alberta Dialogue on Economic Equity for Women* (January 1989), p. 23.

70. Meg Dean, ASWAC, Speech at the University of Alberta, 5 November 1990.

71. See, for example, Julie Anne Le Gras, *Pushing the Limits: Reflections on Alberta Women's Strategies for Action* (Ottawa: Secretary of State Women's Program, 1984).

72. Ibid, p. 37.

73. Tupper, "Alberta Politics: The Collapse of Consensus."

74. The term "feminization of poverty" refers both to the fact that more women live under the poverty line than men and the fact that women experience poverty for different reasons than men. In essence, traditional gender roles

tend to lead women into poverty. See the National Council of Welfare, *Women and Poverty Revisited* (Ottawa, 1990).

75. Ibid., p. 465.

10

Alberta and the Constitution

J. Peter Meekison

Since 1905, successive Alberta governments have engaged in constitutional battles and negotiations. The first question to occupy their attention was the transfer of natural resources, an issue which took 25 years to resolve. When Alberta, Saskatchewan and Manitoba were established as provinces, the public domain, including its natural resources, was owned and controlled ''by the Government of Canada for the purposes of Canada.''[1] For the first 25 years of Alberta's existence, the provincial government tried to convince Ottawa to give it resource ownership. In 1927, agreement was reached in principle and three years later the Constitution was amended to incorporate the terms of the Natural Resources Transfer Act, 1930. A comparison of the Transfer Act with Section 109 of the Constitution Act, 1867, quickly reveals that its provisions are far more detailed and comprehensive. The preamble to the 1930 Act contains the following statement:

> And whereas it is desirable that Alberta should be placed in a *position of equality* with the other provinces of Confederation with respect to the administration and control of its natural resources as from its entrance into Confederation in 1905.[2]

The reference to equality with the other provinces is prophetic when one considers the current position of Alberta on both the amending formula and Senate reform which are both predicated on this principle.

Later began a series of major clashes between the Social Credit government, elected in 1935, and the federal government. Ottawa disallowed

12 statutes during the period 1923-1943, all in Alberta, 11 of them between 1937-1943. The federal government stated in each instance that the provincial statute was either *ultra vires* or it unjustly confiscated property. In addition, three statutes reserved by the Lieutenant Governor were subsequently declared *ultra vires* by the Supreme Court.[3] The initial legislative program of the Social Credit government was derailed by these actions. It is no wonder that Premier Aberhart uncategorically dismissed the recommendations of the Rowell-Sirois Commission which called in 1941 for an expansion of federal legislative authority. The 1943 disallowance was the last time this federal power was used.

One may casually brush aside these early disputes as unimportant or assert that they are no longer relevant. At the time, however, they were central to the development of the federal system. These were clashes over jurisdiction, over centre versus periphery, over provincial equality, and over the role and status of provinces. They represent an important chapter in the constitutional maturation of Alberta. Moreover they have influenced how Alberta governments have viewed the federal system. While recent governments have not harkened back to the past, we know today that disputes over natural resources, provincial jurisdiction, and the principle of provincial equality, have deep historical roots.

The Emergence of the Alberta Constitutional Position

Successive provincial governments have adopted a position best described as one favouring provincial rights. Indeed, Alberta has been unswerving in its belief that strong provinces make a strong federal system. This view is found in the province's reluctance to embrace instantly new cost-shared programs such as Medicare, its use of the courts to challenge federal incursions into provincial jurisdiction and its staking out of a clear position on constitutional reform.

Why has Alberta, along with Quebec, been such a strong defender of provincial rights? There is no single or simple answer. Sheer distance from Ottawa and a belief that decisions are frequently made in Ottawa without taking into consideration the province's interests are two factors. This latter perspective is one of the greatest arguments for Senate reform. Nor should it be overlooked that from 1921 to 1971, Alberta was governed by parties which were considered to be "minor" parties and which in the case of Social Credit had a limited national presence. The national parties had not served the interests of the province, hence the public turned against them. Also throughout much of the province's history the federal and provincial governments have clashed whether or not it was over natural resource transfer or ownership, the National Energy Program, disallowance or the federal spending power. Any one of these factors alone may be insufficient to explain Alberta's strong position on provincial autonomy but taken together a different picture emerges, one favouring provincial rights.

In reviewing the position of the Alberta government since 1971 certain themes are constant. There are parallels between the concerns expressed by Premiers Lougheed and Getty and the Progressive Conservatives and those expressed by Premiers Manning and Strom and Social Credit. One recurring theme is the type of amending formula needed in the Canadian constitution. At the 1964 Premiers Conference held in Alberta the finishing touches were put to the Fulton-Favreau amending formula. Under this proposal, unanimity was required to make amendments to the division of powers or to alter provincial rights or privileges under the constitution. Both as a result of Quebec's repudiation of the Fulton-Favreau formula in 1965 and of the reports of the Royal Commission on Bilingualism and Biculturalism published in the mid-1960s, a series of constitutional conferences were convened. The first was held in February 1968, the last in June 1971. The result was agreement on the Victoria Charter. The Social Credit government, led by Premier Harry Strom, supported the Victoria Charter including the Victoria amending formula. This amending formula was based on the concept of regional vetoes, one for Atlantic Canada, one for Western Canada, one for Ontario and one for Quebec. Shortly after the June 1971 conference, the Government of Quebec stated that it could not support the Victoria Charter, although it continued to support the amending formula contained within.

During the 1971 Alberta election, the Progressive Conservatives rejected the Victoria amending formula because it established two "classes" of provinces. This view was stated by Peter Lougheed in his first major speech in the Legislative Assembly as Premier.

> I want to reiterate and make clear in the record that there is no commitment by the Progressive Conservative Administration to that [Victoria] Charter. We enter into any future negotiations completely uncommitted by any past decision-making . . . There is a provision in this Charter regarding an amending formula that . . . is detrimental

to the Province of Alberta, relative to the Province of British Columbia. But more than anything else, the Charter did not come to basic grips with the basic problem of division of responsibility and allocation of [fiscal] resources.[4]

Under the Victoria formula, the provinces of Ontario and Quebec each had a veto. To secure agreement in the West, agreement of at least two provinces representing 50 per cent of the population of the four was needed. This gave British Columbia a greater say in the West because of its larger population. Put another way, the Alberta government advocated the idea of provincial equality, not regional equality, as the basis upon which amendments should be made to the constitution.

A second theme is control over natural resources. Beginning in 1973, energy became a major point of contention in federal-provincial relations remaining at or near centre stage until 1981. The issue was not confined simply to the subject of proprietary rights but included jurisdictional questions as well. Beginning at the 1974 Premiers Conference and continuing until the Constitution Act, 1982, Alberta pressed for the protection of its ownership rights and the strengthening of provincial jurisdiction over natural resources—two separate but interrelated issues.

It was in this same spirit that the province successfully challenged the constitutionality of an export tax on natural gas—part of the 1980 National Energy Program. In 1973, the province criticized the export tax on crude oil but finally acquiesced when an overall pricing policy was developed in 1974. The province argued that an export tax on natural gas would, in effect, confiscate provincial revenues and was a tax on provincial property prohibited by Section 125 of the Constitution Act. In 1982, the Supreme Court of Canada issued a decision agreeing with the province.

The twin questions of the amending formula and natural resources converged in a seminal resolution approved by the legislature on 4 November 1976. The resolution reads as follows:

Be it resolved that the Legislative Assembly of Alberta, while supporting the objective of patriation of the Canadian Constitution, reaffirms the fundamental principle of Confederation that all provinces have equal rights within Confederation and hence direct the government that it should not agree to any revised amending formula for the Constitution which could allow any existing rights, proprietary interests or jurisdiction to be taken away from any province without the specific concurrence of that province and that it should refuse to give its support to any patriation prior to obtaining the unanimous consent of all provinces for a proper amending formula.[5]

The linkage is clear. Without some kind of constitutional protection or guarantees for proprietary rights, natural resources ownership and/or jurisdiction could be affected through the amendment process. Given the long struggle to acquire the resources in the first place, the province's apprehension was understandable. Moreover, the battles in the mid-1970s with the federal government and some other provinces over energy pricing set off alarms. To be sure, one might argue such a transgression would never happen. While that is probably true, a parallel would be to convince Quebec that protection of the French language should be left to the other provinces. It is unlikely that Quebec would ever agree to such a provision. It is equally unlikely that Alberta would give up ownership of its natural resources. Although the terms energy battles and natural resources are used, the debate focussed almost entirely on crude oil and natural gas most of which is located in Alberta and, to a lesser extent in Saskatchewan and British Columbia. Had other forms of energy such as electricity been included, the dynamics of the debate would have been different.

Other factors shaped Alberta's constitutional position. One was the exercise of the federal spending power. One reason for the establishment of Alberta's Department of Federal and Intergovernmental Affairs in 1972 was to monitor activities in this area and to assess the consequences of federal spending for provincial priorities. These concerns were clearly expressed by both Premier Lougheed and the then minister of the department, Don Getty.[6] Thus it is not surprising that in 1976 Alberta was strongly supportive of the Established Programmes Financing proposal which reduced Ottawa's involvement in the financing and regulation of health care and post-secondary education.

Another event was the 1975 Anti-Inflation Programme and the very significant expansion of emergency powers of the federal government into the economic sphere during a time of peace. Until this time, Ottawa's emergency power had been limited to periods of war. Alberta, and other provinces, challenged the federal government's position and the matter was referred to the Supreme Court in 1976. The Supreme Court limited the claimed scope of federal authority to that of emergency only. The

Court did not accept the key federal argument which would have given new life to the national dimensions doctrine potentially leading to a major increase in federal legislative authority. Use of the federal emergency power surfaced a few years later when the Energy Supplies Emergency Act provided for a rationing program for oil supplies if such were necessary.

In 1974 Mr. Justice Bora Laskin was elevated to the position of Chief Justice of Canada. Laskin was a distinguished jurist but until then, established convention provided that the appointment go to the most senior non-Quebec jurist, at that time Mr. Justice Martland from Alberta. Although Prime Minister Trudeau was within his rights to appoint Laskin, his departure from convention caused the provincial government to look more closely at how the Supreme Court influenced constitutional development.

Alberta and the Constitution Act 1982

After the collapse of the Victoria Charter in 1971, constitutional reform was put on the "back burner." In the mid-1970s, as a result of the emergence of the Parti Québécois as a political force in Quebec, Prime Minister Trudeau raised with the provinces the idea of patriating the constitution, adopting an amending formula and securing a few other amendments. The proposed agenda was very limited in scope. As chance would have it, Alberta was host to the annual premiers conference in 1976 and as a result, Premier Lougheed became the spokesman for the other provinces.

The ten provinces met during the summer and early fall of 1976 to develop a response to the Prime Minister's initiative. Mr. Trudeau continued to support the Victoria amending formula because it was the last one unanimously agreed to (at the 1971 Victoria Conference). In addition to discussing the question of patriation and the amending formula, the provinces insisted that other matters be added to the constitutional agenda. These included a request from Premier Bourassa that Quebec be given constitutional guarantees for its language and culture. Other matters discussed included natural resources, the federal spending power, immigration, communications and the admission of new provinces.[7]

Because of the election of the Parti Quebecois in the fall of 1976, federal-provincial negotiations on the provincial proposals never took place. What resulted from the interprovincial discussions was an agenda to guide future federal-provincial negotiations. These would take place when the federal government had come to terms with the fact that a government had been elected in Quebec pledged to a different political arrangement for Canada. The long-awaited negotiations occurred in the fall of 1978 and late winter of 1979, well into the fifth year of the federal government's mandate.

Thus was Alberta's position on the Constitution shaped as she prepared for the October 1978 Constitutional Conference. The province's position was contained in a paper entitled *Harmony in Diversity: A New Federalism for Canada*. The title reflects two key principles—one that governments can work together cooperatively and, at the same time, retain or preserve their distinct character. In other words, federalism is predicated on diversity and a healthy federal system requires effective provincial governments. The recommendations contained in *Harmony in Diversity* reflected six principles:

(1) Responsible parliamentary government must be the basis of our system of government;
(2) The principles of constitutional monarchy must be maintained;
(3) All provinces have equal constitutional and legal status within Confederation;
(4) Strong provinces make a strong, viable Canada, complementing the role of a strong federal government;
(5) Within their respective spheres of jurisdiction, the two orders of government—federal and provincial—are equal, neither being subordinate to the other;
(6) Each of the two orders of government must respect the responsibilities and jurisdictions of the other.[8]

The position paper contained 29 recommendations which highlighted Alberta's concerns about increasing federal intervention in areas of provincial jurisdiction. It sought to protect existing provincial jurisdictions like natural resource ownership and to limit means whereby the federal government could influence provincial policies through the use of the declaratory power, the emergency power and disallowance. It proposed giving provinces a role in appointments to federal boards and agencies and expanded provincial jurisdiction in transportation, communications and taxation. Underlying the position was the firm conviction that federalism, to be effective, needs strong provinces.

One part of the developing constitutional dialogue—Senate reform—was not referred to in the position paper. Other than for British Columbia, this topic was not then a provincial priority. The division of powers was more important. Until now Alberta's principal concern had been with what one might call the heart of the federal system, the division of powers and the nature of the relationship between the two orders of government. This is clearly the thrust taken in the position paper. Alberta was not alone in adopting this position. At the 1978 Premiers Conference, all ten provinces agreed that the division of powers was the key to constitutional reform.[9]

The first bill introduced by the Progressive Conservative government in 1971 was the Alberta Bill of Rights. Not in question was the province's commitment to human rights as demonstrated by this legislation and the soon to follow Individual's Rights Protection Act. The issue was whether or not there should be an entrenched charter. Alberta was one of a number of provinces which believed that rights, other than language rights, could be protected without "constitutionalizing" them. A similar position was advanced at the 1968 Constitutional Conference by Premier Manning when the matter of an entrenched charter was first raised. The basic concern was the undermining of the role of the legislatures and increasing the role of the courts.

At the February 1979 Constitutional Conference, Premier Lougheed unveiled what eventually became the amending formula entrenched in the Constitution Act 1982. It should be recalled that the Progressive Conservative government of Alberta did not support and was critical of the Victoria formula which up to this point was the only amending formula being given serious consideration. Bearing in mind the 1976 legislative resolution, it was necessary to develop a formula which met the requirements of that resolution. In his presentation, Lougheed outlined six tests which any formula must meet.

(1) The Parliament of Canada must be a participant in all constitutional amendments other than those pertaining to provincial constitutions.

(2) All provinces must have an equal say in constitutional amendments affecting existing provincial rights, proprietary interests and jurisdiction.

(3) Constitutional amendments affecting existing provincial rights, proprietary interests and jurisdiction should not be imposed on any province not desiring it.

(4) Constitutional change must be difficult but not so difficult as to make it impossible. A balance between rigidity and flexibility is essential. Thus any formula must require a high degree of consensus before an amendment can be passed, but no one province should have a veto.

(5) A formula must not be based on regional equality but on provincial equality.

(6) Given our constitutional development to date it will be necessary to devise more than one method of amending the constitution.[10]

Lougheed explained that Alberta did not seek a veto which was one way of meeting the third requirement. It would have made change too difficult, however, thereby conflicting with the fourth test. Instead the province advanced the idea of "opting out" or of having an amendment not apply in a particular province. At first the idea was dismissed and criticized as one which would lead to constitutional chaos. Despite the initial opposition, other provinces and eventually the federal government accepted the concept. It was included in the general amending formula contained in Section 38 of the Constitution Act, 1982.[11]

The amending formula reflects and accepts the existing reality of the Constitution in that there is already a degree of asymmetry contained within it. The differential treatment with respect to natural resource ownership is a good example of this phenomenon. Another is the language provisions of Section 133 which singles out Quebec. Today the concept of symmetry/asymmetry is very much before us as Canadians debate the future of federalism. There is a recognition that a potential solution to our constitutional impasse may need to be constitutional differences among the provinces. Some might argue that this perspective violates the principle of provincial equality. In reality, however, asymmetry already exists within the constitution. The principle of equality in the amending formula gives each province an equal say in making amendments but if the formula is applied as it was designed, there is acceptance that, in the future because of opting out, the distribution of powers may differ from province to province.

The other major concern throughout the 1970s was with natural resources, specifically nonrenewable resources. If one thing characterized

Alberta-Ottawa relations during the 1970s and early 1980s it can best be called the energy wars. Throughout this period Alberta was a strong defender of provincial control of natural resources. It resisted federal incursions into this area. The National Energy Program of 1980 was the ultimate federal intrusion. Alberta, supported by B.C., Saskatchewan and Quebec, pressed for reform in this area. While not achieving all of the province's objectives, Section 92A of the Constitution Act 1982 clarified and strengthened the areas of exclusive provincial legislative jurisdiction over nonrenewable natural resources, including forestry resources. In addition, Section 92A established a new area of concurrent jurisdiction in the area of interprovincial trade subject to federal paramountcy. Section 92A also permits the provinces to levy indirect taxes on nonrenewable resources provided they are nondiscriminatory. This was the first amendment to the Constitution Act since 1867 where provincial legislative jurisdiction had been expanded. The clause permits a sharing of legislative responsibility as opposed to a direct transfer of jurisdiction. For example, giving the province the ability to levy indirect taxes does not preclude Ottawa from doing the same thing.[12]

Another provision of the 1982 Act advocated by Alberta and other western provinces was Section 33 of the Charter of Rights and Freedoms, the so-called "notwithstanding clause." This clause applies to those parts of the Charter dealing with fundamental freedoms, legal rights and equality rights. It gives both provincial legislatures and Parliament the authority to state that a law will stand, notwithstanding the provisions of the Charter. The clause represented a compromise between provinces which opposed entrenching the Charter and the federal government. A further compromise was to limit the exercise of this power to five-year time periods. The clause remains controversial, particularly after its use in 1988 by Quebec in Bill 178 to restrict the language used in signs. The purpose of the clause is to maintain flexibility by balancing parliamentary supremacy with the new role thrust upon the courts.

With proclamation of the Constitution Act 1982, interest in constitutional reform receded. And yet, because the 1982 Act had been adopted over Quebec's objections, the constitution remained unfinished business. The Meech Lake Accord was the next chapter.

Senate Reform

The next phase in the development of Alberta's constitutional position was the quest for Senate reform which started with the 1982 publication of a paper entitled *A Provincially-Appointed Senate: A New Federalism for Canada*.[13] Alberta's position paralleled in most respects reform proposals which had been developed by others over the preceding decade. Why the change of direction? Speaking generally, there are two separate but related events which caused the about-face.

First was the 1980 federal election which saw the defeat of Joe Clark's Conservative government. After the votes were counted, the three western-most provinces found themselves with no members on the government side of the House of Commons. This one event gave a strong impetus to institutional reform. The second event was the by-election victory of a separatist to the Alberta legislature in early 1982. This election took place right after resolution of both the constitutional and energy issues. Nevertheless the message was clear—Alberta is not effectively represented in Ottawa. It was time for new initiatives and the path led to Senate reform.

The proposed Senate would be similar to the German Bundesrat in terms of its composition and functioning. Members would be appointed by provincial governments and would take their direction from the provinces. Representation was a compromise between provincial equality and representation by population. Provinces with populations over five million would have five votes, provinces with populations between one and five million would have four votes, those with less than a million citizens would have three votes. Alberta's proposed Senate would have an absolute veto over matters of concern to the provinces and a suspensive veto over other matters. While the paper still referred to the chamber as a Senate, other proposals referred to it as the Federal Council or House of the Provinces.[14] It soon became apparent that a provincially-appointed Senate had little appeal to Albertans. Had the chamber been called something other than the Senate, public reaction might have been different. Public reaction was negative to this proposal, many critics seeing the change as substituting provincial patronage for federal patronage.

In November 1983, a legislative committee was established by Alberta to look into Senate reform. In 1985, it produced a report calling for comprehensive Senate reform advocating a "Triple-E" model—elected, equal and effective.[15] In only a few years, on the question of Senate reform, Alberta had come from a position of indifference to one of committed advocate. Indeed, Alberta became the leading provincial proponent of Senate reform. In 1985 and 1987, the report's recommendations were supported by all political parties in the provincial legislature.

The most significant difference between the Alberta committee report and other positions advanced to that date was the proposal that the Senate be elected. Most reforms called for a provincially-appointed Senate. Another innovative recommendation is the deadlock-breaking mechanism. The report stated that in the event of a dispute, "the House of Commons should be able to override any amendment (veto) passed by the Senate on a bill other than a money or taxation bill, by a vote that is greater in percentage terms than the Senate's vote to amend."[16] Other recommendations included limiting the size of the Senate to 64 with six members from each province and two from each territory. One-half the senators would be elected during each provincial election and would be elected for the life of two legislatures. Members would sit in provincial delegations and would not be eligible for appointment to the cabinet.[17]

At the 1988 Premiers Conference, Alberta was given the lead responsibility on Senate reform. Other provinces were willing to see Alberta discuss ideas and concepts with all other governments during the following year and present its findings to the 1989 Premiers Conference. In this respect, Alberta played a role similar to that played by Quebec in the discussions leading up to the Meech Lake agreement. Accordingly, Premier Getty established a Task Force on Senate Reform which crisscrossed the country meeting with other governments, the media and university classes explaining the Alberta Legislative Committee Report and listening to other viewpoints. The Hon. James Horsman reported to the premiers at the 1989 Premiers Conference and the mandate from the other provinces was extended for another year. It was soon evident to the task force that most other provinces had given little thought to Senate reform. They were prepared to listen, however, and became increasingly interested in the subject. This is particularly true of the western and the Atlantic provinces. Their interest is understandable given the concentration of population in Ontario and Quebec. Indeed, it became clear in western Canada after the 1980 federal election that western representation in Ottawa needed to be strengthened. If increased representation was not to be gained through the cabinet, which to that point had been the traditional vehicle for balancing regional interests, then a logical alternative was a reformed Senate.

At the marathon meeting of First Ministers convened to save the Meech Lake agreement in June 1990, considerable attention was given to Senate reform and the next phase of constitutional discussions. Had the Meech Lake agreement survived, Senate reform was to have been "the key constitutional priority until a comprehensive reform is achieved." A federal-provincial commission was to be established with a five-year mandate to look at Senate reform utilizing the following principles; elected, more equitable representation and effective powers. If reform had not been achieved within a few years, Ontario's representation was to drop to 18 from 24, that of Nova Scotia and New Brunswick from 10 to 8 and that of the four western provinces and Newfoundland was to increase individually from 6 to 8. Quebec's and PEI's representation would remain at 24 and 4 respectively.[18] Thus what had been seen only as a remote possibility became a key constitutional priority but only if the Meech Lake agreement became part of the constitution.

The election of Senator Stan Waters in 1989 drew national attention to Senate reform. Despite protestations on the part of the federal government about the constitutionality of the election, no attempt was made to challenge it in the courts. While apparently a one-time event, a precedent was established. An integral part of Ottawa's 1991 constitutional proposals included a proposal for an elected senate.

Alberta and Meech Lake

It has been an accident of history that Alberta has thrice hosted the annual Premiers Conference when the constitution was of paramount importance. This was true in 1964 when the Fulton-Favreau amending formula was discussed and in 1976 when the provinces were challenged by Mr. Trudeau to develop a common constitutional position. In 1986, Premier Getty gave the necessary leadership. The 1986 Conference came right after Gil Remillard had outlined Quebec's five conditions for resuming constitutional negotiations. The premiers agreed that Quebec's five conditions should be the "top constitutional priority" and would be negotiated first. A second round would follow when other matters of importance would be negotiated. The process was not to end with the Quebec round. The first two agenda items for the next round—Senate reform and fisheries—were also contained in the "Edmonton Declaration" and subsequently in the Meech Lake agreement.[19] The 1986 Premiers Conference was the first step on the road to Meech Lake.

Two other proposals in the Meech Lake agreement were suggested by Alberta; an interim method of selecting senators and a requirement for annual meetings of first ministers on the economy. The first was introduced as a means of ensuring a federal commitment to Senate reform. If Meech Lake had been approved, the Prime Minister would have had to appoint senators from lists submitted by the provinces. Who knows what the vote would have been on the GST in the fall of 1990 had the flurry of appointments been taken from provincial lists.

The second proposal would constitutionalize the calling of annual meetings of first ministers on the economy. A similar provision was contained in the 1971 Victoria Charter. Moreover, it is something which has often been advocated by Alberta and is one of the recommendations found in both *Harmony in Diversity* and in the 1985 report on Senate reform. Both the agenda and discussion at these annual conferences on the economy reflect the interdependence of governments within the federal system.

Two other provisions of the Meech Lake agreement warrant attention. One is the statement in the preamble endorsing the principle of provincial equality, a phrase inserted at the suggestion of Alberta. The second is the commitment to an early start on Senate reform. Because ratification became protracted, the expected conference did not occur. Nonetheless the priority of Senate reform was reaffirmed at the June 1990 conference. The June 1990 agreement was not reform but it certainly laid a strong foundation.

The Alberta government supported Meech Lake for a number of reasons. Some of the provisions of the agreement were ones previously advocated by the province. These include limits on the federal spending power and annual first ministers' conferences on the economy. The province had tried in the mid-1970s to negotiate an immigration agreement similar to the one between Quebec and Canada (the Cullen Couture Agreement) but had been unsuccesful. Now Alberta was being given that opportunity. Also the agreement ensured a continuing dialogue on Senate reform.

For these reasons and for the more obvious one of national unity, the Alberta government enthusiastically endorsed the Meech Lake agreement. The Legislative Assembly gave its approval to the resolution as

required under the amending formula in December 1987. Premier Getty
continued to support it even though some of his own supporters were
opposed. On many constitutional questions and the role of provinces
within the federal system, Alberta and Quebec have often expressed similar views—essentially a belief in strong provinces and support for provincial autonomy. This link was underlined and reinforced at the 22 April
1991 meeting between Premiers Getty and Bourassa. Their meeting was
of Bourassa's first with another premier since the collapse of Meech Lake.

During the period 1983-1987, the issue of aboriginal rights was the
principal subject of constitutional reform. Although a constitutional
amendment was approved in 1983 and proclaimed in 1984, further constitutional amendments requested by aboriginal people were not realized, much to their disappointment. Alberta adopted the position that
"self government" needed to be clarified before it would consent to any
amendments entrenching this right. Aboriginal constitutional questions
remain as unfinished business today just as Quebec's concerns were in
1982. This reality was dramatically demonstrated in June 1990 by Elijah
Harper, an aboriginal member of the Manitoba Legislature, and his role
in the demise of the Meech Lake agreement.

Alberta has played an important role in recent constitutional discussions. It has developed its positions over a long period of time and, during that time, they have been reasonably consistent. Many constitutional
policies have been the subject of debate in the Legislative Assembly
including ratification of the 1981 constitutional agreement even though
there was no requirement to do so. Alberta's position on Senate reform
was developed as a result of extensive public hearings. To date, Alberta
has been successful in achieving its objectives—from the amending formula to Section 92A of the Constitution Act. Alberta has brought to the
fore debate on Senate reform and through its Senate Election Act
challenged the federal government to pursue Senate reform. It has been
a firm advocate of provincial autonomy and has not hesitated to use the
courts to uphold its position. It has argued that provincial equality must
be a key principle.

Why has Alberta been so successful in achieving its constitutional
goals? Many reasons can be advanced, including the leadership skills and
determination of Premiers Lougheed and Getty who both placed a high
priority on this area. Chance placed Alberta as chair and therefore spokesman of the Premiers Conference in both 1976 and 1986, two important
years in the ongoing constitutional debate. The province developed clear

positions and then looked for allies and supporters amongst the other provinces. These provinces in turn saw and accepted Alberta's leadership role in this area and were content to let it continue. Throughout part of this period, Ontario was seen to be too closely associated with the policies of the federal government, particularly in the area of energy policy. Thus the leadership position which one might ordinarily associate with Ontario amongst the English speaking provinces was filled by Alberta. In this role Alberta was supported by Quebec.

The Future of Canadian Federalism

Canada's future is at best uncertain and at worst lamentable. The collapse of Meech Lake is a watershed in Canada's continuing constitutional evolution. Critics of Meech Lake, who said its failure did not matter have been proven wrong. The Quebec Commission on the Political and Constitutional Future of Quebec, otherwise known as the Belanger-Campeau Commission, and the acceptance by the National Assembly of its call for a referendum on sovereignty cannot be dismissed as either a bluff or as an exercise in public relations. Members of the Quebec commission agreed on one point—the status quo is not acceptable. If Meech Lake was seen as decentralizing it pales by comparison to the Allaire Report of the Quebec Liberal Party released in January 1991. Both committees have called for a referendum to determine Quebec's future within Canada. Opinion polls in Quebec indicate strong support for a very different kind of federal system.

What does all of this mean for Alberta? The answer is a great deal because fundamental restructuring of the federal system now appears likely. If the status quo is being challenged, Albertans must ask some probing questions. To assist in the process of developing an Alberta position, the government established a committee of government MLA's which produced a discussion paper listing a series of questions on the constitution. Those questions subsequently became the focal point for an all-party committee of the Legislative Assembly which reported in March 1992. Among other things the committee endorsed a "Triple-E Senate" and reaffirmed the province's belief in the principle of equality of the provinces.

While the status quo is no longer acceptable what does the status quo mean? What are its benchmarks and its characteristics? For example, would there be agreement on the existing division of powers between the federal and provincial governments? Does provincial equality exist or is it an objective yet to be achieved? Do we agree with the principle of equalization payments? What kind of institutional reforms are necessary? Looking to the future, even more difficult questions arise. Asking some of these questions may cause discomfort but they must be asked, alternatives weighed and solutions which may defy conventional wisdom suggested. Some questions are:

(1) Should a different political arrangement (sovereignty-association asymmetrical federalism, special status) be negotiated with Quebec? If yes, what does this do to the idea of provincial equality? If yes, what is the composition and mandate of the Parliament of Canada and its members from Quebec? If no, does Quebec take precipitious action either through a referendum or a unilateral declaration of independence?

(2) If a different political arrangement is developed with Quebec, will there be a push for "centralization" on the part of the rest of Canada as individuals such as Rene Levesque have suggested would follow? Has Quebec's position on provincial autonomy prevented the rest of Canada from establishing national goals and objectives?

(3) Alternatively, would provinces such as Alberta continue to support provincial autonomy? Indeed, would a more confederal model follow?

(4) What shape would our central institutions, such as the Senate and Supreme Court, take under a different arrangement?

(5) What does provincial equality mean? We know that provinces are not equal in size, population, natural resources, and their economies. Is a redefinition required or does it mean equal legislative authority, equal say in constitutional amendments, equal say in the Senate?

(6) Is cabinet government, with strong party discipline, compatible with federalism?

These and other broad questions need to be addressed. Federalism presupposes differences. In a country as vast as Canada some type of federal arrangement is almost unavoidable. The dilemma is what kind of arrangement will now be acceptable.

Assuming it is in our interests to stay together, can we find creative solutions? Are there values that bind Canadians together? Can the shared experiences since 1867 transcend our divisions? Central to the debate is the division of powers and the debate over centralization and decentralization. Agreement on a new division will be difficult with or without Quebec. Even then, rather than trying to develop a precise list as contained in the Allaire Report, other devices may be considered which allow governments the opportunity to make changes incrementally.

In approaching the division of powers we tend to think in terms of watertight compartments. While such a concept was crucial in drafting the division of legislative responsibilities at Confederation it also assumed no leakage over time. Techniques which will permit change, flexibility and asymmetry need to be considered. Some examples are:

(1) A provision allowing the federal or provincial governments to delegate their legislative authority to each other. This idea is not new and is found in both the Fulton-Favreau formula, in *Harmony in Diversity* and in the federal government paper released in September 1991.

(2) A provision in the Constitution permitting federal-provincial agreements in certain specified areas such as immigration, language, communications and culture. In 1975, Mr. Trudeau proposed this approach as a means of ensuring Quebec's cultural identity. One can see the similarity between this more general approach and the immigration provisions in the Meech Lake agreement.

(3) Greater use of concurrent legislative powers. A classic example is Section 94A which relates to pensions. Under its provisions, the Canada and Quebec Pension Plans have co-existed without the country coming apart. Another example is Section 92A on natural resources.

(4) Finally, a greater use and constitutional sanction of interprovincial agreements. This would allow for a nationwide consensus but on items falling within provincial jurisdiction such as education.

These devices illustrate ways in which flexibility can be achieved within the federal system. Each example makes it possible to accommodate diverse interests. This approach to the division of powers may not be feasible in light of the Allaire report but it makes change possible without requiring a major and too time consuming rewrite of the division of powers.

What are Alberta's interests and concerns? One can expect the province to develop a constitutional position based along traditional lines with insistence on provincial equality, protection of natural resources, improved mechanisms for federal-provincial dialogue, Senate reform, elimination of duplication of effort between the two levels of government and changes to the division of powers. Included with these areas will be support for some means of accommodating Quebec within Canada.

With Alberta's strong support of Meech Lake, the provincial government is held in high regard by the Quebec government. There is another view that Alberta may be marginalized by its strong position on provincial equality and recent criticisms of official bilingualism by Premier Getty. While this is a possibility the links between the Alberta and Quebec governments have been forged over a long period of time. As a result one can expect Alberta's leadership position on the constitution to continue because it is one province that Quebec continues to trust. There is a difference today, however, in that the process of reform is now predicated on the need for public participation. Positions which were originally shaped by governments must now be developed after input from a wide cross-section of Albertans through the all-party committee of the legislature looking into this question. Nevertheless, the principles outlined here will probably continue to underline the province's position. Obviously other constitutional matters such as aboriginal rights will need to be addressed but these questions will be initiated by others and Alberta will respond. In areas such as Senate reform or natural resources, Alberta will take a leadership role.

What of the future? Throughout most of 1990 and 1991 (the period leading up to the collapse of Meech Lake and for the immediate period after) the potential breakup of the country has been debated. To some, such arguments were seen as scare tactics to ensure Meech Lake's passage. To others, disintegration was a real possibility. I believe the possibility of a break-up must be taken seriously.

A key factor to be considered in any new federal system is the dominant position of Ontario. In a Canada without Quebec, Ontario would have about half the population and, thus, about half the seats in a new Parliament. Such hegemony will not sit too well with the other eight provinces. They will demand balancing representation by population in the House of Commons with provincial equality in a new Senate. A federation where one province is so dominant politically and economically will be highly unstable. Should Quebec separate it will not be business as usual. There will be pressure to merge existing provinces into larger units. Is this a good thing? Does it make sense? Are there other alternatives? Any future negotiations will not be confined to a Quebec-Canada axis but will include, of necessity, a new vision of a restructured Canada.

The world is rapidly changing and so too is Canada. The Charter of Rights has had a profound impact on our constitutional development. Immigration from Asia, Latin America, Africa and the Middle East has changed the demography of Canada. We talk of English and French Canada, but in reality these terms no longer accurately characterize Canada. The new constitutional vision must take this reality into account, just as it must take into account Canada's native peoples and the economic conditions created by the Canada-US free trade agreement and the proposed North American free trade agreement. Constitutional matters will come back to center stage and dominate the surroundings. This may well be the final curtain. Perhaps the key difference this time is that along with Quebec's concerns the demands of the West, aboriginals and such groups as women's and multicultural organizations will compete for the spotlight.

Critical to the success of the next round of constitutional negotiations is the need to find an accommodation with Quebec. Many people discuss the potential break-up of the country with a sense of disinterest and detachment. One frequently hears if Quebec wants out, let them go. This is a simplistic and shortsighted response. The economic and political consequences of a rupture will be far-reaching. Canada has achieved a significant degree of recognition on the international scene which will be the first casualty. There will be tremendous logistical problems in administering a country divided in two with Quebec in between. The Alberta-Quebec alliance on provincial autonomy will disappear. This relationship has been an important offset against the influence of Ontario. One can expect Alberta to continue to pursue its interests but its long term interest is in a united Canada.

NOTES

1. See Alberta Act, 1905.

2. See Alberta Natural Resources Transfer Act, 1930, emphasis added.

3. See G.V. LaForest, *Disallowance and Reservation of Provincial Legislation* (Department of Justice: Ottawa, 1955), pp. 75-82.

4. Alberta Legislative Assembly, *Debates*, 29 March 1972, pp. 18-36. Hereafter referred to as *Debates*, date, page.

5. See Alberta, Department of Federal and Intergovernmental Affairs, *Fourth Annual Report*, to 31 March 1977, p. 77.

6. See Hon. D.R. Getty's comments during the Throne Speech Debate, 10 March 1972, pp. 7-22-23. See also remarks of Hon. P. Lougheed during the Budget Speech Debate, *Debates*, 29 March 1972, pp. 18-35.

7. For a complete review of this period, see the exchange of correspondence between Premier Lougheed and Prime Minister Trudeau contained in Alberta, Federal and Intergovernmental Affairs, *Fourth Annual Report*, pp. 55-77.

8. Alberta, *Harmony in Diversity* (Edmonton, 1978), p. 3.

9. See communique from the 1978 Annual Premiers' Conference in Alberta, Department of Federal and Intergovernmental Affairs, *Sixth Annual Report to March 31, 1979*, 1979, pp. 42-46.

10. Ibid., p. 70.

11. For a complete discussion of the amending formula see J. Peter Meekison, ''The Amending Formula,'' *Queen's Law Review* 8, nos. 1 and 2 (Fall 1982/Spring 1983): 99-122.

12. For a more complete discussion on Section 92A, see J. Peter Meekison, Roy Romanow and William D. Moull, *Origins and Meaning of Sec. 92A: The 1982 Constitutional Amendment on Resources* (Montreal: The Institute for Research in Public Policy, 1985).

13. Alberta, *A Provincially-Appointed Senate: A New Federalism for Canada* (Edmonton: Alberta Federal and Intergovernmental Affairs, 1982).

14. See for example the recommendations of the Pepin Robarts Commission, *A Future Together* (Ottawa: Information Canada, 1979) and the 1980 Quebec Liberal Party Position Paper on the Constitution, the so-called ''Beige Paper.''

15. Alberta, Select Special Committee on Upper House Reform, *Strengthening Canada: Reform of Canada's Senate* (Edmonton: Legislative Assembly, 1985.)

16. Ibid., p. 6.

17. See Recommendations, ibid., pp. 4-8.
18. First Ministers Meeting on the Constitution, "Final Communique," Ottawa: 9 June 1990.
19. See Communiques from the Twenty-Seventh Annual Premiers Conference in Alberta, Department of Federal and Intergovernmental Affairs, *Fourteenth Annual Report to March 31, 1987* (Edmonton: 1987).

11

The Lubicon Lake Dispute

Thomas Flanagan

Although the Lubicon Lake dispute has attracted attention around the world, it is oddly difficult for readers to obtain accurate information about it. There is virtually no published scholarship on the subject, and the journalistic accounts are highly partisan.[1] This paper gives an account of the dispute from its remote origins in the signing of Treaty 8 (1899-1900) to the present day. The appendix that follows analyzes the strategic interaction of the three players in the dispute: Canada, Alberta, and the Lubicons. In the appendix I will show that the Lubicons' failure to obtain a settlement is due to their strategic choice of demanding an aboriginal rights (AR) settlement rather than one based on treaty entitlement (TE). Three northern Alberta land claims with similarities to that of the Lubicons—Fort Chipewyan, Sturgeon Lake, and Whitefish Lake— were amicably settled during the 1980s by tripartite negotiations as entitlements under Treaty 8.[2] I will also suggest that the Canadian government has figured out how to counter the Lubicons' position by recognizing and negotiating with neighbouring bands, thus breaking up the Lubicon's solidarity, reducing their numbers, and threatening them with the loss of their treaty entitlement which they have counted on as a fallback position.

My account is based on documents in the public domain such as news-paper stories, legislative debates, and court reports. Many sources will remain confidential to the parties until the dispute is settled, so there are undoubtedly omissions, and perhaps some outright errors, in my interpretation. But since it will be many years before the full story of the Lubicon dispute can be written, I hope this account will be useful in the meantime.

Background

Lubicon Lake lies in a vast wilderness of woods and water north of Lesser Slave Lake between the Peace and Athabasca Rivers. When the two Treaty 8 commissions passed through northern Alberta in 1899 and 1900, there were no trails in the region to accommodate a large party of white men and their supplies. They had to travel by water, making a circle around the area now claimed by the Lubicon Lake band. The commissions stopped at fur trading posts and missions that the Indians were accustomed to visit.[3]

After the initial negotiations at Lesser Slave Lake, each band adhered separately to Treaty 8. The text required the Indian signatories to "cede, release, surrender and yield up . . . all their rights, title and privileges whatsoever" to the lands described in the treaty (all of northern Alberta plus neighbouring bits of British Columbia, Saskatchewan, and the Northwest Territories).[4] When a band adhered to treaty, it surrendered its share of aboriginal title to the entire region; it did not cede a specific parcel of land within the treaty area.

The commissioners received 2217 Indians into treaty in 1899 and 1219 in 1900. Although the government realized that perhaps as many as 500 Indians had not taken treaty, it decided that the Indian title could be considered extinguished and that it was not necessary to send out further treaty parties. The Treaty 8 Inspectors were authorized to add individuals to treaty lists when they made their annual rounds, and many Indians came into Treaty 8 in this way.

Some, however, remained outside of treaty for decades. There was little pressure to enter treaty because the traditional life of hunting and trapping remained viable. Another factor inducing some Indians to stay out was the desire to receive half-breed scrip. A half-breed scrip commission had accompanied the treaty commission of 1899 and had issued certificates for 1195 money scrips ($240 redeemable in Dominion Lands) and 48 land scrips (240 acres). Commissioner J.A. Macrae took 383 additional applications in 1900, and more natives continued to apply for scrip in subsequent years.

Many natives had some white ancestry and could plausibly claim to be either Indians or half-breeds, depending on which appeared more advantageous. Although treaty conferred greater long-term benefits, it paid only an initial gratuity of $7 and an annuity of $5, whereas a certificate for $240 scrip could be sold immediately to speculators for about

$75. A standoff ensued in which some natives living in the area around Lubicon Lake would not enter treaty because they wished to take scrip, while government officials would not grant them scrip because they wanted them to enter treaty, believing that to be in their long-term interest.

Over the years, many Indians added their names to the band list at Whitefish Lake, about 40 miles southeast of Lubicon Lake. In 1933, fourteen men petitioned the government to create a separate reserve for them at Lubicon Lake, pleading that Whitefish Lake was too far away and they did not wish to live there. In 1940, the Indian Affairs Branch gave the Lubicons permission to elect their own chief and treated them afterwards more or less as a separate band,[5] but it was too late for them to obtain a reserve directly from the federal government. The Natural Resources Transfer Act of 1930 had transferred public lands from the jurisdiction of the Crown federal to the Crown provincial, with an obligation upon Alberta to

> set aside, out of the unoccupied Crown lands hereby transferred to its administration, such further areas as the said Superintendent General may, in agreement with the appropriate Minister of the Province, select as necessary to enable Canada to fulfil its obligations under the treaties with the Indians of the Province.[6]

Local officials of the Indian Affairs Branch urged that a reserve be approved and surveyed at Lubicon Lake as quickly as possible. Officials in Ottawa seemed sympathetic but said it could not be done in 1940 due to lack of money and the late season.[7] The Indian Agent, however, visited Lubicon Lake with a federal surveyor and selected an approximate location for the reserve at the west end of the Lake.[8] Under the Treaty 8 formula of one section per family of five, or 128 acres per person, about 25-square miles would be required for the 127 Indians counted at that time.[9]

The Surveyor General claimed he could not afford to do the survey in 1941 because World War II had reduced his budget;[10] but on 17 February 1942, the Indian Affairs Branch requested the Province of Alberta to designate 25 square miles west of Lubicon Lake as a probable Indian reserve.[11] The same year, the Department of Mines and Resources applied for a supplementary appropriation of $5000 to pay for surveying several Indian reserves in northern Alberta, including the one at Lubicon Lake.[12]

But the Surveyor General clearly did not mean to be bothered with this work until after the War was over.[13]

In the meantime, other factors caused Indian Affairs to become less enthusiastic about establishing a reserve at Lubicon Lake. The Branch believed that local officials had registered many persons on Treaty 8 lists in contravention of the strict definitions of the Indian Act. In 1942, an Indian Affairs accountant, Malcolm McCrimmon, removed 663 persons from Treaty 8 band lists for reason such as illegitimacy, adoption, reception of half-breed scrip, and marriage of females to non-Indians.[14] His recommendations reduced the Lubicon Lake band to fewer than half of its former numbers.[15] McCrimmon then advised that a reserve at Lubicon Lake was not necessary because of the band's small size.[16]

McCrimmon's purge of band lists caused such a political uproar that the minister appointed Justice Macdonald of the Alberta Court of Queen's Bench to investigate. Macdonald reported in 1944 that 294 of McCrimmon's recommendations should be overturned, but Indian Affairs reinstated only 129 names out of this group.[17]

After the War ended, the Surveyor General turned to the task of surveying the proposed reserves in northern Alberta. Lubicon Lake was last on a list to be done in the summer of 1946, but the surveyor, who went first to Hay Lake in the far north, could not get to Lubicon Lake.[18] For reasons unknown, the survey at Lubicon Lake was not carried out the following year and was apparently "forgotten."[19]

In 1950, the Lubicon Indians again asked for their reserve,[20] touching off several confusing years. Indian Affairs officials were uncertain whether a reserve had ever been definitely promised or whether Lubicon Lake was the best place for it.[21] In the early 1950s, the ideology of the welfare state was becoming increasingly important in Canada. It was now thought that natives should not be left unsupervised in the bush but should be moved closer to towns and roads so they could receive medical and social benefits and their children could attend school regularly. This was, it will be remembered, the period when the Federal government began to settle the Inuit in villages and to bring the inhabitants of Newfoundland outports into more accessible towns.

Local officials were instructed to ask the Lubicons if they really wanted a reserve at Lubicon Lake or if they might prefer some other location. These consultations proved unsatisfactory because the Lubicons were still actively trapping and hunting. Only a handful might show up for any particular meeting, and opinion about the location of the reserve varied, depending on who was present.[22] Local officials were opposed to locating the reserve at Lubicon Lake because the site was remote and not suitable for farming, logging, or fishing.[23]

While these inquiries and discussions were proceeding, the province of Alberta, which had been carrying a provisional reserve on its books, began to exert pressure for a final decision.[24] The search for petroleum was getting under way in the north, and the province wanted to allow exploration near Lubicon Lake if the land was not to become an Indian reserve. After repeated inquiries, the province issued an ultimatum on 22 October 1953: if the federal government did not commit itself within thirty days, the province would take the Lubicon reserve off its books and open the area to exploration.[25] Indian Affairs, being advised by its local officals that Lubicon Lake was an unsuitable location and that some other solution could eventually be found,[26] made no effort to block Alberta's action, and the Lubicon reserve disappeared.

The Isolated Communities

There was little immediate consequence of the failure to agree upon a reserve. The Lubicons continued to live as they always had—hunting, fishing, and trapping on Crown land which was not otherwise used. There was only minor petroleum exploration around Lubicon Lake—11 wells drilled in the 1950s, 23 in the 1960s—and little production.[27] But the province began an all-weather road from Grande Prairie to Little Buffalo in 1971 and completed it in 1979. Eighty-two wells were drilled around Lubicon Lake in the 1970s.[28] Rising world oil prices also pointed to the development of northern Alberta's oil sands, and Premier Lougheed officially announced on 18 September 1973 that the Syncrude project would go ahead.[29]

Harold Cardinal, a Treaty 8 Cree, was elected President of the Indian Association of Alberta in 1968. In 1969, the federal government released its famous White Paper, proposing the gradual integration of Indians into the Canadian mainstream. In reaction, Cardinal's "Red Paper" of June 1970 vigorously reasserted the separate identity of Indians. The Indian Association of Alberta commissioned an oral history program to capture the elders' understanding of treaties, which seemed to go beyond the written terms.[30]

This new activism of Alberta Indians was related to efforts by the neighbouring Indians of the Northwest Territories to repudiate Treaties 8 and 11 in favour of a new land claims settlement with the federal government.[31] On 2 April 1973, the Indian Brotherhood of the Northwest Territories attempted to register a caveat to the land of the NWT, based on the assertion that aboriginal title had never been extinguished. The registrar of land titles referred this request to the courts, leading to the long legal battle of the *Paulette* case.[32] After an initial success in 1973, the Indians ultimately lost when the Supreme Court of Canada held that the Northwest Territories Act did not allow a caveat to be filed on unpatented land; but they gained much useful publicity for their cause and did finally succeed in getting the federal government to negotiate their claim.

The Indian Association of Alberta borrowed the caveat tactic at a time when it appeared to be working. On 27 October 1975, the Association tried to enter a caveat to about 25,000 square miles lying north of Lesser Slave Lake between the Peace and Athabasca Rivers. This was on behalf of the "isolated communities" —Lubicon Lake and half a dozen other groups of Indians in the area—who claimed to be entitled to reserves under Treaty 8. The normal way to seek a reserve would have been to file a claim with Indian Affairs. By attempting to register a caveat, the isolated communities were asserting an unextinguished aboriginal title to a large part of northern Alberta. They were propounding the novel legal doctrine that Treaty 8 had not extinguished aboriginal title even though the text purported to do so. As a matter of political strategy, they were trying to block Syncrude and other northern oil projects and thereby wring concessions from the provincial government.[33]

The caveat tactic had a modest success in 1976 in bringing about an agreement with Syncrude and the federal government to create a native employment program,[34] but its larger legal and political aims failed. When the Supreme Court of Canada rejected the *Paulette* appeal on 20 December 1976, it noted that one could probably register a similar caveat in Alberta because of the wording of the province's Land Titles Act.[35] Fearing that it might lose the impending court battle,[36] the government of Alberta led the legislature to retroactively insert a new section into the Land Titles Act: "No caveat may be registered which affects land for which no certificate of title has been issued."[37]

Alberta announced at this time what Richard Price calls a "minimal policy." The province would not negotiate directly with Indian groups but only with the federal government. Upon receiving a documented federal request, it would fulfil its responsibilities under the Natural Resources Transfer Act by transferring a land quantum based upon Indian population at time of treaty (1899). All mineral rights would be retained for the province.[38] The province saw no unextinguished aboriginal rights in Alberta, only "unfulfilled land entitlements."[39] The Attorney General challenged Indian groups to go to court if they thought they could prove the existence of unextinguished aboriginal title. "But the government," he said, "cannot be seen to be negotiating settlements to alleged legal rights when there is doubt as the existence of those rights."[40]

Litigation

The province's unyielding position caused the isolated communities coalition to fall apart, and the Lubicon band emerged as a political actor in its own right. After the young and relatively well-educated Bernard Ominayak was elected chief in 1978,[41] he made two decisions that had a profound effect on subsequent Lubicon strategy. First, he hired Fred Lennarson as the band's political adviser. Lennarson, originally from Chicago, was a product of the legendary Saul Alinsky's methods of agitation and organization. Alinsky described his unique approach as "mass jujitsu, utilizing the power of one part of the power structure against another part."[42] *"Wherever possible go outside of the experience of the enemy.* Here you want to cause confusion, fear, and retreat."[43]

Lennarson had worked for Indian groups in eastern Canada before being brought to the Indian Association of Alberta by Harold Cardinal; he also worked as an assistant to Cardinal after the latter left the IAA early in 1977 to become the Alberta Regional Director of Indian Affairs.[44] Under Lennarson's guidance, Lubicon political tactics have borne the Alinsky stamp of "mass jujitsu," pitting parts of government and public opinion against each other with unexpected moves such as appealing to the United Nations and boycotting the Winter Olympics. These tactics have not been successful in achieving a negotiated agreement (Alinsky's advice that "to the organizer, compromise is a key and beautiful word"[45] seems to have been forgotten); but they have earned the Lubicons immense publicity.

Ominayak's second fateful decision was to entrust the Lubicons' legal strategy to a Montreal lawyer, James O'Reilly, who had been instrumental in bringing about the James Bay Agreement. In early 1980 Billy Diamond, Chief of the James Bay Cree, flew in to meet Ominayak. Offering to guarantee a bank loan of $400,000 for the Lubicons plus another $300,000 if necessary, he told Ominayak to hire O'Reilly.[46]

On 15 November 1973, O'Reilly had persuaded Justice Albert Malouf of the Quebec Superior Court to issue an injunction stopping the construction of the giant Hydro-Quebec project at James Bay on grounds of the unextinguished aboriginal title of the Cree and Inuit. The Quebec Court of Appeal quickly stayed Malouf's injunction, but the Quebec government was so shaken that it entered into negotiations with the natives, leading to the James Bay Agreement.[47] O'Reilly played a key role in negotiating the agreement and selling it to the Cree. (In a bizarre twist, O'Reilly went to court again in 1990, claiming that the agreement he had worked so hard to negotiate was unconstitutional.)[48]

The political-legal strategy that had worked for the James Bay Cree in the 1970s—claiming unextinguished aboriginal title, seeking an injunction to hold up natural-resource development, entering into negotiations to achieve a settlement—must have seemed an ideal model for the Lubicon Cree in the 1980s. But there was a key difference between the two situations. Before 1975, there had been no land surrenders of any kind in northern Quebec, so the native claim to possess unextinguished aboriginal title had *prima facie* validity. By contrast Treaty 8 purported to extinguish the Indian title to all of northern Alberta, so the Lubicons have had to make out the far more doubtful proposition that the absence of an adhesion by what may or may not have been a Lubicon band in 1899-1900 created an unceded region in the middle of the Treaty 8 area, like a hole in the middle of a doughnut.

The Lubicons' theory is a departure from the official understanding and administration of treaties in Canada. There have been 80 adhesions, more or less, to the 11 Numbered Treaties in western Canada.[49] In only three of the these cases has the written formula signed by the parties indicated that unceded land was being added to the treaty area: the Green Lake adhesion to Treaty 6 in 1889, the northern Manitoba adhesion to Treaty 5 in 1908-1910, and the northern Ontario adhesions to Treaty 9 in 1929-1930.[50] In each of these three cases, the Indians signing the adhesion lived in an area that the original treaty commission had not visited and that was not contained in the land description of the original treaty document. It was clearly an addition to, or extension of, the treaty. In all other adhesions, as for example Big Bear's adhesion to Treaty 6 in

1882,[51] the chief signed a document surrendering his band's "right, title and interest" in the lands described in the original treaty; no new territory was added to the ceded area. In these cases, the Indians making the adhesion were living within the area described by the treaty.

There is little North American case law to clarify the meaning of adhesion. The closest parallel is a 1976 decision by the Supreme Court of Idaho upholding the validity of the Hellgate Treaty of 1855, even though one group of Kootenai Indians did not sign it.[52] The court held that ratification of the treaty by the Senate and proclamation by the President expressed the sovereign's intent to extinguish aboriginal title in the area described by the treaty. Although this decision was cited favourably by the Ontario Court of Appeal in the *Bear Island* case,[53] its applicability to the interpretation of Canadian treaties has yet to be demonstrated.

The *Bear Island* case resembles the Lubicon dispute inasmuch as the Temagami band, although they live within the land described by the Robinson Huron Treaty of 1850, claim they still possess unextinguished aboriginal title because they did not sign the treaty. There is a difference, however, because the Ontario Supreme Court and the Ontario Court of Appeal have both held that a chief representing the Temagami did in fact sign the Robinson Treaty in 1850.[54] This case, now on appeal to the Supreme Court of Canada, may have considerable relevance to the Lubicon dispute, depending on how the Court deals with it.

Without a victory in *Bear Island* or some other case, the Lubicon theory of continuing aboriginal title must be considered fragile. One can cite no clear judicial precedent in its favour, and it contradicts the consistent Canadian administrative practice of more than a century. O'Reilly must have realized that his chances of making this theory prevail in court were limited, and this perhaps explains why, although he spent much of the 1980s in court on behalf of the Lubicons, he never tackled this proposition directly. His main strategy was to seek an interlocutory injunction against further resource development, on the grounds that the Lubicons' aboriginal rights were threatened with irreparable damage. He tried to hold up resource development first, without actually proving the continuing existence of the Lubicons' aboriginal rights.

This strategy avoided exposing a fragile legal theory to a definitive legal test; it was a political use of the courts to bring government to the negotiating table, as in the James Bay case. O'Reilly clearly wanted to relive the James Bay experience: get an injunction on the basis that native rights are in danger without having to prove that the rights actually exist, then wait for government to come to the table once natural resource development is blocked. It was also straight out of Alinsky: *"No one can negotiate without the power to compel negotiation."*[55] Take hostages first, then talk.

O'Reilly went to work immediately, commencing an action in the Federal Court of Canada on 25 April 1980 against Canada, Alberta, and a number of oil companies. He asked for a declaratory judgment affirming the Lubicons' land rights, without requesting a specific remedy such as damages or an injunction. But the Court held in November that the jurisdiction given to it by the Federal Court Act extended only to suits against the Crown in right of Canada. It had no power to try claims against the province of Alberta or private oil companies, not even against Petro-Canada, which, although federally owned, was not an "officer" or "servant" of the federal Crown.[56] An appeal was quickly dismissed by the Federal Court of Appeal.[57]

From a purely legal standpoint, this seems like an odd case. O'Reilly had almost no time to prepare, and his decision to go to the Federal Court of Canada seems to have been predestined to fail. But the motives may have been as much political as legal: to show the Lubicons some immediate action, to attract publicity for their cause, to build up a sense of moral outrage at yet another Indian loss in the white man's courts. Interestingly, O'Reilly had launched a similar throwaway action in Quebec before bringing his main request for an injunction to halt the James Bay project.[58]

These initial efforts did bring some result. John Munro, Minister of Indian Affairs, accepted the Lubicon claim for negotiation as a treaty entitlement,[59] and in January 1982 there was a federal-provincial meeting to consider the issue.[60] But to negotiate for a reserve within Treaty 8 would undercut the Lubicons' position that they still possessed aboriginal title because they had never adhered to Treaty 8. The potential payoff would be much higher if they could make this latter position prevail.

O'Reilly, therefore, turned to the Alberta Court of Queen's Bench. On 19 February 1982, he filed a statement of claim requesting an injunction against resource development. He asked for a complete cessation of activity in a "reserve area" of 900 square miles around Lubicon Lake, and a reduced level of activity in a surrounding area of 8500 square miles called the "hunting and trapping territory." The theory behind the claim was that unrestricted resource development posed imminent danger to the Lubicons' land rights, which were said to be of three types: (1) aboriginal title that still existed because the Lubicons had never formally adhered to Treaty 8; (2) "in the alternative," as lawyers like to say when they espouse contradictory theories simultaneously, the reserve that had been granted but never implemented by government officials; (3) the Indians' right to hunt, fish, and trap on unoccupied Crown land protected by the Natural Resources Act, 1930.[61]

Ominayak v. Norcen became an immensely complicated case. Numerous procedural arguments took up many days of hearings and resulted in two reported rulings, both of which favoured the Lubicons.[62] The case also generated a massive amount of evidence, filling 32 bound volumes, about such topics as the history of the Cree people, the genealogy of the Lubicon band members, and the reasons for the decline in the moose population. Indeed, an exasperated Justice Forsyth remarked in his second procedural ruling that since much of the evidence required to decide about the injunction was similar to what would be required to determine whether the Lubicons had any land rights, "such time and preparation might better be spent in preparation for the trial itself with the trial going forward at the earliest possible date."[63]

Justice Forsyth declined to grant the injunction. On 17 November 1983, he held that "damages would be an adequate remedy to the applicants in the event they were ultimately successful in establishing any of their positions advanced."[64] That is, the cart could not go before the horse. The Lubicons would first have to prove that their aboriginal title still existed, then seek damages if they could show they had suffered loss. Justice Forsyth did not believe that interference with "their traditional way of life" threatened them with immediate "irreparable injury." He wrote that "the twentieth century, for better or for worse, has been part of the applicants' lives for a considerable period of time."[65] Moreover, an injunction would inflict immediate economic harm on the oil companies, for which the Lubicons would not be able to compensate them should their legal claims prove unfounded.

On 11 January 1985, the Alberta Court of Appeal upheld the lower court's decision. Writing for a 4-1 majority, Justice Kerans said:

> We think that the courts should not forget that an interim injunction is emergent relief. The claimant seeks a remedy without proof of his claim. This inversion should only be considered in cases where the harm is of such seriousness and of such a nature that any redress available after trial would not be fair or reasonable.[66]

Without judging the merit of the Lubicons' theory about their aboriginal rights, the Court held that there was ample time to try the claim and assess damages if any.

In March 1985, the Supreme Court of Canada refused leave to appeal. Two weeks later, after the British Columbia Court of Appeal granted an injunction against logging on Meares Island in circumstances that bore some similarity to the Lubicon case, O'Reilly again sought leave to appeal but was refused a second time.[67]

This defeat marked the end of the Lubicons' attempt to use the courts to achieve their objectives. Having failed to obtain an interim injunction against resource development, they chose not to further litigate their claim of aboriginal title in the Alberta courts, just as they decided not to press their claim for a declaratory judgment in the Federal Court of Canada. Their supporters say "it had become obvious they could in all likelihood never get justice through this route,"[68] whereas skeptics think they realized the weakness of their aboriginal rights claims and had never seriously intended to litigate them. The band did unsuccessfully seek an injunction in the Federal Court of Canada to compel the Department of Indian Affairs to pay their legal fees (more than $2,000,000),[69] but this was a sideshow. They would now rely increasingly on Alinsky/Lennarson tactics of political guerrilla warfare.

The Lubicons and Modern Alberta Politics

During *Ominayak v. Norcen* the Lubicons had already turned to the churches, resulting in a letter dated 23 October 1983 from the World Council of Churches to Prime Minister Trudeau, accusing the Alberta government of genocide.[70] Other churchmen quickly took up the cause. The Task Force of Churches on Corporate Responsibility upbraided Petro-Canada for its role in oil exploration.[71] A delegation of clergymen headed by Ted Scott, the Anglican Primate of Canada, visited Lubicon Lake in the spring of 1984.[72] The Alberta government referred the World Council of Churches letter to the Alberta Ombudsman, who reported in August 1984 that he had found "no factual basis" for charges of genocide.[73] Bernard Ominayak then released a 61-page statement attacking the Ombudsman's report.[74] It was indoor-outdoor political theatre, with NDP members of the Alberta Legislature and the House of Commons recycling the news stories created by ecclesiastical denunciations of the government.

Meanwhile, an important change was taking place in Alberta's position. The provincial government announced in the spring of 1984 that it was willing to transfer mineral rights on Crown lands that might become part of Indian reserves, although it would retain the right to 50% of royalties.[75] This policy change had actually been made in 1982 in the context of negotiations over the Fort Chipewyan claim,[76] but the public announcement at this time was clearly motivated by bad publicity over the Lubicons.

The political situation changed markedly with the election of a Progressive Conservative majority in Parliament in September 1984. The new Prime Minister, Brian Mulroney, had campaigned on a theme of reconciliation with the provinces and with ethnic groups (e.g., payment of compensation to Japanese-Canadians interned during World War II). The new Minister of Indian Affairs, David Crombie, had been mayor of Toronto and was an accomplished practitioner of ethnic politics. He met personally with Ominayak in November and agreed to appoint a federal fact-finder to examine the Lubicons' case.[77] In January 1985, he announced that the investigator would be E. Davie Fulton, onetime federal Minister of Justice and member of the Supreme Court of British Columbia. Fulton's alcoholism had led him into embarrassments and forced him to resign from the bench, but he was now rehabilitated, and he still shared the aura of Red Toryism that Crombie liked to project.

Starting in April, Fulton spent a great deal of time with the Lubicons and ended up virtually as their advocate. On his recommendation, the federal government made an *ex gratia* payment of $1.5 million to the band on 8 January 1986;[78] much of this money was used to repay the loans guaranteed by the James Bay Cree. On 7 February 1986, Fulton submitted a long "Discussion Paper" that isolated contentious issues and highlighted points of common ground among the province, the federal government, and the Lubicons.[79] Suggesting concessions by all parties, it was meant to be the starting point of genuine negotiations.

Perhaps spooked by the prospect of a Fulton Report relatively favourable to the Lubicons, Alberta offered in December 1985 to make an immediate transfer of 25 square miles to the band if they would drop all litigation (although their attempt to gain an injunction had been defeated, their main suit was still theoretically alive).[80] But the Lubicons dismissed this offer out of hand because a reserve of 25-square miles corresponded to their band size in 1940—127 members—and they had grown much larger in the meantime and wanted a correspondingly larger reserve. The size of the band was itself a topic of hot dispute. The band list maintained by federal authorities had 182 names in 1985, but the Lubicons claimed at least 347 members in the same year.[81] The numerical divergence had many causes, including the McCrimmon inquiry of the 1940 and other disagreements about who was entitled to band membership. Parliament also amended the Indian Act in 1985 to allow women, disenfranchised for marrying outside the band, to regain Indian status, along with their children. No one could say what effect this would have on the Lubicon band, but the leadership estimated that a reserve for over 400 people would be necessary. Under the Treaty 8 formula of 128 acres per person, this meant at least 80 square miles.

To an outsider, a quantitative issue such as the size of the band seems like an ideal subject for negotiation and compromise, but for the Lubicons it was a matter of principle. Their theory of aboriginal rights asserted that they were not yet bound by Treaty 8 because they had never adhered to it. When they finally entered the treaty, it would be as a group with all their members. They had to have the power to determine the size and membership of their band, as Indian bands had always done when they entered treaty. To accept any external definition of their size would undercut their claim to continued possession of aboriginal title.

The federal government was not happy with Fulton's report, and Crombie moved on to another portfolio.[82] The Prime Minister then appointed a new negotiator, Roger Tassé, a retired Deputy Minister of Justice and a main architect of the Canadian Charter of Rights and Freedoms. When bilateral discussions between Tassé and the Lubicons began on June 16, 1986, the Lubicons refused to allow Alberta to join, thus rejecting the trilateral approach used for other Treaty 8 claims in the 1980s.[83] But the Lubicons broke off the talks on July 8 when the federal government disputed the band size claimed by the Lubicons and denied their theory of continuing aboriginal title.[84]

With the failure of negotiations, the Lubicons began to put more emphasis on their attempts to influence public opinion. On 14 February 1984, they had filed a complaint before the United Nations Human Rights Committee.[85] They had also established contact with European Green parties; and even as negotiations began with Tassé, a Dutch Green member of the European Parliament was touring Canada in support of the Lubicons.[86] The Lubicons had also spoken of disrupting the 1988 Calgary Winter Olympics, particularly by asking museums around the world not to participate in the Glenbow Museum's Indian exhibition, ''The

Spirit Sings.'' In August 1986 Ominayak, Lennarson, and some Lubicon elders went on a tour of seven European countries to generate support for the boycott.[87]

Such actions continued unabated during 1986 and 1987. The boycott had some success as a number of museums declined to loan artifacts to ''The Spirit Sings,'' but it did not prevent the Glenbow from mounting the exhibit. Lubicon supporters also picketed the cross-country Olympic torch relay, which was sponsored by Petro-Canada.[88] Again, they got some media attention but did not seriously interfere with the relay nor with Petro-Canada's publicity bonanza.

Although not immediately successful, these efforts did indirectly lead to results. In October 1987, the federal government appointed a new negotiatior, Calgary lawyer Brian Malone.[89] A meeting involving two cabinet ministers, Bill McKnight and Joe Clark, was set up in Ottawa for 21 January 1988, in an attempt to get movement before the Winter Olympics opened in February. But the meeting got nowhere, and the Minister of Indian Affairs, Bill McKnight, gave the Lubicons an ultimatum. If they did not return to the table within eight days, the federal government would take further steps toward a legal resolution.[90]

The Lubicon strategy at this time was to demand a prominent role for Davie Fulton as a mediator. Archbishop Ted Scott telexed the Prime Minister to appoint Fulton, and Fulton told the *Globe and Mail* on 9 February that he could settle the Lubicon dispute in three to six months.[91] He appeared the same day before the House of Commons Standing Committee on Aboriginal Affairs, which then voted to ask the government to appoint him as mediator for bilateral negotiations.[92]

McKnight, however, pushed ahead with his own strategy. On 3 February 1988, he wrote to Jim Horsman, the Alberta Attorney General and Minister of Federal and Intergovernmental Affairs, to request that Alberta provide a land quantum for a reserve according to what became known as the ''McKnight formula,'' and he made scarcely veiled threats to sue the province if it did not quickly comply. The McKnight formula accepted the full band size and kept it open to allow for natural increase until the reserve was actually surveyed and for the return of disenfranchised Indian women and their children under the Indian Act amendments of 1985. However, it did not include the many nonstatus Indians and members of other bands that the Lubicons had on their own list. It also would have made deductions for persons whose ancestors had received half-breed scrip in the past as well as for those who in the future might choose to take land in severalty, as allowed by Treaty 8.[93] The McKnight formula would have produced a reserve larger than Alberta had previously been willing to grant but smaller than the Lubicons demanded.

The provincial cabinet did not like being threatened, and it was increasingly exasperated by the federal government's inability to come to terms with the Lubicons. It also embarrassed itself by announcing the Daishowa pulp mill and then having to admit that the timber-cutting licenses for this project would overlap with the Lubicons' "Hunting and Trapping Territory."[94] Around this time, the cabinet decided that Premier Don Getty should approach Bernard Ominayak personally and try to work something out.[95] Ominayak proved receptive to the overture, and the two men met for the first time on 4 March 1988.[96]

McKnight's initiative had led to an unexpected realignment of forces. Up to this point, the Lubicons, while denouncing both governments, had saved their worst rhetoric for the province and insisted on talking only with the federal government, under the constitutional principle of federal responsibility for Indians. Why did Ominayak now start to deal with Getty? Perhaps because McKnight's threats to litigate the matter would have forced O'Reilly to justify his aboriginal-rights theory in court.

In any case, Getty and Ominayak got on very well personally, and Getty became almost an advocate for the Lubicons in the spring of 1988. He tried to get the federal government to accept a proposal for arbitration in which there would be a three-person tribunal. The Lubicons would name Davie Fulton, the two governments would agree on another choice, and the two arbitrators would agree on a neutral chairman.[97] But the federal government would not accept the proposal, perhaps because the Lubicons did not want the arbitration to be binding,[98] perhaps for other reasons not made public.

McKnight, therefore, made good on his threat to litigate. On 17 May 1988, federal lawyers filed a statement of claim in the Calgary District of the Alberta Court of Queen's Bench demanding that the province make available a land quantum for a reserve according to the McKnight formula. Alberta and the Lubicon band were joined as defendants.[99] It was a strange reversal of the litigation of the early 1980s.

It quickly became evident that the Lubicons would do everything possible to avoid proving their claim in court. In early June, Bernard Ominayak began to say openly that the Lubicons were ready to "assert jurisdiction," i.e., to assume governmental control over their traditional territory in validation of their claim that they had never relinquished their aboriginal rights.[100] On 21 September, Ominayak announced that his band would assert jurisdiction on 15 October if an agreement was not reached; this would mean a blockade of roads into oil-producing lands.[101] On 6 October, O'Reilly read a statement in court that the Lubicons were asserting jurisdiction and would not participate in any further judicial proceedings.[102] They had no hope of obtaining justice in Canadian courts, and they rejected the jurisdiction of Canadian authorities over them. Observers noted that O'Reilly trembled as he spoke. It was a paradoxical moment for one who had built his career on the strategic use of Canadian courts.

Events now moved quickly in elaborate choreography. Although the province declared that it would enforce the law, the Lubicons set up their blockade on 15 October. The province secured an injunction against it on 19 October; and early on the morning of 20 October, heavily armed RCMP officers took down the blockade and arrested 27 people.[103] Getty and Ominayak, who had certainly been in contact behind the scenes, then met on 22 October in the little town of Grimshaw. The same day, Getty agreed to sell the federal government 79-square miles with mineral rights, and another 16-square miles without mineral rights, for a reserve.[104] The total of 95-square miles conformed to the Lubicons' own count of their membership.

In the trilateral treaty-entitlement negotiations with the Whitefish Lake band and the federal government, Alberta had already decided to depart from its "minimal policy" that reserves should be determined by band size at time of treaty. It was now willing to accept the federal "date of first survey" (DOFS) position.[105] The Whitefish Lake settlement was announced on 21 December 1988.[106] Getty, however, went even farther in the Lubicon case. In approving the 95-square-mile reserve, he was accepting not only the DOFS principle but also the band's own count of its membership in preference to the federal count—an issue that had not arisen in the Whitefish negotiations.

But no settlement was possible without the agreement of the federal government. Negotiations began well when Ottawa accepted the 95-square-mile reserve but broke down on 24 January 1989. Many minor disagreements, such as whether Canada should pay for a hockey rink on the reserve, contributed to the stalemate, but the biggest single issue was compensation. Maintaining they had a "comprehensive" claim based on aboriginal rights, the Lubicons demanded compensation from the federal government for failure to extinguish their aboriginal title in

1899. The amount owed—$167 million according to one calculation—would compensate the Lubicons for various federal benefits that they had allegedly not received since 1899 because they had no reserve. The Lubicons were willing to negotiate the amount of compensation but not the principle that something had to be paid. The federal government viewed this as only a "specific" claim based on treaty entitlement. It recognized the Lubicons' right to a reserve, and it was willing to pay to set up the reserve—$45 million, according to its calculations. But it refused to pay a general amount for extinguishment of aboriginal title, because in its view aboriginal title had been extinguished all over northern Alberta with the signing of Treaty 8. It was not so much the amount of money that was at stake, although that was certainly important. The federal government could not accede to the Lubicons' claim for compensation without undercutting the validity of the treaties, on which it had always insisted. If it deviated from this principle in the Lubicon case, it might be forced to regard many other current and potential claims across Canada as "comprehensive" (aboriginal rights) rather than "specific" (treaty entitlement) claims.[107]

The actual collapse of the negotiations was little short of bizarre. When the federal representatives delivered a formal offer on 24 January, Fred Lennarson reacted by evoking a "Jonestown scenario." The Lubicon, he said, were "not afraid to die if they must." After lunch, he gave Ken Colby, the federal public relations specialist, a photocopy of the chapter entitled "Of Voluntary Death," from Friedrich Nietzsche's *Thus Spoke Zarathustra*. The chapter begins:

> Many die too late and some die too early. Still the doctrine sounds strange: "Die at the right time."
> Die at the right time: thus Zarathustra teaches.

Not surprisingly, talks broke off in the afternoon after only twenty minutes.[108]

Since the breakdown of negotiations, the Lubicons have persisted in their refusal to compromise. They tried to widen their support by creating a "Treaty Alliance of North American Aboriginal Nations,"[109] sometimes described (rather grandiosely) as an "Indian NATO." They also continued to "assert jurisdiction" by delivering an ultimatum to oil companies: obtain permits from us or shut down your operations.[110] On

1 December 1989, Petro-Canada and Norcen shut in 20 wells rather than make an issue of it.[111]

Simultaneously, however, the solidarity of the Lubicons began to break up. Only days after the failure of negotiations, Brian Malone was contacted by Lubicon band members who complained that they had been dropped from the band because of their opposition to Ominayak's tactics. They said they now wanted land in severalty, an option provided by Treaty 8. After repeated discussions with these dissidents, it emerged that, while some really wanted severalty, others favoured forming another band and negotiating a separate settlement. Talks with federal officials were well underway by spring 1989.

Ominayak called a snap band election for 31 May to dispell rumours of opposition to his leadership. He was re-elected chief by a unanimous show of hands,[112] but this could not stop the defectors. On 28 August the Department of Indian Affairs recognized a new Woodland band of about 350 members, including 117 names previously on the Lubicons' own list. About 30 of these had been expelled by the Lubicons; the rest seem to have left voluntarily.[113] The new band is an amalgamation of Lubicon dissenters with Indians from nearby "isolated communities," such as Cadotte Lake, that had not previously been recognized as bands.

The Woodland leaders immediately began to negotiate a specific claim, resulting in an agreement in principle on 26 March 1990. Its terms are similar to the final offer that the Lubicons rejected.[114] There is to be a reserve at Cadotte Lake (which will not interfere with the site promised to the Lubicons), and a financial package to build homes and other facilities. The completed deal was signed in December 1990, with an announced value of $56 million.[115] Meanwhile, the federal position is that it will extend similar treatment to any other bands in the isolated communities area that want to enter negotiations.[116] If this policy is successful, it will leave the Lubicons isolated and may lead to further defections from their ranks.

On 26 March 1990, the United Nations Human Rights Committee handed down a ruling on the complaint the Lubicons had made six years earlier, but the rather inconclusive nature of the judgment deprived it of any political impact. The Committee found that, while the Lubicons had a right to protection of their culture and identity under international agreements, Canada "proposes to rectify the situation by a remedy that the committee deems appropriate."[117] The Committee also rejected the Lubicons' charges that Ottawa had conspired to form the Woodland Cree

Band in order to undermine the Lubicons' claim. At the time of writing, the stalemate continues.

The Lubicons' latest tactic is to try to keep out logging contractors who wish to cut wood for the Daishowa mill. The events that took place at Oka, Quebec, in the summer of 1990 have strengthened the Lubicons' hand by making an outbreak of violence in Alberta seem more plausible. In November 1990, there was an attack upon a contractor's camp, after which 13 Lubicon band members were charged with arson.[118]

Strategy and Stalemate

The Lubicons want, above all, a settlement based on their theory of aboriginal rights, which would give them, in addition to a reserve of 95-square miles, a large amount of money, including perhaps $100 million compensation for extinguishment of aboriginal title, and many other rights, including self-government and management of wildlife in the region. The main alternative at this stage is a reserve of 95-square miles based on the theory of treaty entitlement, with less cash and other benefits. At earlier stages in the dispute, there were even less generous options with smaller reserves; but these dropped out of consideration with the events of fall 1988. But the Lubicons will not accept the treaty option, even though it is now more generous than ever before. They are willing to remain without a treaty settlement in hopes of obtaining the more lucrative aboriginal rights settlement. (Note, however, that their acceptance of the status quo hinges upon the belief that it is only a temporary stage preparatory to obtaining the bigger prize. It would be irrational to prefer the status quo to the treaty settlement if the status quo were to be permanent. We will return later to this point.)

The preferences of the federal government are a mirror image of the Lubicons'. The government's first choice is a treaty settlement, which it acknowledges itself obliged to make under the law. Its last choice is an aboriginal rights settlement, which by accepting the Lubicons' novel theory of adhesion might have repercussions on other pending claims and perhaps even on existing treaty obligations. It prefers the status quo of no settlement at all to recognizing the Lubicons' aboriginal rights claim.

After years of supporting less generous options, Alberta's first choice is now the 95-square-mile reserve that Getty and Ominayak agreed to on 22 October 1988. But Alberta's second choice is not so clear, perhaps because it has blurred its preferences in trying to broker a deal between the other two parties. I assume, however, that the province prefers no deal at all to an aboriginal rights deal because recognition of the Lubicons' aboriginal title might jeopardize its control of natural resources in the area.

However, the preferences of Alberta are not critical at this stage. Canada and the Lubicons are required by the Canadian constitution to reach a bilateral agreement. Only after an accord is made will Canada request land from Alberta. The important issue is to understand why Canada and the Lubicons have not been able to reach agreement.

Until the band actually has a reserve, it has little purchase over the federal government. Most of the things it has done in the past, such as interfering with oil and gas development, affected Alberta more than Canada. The band may be able to impede Daishowa, but this also will have much more provincial than federal impact. The Lubicons perceived an opportunity to embarrass Canada in the 1988 Winter Olympics and did their best to exploit it, but they still did not succeed in changing Canada's preference structure. Nor has their appeal to the United Nations Human Rights Committee had any great impact.

The Lubicons have been reluctant to pursue their legal option, presumably because they realize their theory is novel and has a high chance of rejection in court. Even worse, a judicial defeat for the aboriginal rights principle would decisively undermine its political credibility. The political strategy of demanding aboriginal rights does not require that the legal theory be demonstrably valid, but it does require that it not be demonstrably invalid. The Lubicons thus have much to lose by going to court.

What are the federal government 's options for influencing the Lubicons' choices? It could try to make them forget about aboriginal rights by winning a conclusive battle in court, which seems to have been the federal strategy in 1988 when it initiated a lawsuit. But this strategy proved difficult in two respects. First, it was necessary to sue Alberta as well as the Lubicons, thus poisoning intergovernmental relations, which as the Meekison and Gibbins chapters reveal are already decidedly complex and factious. Second, since this was a civil, not a criminal action, the Lubicons could not be compelled to co-operate. It might have been possible to win a legal judgment even after the Lubicons refused to appear in court, but such a result would have made the federal government look like a bully and would probably have backfired in the wider realm of public opinion. Thus it is not surprising that Canada decided not to proceed with its litigation.

It appears rather than the federal government is attempting to break the stalemate by recognizing and dealing with new bands such as the Woodland Cree. If they continue to succeed in drawing members of the Lubicon band into other bands, the Lubicons at some point will no longer be able to maintain even their treaty entitlement claim to a 95-square-mile reserve. The Lubicons thus have a great deal to lose if they refuse to negotiate while the federal government cultivates other partners.

It is, therefore, perhaps not surprising that the Lubicons re-entered into negotiations in early 1992. Although the dispute is far from settled, Canada may have found the right strategy for breaking the stalemate and coming to a negotiated settlement . At that point, the full consequences of the Lubicons dispute for Alberta politics will become clearer. Readers interested in a more formalized statement of this interpretation, based on rational-choice analysis, can now turn to the appendix.

Appendix
A Study in Strategy

Let us attempt to model the final stage of the Lubicon dispute using the techniques of rational-choice analysis.[1] Each actor—the Lubicon band, the federal government, and the provincial government—will be considered as rationally pursuing its own interests and ranking its preferences in a consistent way. Conflict arises because the three players have different interests and different priorities.

If we call an aboriginal rights settlement "AR," the status quo of no deal "ND," and a treaty entitlement settlement "TE," the preferences of the three parties may be summarized in Matrix 11-1:

MATRIX 11-1   Collective Choice Problem

		PREFERENCES				
		1		2		3
	Lubicons	AR	>	ND	>	TE
PLAYERS	Canada	TE	>	ND	>	AR
	Alberta	TE	>	ND	>	AR

This situation represents considerable, if not complete, agreement. Canada and Alberta agree upon the ranking of all three options, and all three parties agree upon the status quo as second choice. There is enough agreement to generate a "Condorcet winner," that is, a collectively transitive majority choice.

To see this, imagine that the three parties each have one vote to cast in a series of choices between the options taken two at a time. In a contest of AR against ND, Canada and Alberta prefer ND, so ND > AR. In a contest of AR against TE, Canada and Alberta prefer TE, so TE > AR. And in a contest of ND against TE, Canada and Alberta again prefer TE to ND, so TE > ND. But if TE > ND, and if ND > AR, then TE > AR, which is also true. Overall, there is a transitive "collective" or "social choice" of TE > ND > AR (treaty entitlement > no deal > aboriginal rights). TE would thus be a so-called "Condorcet winner" (an alternative that wins every pairwise comparison) in the problem of collective choice.

Why then has TE not emerged as a final outcome, at least not yet? Because the real-world stituation is not adequately modelled by a three-person voting game. The Canadian constitution requires Canada and the Lubicons to reach a bilateral agreement, after which Canada will request land from Alberta. In this scenario, there is not a single-stage three-person voting game but a two-stage sequence of two-person games in which Canada is the common player. To see why Canada and the Lubicons have not been able to reach agreement in their game will require further analysis.

Let us model the conflict between Canada and the Lubicons using a two-person, binary-choice game. Each player has two strategies: to offer an aboriginal rights (AR) or a treaty entitlement (TE) settlement. No deal (ND) is not a strategy, only an outcome. As in the well known game of assurance, the parties only have to adopt the same strategies to achieve a settlement, as shown in Matrix 11-2:

MATRIX 11-2   Assurance Model of Lubicon-Canada Game

| | | CANADA | |
		AR	TE
LUBICONS	AR	AR settlement	no deal
	TE	no deal	TE settlement

LUBICONS: AR > ND > TE
CANADA: TE > ND > AR

Since the players are allowed to communicate with each other, it would be a simple matter to co-ordinate their strategies and achieve a settlement; but their preference rankings dictate otherwise, as we can see in Matrix 11-3, where we use their preferences as ordinal payoffs in the game matrix (we follow the convention of reversing the verbal order when we assign numbers to represent ranks; i.e., 3 = most preferred alternative, 2 = next, 1 = least preferred) .

MATRIX 11-3   Lubicon-Canada Game with Ordinal Payoffs

		CANADA	
		AR	TE
	AR	3, 1	**2, 2**
LUBICONS			
	TE	2, 2	1, 3

Given these payoffs, each player has a dominant strategy. The Lubicons should offer AR because they get a higher payoff no matter what Canada does. If Canada offers AR, then the Lubicons get their first choice (AR), which is better than their second (ND); and if Canada offers TE, the Lubicons get ND, which is better in their eyes than TE. For similar reasons, Canada has a dominant strategy of TE. If the Lubicons also play TE, the result is TE, which is Canada's first choice; and if the Lubicons play AR, the result is ND, Canada's second choice.

The game thus has a saddlepoint (shown in boldface) in the upper right cell of the matrix: no deal, which is the second choice of both players. This is an equilibrium outcome in the sense that neither player has an incentive to make a unilateral move. Movement for either player without movement by the other will result in the moving player dropping from second to third choice in his payoff. In nontechnical language, we have a stalemate because each side prefers to continue without an agreement rather than to accept the other's first option, since the other's best choice is its own worst choice. What initially appeared to be a game of assurance turns out to be the game known in the literature as "deadlock."[2]

Deadlock or stalemate ensues because neither party will accept the other's preferred principle of co-operation. A break in the stalemate will require a change in the payoff matrix, which means a change in the way in which either or both of the players rank the outcomes. Let us look at the possibilities for the players to induce such changes in their opponents' preferences.[3]

The Lubicons' political strategy has always been to cause embarrassment for the federal government, thus inducing it to prefer AR to ND in order to end the conflict. Success in this Alinsky-Lennarson strategy would produce a federal preference ranking of AR > TE > ND, resulting in the payoffs shown in Matrix 11-4:

MATRIX 11-4   Lubicon-Canada Game after Lubicon Political Success

		CANADA	
		AR	TE
LUBICONS	AR	**3, 2**	2, 1
	TE	2, 1	1, 3

LUBICONS: AR > ND > TE
CANADA: TE > AR > ND

In this version of the game, Canada no longer has a dominant strategy. Canada should play AR if the Lubicons play AR, and TE if the Lubicons play TE. In other words, Canada is now in an assurance game where it profits by playing the same strategy as the Lubicons. Canada, of course, prefers the Lubicons to play TE, but will accept AR rather than miss an agreement altogether. The Lubicons, for their part, still have AR as a dominant strategy. Knowing that the Lubicons will play AR, Canada will do likewise, and the game will have a saddlepoint in the upper left cell, representing an aboriginal rights settlement.

The Lubicons' political strategy is formally rational, but the evidence suggests that it is not empirically feasible. The Lubicons will not have much weight with the federal government until the band actually has a reserve. During the 1988 Winter Olympics the Lubicons did their best to embarrass Canada but their actions did not change Canada's preference structure. And their efforts to interfer with oil and gas development or to impede Daishowa have much more provincial than federal impact. As well, their appeal to the United Nations Human Rights Committee has not had any major effect.

The Lubicons could also resort to testing their aboriginal rights theory in court, and a legal victory would decisively change the federal government's preference order. If the courts held that the Lubicons still had unextinguished aboriginal title, the rule of law would compel Canada to make AR its first priority, (AR > TE > ND), yielding Matrix 11-5:

MATRIX 11-5   Lubicon-Canada Game after Lubicon Judicial Victory

		CANADA	
		AR	TE
LUBICONS	AR	**3, 3**	2, 1
	TE	2, 1	1, 2

LUBICONS: AR > ND > TE
CANADA: AR > TE > ND

Once again, the game has a saddlepoint in the upper left cell. AR remains a dominant strategy for the Lubicons. Knowing that, Canada does better by offering AR, which is also its first preference. Both sides get the outcome they value most highly.

Presumably because the Lubicons realize their theory is unprecedented and is likely to be rejected in court, the Lubicons have been disinclined to pursue their legal option. The Lubicons have much to lose by going to court. A judicial defeat for the AR principle would decisively undermine its political credibility. The political strategy of demanding AR does not require that the legal theory be demonstrably valid, but it does require that it not be demonstrably invalid.

This reasoning can be formalized. Assume that the advantage of AR over TE is about $100 million (this figure is not exact, but it is probably the right order of magnitude). Assume further that the Lubicons' costs of obtaining AR can be ignored at this point. Whether AR is obtained by litigation or political negotiation, there will be lawyers' fees of several million dollars; but these will in the end be paid from some government account, since the Lubicons have few resources of their own. The expected utility of undertaking litigation (EU_L) for AR is about $100 million multiplied by the probability of winning the action (p_L), or

(1) $EU_L = 100p_L$

Similarly, the expected utility of negotiating for AR (EU_N) is $100 million multiplied by the probability of success in the negotiations (p_N), or

(2) $EU_N = 100p_N$

However, these simple equations neglect the effect of unsuccessful litigation upon negotiation. In fact, the expected utility of litigation must be reduced by the effect that failure in litigation will have upon the prospects of negotiations. If the probablility of success in negotiations is p_L, the probability of failure is $1-p_L$, so

(3) $EU_L = 100p_L - 100p_N(1-p_L)$

It will be rational to pursue litigation if the expected utility of litigation as expressed in equation (3) is larger than the expected utility of negotiation as expressed in equation (2), or if

(4) $100p_L - 100p_N(1-p_L) > 100p_N$

Dividing both sides by 100 and rearranging terms,

(5) $p_L - p_N + p_Lp_N > p_N$ or $p_L(1-p_N) > 2p_N$

yielding

(6) $p_L > 2p_N / (1 - p_N)$

Inequality (6) represents the condition under which it will be rational for the Lubicons to prefer litigation to negotiation as a way of pursuing AR. There is no unique solution because p_L and p_N are independent of each other. But for any value of p_N, it is easy to compute the minimum value of p_L required to justify litigation. For example, if p_N is 1/3, the threshhold value of p_L is 1/2. For realistic values of p_N, the conclusion is always the same: it is rational for the Lubicons to resort to litigation only if they are appreciably more certain of its success than they are of success in negotiation. In case of doubt, prefer the political strategy.

What are the options of the federal government for affecting the preferences of the Lubicons? The federal strategy in 1988, it seems, was to try and make them forget about AR by winning a conclusive battle in court. But it was necessary to sue Alberta as well as the Lubicons. As well, the Lubicons could not be compelled to co-operate since this was a civil, not a criminal action. Even if the Lubicons refused to appear in court, the federal government might have been able to win a legal judgment. However, public opinion may not have viewed this course of action favourably. Canada decided not to proceed with its litigation.

A more realistic strategy is to induce the Lubicons to prefer TE to ND, i.e., reorder their preferences from AR > ND > TE to AR > TE > ND. The reason that the Lubicons now prefer ND to TE is probably a belief that ND is temporary, and that they have the option to accept TE whenever they choose. They are correct in this belief to the extent that the federal government has repeatedly acknowledged that the Lubicons have a right to a reserve under Treaty 8. Should the government try to repudiate this obligation, the Lubicons could almost certainly win a court judgment in their favour.

The government, however, is now undermining the Lubicons' position by dealing with the Woodland Cree, who number many breakaway Lubicons. Conclusion of an agreement with the Woodland Cree and perhaps with other such bands in the future might reduce the numbers of the Lubicon band to the point where they could no longer justify the offer that is still on the table. Over time, the federal policy threatens to replace the 95-square-mile reserve (call it TE_1) with a smaller one (TE_2), probably accompanied by correspondingly lesser financial benefits. TE_1 remains on the table for now but with an undefined time limit attached. A settlement will result if the Lubicons react to the implicit threat by putting TE_1 ahead of ND, perhaps in this ordering: AR > TE_1 > ND > TE_2. Assuming the government's new ordering to be TE_2 > TE_1 > ND > AR, Matrix 11-6 will result:

MATRIX 11-6   Lubicon-Canada Game with Threat of Smaller Reserve

		CANADA		
		AR	TE_1	TE_2
	AR	4, 1	2, 2	2, 2
LUBICONS	TE_1	2, 2	**3, 3**	2, 2
	TE_2	2, 2	2, 2	1, 4

LUBICONS: AR $>$ TE_1 $>$ ND $>$ TE_2
CANADA: TE_2 $>$ TE_1 $>$ ND $>$ AR

The Lubicons no longer have a dominant strategy, but they do have a worst strategy, namely TE_2, in which they can do as poorly as their fourth choice, whereas with AR or TE_1 they can do no worse than third. That is, TE_2 is a weakly dominated strategy for the Lubicons; they will not play it because they can always do at least as well by playing something else. Canada, realizing that the Lubicons will not play TE_2, now has a weakly dominant strategy: TE_1. Knowing that, the Lubicons will achieve their best result by also playing TE_1, and an agreement will be reached in the central cell of the matrix.

Game theory is not prophecy. It cannot tell us whether the Lubicons will adjust their priorities as the government seems to hope, or whether they will think the government is bluffing. It cannot predict whether the federal or provincial governments might change their priorities, perhaps in response to an election or other political pressures. But it does show us that all sides in this intractable dispute have behaved rationally in the sense of trying to obtain their objectives as they define them. In particular, Canada is now pursuing a realistic strategy that could induce the Lubicons to settle.

NOTES

1. Boyce Richardson, "The Lubicon of Northern Alberta," in Boyce Richardson, ed., *Drumbeat: Anger and Renewal in Indian Country* (Toronto: Summerhill Press for the Assembly of First Nations, 1989), pp. 229-64; John Goddard, "Forked Tongues," *Saturday Night* (February 1988), pp. 38-45; John Goddard, "Last Stand of the Lubicon," *Equinox* 21 (May/June 1985), pp. 67-77. Goddard is writing a book on the subject.

2. Richard T. Price, "Indian Treaty Land Entitlement Claims in Alberta: Tripartite Negotiations and Settlements (1971-1988)," Canadian Historical Association Annual Meeting, June 1989.

3. Thomas Flanagan, "Some Factors Bearing on the Origins of the Lubicon Lake Dispute, 1899-1940," *Alberta* 2, no. 2 (1990): 47-62.

4. The text of Treaty 8 is reprinted in Dennis F.K. Madill, *Treaty Research Report: Treaty Eight* (Ottawa: Indian and Northern Affairs Canada, Treaties and Historical Research Centre, 1986), pp. 127-35.

5. Their band status was reconfirmed 13 November 1973, by federal Order in Council P.C. 1973-3571.

6. Memorandum of agreement, 14 December 1929, s. 10, enacted by the Alberta Natural Resources Act, S.C., 1930, c. 3.

7. H.W. McGill to C.P. Schmidt, 14 August 1940. This and following correspondence is found in Exhibit B attached to Affidavit 2 of Chief Bernard Ominayak, filed 23 September 1982, in *Ominayak v. Norcen*. Contained in the papers of Judge N.D. McDermid, Glenbow-Alberta Institute, 6992, appeal book 3.

8. N.-P. L'Heureux to Secretary, Indian Affairs Branch, 1 October 1940, ibid.

9. F.H. Peters to D. J. Allan, 19 October 1940, ibid.

10. T.R.L. MacInness to N.-P. L'Heureux, 9 September 1941, ibid.

11. H.W. McGill to N.E. Tanner, 17 February 1942, ibid.

12. Minister's Chief Executive Assistant to H.W. McGill, 18 April 1942, ibid.

13. F.H. Peters to H.W. McGill, 20 August 1942, ibid.

14. A.G. Leslie to T.R.L. MacInnes, 11 January 1951, ibid.

15. McCrimmon wrote that he deleted 58 names from the Lubicon Lake band list, Report, 14 July 1942, ibid. Goddard, "Last Stand of the Lubicon," claims that McCrimmon "cut 90 names from a list of 154" at Lubicon Lake. Different points in time may be involved.

16. Malcom McCrimmon to D.J. Allan, 11 August 1943, ibid; idem to Acting Director, Indian Affairs Brach, 4 July 1945, ibid.

17. A.G. Leslie to T.R.L. MacInnes, 11 January 1951, ibid.

18. C.D. Brown to R.A. Hoey, 29 October 1946, ibid.

19. D.J. Allan to G.H. Gooderham, 15 March 1952, ibid.

20. G.S. Lapp to G.H. Gooderham, 21 July 1950, ibid.

21. D.J. Allan to G.H. Gooderham, 15 March 1952, ibid.
22. Compare G.S. Lapp to G.H. Gooderham, 13 June 1952, ibid, with Lapp to Gooderham, 17 June 1953, ibid.
23. G.H. Gooderham to Acting Superintendent, Reserves and Trusts, 28 November 1952, ibid.
24. T.W. Dalkin to D.J. Allan, 11 February 1952, ibid.
25. T.W. Dalkin to G.H. Gooderham, 22 October 1953, ibid.
26. G.S. Lapp to E.A. Robertson, 5 May 1954, ibid.
27. I have compiled the figures on petroleum exploration from the Map Book, pp. 13-16, in the McDermind Papers, GAI.
28. Ibid.
29. Larry Pratt, *The Tar Sands: Syncrude and the Politics of Oil* (Edmonton: Hurtig, 1976), p. 18.
30. Richard T. Price, ed., *The Spirit of the Alberta Indian Treaties* (Montreal: Institute for Research on Public Policy).
31. René Fumoleau, *As Long as This Land Shall Last: A History of Treaty 8 and 11* (Toronto: McClelland & Stewart, [1975]); Mel Watkins, ed., *The Dene Nation: The Colony Within* (Toronto: University of Toronto Press, 1977).
32. *Chief François Paulette v. R.*, 1974, 39 D.L.R. (3d) 81; 1974, 42 D.L.R. (3d) 8; 1976, D.L.R. (3d) 1; [1977] 2 S.C.R. 628.
33. Richard Charles Daniel, *Indian Rights and Hinterland Resources: The Case of Northern Alberta* (University of Alberta: MA thesis in sociology, 1977), pp. 195-203.
34. Ibid., p. 202.
35. *Paulette v. R.*, [1977] 2 S.C.R. 628 at 638, 645.
36. *Alberta Report*, 21 March 1977, p. 14.
37. (Bill 29) The Land Titles Amendment Act, S.A, 1977, c. 27, s. 10, amending s. 141 of the Land Titles Act. Royal assent 18 May 1977.
38. Price, "Indian Treaty Land Entitlement Claims," p. 18.
39. Bob Bogle, *Alberta Hansard*, 17 March 1978, p. 262.
40. Jim Foster, *Alberta Hansard*, 6 April 1977, pp. 672-73.
41. Goddard, "Forked Tongues," p. 43.
42. Saul D. Alinsky, *Rules for Radicals* (New York: Vintage Books, 1972), p. 148.
43. Ibid., p. 127. Italics in original.
44. *Alberta Report*, 18 April 1977, p. 16.
45. Ibid., p. 59
46. Roy MacGregor, *Chief: The Fearless Vision of Billy Diamond* (Markham, Ont.: Viking, 1989), pp. 257-58.
47. Billy Diamond, "Aboriginal Rights: The James Bay Experience," in Menno Boldt and J. Anthony Long, eds., *The Quest for Justice: Aboriginal Peoples and Aboriginal Rights* (Toronto: University of Toronto Press, 1985), pp. 265-91.

48. *Globe and Mail*, 4 April 1990.

49. Counted from the *Treaty Research Report* series, containing a separate volume on each treaty, published by the Treaties and Historical Research Centre of the Department of Indian Affairs and Northern Development. I say "'80 adhesions, more or less," because it is not always clear whether events amounted to a separate adhesion or to different signatures on the same adhesion.

50. See the synopsis published in May 1979 by the Treaties and Historical Research Centre, entitled "Treaty Agreements between the Indian People and the Sovereign in Right of Canada," as well as the map.

51. Printed in John Leonard Taylor, *Treaty Research Report: Treaty Six* (Ottawa: Indian and Northern Affairs Canada, Treaties and Historical Research Centre, 1985), p. 74.

52. *State v. Coffee*, 556 P. 2d 1185 (1976).

53. *A.G. Ontario v. Bear Island Foundation et al.*, 68 O.R. (2d) 394 (1989), at 413.

54. *A.G. Ontario v. Bear Island Foundation*, 49 O.R. (2d) 353 (1985); 68 O.R. (2d) 394 (1989), at 408.

55. Alinsky, *Rules for Radicals*, p. 119. Italics in original.

56. *Lubicon Lake Band v. the Queen*, [1981] 2 F. C. 317.

57. Decided 5 May 1981, 13 D.L.R. (4th) 159.

58. MacGregor, *Chief*, p. 74.

59. *Alberta Hansard*, 12 May 1983, pp. 953-54.

60. Richardson, "The Lubicon of Northern Alberta," pp. 242-43.

61. The theory of the case is best summarized in the appellants' factum, GAI, McDermid Papers.

62. *Ominayak v. Norcen*, 23 Alta. L.R. (2d) 284 (1983); 24 Alta. L.R. (2d) 394 (1983).

63. 24 Alta. L.R. (2d) 394 at 400.

64. *Ominayak v. Norcen*, 29 Alta. L.R. (2d) 152 (1984) at 157.

65. Ibid., pp. 157-58.

66. *Ominayak v. Norcen*, 36 Alta. L.R. (2d) 138 (1985) at 145.

67. Richardson, "The Lubicon of Northern Alberta," p. 246; [1985] 1 S.C.R. xi.

68. Richardson, "The Lubicon of Northern Alberta," p. 246.

69. *Ominayak v. Canada (Minister of Indian Affairs and Northern Development)*, [1987] 3 F.C. 174.

70. *Alberta Hansard*, 20 March 1984, pp. 233-35.

71. House of Commons Debates, 8 May 1984, pp. 3512-13. The letter was sent in December 1983.

72. House of Commons Debates, 6 April 1984

73. *Alberta Hansard*, 13 November 1984, pp. 1494-95.

74. *Alberta Multi-Media Society of Alberta* (a weekly Indian newspaper; hereafter cited as AMMSA), 14 September 1984, p. 3.

75. Peter Lougheed, *Alberta Hansard*, 16 April 1984, pp. 507-10; Milt Pahl, *Alberta Hansard*, 25 May 1984, p. 2.

76. Price, "Indian Treaty Land Entitlement Claims," p. 16.

77. *AMMSA*, 30 November 1984, p. 3.

78. United Nations Human Rights Committee, decision of 26 March 1990, CCPR/C/38/D/167/1984, p. 8, hereafter cited as UNHRCO.

79. E. Davie Fulton, "Lubicon Lake Indian Band—Inquiry: Discussion Paper," 7 February 1986, photocopy.

80. *AMMSA*, 13 December 1985, pp. 1, 3.

81. Fulton Report.

82. Richardson, "The Lubicon of Northern Alberta," p. 252.

83. *Alberta Hansard*, 13 August 1986, pp. 1055-56.

84. *Windspeaker* (successor to *AMMSA*), 12 December 1986, pp. 3, 5; Richardson, "The Lubicon of Northern Alberta," p. 253.

85. UNHRC, p. 1.

86. *Windspeaker*, 27 June 1986, pp. 1, 3.

87. *Windspeaker*, 12 December 1986, pp. 3, 5.

88. *Windspeaker*, 20 November 1987, p. 3.

89. Richardson, "The Lubicon of Northern Alberta," p. 254.

90. Ibid., p. 256; *Windspeaker*, 22 January 1988, p. 2; House of Commons Debates, 21 January 1988, pp. 12151-53.

91. House of Commons Debates, 28 April 1988, p. 14911.

92. House of Commons Debates, 9 February 1988, pp. 12786-87.

93. The letter of 3 February 1988, containing the McKnight formula, is quoted in the federal statement of claim, *A.G. Canada v. A.G. Alberta and the Lubicon Lake Band*, pp. 7-9, Alberta Court of Queen's Bench, 17 May 1988.

94. House of Commons Debates, 10 February 1988, pp. 12822-23.

95. Interview with Dave Russell.

96. *Windspeaker*, 11 March 1988, p. 1.

97. Don Getty, *Alberta Hansard*, 6 May 1988, pp. 876-77.

98. Bill McKnight, House of Commons Debates, 18 May 1988, pp. 15577-78.

99. *A.G. Canada v. A.G. Alberta and the Lubicon Lake Band*, Alberta Court of Queen's Bench, no. 8801-07584.

100. *Windspeaker*, 3 June 1988, p. 3.

101. Richardson, "The Lubicon of Northern Alberta," p. 258.

102. *Windspeaker*, 7 October 1988, p. 1.

103. Richardson, p. 260; *Windspeaker*, 21 October 1988, p. 1.

104. *Windspeaker*, 26 October 1988; Richardson, p. 261.

105. Price, "Indian Treaty Land Entitlement Claims," pp. 15-19.

106. Government of Canada, news release, 21 December 1989, included as Appendix 2 to Price, 1989.
107. *Calgary Herald*, 7-8 February 1989, p. A5.
108. From notes prepared by Brian Malone, Robert Coulter, Fred Jobin, and Ken Colby, 9 February 1990. In the author's possession.
109. *Windspeaker*, 14 July 1989, p. 1.
110. *Windspeaker*, 3 November 1989, p. 1.
111. *Windspeaker*, 1 December 1989.
112. *Windspeaker*, 2 June 1989, p. 1.
113. *Windspeaker*, 28 July 1989, pp. 1-2; 15 October 1990, pp. 1, 3; UNHRC, pp. 20-21, 25.
114. Canada, press release, 26 March 1990.
115. *Calgary Herald*, 20 December 1990.
116. Interview with Brian Malone, 4 July 1990.
117. UNHRC, p. 29; *Calgary Herald*, 4 May 1990, p. B6.
118. *Alberta Report*, 28 January 1991, pp. 10-11.

APPENDIX NOTES

1. The analysis in this section, particularly the use of ordinal games, is modelled on the examples in Steven J. Brams, *Rational Politics: Decisions, Games, and Strategy* (San Diego: Academic Press, 1985).
2. George Tsebelis, *Nested Games: Rational Choice in Comparative Politics* (Berkeley: University of California Press, 1990), p. 63.
3. Those familiar with game theory will recognize the situation as that of the "nested games" analyzed by Tsebelis, but I hope this presentation is simpler.

Index